Politics of Education in Latin America

Comparative and International Education

A DIVERSITY OF VOICES

VOLUME 49

The titles published in this series are listed at *brill.com/caie*

Politics of Education in Latin America

Reforms, Resistance and Persistence

Edited by

Carlos Ornelas

BRILL
SENSE

LEIDEN | BOSTON

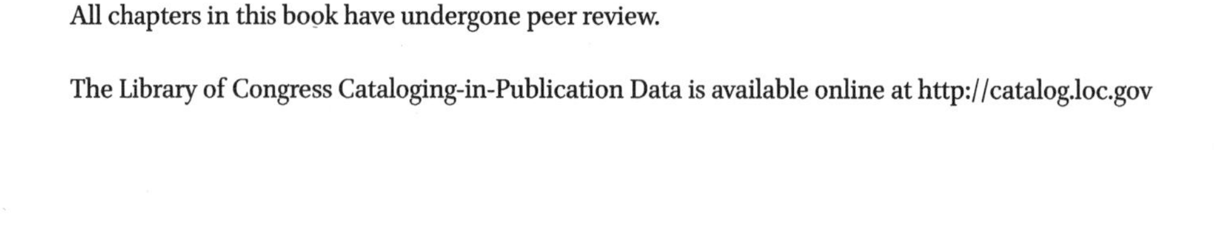

All chapters in this book have undergone peer review.

The Library of Congress Cataloging-in-Publication Data is available online at http://catalog.loc.gov

Typeface for the Latin, Greek, and Cyrillic scripts: "Brill". See and download: brill.com/brill-typeface.

ISSN 2214-9880
ISBN 978-90-04-41335-1 (paperback)
ISBN 978-90-04-41336-8 (hardback)
ISBN 978-90-04-41337-5 (e-book)

This book is printed on acid-free paper and produced in a sustainable manner.

Printed by Printforce, the Netherlands

Contents

Foreword

Politics of Education in Latin America: Reforms, Resistance and Persistence is a unique collection of reflective chapters on major efforts to reform education systems in Latin America. That is evident from the introductory chapter by editor Carlos Ornelas, who provides a conceptual framework drawing on a diverse range of sociopolitical philosophers from Machiavelli and Marx, Weber and Durkheim to Nussbaum and Giddens. The four essential elements of the framework—purpose, tradition, context, and tools—may seem idiosyncratic, but, turn out to be provident as the various chapters make place reform efforts in historical contexts and describe the driving forces and dynamics of attempts to overcome and, in some cases, radically change inequitable policies and practices.

As cases in point, the book begins with attempts in Argentina and Chile to include more inclusive education systems in the aftermath of military dictatorships. Chile is particularly notable for how privatized the entire system was as the result of neoliberal economic and education policies that were implemented. Diminishing the privileged position of those previous favored by the Pinochet regime, however, does not go uncontested. By contrast, the second chapter on Chile documents how best practices in teacher education and professional development have been implemented, to all purposes, without significant opposition.

In addition to the quality of a country's teaching force, one significant element of reform efforts to achieve more inclusive, equitable education system involves multiculturalism; this is true of many of the countries in the region with either majority or pluralist indigenous populations. Brazil, despite its multiracial image, has a long history of discrimination against the descendants of African slavery in the impoverished Northeastern Region. Chapter 4 points out that multiculturalism is a comprehensive term embracing major identity markets other than race and ethnicity. The recent election of a racist, homophobic, misogynist President, poses major problems for continued success in achieving a genuinely multicultural education system in Brazil.

Issues of transformation and opposition, accomplishments and unfulfilled purposes and promises, further highlight the Ecuadorian case (Chapter 6), where far-reaching reforms of the populist Rafael Correa government exerted state power to take control of an unwieldy system. Despite resistance to such effort, significant progress was made in equity and quality. The Mexican case (Chapter 10) is an example of efforts by the state to take control of a system dominated by the national teachers' union affiliated with the *Partido Revolucionario Institutional* (PRI). The chapter raises the issue of whether one vertical hegemonic structure is now being replaced by another, while contestation continues between those favored or not by the status quo in schooling and society. Whether or not fundamental change for the better has occurred remains problematic. The Peruvian case (Chapter 5) illustrates how constant turnover in the Ministry of Education and inconsistency in policy formulation and implementation—common to the region as to other parts of the world—have resulted in only modest improvements in the overall running and outcomes of schooling.

Contradictions and opposing forces are placed in specific historical, sociocultural, and economic contests, that go from the national and regional to the international. Illustrative of this point is the Cuban case (Chapter 9) that examines six decades of education innovations in the context of Cold War changing relations of the island with the United States and the Soviet Union. The chapter on El Salvador (Chapter 8) provides a detailed description of how national as well international factors are essential to understanding the trajectory of education reforms, both their successes and failures. The role of one particular significant international actor—the Organization for Economic Cooperation and Development (OECD)—is illustrated in what reform initiatives were undertaken in Colombia.

The concluding chapter of the volume is different in that it involves a cross-national analysis of the response of different teacher organizations to reform efforts in Argentina, Brazil, and Mexico that may or may not be favorable to them and the education system. Here it needs to be pointed out that I take a stand against the attempts to pin the failure of education reform on teacher unions. Historically, in Latin America as elsewhere, teacher unions have been the single most significant force for expanding and strengthening public education as a fundamental citizenship right that serves the common good.

In addition to studying education reforms within the overarching framework of "the dialectic of the global and the local," another unique feature of the book is the process employed by the editor to achieve a complementary set of chapters. As described in his introduction, Ornelas arranged for the various contributing authors to make presentations at two sessions at the 2018 Mexico Conference of the Comparative and International Education Society (CIES). The authors then met for two days at CREFAL (Centro de Cooperación Regional para la Educación de Adultos en América Latina y el Caribe) in Patzcuaro, with the goal of providing an opportunity for each chapter to be critiqued and improved in extraordinarily collegial ways.

The result of this carefully planned undertaking is a volume that offers fresh perspectives by distinguished Latin American and North American scholars, who have dedicated their careers to understanding how education systems play significant roles in shaping their societies and are in turn shaped by them. Their abiding concerns have been with what it takes to create equitable, quality education systems that contribute to the individual and collective well-being of all. I believe *Politics of Education in Latin America: Reforms, Resistance and Persistence* is a worthy representation of their scholarship and policy involvements that have benefited so many not only in their societies but others around the Americas and the globe.

Robert F. Arnove
Chancellor's Professor Emeritus of Education
Indiana University, Bloomington

Acknowledgments

This book would not have been possible without the CIES conferences. In them, intellectual discussion, debates about theories and practical perspectives, and the emphasis on making useful comparisons for academia and decision-making provide an exceptional framework for peer cooperation. I am pleased that colleagues who wrote the chapters of this book accepted my invitation. They worked hard and responded to my demands that, I hope, were not many or exaggerated.

Regina Cortina and Sergio Cárdenas are in some way jointly responsible for this publication. Regina not only invited me to organize the two sessions—and she entrusted me with other tasks for the Mexico City Conference—but she also motivated me to make sure that the papers did not remain in the annals of the CIES. Sergio, then general director of CREFAL, sponsored the conference in Pátzcuaro and, with that, he contributed to the authors getting to know each other a bit more. We stayed together and spoke about matters beyond our scholarly work. CREFAL staff always collaborated and supported us on both more substantial organizational matters and minor details. They are too many to mention individually.

Also, the students of the MA in Learning and Educational Policies of the CREFAL are too numerous and have our appreciation. They provided sharp comments, some of them very critical, in response to the presentations of our essays. Bob Arnove was more than a commentator; he acted as an advisor who told us how to improve content and performance. I value that he has agreed to write the Foreword.

My friend Bradley Levinson translated and edited (even in Spanish) the work of René Guevara and Sandra Milena Téllez, from Colombia. He also helped me to put my chapter and this introduction in better English form. I thank him very much.

The final outcome is in a better shape thanks to our series editor at Brill Sense, Allan Pitman, who put many hours of his work to polish the presentation, and to Jolanda Karada, our book's production editor. We all express gratitude to them for their hard work and kind comments.

Figures and Tables

Figures

Tables

Notes on Contributors

Robert F. Arnove
is Chancellor's Professor Emeritus of Education, Indiana University, Bloomington. He is an Honorary Fellow and Past President of the Comparative & International Society based on his distinguished contributions to the advancement of this interdisciplinary field. Over the last five decades, he has written extensively on education and sociopolitical change in Latin America, and, more generally, on the dynamics of globalization. Among his many publications excels *Comparative Education: The Dialectic of the Global and the Local* (with Carlos A. Torres & Stephen Franz, 4th ed., Roman & Littlefield Publishers, 2013).

Beatrice Ávalos
is professor and researcher at the University of Chile's Institute of Advanced Studies in Education, charged with its teachers' research strand. She earned a Ph.D. from Saint Louis University. In 2013 she was awarded the National Prize for Educational Sciences in Chile. She directed and published studies on the teaching profession, teacher education and education policies with a focus on less developed countries. Among her recent publications is *Heroes o Villanos: La Profesión Docente en Chile* (2013), and with P. Razquin on teacher education international policy in *The Sage Handbook of Research on Teacher Education* (edited by D. J. Clandinin & and J. Husu, Sage, 2017).

María Balarin
works as a Principal Researcher at the Group for the Analysis of Development (GRADE) in Peru, where she is also Director of Research. She holds a Ph.D. in Education Policy from the University of Bath, an M.A. in Psychoanalytic Theory from the University of Essex, and a B.A. in Philosophy from the Pontificia Universidad Católica of Perú. Her work, which has been published in academic books and journals, focuses on education policymaking and implementation, on the role of markets in education and their impact on educational segregation trends, and on the transitions to adulthood among young people living in marginal urban areas in developing countries.

Jorge Baxter
is an Associate Professor in the Faculty of Education at the Universidad de Los Andes in Bogota, where his teaching and research focus on comparative education policy, communication for social change, and international

development. He has a Ph.D. in international education policy from the University of Maryland. Jorge has worked for over 20 years in the education, health, arts, and media fields. He was the Latin American Director of Social Impact at Sesame Workshop from 2013–2016, an education specialist at the Organization of American States from 2002–2009 where he worked with Dr. Bradley Levinson of Indiana University to launch the *Inter-American Journal on Education for Democracy*.

Jason Beech
teaches Comparative Education and Sociology of Education at Universidad de San Andrés in Buenos Aires. He is a researcher of the National Council for Scientific and Technical Research of Argentina (CONICET), and Director of the Ph.D. in Education at Universidad de San Andrés. He holds a Ph.D. in Education from the Institute of Education, University of London, and has taught in several universities in the Americas, Europe, and Australia. He is interested in the globalization of knowledge and policies related to education and in exploring the link between cosmopolitanism and education.

Cristián Bellei
is a researcher at the Center for Advanced Research in Education and Professor of Sociology at the University of Chile. He obtained a master's degree in educational policy and a doctorate in education from Harvard University. His research and publications refer to education policy, quality and school improvement, equity, segregation, and the education market. His most recent book is *El gran experimento: mercado y privatización de la educación chilena* [The great experiment: Market and privatization of Chilean education] (LOM Ediciones, 2016).

D. Brent Edwards Jr.
is an Assistant Professor of Theory and Methodology in the Study of Education at the University of Hawaii, Manoa. He was a Visiting Scholar at the University of Amsterdam, a Fulbright Scholar at the University of Central America, and a Post-doctoral researcher at The University of Tokyo. His work focuses on (a) the global governance of education and (b) education policy, politics and political economy, with a focus on low-income countries. He has two recent books: *Global Education Policy, Impact Evaluations, and Alternatives: The Political Economy of Knowledge Production*; and *The Trajectory of Global Education Policy: Community-based Management in El Salvador and the Global Reform Agenda* (both with Palgrave Macmillan).

Gilberto García Batista
is Professor Emeritus at the University of Pedagogical Sciences Enrique José Varona, and guest professor at the University of Holguin. He is Doctor of Sciences and Doctor of Biological Sciences. He presides the Association of Pedagogues of Cuba since 2013. His interests include teacher training, higher education, school hygiene and methodology of educational research. He directs the Section of Pedagogical Sciences in the National Commission of Scientific Degrees of the Republic of Cuba. He is also a member of the National Accreditation Board and was the national coordinator of the Master of Science in Education of broad access. He has more than 30 years of experience in education research.

Mark Ginsburg
retired in 2016 from FHI360. He is a visiting scholar at the University of Maryland (USA) and a visiting professor at the Universidad de Ciencias Pedagógicas (Cuba), and was a faculty member at other universities: Aston (England), Houston, Pittsburgh, and Columbia (USA) as well as a visiting professor at George Washington University (USA) and Kobe University (Japan). He was President of the Comparative and International Education Society (1991) and coeditor of *Comparative Education Review* (2003–2013) as well as President of the United Faculty of the University of Pittsburgh (affiliated to the American University of Professors and the American Federation of Teachers, 1992–2004).

René Guevara Ramírez
is a Professor of the Graduate Department at the National Pedagogical University (Colombia). He earned Ph.D. in Social Sciences from the Autonomous Metropolitan University (Mexico). He also holds a master's degree in University Management from the Universidad de Los Andes (Colombia), and a Bachelor of Arts degree in Social Sciences from the Francisco José de Caldas District University (Colombia). He coordinates the Politia-UPN Research Group. He is author of the book *El campo político en universidades públicas latinoamericanas*, and a number of articles on politics and higher education in Colombia.

Ana Ivenicki
is a Full Professor at the Department of Educational Studies at the Federal University of Rio de Janeiro (UFRJ). She holds a Ph.D. in Education, from the University of Glasgow. She also is a Researcher 1A (top classification) for the Brazilian National Research Council (Conselho Nacional de Desenvolvimento Científico e Tecnológico). She has been widely publishing in Brazil and abroad. Her research interests include multicultural and comparative education,

international education, teacher education and evaluation of higher education in multicultural perspectives.

Aurora Loyo
labors as a senior researcher at the Social Sciences Institute of the National Autonomous University of Mexico. She earned a BA degree in Sociology from the UNAM and completed her graduate studies at La Sorbonne and El Colegio de México. Her main lines of research are educational policy and social actors, basic education, and teachers' organizations in Mexico and Latin America. She has taught at the Graduate Division of UNAM and the Dr. José María Luis Mora Institute. Since 1989, she has reported uninterruptedly on the development of educational policy in Mexico. She has published books, book chapters, and articles in academic journals.

Gonzalo Muñoz Stuardo
is a professor of the Faculty of Education and Director of the Master's in Leadership and Educational Management Program, at Diego Portales University. He earned an MA honors in Sociology and Master in Sociology at the Catholic University of Chile. He was Head of the General Education Division of the Ministry of Education of Chile, between 2014 and 2016. He previously worked as Director of Studies of the Center for Innovation in Education at Fundación Chile. In October 2012, he was appointed Board Member of the Quality Agency of Education. He has published books and articles in educational policies, school effectiveness and improvement, and educational leadership.

Carlos Ornelas
is professor of Education and Communications at the Metropolitan Autonomous University, in Mexico City and Honorary Fellow at Center for Regional Cooperation for Adult Education in Latin America and the Caribbean. He earned a Ph.D. in Education from Stanford University. The Fondo de Cultura Económica just published his most recent book, *La contienda por la educación: globalización, neocorporativismo y democracia.* His research interests include a comparative analysis of Mexican education and other countries. He has published widely on education reforms and the politics of education. He writes two columns per week in *Excelsior*, a Mexican national newspaper.

María Fernanda Rodríguez
has worked as a Research Assistant in the Group for the Analysis of Development (GRADE), where she gained experience in the research on youth, education, and labor, in the evaluation of educational programs by the Ministry of Education and consultancies for the OCDE and UNESCO. She holds a bachelor's degree in

social sciences with a major in Sociology by the Pontificia Universidad Católica del Perú. She specializes in qualitative methodologies, education, urban issues, politics and gender studies and currently works in the Ministry of Education of Perú.

Sandra Milena Téllez Rico
teaches at the Graduate Department at the National Pedagogical University (Colombia) where she obtained her bachelor's degree in Psychology and Pedagogy and her master's degree in Education. She earned a Ph.D. in Sociology from the Autonomous Metropolitan University (Mexico). She is a member of the Politia-UPN Research Group. Author of chapters of books and articles on academic work and higher education in Colombia.

José Weinstein Cayuela
is the Director of the Center for Development of School Leadership at Diego Portales University, where he is Full Professor. A sociologist from the University of Chile, with a Ph.D. in Sociology from the Université Catholique de Louvain (Belgium). He was Undersecretary of Education (2000–2003), and the first Minister of Culture (2003–2006) of Chile. He created and directed programs on school improvement and youth development. Important international organizations have requested his expertise. He has published over 60 articles in books, reviews, and journals focusing on education, poverty, youth, and culture. His recent work has significantly focused on school leadership development and capacity improvement of vulnerable schools.

INTRODUCTION

Reforms, Resistance and Persistence

Carlos Ornelas

Since the mid-1980s there has been a fever for education reforms around the globe. In Europe, some governments planted the tendency since the postwar period with the purpose of banishing the National Socialist ideology and Fascist inclinations; the idea of democracy pushed the efforts of change, especially in what was to be the Federal Republic of Germany (Max Planck Institute for Human Development and Education, 1983). In the United States, reform initiatives in education appeared in school districts and states since early in the twentieth century (Levin, 1976; Sack, 1981). In Asia, Korea, Taiwan, Hong Kong and, to some extent, Singapore, tried to emulate the successes of Japan's education (Goh & Gopinathan, 2008). Along with the purposes of democratization—which manifested itself more than anything in the expansion of schooling—in many European and Asian, and to some extent in Latin America countries, governments sponsored the training of teachers based on meritocratic postulates (Takayama, 2013).

The embryo that perhaps most strongly fueled the epidemic of global reform began when in the United States the famous report, *A Nation at Risk*, blamed poor school quality for the troubles that—from a catastrophic perspective—afflicted the economy, the loosening of social cohesion, and the loss of competitiveness of that country in the world. The United States was no longer the power that dictated the rules in world politics and economics, even as it maintained the vanguard in scientific and technological innovations (Goldberg & Harvey, 1983). The scarcity of competent "human capital" was threatening its hegemonic position on the planet. Although human capital theory had already advanced in academic spheres, it was with the effects of *A Nation at Risk* that human capital became the dominant political slogan in education.

At the same time, the market economy became the ideological nucleus of reforms in education. Educating for work became the mandate for education; to educate for a full life was a hindrance. Martha Nussbaum puts it plainly: "Education for economic growth needs basic skills, literacy, and numeracy ... The student's freedom of mind is dangerous if what is wanted is a group of technically trained obedient workers to carry out the plans of elites who are aiming at foreign investment and technological development" (Nussbaum, 2010, p. 18).

 | DOI: 10.1163/9789004413375_001

Intergovernmental organizations, like the World Bank, in the first place, regional development banks, such as the Interamerican Development Bank (IDB), the Organization for Economic Cooperation and Development (OECD), and others embraced the focus on human capital. UNESCO did not abandon its humanistic ends, but its influence diminished. The theory of human capital fit well with the neoliberal ideology in its efforts to banish from educational systems humanistic, obsolete pedagogical traditions, far from the aims of economic growth. The instruments used by the agents of neoliberalism were shrinking of state budgets, applied research, international assessments, rankings, and subtle propaganda wrapped in catchy phrases such as "skills for life," "knowledge society" or "learning for all" (Klees, Samoff, & Stromquist, 2012; Stromquist & Monkham, 2014). Those organizations framed an "international model for the information age." Their main components were: Decentralization/school autonomy; lifelong learning; a centralized curriculum based on competencies; central evaluation systems; and professionalization of teachers (Beech, 2008). That common core became the Global Education Reform Movement, or GERM, as Pasi Sahlberg called it (Hargreaves, 2015).

Until recently, it would seem that Latin America has been reluctant to promote reforms of this type; except for Chile, which became a global example, even as a laboratory, where the privatization of education took command, and General Pinochet's government introduced a voucher system to promote "fairness" (Colegio de Profesores de Chile; Cox, 2005). However, the slogan of educational reform has long stood in the Latin American region; Córdoba's movement for university reform in 1918 is the antecedent that formed the foundations of more recent adventures.

In general terms, after the struggles between Liberals and Conservatives throughout the nineteenth century, the educational systems of Latin America were molded under the inspiration of the Napoleonic model: centralized, uniform, elitist and career-oriented. The Anglo-Saxon liberal tradition, although it had some influence throughout the twentieth century on segments of private education, did not fare well against this hegemonic model (Levy, 1986). Latin American school systems, moreover, were constituted under the aegis of the State, which favored the institution of trade unions that impregnated with their politics the shaping of education; these encouraged clientelist practices among teachers, thereby moving further away from the ideals of meritocracy.

The reform projects in education compiled in this book offer a broad outlook of transformation trends, but also of the resistances that those reforms generate and the persistence of certain traditions. The cases emphasize the study of national projects, but they do not fail to mention the influence of global proclivities and learnings as well. It is worth starting with conceptual definitions, before addressing the relationships between reforms in Latin America and those in other latitudes.

1 Reform

The expression "education reform" is perhaps one of the most employed in the international literature of comparative education. Writers take for granted that everyone understands the concept and do not define it or delineate its characteristics. The watchword of education reform is used to justify policies of governments, or to promote changes in schools to improve student learning; the same notion is used to align projects led by intergovernmental organizations, or to explain the push of communities that would like to seize the destiny of their schools. Movements of change range from those that try to transform a complete school system to those that focus on a particular practice or institution. There are restructuring movements that promote the teaching of religious values, while others oppose such designs.

There is not a satisfactory conceptual definition of what education reform is, or should be. Still, there are many ways to make sense of changes in education. It may result from the goals of the reformers themselves. These may include, for example, addressing the perceived needs of their education system, or resolving a crisis; serving political ends, or legitimating a given government policy (Bacharach, 1990; Bajaj, 2012; Gorski, 2014; Iturralde Guerrero, Maya, & Silva, 2017; Tyack & Cuban, 2001). Burton Clark argued: "Change is the most used concept in the social sciences." Swapping the term change for reform can be useful: both extensive system reforms and micro reforms are vital to the field. The reforms can be designed and implemented by way of a top-down approach in which an authority targets the school setting or teachers. Alternatively, it can come locally from grassroots organizations, gain momentum, and spread to other branches of the system (Clark, 1984).

Another issue is the course of educational reforms. A selective review of the literature shows that most of them, especially those that use a top-down model, follow a similar path: an appeal for action, legal formulation of strategies; policy implementation; changes in curriculum; new textbooks; and teacher training enhancement. Others attempt to institute a given model of pedagogy, such as the competency-based approach or the constructivist paradigm. Another type of reform endeavors to establish a centralized evaluation system in tandem with decentralized school management; this makes use of external accountability and corrective procedures for teachers (Anderson, 2005; Burns, Köster, & Fuster, 2016; World Bank Group, 2011). The neo-liberal ideal, alternatively, advocates for privatization and deregulation of educational systems (Turner, 2014; Zajda, 2006).

Still, there is a need for a guiding framework to gauge the main features of any given education reform. If we consider four essentials—purpose, tradition, context, and tools—utilizing such a structure is feasible. The scaffold starts from the premise that there is a philosophical precept, a fundamental principle, that governs the action of those who propose reforms: a purpose. It may be implicit, but most of the time the resolve is evident: the search for social justice, equity, freedom or merit. Other times, the exposition of these principles may provide rhetorical cover for rather more utilitarian resolutions, although these may have sound qualities, too, such as competence, transparency or accountability. In any case, it is not philosophy, but political action that gives substance to a particular reform.

The noun *purpose* has several meanings. In the pages of this text, we use it to denote the political interest of the proponents of educational reforms. It includes their aspirations to transcend, or longings to maintain or expand their power, the determination to achieve goals, the passion—or passivity—in their work, and the ambition that the reform will increase their legitimacy. Typically, the most salient purpose of systemic reform is to dismantle or root out the dominant traditions that the reformist group considers harmful. The advocates of the changes assume that those who guard such traditional practices only justify their legitimacy in the sense in which Weber pointed out in *Politics as a vocation*: legitimacy based on "the authority of the eternal yesterday (*fieterno ayerfl*), i.e., of the mores sanctified through the unimaginably ancient recognition and habitual orientation to conform... like the domination exercised by the patrimonial prince of yore" (Weber, 1946, pp. 78–79).

By *tradition*, one may understand the current political customs, which could include conceptions about the uses of power. It also encompasses the dominant practices, both in the administration of the system and in teaching; the beliefs around those practices, as well as the even more deeply ingrained bureaucratic methods—which are therefore more difficult to eradicate because they have iron-armed defenders. In the same way, the tradition includes myths and legends built around a school system, which becomes part of the dominant ideology. The set of traditions forms a link with existing social relationships, and this tie thus defines the convoluted context that conditions the political action of reformist groups. A savvy reformer identifies profitable myths—or those which they presume virtuous ones, as Machiavelli would say—that can favor her/his endeavor and tries to rescue them and align them with her/his goals.

The description of this type of political *context* derives from Karl Marx's famous quote in *Luis Bonaparte's Eighteenth Brumaire*: "Men make their own history, but they do not make it as they please; they do not make it under circumstances chosen by themselves, but under circumstances directly found, given and transmitted from the past. The tradition of all the dead generations weighs like a nightmare on the brains of the living" (Marx, 1972, p. 437). Anthony Giddens revises Marx's phrase and instead of men proposes "Human beings make their own history." The context, claims Giddens, "includes the reflexive register, by the art of the interested agents, of the conditions in which they 'make history" (Giddens, 1995, p. 272).

The *context* for reform, consequently, always incorporates the changing political environment, the social conditions, the reception given to some initiative, the social relations between segments, groups, organizations, and citizens, as well as the historical fabric—the remnant of former generations. All of these determine the fate of the reforms. The reformers package their proposals in philosophical or doctrinal principles while incorporating components of practical life, such as raising productive capacities, encouraging citizen participation, or offering a quality service.

The reformers use a separate type of apparatuses, devices or instruments, which we incorporate into the concept of *tools*, to achieve the goals of the education reform project. These may be varied but unified by the resolve to put into practice the purposes of the reform, or at least part of them. There are three categories of tools: institutional, political, and educational. All processes of reform involve a form of political battle. On one front are the reformist militants, those who would like to change the order of things and believe they have the legitimacy to do so. On the other front are the defenders of the status quo: those who are its direct beneficiaries, others who live in a sort of comfort zone and fear any alteration that may jeopardize their way of life. These last groups of people are often labeled as conservatives.

Machiavelli said: "There are two methods of fighting, one with laws, the other with force: the one is proper to man, the second to beasts; but because the first one often does not suffice, one has to have recourse to the second" (Machiavelli, 2003, p. 75). Machiavelli was referring to the use of power as a kind of warfare, and that politics has at its base the struggle for power. Thus, the reformist, especially if she/he heads the state, must lead her/his parties to use available instruments.

The institutional tools are fundamental in the modern state and the global arena. Although political scientists have used institutional theory at least since Emile Durkheim established the principles of modern sociology, there are debates and schools of thought around the meaning of an institution (Durkheim, 1989). For Sue Crawford and Elinor Ostrom—who base their analyses on individual behavior—there are three types of concepts about what is an institution: (1) institutions-as-equilibria; (2) institutions-as-norms; (3) institutions-as-rules. Each is part of a different set of assumptions that try to explain political order and are "based on a view that institutions are enduring regularities of human action in situations structured by rules, norms, and shared strategies, as well as by the physical world." Institutional change thus implies that the "rules, norms, and shared strategies are constituted and reconstituted by human interaction infrequently occurring or repetitive situations" (Crawford & Ostrom, 1995, p. 582). The functioning of any government relies on the efficiency—and evolution—of political institutions.

To reform education, then, crusading reformers consider tools to promote institutional changes in line with their purposes, using their legal (bureaucratic rationality) powers and the monopoly of force, as Max Weber (2014) would say. Victor Baldridge (1978) and, from another perspective, Douglas North (1990), suggest that the classical Weberian analytic model is useful for elaborating typologies, examining the mechanisms of power, and evaluating the degree to which a government policy increases or diminishes its legitimacy. However, the Weberian bureaucratic prototype and the institutional analysis are insufficient to explain the decision-making process, since it ignores the informal types of power and influence—which might include groups like entrepreneurs or unions—that impose illegitimate constraints on the State policies. Nor is it adequate to explain struggles for power or changes in the relationships between political actors.

For these reasons, several chapters in this book combine institutional analysis with concepts of classical political theory, without a clear border between one or another type of tool. Still, the encompassing phrase of education reform constitutes their core. In abstract terms: the governing authorities who embark on processes of institutional change have the purpose of reforming specific patterns of behavior within the educational institutions of the apparatus of the State as a whole. The explicit goal of undertaking reform may best state vague or ambiguous, but the implicit one is not: maintain power. In this attempt, the traditions of political actors that coexist within—and give life to—institutions are affected. These actors may be able to accept—either by belief, convenience, or conformity, as Weber said—some of the proposed changes, but they will also always generate specific types of disputes.

Given these quarrels, although their design can be rational, correct and necessary, the fate of educational reforms is never inevitable. Their project is not a film script where the entire cast obeys the director to achieve the desired end. It is a plot open to public scrutiny and the vagaries of politics, where performers can be fickle and even treacherous. Besides, uninvited social actors often intervene, and certainly make themselves heard.

The education reform initiative has an origin that meets a purpose of change. Although the startup could respond to global demands, always alludes to national and local needs. On a few occasions, local initiatives expand to a whole system. The manifesto of reform still expresses a determination for transformation. That can be institutional—which includes legislation—or structure. Those who propose it, regularly aspire that the changes they promote reach depth and permanence. They wish the move had a course that does not allow many deviations, but flexibility to shift or dismantle certain traditions. Usually, that enterprise starts from above and spreads through the system. The reform contains the impulse of an ideology, which can be expressed or hidden, but present in the implementation's tools; it demands political action to convince that its purposes are prominent and necessary. This statement always refers to education as a factor of economic development, social cohesion, and citizen's virtues, as well as it suggests that the reform is a guardian and promoter of culture.

The final goal of education reform is to transform—either at the root or in the daily behavior of the actors of the educational act—the practices that their advocates considered remiss in the advancement of education, especially in schools and classrooms. The search to increase political legitimacy is a veiled, but present, purpose. For this motive, the reformist discourse always starts from diagnoses that show realities that it is urgent to modify and appeals to society as a whole to support change projects. They exhibit the promise of reform under an alluring discursive cover.

2 Resistance

Proposals for change face the defiance of those who benefit from the status quo, while the potential beneficiaries are not always their most fervent defenders. Reforms that last result from leaders who acted effectively in the context, such that they could even overcome an adverse political environment. It is not a matter of luck—fortune favors the prince who perseveres, said Machiavelli—it is the consequence of the political action (Machiavelli, 2003).

Opposition to education reform initiatives is manifold; it may be owing to the defense of certain traditions—some legitimate, others dishonest, or to the durability of cultural patterns. For many reasons, teachers are often the target of criticism, and institutional change is directed towards them, especially most of the pedagogical and curricular proposals. In many instances, teachers charge the blame for the failures of education, the low quality of training, the poor performance of students in international evaluations, and even for the shortcomings of the bureaucracy. Intergovernmental organizations and scholars aligned with the neoliberal perspective are typically responsible for reproaching and targeting teachers (Bruns, Filmer, & Patrinos, 2011; World Bank, 1995; World Bank Group, 2011), for instance. Other institutions, such as the OECD, criticize teachers in a somewhat more encouraging fashion, arguing to recruit the best prospects for the teaching profession. Yet, this still implies that current teachers lack the attributes—even the essential qualities—of professionalism (OECD, 2005).

Teachers and intellectuals sympathetic to their cause tend to see them as victims of an unjust social and political system, and of neoliberal forces. For those reasons, teachers and teachers' organizations are natural opponents to the attempts to upend the established arrangement (Hernández Navarro, 2011). Many times, leaders of the teachers' unions defend the status quo to protect their privileges, and so they mobilize their membership to embark in struggles against the reformist government. Also, the reformist government faces the rebelliousness of opposition political parties that pursue their ideological standpoints and political agendas. Education reform movements thus either walk a path filled with landmines, or the bureaucrats charged with hiking the trails are themselves incompetent or reticent.

3 Persistence

There are at least three ways of looking at the stability of school systems all over the world. Jacques Delors, in his recent visit to the four pillars of education, argues that: "Schools focus on continuity, memory—there is no future without memory—and so they try to resist the fast pace of modern life and the dominance of the present, which prevents us from taking a step back, exercising our judgment and thinking about the future" (Delors, 2013). That would be the best drive to maintain things that work out well or healthy at the education systems. That means that not always reform movements are driven by reasonable motives; some may generate out of capricious leaders.

Another path may be what neoinstitutionalist sociologists' term as the cultural persistence of teachers and other actors of the education realm (Zucker, 1999), or what Torsten Husen identifies as opportunistic ignorance: "people with interest in the status quo simply do not want to know disturbing facts." Furthermore, Husen argues that "The Common problem in the school systems of modern societies is the bureaucratic 'Cement cover' which stifles initiative and the innovative spirit" (Husen, 2007, p. 5).

The third perspective that may explain institutional persistence, according to Elinor Ostrom, is that "the creation and modification of effective social institutions are closer to an evolutionary process than from a top-down engineering design process. Social institutions evolve when human beings build from the existing rule structures, adding rules for some activity, modifying others and discarding others" (Ostrom, 2009, p. 18). See also Mahoney and Thelen (2010). Thus, radical or fast-track reforms are more difficult to implement.

These approaches provide rationales for both the persistence of existing school systems—or even an insurmountable defense of present conditions—as well as the reform that someone (usually political and business leaders) contend be necessary because schools are not working correctly. However, in most cases the meaning of reform is both inclusive—everything fits in it—or elusive, without content. Thus, we should outline ways of approaching the notion.

4 The Local and the Global

The dialectic between the local and the global, as Robert Arnove puts it, is a complex issue, not reducible to comparisons that only consider the similarities between international trends and the engineers of particular arrangements in each nation or region of the planet. "The school system of each country reflects the corresponding sociocultural systems within which they are embedded" (Arnove, 2013, p. 7). Each country has its history, its political dynamics, and particular social features. However, certain principles from the study of school systems in other societies may conceivably show likenesses with what is going on in another country. Even if those principles are very general, such as the structure of a system (primary, secondary, superior), the status of teachers, teaching practices in the classroom, or curricular rigidity in contrast to the autonomy of teachers to teach. Each country has cultural particularities or traditions and rituals of the social organization that may be unique, although with the growth of globalization these particularities may tend to become more and more invisible.

In my essay in this book, I expound upon the interpretative perspectives that scholars use to explain the convergence, or isomorphism, in the transfer of educational policies. These perspectives cover how governments or certain national social segments incorporate borrowed strategies in their reform projects: world culture theory, the approach of cultural neo-imperialism, and the perspective of the lender and the borrower (The discussion of these theoretical perspectives is more illustrative than prescriptive). The essay by Brent Edwards pinpoints a framework to study the political economy of policy implementation and tracks the influence of foreign aid institutions over El Salvador. Nonetheless, by intellectual conviction and the design of the anthology, each author in this volume has constructed her/his theoretical scaffolding, according to her/his object of study.

5 Regarding This Volume

The idea of composing a text like the one we put at your disposal today came up in a conversation I had with friends and colleagues of the Comparative and International Education Society, at the annual meeting held in Atlanta, in March of 2017. There I began to outline a map that would show the reforms of education in Latin America from the 1980s forward. The stars aligned correctly. My friend, Regina Cortina, who is the president of CIES and who worked hard to organize the 2018 Conference in Mexico City, invited me to convene a session (which resulted in two) on the hot topic of education reform in Latin America. I called ten colleagues from seven countries to participate in the adventure.

In March 2018 we held the panel, "The Blossom of Educational Reforms in Latin America," with eight papers. In the first session we had: Jason Beech, from the San Andrés University of Buenos Aires; Ana Ivenicki, Professor of Education at the Federal University of Rio de Janeiro; Beatrice Ávalos and Cristián Bellei, from the Center for Advanced Research in Education of the University of Chile; and José Weinstein and Gonzalo Muñoz, from Diego Portales University from Santiago, Chile. In the second session, those presenting their papers were René Guevara Ramírez and Sandra Milena Téllez Rico, from the National Pedagogical University of Colombia; Brent Edwards, from the University of Hawaii; Carlos Ornelas, from the Autonomous Metropolitan University in Mexico City; and Aurora Loyo, from the National Autonomous University of Mexico. We had two distinguished discussants, Martin Carnoy, from Stanford University, and Robert Arnove, from Indiana University.

Except for José Weinstein, Gonzalo Muñoz, and Sandra Milena Tellez, who could not travel, the rest of the attendees also participated in a day and a half conference at the Center for Regional Cooperation for Adult Education in Latin America and the Caribbean (CREFAL), in Pátzcuaro, Michoacán. Bob Arnove accompanied us. In addition to presenting the papers in Spanish, in this conference, we discussed the overall outlook of education reform, noted significant absences for a broader understanding of the phenomenon, and agreed to improve each one of the works. Then I called Jorge Baxter, to illustrate the case of Ecuador, and María Balarín, who in turn invited María Fernanda Rodríguez, to analyze the education system in Peru. In Patzcuaro, we noted the absence of the analysis of Cuban education, with its history of achievements in their education system. I invited Mark Ginsburg, who spends long periods on the island; for our great fortune, he agreed to write an essay together with Gilberto García Batista.

The theme of the CIES 2018 Conference in Mexico City was "Re-Mapping Global Education. South-North Dialogue," with a clear intention to distance itself from the North-South idea (all good education reform ideas get diffused from the Global North to the South), which is still dominant in academia, the press, and popular literature. For that reason, instead of organizing the content of the book by themes or regions, I decided to present the chapters simply according to the geography of the countries, from South to North.

In Chapter 1, Jason Beech, starting from the standpoint that the notion of inclusion has been central in global discourses about education in recent decades, analyzes policies and controversies for basic training in Argentina from 2003 to 2015. He makes the argument that such policies have aimed at the inclusion of the country's most disadvantaged groups, at least at the normative and rhetorical levels. He also argues that, by highlighting inclusion, such policies have resulted in contradictory outcomes. Even though some positive results have emerged, the overall situation of exclusion of a significant portion of society has not been resolved and remains a challenge for the educational system.

In Chapter 2, Beatrice Avalos and Cristián Bellei present how the Chilean government responded to the demands of the 2006 and 2011 student movements by employing two new laws, "Inclusion" (2015) and "Teacher Professional Development" (2016). Their analysis includes the debates between different social sectors about the rise and gradual dismantling of privatization and socioeconomic school segregation. They consider how the Bachelet administration (2014–2018) launched reforms to diminish the salience of market dynamics in Chilean education, including the ending of public subsidies to for-profit schools and supporting inclusive policies and ending selection practices in publicly-funded schools. The reform promotes quality in schools through improved teacher working conditions and training.

Still in Chile, Gonzalo Muñoz Stuardo and José Weinstein Cayuela, in Chapter 3, examine the 2014 "Inclusion Law." They illustrate how, even in the history of a short time, it modified the relationship of the state to private instruction, establishing free education in all schools, ending discrimination in student selection, and terminating profits from schools receiving public resources. From comparative and normative perspectives, their analysis shows that the Inclusion Law helps in three areas. First, treating quality education as a right for all. Second, eliminating the differences that acted against public school. Third, potentially decreasing socio-educational segregation. Nonetheless, its implementation faces challenges regarding better learning in Chilean schools.

The text then jumps a bit to the north. In Chapter 4, Ana Ivenicki takes multiculturalism as one of the salient features of Brazil and yet often unaddressed in education policies. Although not delving into curricular guidelines, she discusses a recent document of education reform in Brazil that modifies primary school programs, with implications for teacher education institutions: the Brazilian National Curricular Guidelines for Primary Education, approved in 2017. These guidelines advance a multicultural approach that should contribute to linking the search for excellence in education to social inclusion and to the development of citizens who value diversity and take a clear stand against prejudices along the lines of race, gender, ethnicity, and other identity markers.

Farther north, María Balarín and María Fernanda Rodríguez in Chapter 5 develop a history of turbulent times in Peru that brought an education reform movement which in three decades could not change many problems identified in the 1990s. The goal of Peru's subsequent governments has focused on improving the efficiency and effectiveness of schools. Although there have been constant changes in teams at the Ministry of Education, the reforms have only achieved some modest improvements in first-order policies such as students' achievement, enrollment growth, and infrastructure. The authors argue that several administrations have postponed much needed second order pedagogical reforms that seek to bring more fundamental changes to the core of educational practice.

Chapter 6 goes to the center of the Andean region, where Jorge Baxter identifies and compares competing policy stories of principal actors involved in the Ecuadorian education reform under President Rafael Correa, from 2007–2015. This essay is a study on the uses of political power. Baxter argues that since the 2007 presidential elections, President Correa focused his political capital on reconstituting the state's authority and ability to formulate and implement public policies. Before Correa's time, neoliberal politics eroded the state capacity to govern over the education sector. The concentration of power, combined with a capacity building agenda, allowed the Correa government to make progress on education reform with significant outcomes in equity and quality.

René Guevara Ramírez and Sandra Milena Téllez Rico engage in a debate over public policies in Colombian education in Chapter 7. They discuss the background politics that president Juan Manuel Santos (2010–2018) undertook to make Colombia acceptable as a member of the OECD. The evaluation of its education system turned out to be a matter of fundamental significance. The authors review the assessment that OECD staff and members of the Colombian Ministry of Education carried out to align the goals of national education with global trends championed by the OECD. They highlight four issues that would support education reform and assessment conducive to entering the OECD: quality, relevance, use of information, and funding.

Central American countries have spent decades in nearly constant turmoil. In Chapter 8, D. Brent Edwards Jr. takes the political economy of educational policy implementation in El Salvador as a case where education is a disputed landscape, and at the same time, political actors see it as a tool to move their agendas ahead. The analysis of Edwards goes beyond a focus on reform processes at the national level to examine the role of international organizations and global trends on current reform dynamics worldwide. By being mindful of the conditions in which education policies are more or less likely to be executed elsewhere, the chapter derives lessons that may be relevant well beyond El Salvador.

In Chapter 9, Mark Ginsburg and Gilberto García Batista review much of the Cuban education reform undercurrents since the early 1960s. They provide a long-term perspective on the struggle of Cuban revolutionaries to improve education. The authors explain how such reforms are paying attention to both national and global economic and cultural trends, as well as underlying political forces. They focus on the four revolutions or *perfeccionamiento* initiatives in education that the Cuban government has carried out since 1961. They conclude by noting that the reforms of education and teacher education enabled Cuba to continue on its socialist path, in the face of significant challenges, and contributed to Cuba's excellent achievements in access, equity, and quality of education.

In the chapter that follows (Chapter 10) I enter into a discussion of the main political components of the Mexican education reform of the Peña Nieto administration (2012–2018). I synthesize how both the reform proposal itself and the reactions of diverse actors contributed to re-mapping the Mexican basic education system. I bring into consideration opposing theoretical perspectives to discuss the Mexican reform. Although the change achieved notable success in political terms—diminishing the power of the corporatist union, for example—it is now on the verge of vanishing because the president elected in July 2018 threatens to dismantle it completely.

In the final chapter (Chapter 11), Aurora Loyo examines how and why Latin American teachers' unions oppose most education reforms. Such unions represent a tradition of struggle, and some of them constitute power which governments have to reckon with. She takes the cases of powerful guilds, such as the Confederation of Workers of the Argentine Republic (CTERA), the National Conference of Workers in Education of Brazil (CNTE), and the National Union of Workers of Education (SNTE) in Mexico, and its dissident groups. Loyo carefully reviews the main features in the repertoire of the teachers' organizations responses, which the leaders of those organizations foster to maintain the status quo and to strive to preserve their power.

References

Anderson, J. A. (2005). *Accountability in education.* Paris: UNESCO.

Arnove, R. F. (2013). Introduction: Reframing comparative education: The dialectic of the global and the local. In R. F. Arnove, C. A. Torres, & S. Franz (Eds.), *Comparative education: The dialectic of the global and the local* (4th ed., pp. 1–24). Lanham, MD: Roman & Littlefield Publishers.

Bacharach, S. B. (1990). *Education reform: Making sense of it all.* Boston, MA: Allyn & Bacon.

Bajaj, M. (2012). *Schooling for social change: the rise and impact of human rights education in India*. New York, NY: Continuum.

Baldridge, V. E. A. (1978). *Policy making and effective leadership*. San Francisco, CA: Jossey-Bass.

Beech, J. (2008). The institutionalization of education in Latin America: Loci of attraction and mechanisms of diffusion. In D. P. Baker & A. Wiseman (Eds.), *The impact of comparative education research on institutional theory* (pp. 281–303). Wagon Lane: Emerald.

Bruns, B., Filmer, D., & Patrinos, H. A. (2011). *Making school work: New evidence on accountability reforms* (Human Development Perspectives). Washington, DC: The World Bank.

Burns, T., Köster, F., & Fuster, M. (2016). *Education governance in action: Lessons from case studies*. Paris: OECD Publishing.

Clark, B. R. (Ed.). (1984). *Perspectives on higher education: Eight disciplinary and comparative views*. Berkeley, CA: University of California Press.

Colegio de Profesores de Chile. Informe Chile. In P. Gentili & D. Suárez (Eds.), *Las reformas educativas en los países del cono sur: un balance crítico* (pp. 277–358). Buenos Aires: Consejo Latinoamericano de Ciencias Sociales.

Cox, C. (2005). Las políticas educacionales de Chile en las dos últimas décadas del siglo XX: compromiso público e instrumentos de Estado y mercado. In M. Carnoy, G. Cosse, & C. Cox (Eds.), *Las reformas educativas en la década de los 90: Un estudio comparado de Argentina, Chile y Uruguay* (pp. 73–146). Buenos Aires: Ministerio de Educación, Ciencia y Tecnología.

Crawford, S. E. S., & Ostrom, E. (1995). A grammar of institutions. *American Political Science Review, 89*(3), 582–600.

Delors, J. (2013). The treasure within: Learning to know, learning to do, learning to live together and learning to be. What is the value of that treasure 15 years after its publication? *International Review of Education, 59*, 319–330.

Durkheim, E. (1989). La educación, su naturaleza y su función. In E. Durkheim (Ed.), *Educación y sociología* (pp. 55–98). Mexico City: Colofón.

Giddens, A. (1995). *La constitución de la sociedad: bases para la teoría de la estructuración* (J. L. Etcheverry, Trans.). Buenos Aires: Amorrortu.

Goh, C. B., & Gopinathan, S. (2008). Education in Singapore: Development since 1965. In B. Friedriksen & J. P. Tan (Eds.), *An African exploration of the East Asian Education* (pp. 80–108). Washington, DC: The World Bank.

Goldberg, M., & Harvey, J. (1983). A Nation at risk: The report of the National Commission for excellence in education. *The Phi Delta Kappan, 65*(1), 14–18.

Gorski, P. C. (2014). Poverty, economic inequality, and the impossible promise of school reform. In P. C. G. K. Zenkov (Ed.), *The big lies of school reform: Finding better solutions for the future of public education* (Kindle edition). New York, NY: Routledge.

Hargreaves, A. (2015). Foreword to the first edition. Unfinnished business. In P. Sahlberg (Ed.), *Finish lessons 2.0: What can the world learn from education in Finland.* New York, NY: Teachers College Press.

Hernández Navarro, L. (2011). *Cero en conducta: crónicas de la resistencia magisterial.* Mexico City: Para Leer en Libertad.

Husen, T. (2007). Problems of educational reform in a changing society. In V. D. Rust (Ed.), *Education reform in international perspective* (pp. 3–22). Bingley: Emerald.

Iturralde Guerrero, D., Maya, S. P., & Silva, M. L. G. (2017). *La reforma educativa en México, Chile, Ecuador y Uruguay: aportes para un análisis comparado.* Pátzcuaro, Michoacán: Crefal.

Klees, S. J., Samoff, J., & Stromquist, N. P. (Eds.). (2012). *The World Bank and Education.* Boston, MA: Sense Publishers.

Levin, H. M. (1976). Problems of educational reform in a changing society. In M. Carnoy & H. M. Levin (Eds.), *Education reform in international perspective.* New York, NY: David McKay.

Levy, D. C. (1986). *Higher education and the state in Latin America: Private challenges to public dominance.* Chicago, IL: University of Chicago Press.

Machiavelli, N. (2003). *The Prince and other writings* (W. A. Rebhorn, Ed.). New York, NY: Barnes and Noble Classics.

Mahoney, J., & Thelen, K. (2010). *Explaining institutional change.* Cambridge: Cambridge University Press.

Marx, K. (1972). The Eighteenth Brumaire of Louis Bonaparte. In R. C. Tucker (Ed.), *The Marx-Engels reader* (pp. 436–525). New York, NY: W. W. Norton & Company.

Max Plank Institute for Human Development and Education. (1983). *Between elite and mass education: Education in the Federal Republic of Germany.* Albany, NY: State University of New York.

North, D. C. (1990). *Institutions, institutional change and economic performance.* Cambridge: Cambridge University Press.

Nussbaum, M. C. (2010). *Not for profit: Why the democracy needs the humanities* (Kindle edition). Princeton, NJ: Princeton University Press.

OECD. (2005). *Teachers matter: Attracting, developing and retaining effective teachers.* Paris: Organisation for Economic Cooperation and Development.

Ostrom, E. (2009). Las reglas que no se hacen cumplir son mera palabrería. *Revista de Economía Institucional, 11*(21), 15–24.

Sack, R. (1981). Una tipología de las reformas en educación. *Perpectivas, XI*(1), 45–60.

Stromquist, N. P., & Monkham, K. (2014). *Globalization and education: Integration and contestation across cultures* (2nd ed.). Lanham, MD: Rowman & Littlefield.

Takayama, K. (2013). Not just tiger mums and rote learning: It's time for a balanced view of Asian education. *The Conversation.* Retrieved from https://theconversation.com/not-just-tiger-mums-and-rote-learning-its-time-for-a-balanced-view-of-asian-education-21154

Turner, D. A. (2014). Neo-liberalism and Public Goods. In D. Turner & H. Yolcu (Eds.), *Neo-liberal educational reforms* (Kindle book). New York, NY: Routledge.

Tyack, D., & Cuban, L. (2001). *En busca de la utopía: un siglo de reformas de las escuelas públicas*. Mexico City: Fondo de Cultura Económica.

Weber, M. (1946). Politics as a vocation. In H. H. Gerth & C. W. Mills (Eds.), *From Max Weber: Essays in sociology* (pp. 77–128). New York, NY: Oxford University Press.

Weber, M. (2014). *Economía y sociedad* (New edition, reviewed, commented and annotated by Francisco Gil Villegas; J. M. Echavarría, J. RouraParaella, E. Ímaz, J. F. Mora, & F. G. Villegas, Trans). Mexico City: Fondo de Cultura Económica.

World Bank. (1995). *Priorities and strategies for education: A World Bank review*. Washington, DC: The World Bank.

World Bank Group. (2011). *Education strategy 2020: Learning for all: Investing in people's knowledge and skills to promote development*. Washington, DC: The World Bank.

Zajda, J. (2006). Introduction. In J. Zajda (Ed.), *Decentralisation and privatisation in education: The role of the state* (pp. 3–27). Dordrecht: Springer.

Zucker, L. G. (1999). El papel de la institucionalización en la persistencia cultural. In W. W. Powell & P. J. DiMaggio (Eds.), *El nuevo institucionalismo en el análisis organizacional* (pp. 126–153). Mexico City: Fondo de Cultura Económica.

CHAPTER 1

The Long and Winding Road to Inclusion: Educational Policies in Argentina (2003–2015)

Jason Beech

Abstract

This chapter analyses policies for basic education in Argentina from 2003 to 2015. I argue that such policies have aimed at the inclusion of the most disadvantaged groups, at least at the normative and rhetorical levels. However, I also will contend that the emphasis on inclusion has resulted in contradictory effects. Even though the reform has some positive signs, the overall situation of exclusion of a significant portion of society remains a challenge for the educational system. The results of PISA, for instance, and national assessments do not show improvement concerning the quality of education. The notion of inclusion has been central in global discourses about education in the last decades. The malleability of the concept partly explains its preeminence in international discussions. The binary inclusion/exclusion works as a worldwide slogan with certain stability and adapts to the situation of different places. For example, in Sweden or Finland, the focus on inclusion aims at unsuccessful students, usually from low educated and immigrant families. South Africa reads inclusion/exclusion through the lens of ethnic categories, and it relates to "salvation from the dead hand of apartheid." Having as background the collapse of the Argentine socio-economic structure, starting in the 1970s and culminating in 2001 the crisis, I analyze the most relevant education policies during the Kirchner administrations (2003–2105).

1 Introduction

This chapter analyzes policies for basic education in Argentina from 2003 to 2015. I argue that such policies have aimed at the inclusion of the most disadvantaged groups, at least at the normative and rhetorical levels. However, I also contend that the emphasis on inclusion has resulted in contradictory effects. Even though some positive signs accounted for, the overall situation of

 | DOI: 10.1163/9789004413375_002

exclusion of a significant portion of society has not been resolved and remains a challenge for the educational system.

The notion of inclusion has been central in global discourses about education in the last decades. The malleability of the concept partly explains its preeminence in international discussions. The binary inclusion/exclusion can work as a worldwide slogan with certain stability and adapt to the territorial situation of different places. So, for example in places like Sweden or Finland, the focus on inclusion is aimed at unsuccessful students, usually from low educated and/or immigrant families (Lindblad & Popkewitz, 2004). In South Africa, inclusion/exclusion is read through the lens of ethnic categories and is related to "salvation from the dead hand of apartheid" (Muller, 2004, p. 144).

In the case of Argentina, after the sustained growth of inequalities and poverty that started in the 1970s and culminated in the socioeconomic and political crisis of 2001, educational inclusion has been associated to the need to attend the educational needs of those most affected by the debacle of the socioeconomic structure. To give an idea of the magnitude of the challenge, in 1980 10% of the population in Argentina was living in poverty, a number that grew to 56% in 2002 (Gasparini & Cruces, 2008; Gasparini, Marchioni, & Sosa Escudero, 2000). The situation is even worse when considering that children are over-represented among the poor. In the second semester of 2003 71% of children lived in poor households (Kessler, 2014). In this context of severe socio-economic decline, the global and local demands for increasing access to education generated a considerable challenge to include the most disadvantaged groups, especially in early childhood, secondary and post-secondary levels of the educational system.

I present an analysis of the most relevant education policies during the Kirchner administrations (2003–2105). In the context of the "turn to the left" in most of Latin America, there was strong rhetoric against "the 1990s," "neoliberalism" and—to a certain extent—globalization. The government articulated its political discourse and action around the notion of inclusion. For example, it expanded the access to pensions, legalized gay marriage, and implemented the Universal Child Allowance, a massive conditional cash transfer program. Also, the program Conectar Igualdad provided more than five million computers to secondary school students and teachers, the Fines program created an alternative educational track for young people and for adults who had dropped out of secondary education, and a new national education law made secondary education compulsory. Investment in education and teacher salaries also improved significantly in the first half of the Kirchner administrations.

The chapter shows that the overall results of these initiatives regarding inclusion have been quite contradictory. Even though more students are accessing secondary education, repetition and dropout rates are still very high and are strongly correlated to socio-economic status. The results of national assessments show mixed results without a clear tendency towards improvement concerning the quality of education. Also, the growing exodus of students across the socioeconomic spectrum to private schools is another indicator of the failure of state policies aimed at improving the public system.

Thus, a steady movement towards educational inclusion in Argentina is still a utopian dream. I will argue that the approach to education policies during the analyzed period was based on a series of strategies and programs that operated at the margins of the educational system but did not have profound effects on actual structures and practices that have been excluding the most disadvantaged groups.

To further explore these arguments, I will divide the chapter into five sections. The first one describes the socioeconomic debacle of Argentina during the last decades of the Twentieth Century and briefly describes the reform of the 1990s and main educational indicators by the end of the century, to present a panorama of the situation by the beginning of the 2000s. The second section analyses the overall characteristics and political orientations of the Kirchner administrations and their whole approach to education policies. I will contend that one of the main features of education policies during that period was the fragmentation of state intervention into a series of isolated programs. Thus, the third section offers an analysis of some of the leading programs aimed at impacting the educational system during the Kirchner administration: Conectar Igualdad, Fines, and Asignación Universal por Hijo. In the fourth part, I review the primary indicators of inclusion in education, regarding access, permanence, graduation, and quality of learning. I will also show that one of the main trends concerning results (even if it was not necessarily an intended outcome) was the growth of private enrollments, especially in Greater Buenos Aires and, to a lesser extent, in other big urban centers. In the concluding section, I offer interpretations of the difficulties that Argentina is experiencing to promote inclusion in education.

2 The Political, Economic and Educational Situation in Argentina at the Start of the Twenty-First Century

Political instability has been a salient characteristic of Argentina in the second half of the Twentieth Century. Since the first presidency of Peron from 1946 to 1951, no constitutionally elected president finished its full term until Carlos Menem in the 1990s. Except for two brief democratic periods interrupted by military coups, the armed forces took control of the state between 1955–1973. In the 1960s and especially in the 1970s, guerrilla groups emerged. In 1976, the infamous Proceso de Reorganización Nacional started the darkest period in Argentine history, when state-sponsored violence against citizens resulted in tens of thousands of people made to "disappear."

Economic indicators between the 1970s and 2000s show a persistent growth of inequalities and poverty. The Gini coefficient in Argentina went from 0.36 in 1974 to 0.51 in 2000 (Altimir et al., 2002). Poverty also increased. In 1980 the index of poverty in Argentina was almost 10%, and the level of extreme poverty or indigence was close to 2% (Gasparini, Marchioni, & Sosa Escudero, 2000). Since then, these indexes had consistently increased, reaching their peak in 2002 when 56% of the population was below the poverty line. As Gasparini and Cruces (2008) describe:

> To some extent, the dramatic increase in income inequality experienced by Argentina between the mid-1970s and the mid-2000s is easy to understand. The country experienced in three decades most of the phenomena that are linked to increases in inequality in economic theory: macroeconomic severe crises; hyperinflation; high unemployment; repressive dictatorships; processes of deep trade liberalization; episodes of sudden and rapid capital accumulation, technology upgrading and modernization; weak labor institutions; and un-equalizing demographic changes. (p. 4)

In 1973 the external debt was 4.89 billion dollars, Menem started his presidency in 1991 with 62.2 billion dollars, and by the end of 1999, the debt had risen to 146.2 billion dollars. In December 2001, faced by a severe economic crisis, President De la Rua froze all bank accounts. People took to the streets, and the president stepped down in response to the violent riots in which security forces killed close to 40 people. After a period of political uncertainty, with three different interim presidents named in the same week, a Legislative Assembly designed Senator Eduardo Duhalde to complete De la Rua's term.

Thus, by 2002, Argentina was going through its worst political, economic and social crisis. It was the culmination of a significant process of socio-economic and political debacle. Governmental authorities had insignificant legitimacy, the economy was devastated, and severe poverty and massive inequalities struck the country. Besides, one of the interim presidents had declared Argentina's default of its foreign debt. The country was politically and economically isolated from the world system and in a very fragile situation.

In general, educational policies in the second half of the Twentieth Century followed the unstable logic of the political context. The most relevant initiative to consider regarding its influence on the post-2001 period is the reform of the 1990s that attempted to make a substantive and overreaching overhaul of the Argentine educational system. The reform of the 1990s, based on the Ley Federal de Educación (LFE), for the first time in Argentine history regulated in one normative document most aspects of basic education. Tiramonti (2001) notes that while structural adjustment policies tended to reduce the functions of the state, the National Ministry of Education acquired with the educational reform an increasingly prominent role that is only comparable with the importance assigned to education during the foundational period of the Argentine educational system in the nineteenth century. This same author refers to the "hyperactivity" of the national state in the production of proposals for action, plans, and programs. The Law of the Transfer of Educational Services transferred the responsibility of basic education (including tertiary institutions where most of the teacher education takes place) to the provinces.

There was also a Higher Education Law; a Federal Council of Education was re-established; a Federal Educational Pact was signed; and the whole structure of the Argentine educational system—traditionally divided into seven years of primary education and five years of secondary school—was changed into a 6-3-3 configuration. In addition, the reform established several programs, such as the National System of Evaluation (SINEC), the National Commission for the Evaluation of Universities (CONEAU), a Social Educational Plan, a Federal Net of Continuous Teacher Training, and Curricular Reforms for Pre-school Education, General Basic Education, Polimodal (secondary education) and for Teacher Education. Curricular reforms changed the locus of decision making, passing from a model that was very centralized in the National government to give room for decisions at the levels of provincial administrations, schools, and even teachers. At the same time, the government promoted a change in the whole logic of school contents through a sharp critique of the existing encyclopedic culture, based on factual knowledge, and the promotion of a curriculum based on the development of competencies (Beech, 2011).

Although the above description of the reform is not exhaustive, it is enough to show that the change of the 1990s was a very ambitious attempt to reform almost every aspect of the educational system at once.

Thus, by 2001, when the socio-economic crisis broke out, the educational system was going through a process of an incomplete overreaching reform that had been appropriated quite differently in each of the 23 provinces and the City of Buenos Aires, generating what many authors refer to as a "disarticulation of the school system" (Terigi, 2016). Schools and teacher salaries were also affected by the growth in poverty, inequality, and unemployment. Thus, the challenge of reconstruction was massive.

3 Education Policies during the Kirchner Administrations

In 2003 elections were called to replace president Duhalde. In a context of distrust for political parties and politicians in general, Menem won the first round of elections with only 24% of votes. He had to compete in a second vote with Nestor Kirchner who had been voted second. Aware that most of the population had a very negative view of his figure and that he had no chance of winning, Menem withdrew from the ballotage, and Nestor Kirchner was made President.

The Kirchner administration defined itself discursively against Menem, 'the 1990s' and 'neoliberalism.' It was part of the turn to the left in Latin America, governing for three consecutive four years periods: Nestor Kirchner from 2003 to 2007, and Cristina Fernandez de Kirchner from 2007 to 2015. The Kirchner administration reversed some of the privatizations of the 1990s with the nationalization of Aerolineas Argentinas, postal services, retirement and pension funds and the water company. Kirchner also made a strong move to minimize Argentina's link to international credit organizations such as the International Monetary Fund. The government articulated its political discourse and action around the notion of inclusion. It expanded the access to pensions, legalized gay marriage, and implemented the Universal Child Allowance, a massive conditional cash transfer program.

In 2003 started the period of significant economic recovery, with annual growth rates of close to 9% of the GDP until 2007. From 2008 to 2011 the GDP continued to grow at a smaller rate with a recession in 2009. From 2012 onwards, the economy stagnated with years of modest growth followed by years of small recessions (Rivas & Dborkin, 2018). Similarly, poverty was reduced significantly from 2003 to 2007; the trend continued but at a slower pace from 2007 to 2011, and stagnated close to 30% since then (Figure 1.1). Thus, the level of poverty that Argentina has since 2011without significant variations is similar to the one it had in the first years of the 1990s. Nevertheless, economic growth and poverty reduction were substantial during the first two terms of the Kirchner administration, contributing to the reduction of poverty, inequalities, and unemployment.

In this context, the Kirchner administration was very active regarding education policies during their three successive presidential periods. In a federal country with 24 different educational systems not all initiatives, failures and success are attributable to the national government. Nevertheless, the analysis of education policies in each jurisdiction exceeds the possibilities of this chapter which focuses on examining the main characteristics of national policies. In some cases, when available, I present some indicators of each province when they are relevant to show regional differences or inequalities, but I

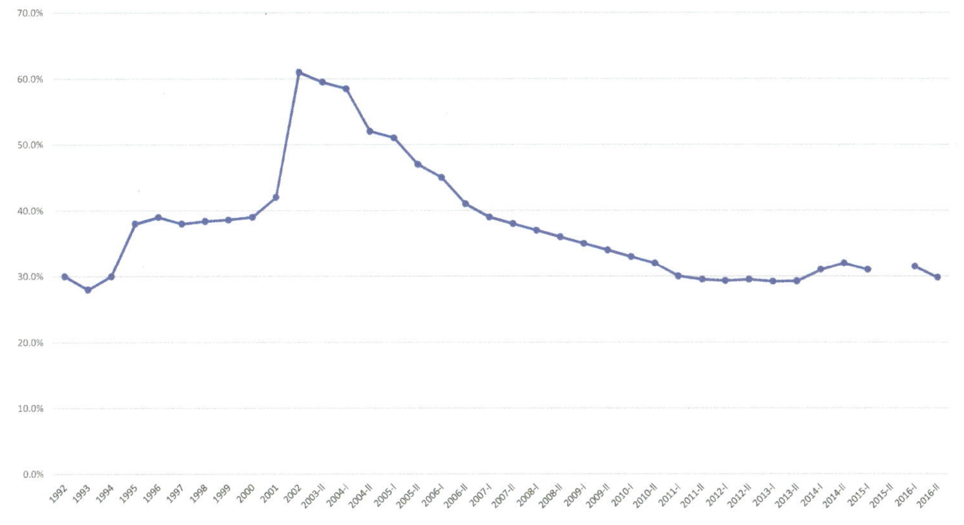

FIGURE 1.1 Poverty in Argentina (1992–2016) (from Gasparini, 2017, p. 572)

do not offer a detail exploration of these dissimilarities. During the analyzed period, the national government was also very active in its policies for universities, especially concerning the creation of new institutions. However, given space constraints, I center this chapter on strategies for basic education.

During the first years, between 2003 and 2006, the initiatives of the national administration focused on the need to overcome the crisis of the educational system. Overall, the emphasis was on improving financial investments in education and recovering teachers' salaries that had been steadily declining since the 1970s and were further struck by the crisis of 2001 (see Figure 1.2). These efforts were visible in the laws passed during the period. In 2003, a Law of Guarantee of Teacher Salaries and 180 School Days aimed at assuring a minimum salary for teachers in all provinces. It also ruled the minimum number of school days in each province that was (and still is) in some cases affected by teacher strikes demanding salary improvements. In 2004 the Law of the National Fund for Teacher Incentives renewed a mechanism created in 1998 through which the national government transferred funds to the provinces to pay teachers an extra compensation. In 2005, a Law of Educational Financing was passed establishing annual targets that set the minimum investments that the national and provincial administrations had to dedicate to education, science, and technology. It defined the aim of reaching a total investment of 6% of the GDP by 2010. The National Law of Education in 2006, established that once reached the target of 6%; the next step was for the national and provincial govrnments to invest at least 6% of the national GDP in education, excluding science and technology (Rivas & Dborkin, 2018).

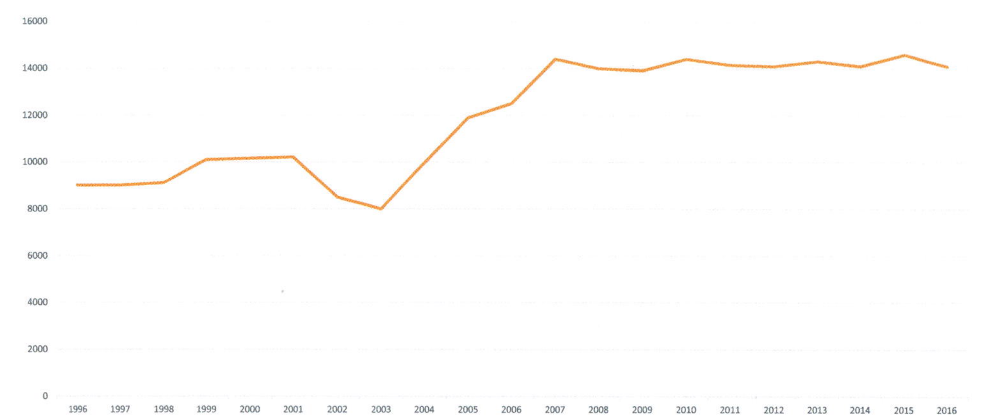

FIGURE 1.2 Evolution in teacher salary in Argentina (1996–2016) in Argentine pesos 2016 (based on Rivas & Dborkin, 2018)

The financial aims of the Law were achieved, passing from an investment of 4.6% of the GDP in 2005 to 6% in 2010 (Bezem, Mezzadra, & Rivas, 2012, 2014). Between 2003 and 2015 investment per student increased 158%. However, the increase was not stable during the whole period. Given the crisis of 2001, investment per student in 2003 was meager. With the economic recovery and the decision to increase investments in education between 2003 and 2007 per student expenditure almost doubled with an increase of 99%. From 2007 to 2011 the increase was 24% and between 2011 and 2015 only 4% (Rivas & Dborkin, 2018).

Similarly, changes in teacher salary show that there was an overall increase during the whole period, but with three different cycles (Figure 1.2). After a decrease of 20% in 2002 and 7% in 2003 teacher salaries were very low. From 2003 to 2016 the increase was 80%. From 2003 to 2007 it was 69%, from 2007 to 2011 7% and from 2011 to 2015 4% (Rivas & Dborkin, 2018).

The second phase of educational policies during the Kirchner administration started with the passing and implementation of the Law of National Education (LEN for its acronym in Spanish) in 2006 (Terigi, 2016). The Ministry of Education initiated a participatory deliberation, inviting teachers and all sectors of society to give their opinion on the forthcoming changes. In line with the overall discursive political positioning of the government, the document that promoted the debate took the criticism of the economic and educational reforms of the 1990s as a starting point. The LEN was passed in 2006, replacing the Ley Federal de Educación (LFE) of 1993.

The LEN established the expansion of compulsory education, from 10 to 13 years by making the last three years of secondary education mandatory. That was the most consequential change that had a considerable impact on future education policies, focusing the attention of policymakers on secondary school, and impacting on student and families' behavior, resulting in an expansion of enrollments (I will offer accurate indicators later).

Another essential objective of the LEN was to overcome the disarticulation of the educational system. On the one hand, as a consequence of the freedom that provincial governments had to adopt the 6-3-3 structure promoted by the LFE, basic education was organized in many different formats in the provinces. The LEN returned to the traditional division between primary and secondary school, giving local governments the option of a 6-6 or a 7-5 structure (Míguez, 2014).

On the other hand, the reform of the 1990s had shifted most formal power to make decisions about education from the national to the provincial authorities. However, in practice, the challenge of developing a proper articulation between the federal and provincial levels was not met. To address this issue, the LEN revised the role of the state, giving more participation to the national government in education policy, and making it the principal responsible for guaranteeing access for all to the educational system (Filmus & Kaplan, 2012; Míguez, 2014; Terigi, 2016) This had two related consequences. One was a process of "recentralization" expressed in the LEN and in general in the whole approach to education policies during the Kirchner administrations. The LEN established that the resolutions of the Federal Council of Education could be mandatory for the provinces if stipulated by the Council (Míguez, 2014; Terigi, 2016). The Federal Council is an institution comprised of the Ministers of Education of all provinces lead by the National Minister, that has the role of coordinating educational policies among the different provinces. Also, during the Kirchner period, the central government developed many national programs that recentralized educational policymaking from the provincial to the national level.

The other way in which the LEN aimed at strengthening the role of the national government was more symbolic, by emphasizing the responsibility of the state in promoting "educational justice" and in overcoming educational inequalities. Probably one of the most eloquent expressions against privatization is contained in article 10 that establishes that "the National State will not sign bilateral or multilateral free trade agreements that imply conceiving education as a lucrative service or promote any form of commodification of public education" (Art. 10).

For some, the way in which the LEN defines the responsibility of the state in guaranteeing education equality is a fundamental feature of the Law that marks a significant shift from the "neoliberal program" of the LFE (Filmus & Kaplan, 2012). Others (Míguez, 2014; Terigi, 2016), recognize the emphasis of the LEN on state responsibilities, but do not see it as such a significant change when compared with the LFE. As Miguez (2014) suggests: "These differences were not expressed in statements that were very different from those present in the Ley Federal; in any case, they appear through the reiteration of the responsibility of the state in successive articles…" (p. 31). He later emphasizes this position by noting that the change in paradigm that the LEN was promoting could not be expressed in a completely new language. Nevertheless, the positions in this debate are not based on distinct interpretations of the definitions in the LEN, but rather on different readings of the LFE and the extent to which it expressed a neoliberal approach to education policies (Beech & Barrenechea, 2011).

The LEN also established the creation of the National Institute for Teacher Education (INFD for its acronym in Spanish). Teacher education was (and still is) considered to be one of the weakest aspects of education in Argentina, partly due to the existence of an extensive and disarticulated system of teacher education with more than a thousand tertiary institutions and some universities that also prepare teachers. The law gave the INFD the responsibility of planning and implementing policies aimed at articulating the system of initial and continuous teacher training. Even though the INFD designed new national curricular guidelines for teacher education and was very active in offering professional development options to teachers all over the country, it did not adequately fulfill its role as an agency of evaluation and accreditation of institutions.

Thus, the LEN was a very ambitious legislation. Following the tradition of seeing changes in the law as representing a reform, many analysts consider these alterations as an educational reform (Míguez, 2014; Ruiz, 2009). The two significant changes are the extension of compulsory education and revisions in structure, returning to the traditional distinction between primary and secondary school. There are also many structural continuities with previous legislation. The LEN did not promote major reforms in the governance of education, nor was the curriculum changed. Thus, it is debatable to what extent the sanction of the LEN can be considered to represent an educational reform or not.

Another critical issue is that legislation in itself does not change education. Terigi (2016) notes that one of the problems with the law was that no prior planning was made to assess the feasibility of the made decisions, setting priorities and progressive plans that could organize human and material efforts in reaching the aims set by the law. Feldfeber and Gluz (2011) also mention the difficulties in attaining some of the objectives but attribute them to the lack of effective policies that could materialize the contents of the LEN, and to the dynamics of the Argentine federal system which sometimes creates obstacles for the effectiveness of education policies.

Nevertheless, the LEN became a fundamental guide for education policies in the years following its approval (Feldfeber & Gluz, 2011; Terigi, 2016). Most efforts were in addressing the challenges of including all students in secondary education and reducing dropout and repetition rates. Another important initiative was a new Law in 2014 that made early childhood education compulsory for 4-year-old children (before, since the LFE it was only mandatory for 5-year-olds).

4 Fragmented Education Policies: The Emphasis on Programs

A characteristic of education policies in Argentina in the 2000s was the fragmentation of state initiatives into a series of individual and isolated programs. That is not significantly different from previous administrations. Some of the programs, such as the National Program for Scholarships for Students continued of earlier ascendancies. Similarly, negotiations for the Program for the Improvement of the Educational System that had the financial support of the Inter-American Development Bank started in 2001. The government approved such Program in 2003. Nevertheless, the Kirchner administration was very active in developing new programs, such as the Integral Program for Equality in Education, National Program for Educational Inclusion, Program for Sex Education, Program of Support to the Policy of Improvement of Equity in Education.[1] Especially after the LEN that made secondary education compulsory, many of these programs focused on secondary school.

Out of the programs created, there are three that I will analyze in more detail given their significance regarding the financial resources invested and their social and educational repercussions: Universal Child Allowance, *Conectar Igualdad*, and *FinEs*.

4.1 *Universal Child Allowance*

The Universal Child Allowance (AUH) is a Conditional Cash Transfer Program (CCTP). This kind of programs represent the efforts of governments in Latin America to reposition the state at the center of a welfare system. CCTP programs in Latin America developed in two different ways. Some countries created utterly new programs, such as Progresa (later transformed into Oportunidades) in Mexico and Bolsa Familia in Brazil. Other countries such as Chile and Uruguay decided to extend the coverage of already existing programs. The Argentinian government created AUH as an extension of the Contributory Family Allowances (AFC) (Bertranou & Maurizio, 2012).

In 2008 Nestor Kirchner's administration decided to re-nationalize the pensions system, privatized during the 1990s. Then, "the reserves of the privately-managed pensions system (equating to about 10 percent of the GDP) were transformed into the Sustainability Guarantee Fund (FGS), which is part of the public social security system (Bertranou & Maurizio, 2012, p. 56). Since its origin, that program targeted households in which parents were unemployed, or working in the informal sector and earning less than the minimum wage, and those working in domestic service. The AUH covers all children from their birth until they are 18 years old, up to a maximum of five children per household. The age cap does not apply to children with disabilities, but beneficiaries of the AUH must be Argentine or must have been a legal resident in the country for more than three years.

According to Cecchini (2014), CCTP programs in Latin America mostly fall into two different types of programs. There were those with strong conditionalities and those with soft conditionalities. The AUH is an example of the latter category because beneficiaries are entitled to 80% of the benefit—paid monthly—irrespective of the fulfillment of the obligations established in the Program. The remaining 20% is to be transferred at the beginning of the following school year; that percentage is contingent on the fulfillment of the sanitary and educational conditionalities. Beneficiaries must show evidence of attainment of vaccination requirements and medical check-ups for all children under five years old. Besides, for the recipients to receive the transfer, all those children older than five years old must attend school and complete the school year.

By 2015 there were more than 3.6 million beneficiaries from the AUH; the overall amount of the transfers represented 0.8% of the national GDP (Edo, Marchionni, & Garganta, 2017). According to ANSES—in collaboration with CEDLAS, CONICET, and UNICEF (2017)—by the end of the year 2015, 12.5% of the households benefited by the program were no longer deemed as being poor. Kliksberg and Novacovsky (2015) noted that children pertaining to households that benefited from the AUH experienced an 8.4% increase in consumption of basic nutriments and a 7.1% increase in the assistance to medical check-ups.

Although linear causality between the AUH and enrollments cannot be assumed, the data suggests that the program had a stronger educational outcome on older secondary students than in primary level and lower secondary students. A report by UNICEF (2017) states that by the year 2004 net enrollment rates for primary education and early secondary schools where over 97%, while net enrollment rates for youth between 15 to 17 years old were close to 82%. For this age group, AUH appears to have had a substantial effect because although that 82% remained relatively constant until 2009, as from 2010—when the government launched AUH—enrolments had continuous growth, reaching 87% by 2014. This growth affected, mainly, beneficiaries of the AUH. The report goes on to explain that while non-beneficiary's enrollment levels incremented by 1.9%, the rate for those benefitted by the AUH was of 5.1%.

According to Edo, Marchionni, and Garganta (2015) "... the impact seems to be higher for boys than for girls and among single-parent households where the head has lower education levels" (p. 3). Moreover, although the evidence shows that regarding the educational outcomes of the program, girls were not benefited by the AUH as much as boys did, they still benefited from a reduction of inter-annual dropout and retention rates.

Thus, the influence of AUH was very positive both in contributing to reducing extreme poverty and in promoting access to health and education services. The AUH has gained much social support and has been sustained and even expanded by Fernandez de Kirchner's successor.

4.2 *Conectar Igualdad*

In 2009 President Fernandez de Kirchner gained massive support from the Argentine population, obtaining almost 55% of the votes for her reelection. The social security system had substantially increased available funds after the re-nationalization of the pension system. The Program Conectar Igualdad, launched in 2010, used part of those funds.

Conectar Igualdad aimed at giving a computer to every student and every teacher in state secondary schools, in public teacher education institutions and individual schools, to provide connectivity to their establishments, and to train participating teachers. The model that inspired such a program was the One Laptop per Child (OLPC) initiative, but instead of using the computers produced by OLPC, it bought the Classmate computers developed by Intel, a private corporation. At the time, the one to one model was quite popular in Latin America. By 2015 86% of OLPC devices and 89% of Classmates had been sold in countries such as Brazil, Colombia, Paraguay, Venezuela, Peru, Honduras and Uruguay (Beech & Artopoulos, 2017). Especially crucial in influencing the decision of launching Conectar Igualdad was the Uruguayan Plan Ceibal that distributed the OLPC computers to all primary school students in the country. In 2010, Conectar Igualdad became the most significant program of netbook distribution to students in the world. By the end of 2015, it had already distributed more than 5.3 million netbooks in the country (Gvirtz, 2016).

Conectar Igualdad was one of the initiatives that helped to portray the image of an inclusive and effective government that had sought to reoccupy a central role in promoting social inclusion.

The design, implementation, and evaluation of Conectar Igualdad were carried out through different units that reported to the President. The central unit was the Administración Nacional de la Seguridad Social (ANSES), the institution in charge of social security that had the funds of the pension system. It was its responsibility of buying and distributing the netbooks. The National Ministry of Education oversaw teacher education and the pedagogic side of the project, and the Ministry of Federal Planning, Public Investment and Services managed connectivity. Thus, it was a complex organizational structure that had two significant effects. As the program became the most visible and disruptive education policy of the time, it contributed to recentralize influence on education at the national level, but at the same time displaced power from the Ministry of Education to other state agencies.

The three primary objectives of Conectar Igualdad were to recuperate and revitalize public schooling, to reduce the digital gap and to build a universal policy of digital inclusion of federal reach. The promotion of technology and the use of netbooks not only by students but also by all family members seemed particularly relevant in a scenario where according to the last census, in 2010, 41% of Argentines between 25 and 50 years old, did not use computers.

At the beginning of the program, official voices claimed that Conectar Igualdad was going to revolutionize the whole education system. The plan appeared as an initiative that could, almost on its own, reduce drop-out and repetition rates amongst secondary school students, by invigorating their engagement to the new technology-mediated activities that it promoted (Lago Martínez, 2015). After all, in Argentina, many of the students that abandon schools in the last years of secondary education are very much motivated by a lack of interest in what schools offer (Sibila, 2012). Therefore, through the incorporation of technology, it was thought that students would find it easier to reconnect with school practices. Once students graduated, they could keep the device as their property. The expectation was that this would act as an incentive to improve graduation rates. The authorities also thought that giving students access to these computers would revitalize public schools, making them more attractive for families, creating a discouragement to move to private schools.

Fernandez de Kirchner expressed, during the official launch of the program Conectar Igualdad on April 6th, 2010, that:

> I feel a little bit as the Sarmiento of the 200th Bicentenary, because if Argentina was revolutionized with public education, with the compulsion of primary schools, with the education that always characterized our country as a distinctive feature in the training of its human resources, in its degree of literacy, in its level of instruction.[2] I feel that the same thing

> happens with this program that we are launching today, Conectar Igualdad, a name, I clarify, was not aleatory. I wanted it to include the term equality because I think it is the distinctive term that all those Argentines that have been committed to the development of our country since 1810 have always pursued.[3]

According to Dussel (2014), the discourse behind *Conectar Igualdad* was that citizens had rights, and to achieve such entitlements was a state task. Hence, given the technological innovations in society at large, it was the state's responsibility to allow the most marginalized populations to have access and to learn how to become literate in the use of technology.

Overall, the program was very efficient in distributing the netbooks, but not as successful concerning teacher education and, especially regarding providing connectivity to schools. One of the most significant technical challenges of *Conectar Igualdad* was connecting schools to the internet and installing the local area network at schools. The process proved to be a big problem for the central administration and one of the most significant obstacles for the practical use of technology in the methods of teaching and learning.

In assessing the outcome of the program, it is essential to distinguish between its social implications and its pedagogic results. *Conectar Igualdad* was beneficial in providing access to technology to many students and families that had never owned a computer before. Thus, it had a noticeable impact in contributing to diminishing the digital gap in a context of significant inequalities (Kliksberg, 2016).

However, during its first five years of implementation *Conectar Igualdad* did not have a significant pedagogical imprint, especially when compared to the importance it had in the social inclusion arena. Critical voices have affirmed that by 2015 *Conectar Igualdad* had failed to re-shape educational practices; students barely used computers in schools. Also, the usage was not transformative; students mostly used the notebooks for word processing, group presentations or web searches (Lago Martinez, 2015). A recent study (Benítez Larghi & Zukerfeld, 2015) analyzed the kind of use that students make of the netbooks through a survey. In terms of the application for educational activities, only 7.3% say that they use the computer every day in school, 33% say they use it in school more than once a week, while 28.7% say they use it less than once a week in school, and 31.1% say they never use it in school for educational activities. The use for educational activities at home is a bit higher: 9.5% say they use it every day, 41.8% say they use it once a week, 27.3% less than once a week and 21.4% never. Consistent with the view that the program had a stronger impact regarding overall digital inclusion, the use for non-educational activities is higher in school and at home.

Thus, even though the government conceived *Conectar Igualdad* as a program, which could potentially revolutionize public education in Argentina, its pedagogical outcome represented one of its most significant shortcomings. Furthermore, it received two more relevant critiques. One the one hand, based on statistics that show that 34% of benefited students did not have a computer at home before the program, Tedesco, Steinberg, and Tófalo, (2015, p. 82) note how important the plan was for these students. However, they also argue that it is necessary to revise in the future "the viability of sustaining initiatives of massive distribution of personal computers, and maybe concentrate efforts in particular contexts in which there are significant gaps." Besides, Terigi (2016, p. 28) points to the huge investment made and to a controversial aspect of the program: "the provision of netbooks is a recurring expense...which is operationally financed with funds of ANSES, that should be destined to pensions and social security. Maybe in the future, this mode of financing should be revised."

In 2018 *Conectar Igualdad* was replaced with a new plan called Plan Aprender Conectados (Learning Connected).[4] It virtually implies closing down *Conectar Igualdad* since the new project does not consider the distribution of notebooks to students and is in charge of the Ministry of Education, displacing ANSES. Within the structure of the new Plan, there is a section dedicated to *Conectar Igualdad* which seems to work exclusively to give support to students who already have the netbooks distributed.[5]

4.3 *FinEs*

In 2008, the Federal Council of Education created the Plan for the Completion of Primary and Secondary Education for Youth and Adults (known as FinEs for its Spanish acronym). The purpose of the program is to offer young people and adults excluded from the educational system, the possibility of finishing primary and secondary education. FinEs responded to a mandate of the LEN that made secondary education compulsory. By 2008 almost 42% of the population between 18 and 60 years old (5.5 million people) had not completed that cycle. Among them, 1.6 million were between 18 and 30 years old (Viego, 2015). The LEN established that extraordinary measures had to be taken to support those vulnerable populations so that they could complete the requirements imposed by the legislation.

However, the Argentine education system already had alternative possibilities for individuals to end their secondary education, even as 'adults,' through a compensatory system. Viego (2016) explained that by 2008 6,546 schools operated under this system. Thus, FinEs functions as a parallel structure to existing educational options for adults that had not finished compulsory educational levels.

Between April and November of 2008, the program FinEs arrived at all Argentine provinces and the City of Buenos Aires. Although the national government promoted the Plan, it was local provinces which administered it in their territories, making specific arrangements in local contexts. Since its conception, the project had two distinct phases. The first one (FinEs I) targeted students who had persisted in school for the last year of secondary education but were not able to pass all required courses. The second phase (FinEs II) extended the realm of beneficiaries to all other individuals that had not finished either primary or secondary education.

A salient characteristic of FinEs is that it promotes the articulation of local states with organizations of civil society in its implementation. Thus, unlike most programs that targeted older youth and adults, FinEs often operated in places different to regular schools: local clubs, NGOs' headquarters, places where members of political parties meet, unions' headquarters, and churches, among other places (Facioni, Ostrower, & Rubinsztain, 2013). The participation of organizations of civil society gave a powerful local community imprint to FinEs. Crego and Gonzalez (2015) point out that FinEs allowed students who did not have easy access to schools to have an educational experience in a place closer to them. The role of social organization and grassroots movements was a very relevant aspect of the program. These organizations did not only host many of the in-person sessions between tutors and students but also helped with the recruitment of beneficiaries of the program.

There is little information as to actual spending in the program, and there are few official statistics regarding graduation rates. Nevertheless, using some of the available data, Viego (2016) provides some evidence on the effects of the Plan. Between 2008 and 2013 the percentage of individuals aged 18 to 60 years old that had neither completed the secondary level or were not attending schools decreased from 46.3% to 42.8%. Nonetheless, Viego (2016) states that the available evidence suggests that this declining trend had begun before the implementation of FinEs and that it did not accelerate with the Plan.

Taken as a whole, the Plan triplicates the global rate of graduation of the existing schools for Adults. However, when distinguishing between FinEs I and FinEs II the situation is entirely different. In the case of FinEs II, the graduation rate is not much higher than the one of the existing schools for adults. Furthermore, Viego (2016) notes that an official report shows a sustained growth of enrolments in schools for adults between 2001 and 2010. Since 2010, once FinEs was operational in all provinces, enrolments in schools for adults started to decrease at a very similar rate to the growth of registrations in FinEs II. That suggests that in practice rather than becoming another available option for adults, Fines II almost replaced existing schools for adults regarding the students it attracted (Viego, 2016).

On the other hand, the graduation rates of FinEs I, that was aimed at regular secondary school students that had some pending exams to graduate, were much lower than rates of graduation in common secondary schools. While in common schools one out of two students graduate, in FinEs I the proportion is one to four (Viego, 2016).

It is tight with available data to have a definitive view of the merits of the Plan regarding its results. On the one hand, it is clear that it had an inclusive effect by contributing to the graduation of many people excluded from the system. Nowadays, having a secondary school certificate is almost indispensable to access the formal job market, and FinEs has helped people from some of the most vulnerable social groups to have entrance to this capital. It is not clear what the fiscal cost is, and, for FinEs II, if the coexistence of this Plan with the existing schools for adults is needed.

Within the literature there are critiques to FinEs. One of the negative issues mentioned is the quality of the education that it offers. The content of the courses of this program (in its two versions) was believed to be much less demanding than that of the mainstream system. Besides, most jurisdictions determined that tutors be those that had to decide whether the students had fulfilled the curricular content successfully. Authors such as Viego (2016) found that many tutors felt compelled to pass students, who needed the high school diploma to apply for jobs. Most of the recipients of these programs were socially disadvantaged individuals. Hence, it is understandable that tutors could feel somehow compelled to pass students so that they could move forward and have a better chance of improving their economic situation.

Other critiques were based on the sub-standard working conditions of tutors, that had unstable short contracts (Huenchunao & Muñoz, 2016), and earned much less than mainstream teachers (Viego, 2016). Diaz (2016) also highlights the lack of preparation of many of the tutors. Although many of them also work in schools within the mainstream system, some jurisdictions have allowed university students—even from other fields, with no pedagogical experience—to act as trainers. Finally, Facioni, Ostrower, and Rubinsztain (2013) suggest that even though the fact that the Plan operated in settings of organizations of civil society had some advantages concerning facilitating access, many of those physical spaces were ill-equipped for educational practices.

Thus, FinEs has been quite useful for providing access to a school diploma to some of the most excluded populations, but at the same time, the Plan is poor concerning the quality of the education it offers and the working conditions of its teachers. Moreover, there are not many available data to evaluate its efficiency regarding investment of resources vis a vis its contribution.

Overall, the three programs analyzed in this section had mixed results in their educational aims. The objective of promoting education inclusion guides all of them. In general, the three were successful concerning supporting access to education or digital technologies. However, none of these programs has had a significant effect in transforming the mainstream educational system or in improving the quality of teaching and learning within it, nor have they made it more inclusive, changing the structural conditions that create exclusions and inequalities within the system.

5 Assessing Inclusion in Education in Argentina

Since 2003 Argentina has gone through a process of steady economic growth (at least until 2009). Programs to attend the economic needs of the most disadvantaged were created, investments in education increased, and teacher salaries were improved. At the same time, the state established a series of education policies and programs aimed at educational inclusion. Thus, in principle, an improvement in indicators could be expected. Typically, measuring inclusion includes two main issues. On the one hand, access and permanence in the educational system, and on the other, the quality of learning outcomes in schools.

Regarding access, enrollments grew significantly in early childhood education (38%) and secondary school (16.6%) between 2003 and 2015.[6] The extension of compulsory schooling to 4-year-olds and all secondary education mostly explains these changes that were also fueled by the creation of new schools, especially for early childhood. Meanwhile, in primary, enrolments were reduced by 3.6%. Considering that access at this level has been already universal in Argentina for several decades, the reduction is probably related to a combination of three factors. First, a slight demographic decrease from 2001 to 2010 in population between 5 and 12 years old. Second, as I later discuss in more detail, there was a significant reduction in repetition rates in primary education, which contributed to having fewer over-aged students. Finally, before the LEN provinces had very different ways of dividing primary and secondary school. The arrangements that were made to adapt the provincial systems to the mandates of the new law tended to reduce the number of years included within primary education as they are part now of secondary school.

An important aspect to consider concerning analyzing access to education is the distinction between state-run and privately run schools since changes were not homogeneous in both subsystems. In all levels of basic education, enrollments in the private sector grew more than enrollments in the public sector. The most significant difference was at the primary level that had a growth of 27.3% in the private sector, while the public sector had a reduction of 11.6%. Enrollments in early childhood grew 64.7% in the private sector and 27.6% in official schools. In secondary education, the difference is not as big, with a growth of 23.3% in private schools and 14.1% in the public subsystem.

Thus, there is a definite tendency towards a higher growth of enrolments in private schools. This general tendency at a national level is manifested very differently in different provinces. While the overall percentage of enrollments in the private sector is 29% on average in the country as a whole, in the City of Buenos Aires it is 51% and 40% in Buenos Aires conurbation (formally part of the Province of Buenos Aires). Cordoba (33%) and Santa Fe (29.5%) are closer to the national average, while in Chaco, Formosa and La Rioja private enrollments are close to 10%.[7]

Concerning permanence in schools, another key indicator to measure inclusion, the data show significant improvements in primary education where the percentage of over-aged students was reduced from 22.8% in 2003 to 11.4% in 2015. In the same direction, repetition rates reduced by 69% between 2003 and 2014. Meanwhile, in secondary education, there are mixed results, without significant improvements and some setbacks. In basic secondary school (the first three years) the proportion of overaged students increased 4% from 32.2% in 2003 to 33.3% in 2015, while repetition rates augmented 18% in the same period. In the case of upper secondary, the proportion of overaged students decreased by 6% and repetition by 13% between 2003 and 2015. Therefore, considering permanence, there were significant improvements in primary education, but in the case of the secondary school that included many new students that are the first generation in their families to access this level, the challenge to improve trajectories persists.

Graduation rates had improved from 39.5% in 2003 to 45.6% in 2013. In the public subsystem graduation rates are lower, but the improvements are more significant, from 30.6% in 2003 to 38.5% in 2013 (Terigi, 2016). Thus, a higher percentage of students are advancing from secondary education, but the proportion is still deficient.

The last issue to consider is the quality of learning outcomes for those who accessed and remained in the system. National evaluation systems report results by grouping students into three levels: low, mid and high performance. At primary level, in both the 3rd and 6th grades, the percentage of low performing students reduced in Language and Mathematics between 2005 and 2013. At the same time, the portion of high achieving students increased in all cases. However, in Mathematics most students are in the low and mid performance categories (the percentage varies between 70% and 86%), while very few students are in the high performing group. The highest rate was 28% for 3rd grade and 26% in 6th grade in 2010. Performances in other subjects are similar.

In secondary education, in all subjects—Mathematics, Language, Social Sciences and Natural Sciences—the fraction of students in the low performing group diminished between 2003 and 2013. That was especially visible in Mathematics. On the other hand, the percentage of students with high performance in the assessments of 2013 in most disciplines was similar or smaller than in 2005. In Mathematics, the highest rate of students in the top performing group was recorded in 2007, while in all other disciplines it was in 2005. Thus, overall, in most subjects, improvements in the reduction of students performing in the low level implied an increase in the mid-level, without increases in the high performing group. The other vital tendency to report is that changes in performance did not move in time in an apparent trend towards improvement. Instead, results in learning assessments have moved irregularly with enhancements alternating with setbacks. Furthermore, for all curricular areas and all evaluations, the clear majority of students is in the low and mid performing groups. Consequently, for the analyzed period, there are no reports of significant improvements in the quality of learning.

Regarding the relationship between learning outcomes and the socioeconomic status of students, there is a definite tendency in which as the socioeconomic students' status augments, the proportion of students in the high performing group increases and the percentage of students in lower levels of performance shrank. Overall, both for primary and secondary and in all the disciplines that are evaluated, in the low socioeconomic group, the proportion of students below the basic expected level is more than three times higher than for the top socio-economic group (Aprender, 2016).

Consequently, since the collapse of the socioeconomic structure of Argentina that culminated in the crisis of 2001, the aim of including the most disadvantaged groups in the educational system has been emphasized in the official rhetoric and in some specific policies and programs. However, this stress on inclusion resulted in contradictory effects. There are some positive signs, such as the increased access in early childhood and secondary education and the improvements in educational trajectories in primary schools. The increase in graduation rates in secondary education is also a positive sign. However, there are no significant enhancements in quality of learning outcomes nor in the trajectories of secondary school students coming from the most disadvantaged backgrounds, and even though graduation rates in secondary schools have improved, they are still deficient. This educational level continues to be the biggest challenge concerning inclusion and one of the most defiant levels to improve.

6 Conclusions

Throughout this chapter, I analyzed education policies between 2003 and 2015. I exhibited that the national state has been very active in promoting educational inclusion, in a context of a government that had a robust discursive emphasis on the responsibility of the state in improving the opportunity of the most disadvantaged groups. The government faced the need to reconstruct the country after three decades of political instability and socio-economic collapse that ended in the most severe social, economic and political crisis ever experienced in Argentina. From this very complex point of departure, the economy grew steadily for the first half of the period, significantly reducing unemployment, inequalities, and poverty. However, since 2011 the economy has overall stagnated, and poverty has remained close to 30%. Argentina seems to have structural difficulties to improve the socio-economic situation of its most vulnerable population beyond that point. The level of poverty since 2011 is similar to the one in the beginnings of the 1990s.

In education, the incomplete reform of the 1990s left a disarticulated system that also suffered from the impact of the overall crisis, affecting the social conditions of families, and with teacher salaries and investments at a shallow level. The Kirchner administrations significantly augmented expenditures and teacher salaries and were very active in terms of creating educational initiatives to promote inclusion. When considering the point of departure, results were largely positive. However, there were also limits regarding promoting inclusion. Still, low graduations rates in secondary education, the need to improve student trajectories in this level, and severe difficulties to steadily improve the quality of learning outcomes are some of the indicators of these limits to educational inclusion.

The difficulties to promote a generalized inclusion in education do not a have a linear nor straightforward explanation. Nevertheless, one of the reasons seems to be the fact that most of the policies established aimed at compensating for some of the problems of the system, but they did not have an impact on the structural conditions that generate exclusion from the educational system. For example, FinEs provided a valuable alternative to compensate for exclusions, but it operates outside the formal educational system, without any influence on the mechanisms that generate the injustices that it tries to overcome. Meanwhile, there has been no significant interventions on fundamental aspects, such as governance mechanisms, how resources are assigned (for example teachers to schools), the teaching career, and the encyclopedic curriculum fragmented into 12 to 14 subjects in secondary education. In this way, the educational system in Argentina continues to operate as a mechanism that tends to the reproduction and widening of inequalities.

Another relevant tendency is the growing movement of families towards private schools that have taken place in the last 15 years in the big urban centers, especially in the Buenos Aires conurbation. It is no longer only the most affluent groups that opt for private schooling for their children, but also those in the second- and third-income quintile. The process of privatization contributes to widening inequalities, fragmentation and segregation. Furthermore, since most private schools that cater for the lowest socioeconomic groups belong to the Catholic Church and have subsidies from the state, those movements to private education contribute to the erosion of the laicity of some provincial educational systems. It is an incremental process that is almost imperceptible and is happening without proper public debate in society and its institutions of democratic deliberation.

Thus, educational inclusion in Argentina is still a huge challenge that requires policies that address the structural problems of the educational system to pass from rhetoric to practice so that formal education can become an instrument of inclusions, social development, and equality.

Notes

1 This is not a complete list. To see all the programs created in the period see the balance made by the Ministry of Education (Ministerio de Educación, 2015 #605).
2 Domingo Faustino Sarmiento is considered to be the founding father of the Argentine educational system.
3 The speech of the president introducing the program Conectar Igualdad can be accessed from https://www.casarosada.gob.ar/informacion/archivo/22068-blank-11525813
4 Decree 386/2018.
5 https://www.argentina.gob.ar/educacion/aprender-conectados/conectar-igualdad
6 Unless specifically stated, all data in this section is taken from the 2015 Annual Report of the Ministry of Education.
7 Given the way in which the state reports the data, average privatization data used in this paragraph includes non-university higher education.

References

ANSES. (2017). *Análisis y propuestas de mejora para ampliar la asignación universal por hijo*. Buenos Aires: UNICEF.

Argentina, M. d. E. y. D. (2016). *Aprender 2016*. Primer Informe de Resultados.

Beech, J. (2011). *Global panaceas, local realities: International agencies and the future of education*. Frankfurt am Main: Peter Lang.

Beech, J., & Artopoulos, A. (2017). *Knowledge, computers and development: Mobilizing knowledge related to 1:1 Programs in Latin America*. Paper presented at the 2017 AERA Annual Meeting, San Antonio, TX.

Beech, J., & Barrenechea, I. (2011). Pro-market educational governance: Is Argentina a Black swan? *Critical Studies in Education, 52*(3), 279–293. doi:10.1080/17508487.2011.604077

Benítez Larghi, S., & Zukerfeld, M. (2015). *Flujos de conocimientos, tecnologías digitales y actores sociales en la educación secundaria. Un análisis socio-técnico de las capas del Programa Conectar Igualdad*. La Plata: Universidad Nacional de La Plata Universidad Maimonides.

Bertranou, F., & Maurizio, R. (2012). Semi-conditional cash transfers in the form of family allowances for children and adolescents in the informal economy in Argentina. *International Social Security Review, 65*(1), 53–72.

Bezem, P., Mezzadra, F., & Rivas, A. (2012). *Informe final de Monitoreo de la Ley de Financiamiento Educativo. Informe de monitoreo y evaluación*. Buenos Aires: CIPPEC.

Bezem, P., Mezzadra, F., & Rivas, A. (2014). *¿Se cumplió la Ley de Financiamiento Educativo?* Buenos Aires: CIPPEC.

Cecchini, S. (2014). Educación, programas de transferencias condicionadas y protección social en América Latina y el Caribe. In M. Feijoó & M. Poggi (Eds.), *Educación y políticas sociales: sinergias para la inclusión*. Buenos Aires: IIPE-UNESCO.

Crego, M. L., & González, F. M. (2015). *Jóvenes y posiciones desiguales. Relaciones entre experiencia e igualdad en el caso del Plan FinEs en el Gran La Plata*. Paper presented at the III Seminario Internacional Desigualdad y Movilidad Social en América Latina, Bariloche.

Díaz, M. P. (2016). *Acceso, experiencias y expectativas de los egresados del plan finalización de estudios secundarios (FINES) en profesorados secundarios*. Paper presented at the IX Jornadas de Sociología de la Universidad Nacional de La Plata.

Dussel, I. (2014). Programas educativos de inclusión digital. Una reflexión desde la Teoría del Actor en Red sobre la experiencia de Conectar Igualdad (Argentina). *Versión. Estudios de Comunicación y Política, 34*, 39–56.

Edo, M., Marchionni, M., & Garganta, S. (2015). *Conditional cash transfer programs and enforcement of compulsory education laws: The case of Asignación Universal por Hijo in Argentina* (Working paper, No. 190).

Edo, M., Marchionni, M., & Garganta, S. (2017). Compulsory Education Laws or Incentives From CCT Programs? Explaining the rise in secondary school attendance rate in Argentina. *Education Policy Analysis Archives, 25*(76). http://dx.doi.org/10.14507/epaa.25.2596

Facioni, C., Ostrower, L. A., & Rubinsztain, P. (2013). *Cuando el Estado se hace presente: los Bachilleratos Populares a partir del Plan FinEs.* Paper presented at the X Jornadas de Sociología. Facultad de Ciencias Sociales, Universidad de Buenos Aires.

Feldfeber, M., & Gluz, N. (2011). Las políticas educativas en Argentina: herencias de los '90, contradicciones y tendencias de "nuevo signo." *Educação & Sociedade, 32*(115).

Filmus, D., & Kaplan, C. (2012). *Educar para una sociedad más justa. Debates y desafíos de la Ley de Educación Nacional.* Buenos Aires: Aguilar.

Gasparini, L., & Cruces, G. (2008). *A Distribution in Motion: The case of Argentina.* La Plata: Centro de Estudios Distributivos, Laborales y Sociales, Universidad Nacional de la Plata.

Gasparini, L., Marchioni, M., & Sosa Escudero, W. (2000). *La distribución del ingreso en la Argentina y en la provincia de Buenos Aires.* Buenos Aires: Ministerio de Economía de la provincia de Buenos Aires.

Gasparini, L., & Tornarolli, L. (2017). *La pobreza en Argentina: recuperando la comparabilidad.* Retrieved from http://focoeconomico.org/2017/04/01/la-pobreza-en-argentina-recuperando-la-comparabilidad/

Gvirtz, S. (2016). Tres decisiones claves para definir una política de integración de TIC: el Programa Conectar Igualdad. In M. T. Lugo (Ed.), *Entornos digitales y políticas educativas: Dilemas y certezas* (pp. 137–161). Buenos Aires: IIPE – UNESCO.

Huenchunao, V. G., & Muñoz, H. B. (2016). *La configuración del trabajo docente pedagógico desde las nuevas relaciones laborales en la escuela media de la norpatagonia: el caso Plan FinEs.* Paper presented at the Actas del III Seminario Nacional de la Red Estrado.

Kessler, G. (2014). *Controversias sobre la desigualdad: Argentina 2003–2013.* Buenos Aires: Fondo de Cultura Económica.

Kliksberg, B. (2016). *Hacia la inclusión digital: Enseñanzas de Conectar Igualdad.* Buenos Aires: Ediciones Granica.

Kliksberg, B., & Novacovsky, I. (2015). *El gran desafío: romper la trampa de la desigualdad desde la infancia: aprendizajes de la Asignación Universal por Hijo.* Buenos Aires: Editorial Biblos.

Lago Martínez, S. (2015). La inclusión digital y la educación en el Programa Conectar Igualdad. *Educação, 38*(3).

Lindblad, S., & Popkewitz, T. S. (2004). Education restructuring: Governance in the narratives of progress and denials. In S. Lindblad & T. S. Popkewitz (Eds.), *Educational restructuring: International perspectives on traveling policies* (pp. 69–94). Greenwich: Information Age Publishing.

Míguez, D. (2014). Las reformas educativas argentinas en el contexto latinoamericano. Los sentidos de igualdad y democracia (1983–2006). *Revista Latinoamericana de Estudios Educativos, XLIV*(3), 11–42.

Ministerio de Educación. (2015). *La política educativa nacional 2003–2015: Inclusión y mejores aprendizajes para la igualdad educativa.* Buenos Aires: Ministerio de Educación.

Muller, J. (2004). Responsiveness and Innovation in Higher Education Restructuring: The South African case. In S. Lindblad & T. S. Popkewitz (Eds.), *Educational restructuring: International perspectives on traveling policies* (pp. 143–165). Greenwich: Information Age Publishing.

Rivas, A., & Dborkin, D. (2018). *¿Qué cambió en el financiamiento educativo en Argentina?* (Working paper No. 162). Buenos Aires: CIPPEC.

Ruiz, G. (2009). La nueva reforma educativa argentina según sus bases legales. *Revista de Educación, 348*, 283–307.

Sibila, P. (2012). *¿Redes o paredes? La escuela en tiempos de dispersión.* Buenos Aires: Tinta Fresca.

Tedesco, J. C., Steinberg, C., & Tófalo, A. (2015). R*esultados de la encuesta nacional sobre integración de TIC en la educación básica Argentina.* Buenos Aires: UNICEF.

Terigi, F. (2016). Políticas públicas en educación tras doce años de gobierno de Néstor Kirchner y Cristina Fernández. *Análisis, 16.*

Tiramonti, G. (2001). *Modernización educativa de los 90 ¿El fin de la ilusión emancipadora?* Buenos Aires: TEMAS Grupo editorial.

Viego, V. (2015). Políticas públicas para la terminalidad educativa: el caso del Plan Fines en Argentina. *Archivos Analíticos de Políticas Educativas, 23*(116), 1–21.

CHAPTER 2

Recent Education Reforms in Chile: How Much of a Departure from Market and New Public Management Systems?

Beatrice Ávalos and Cristián Bellei

Abstract

Chilean education is an extreme case of a market-oriented educational system. The Chilean government implemented policy instruments associated with this view for several decades. These policies entail privatization and socioeconomic school segregation. Teachers suffered the effects of such policies. As a response to the demands of the 2006 and 2011 student movements, the Chilean government (2014–2018) launched reforms to diminish the relevance of the market dynamics in Chilean education, including ending public subsidies to for-profit schools. Specifically, two new laws aim to reduce school selection in publicly funded schools and to improve the management system of public schools. A third law addresses teaching and teacher conditions by establishing requirements for teacher education and a new teacher career system. Based on a literature review and the study of policy documents, this Chapter discusses two aspects of the Chilean education reform. First, it deals with the challenges this change will face and the extent to which it moves away from the market model. Second, it focuses on the teacher reform that sectors of civil society and political groups consider essential to improve teachers working conditions and preparation.

1 Introduction

Education reforms in Chile became one of the most critical change areas occurring during the four years of the center-left government of President Michelle Bachelet (2014–2018) and took place in the context of much political and educational discussion. As we argue in this article, these reforms attempted to correct the adverse effects of the neo-liberal market system inherited from the military dictatorship period (1973–1990) and lessen the operation of "new public management" principles over the school system and its structure, including

 | DOI: 10.1163/9789004413375_003

the conditions of teachers and teacher education. The article deals with three of such reforms embedded in laws known as "Inclusion," "Public Education" and "Teacher Professional Development." Concerning the first two, we analyze the degree to which they move towards establishing a less market-driven publicly funded school system and set out conditions for non-discriminatory access to them. We consider the nature of the opposition to these changes and how to deal with in the final versions of the two laws. About the policy affecting teachers, we focus on the establishment of a career system expected to better teacher working conditions and on measures to improve the quality of initial teacher education, noting the extent to which it sets out quality assurance mechanisms less marked by narrow accountability considerations.

In this article, we attempt to highlight whether and how these three policies succeed in providing better conditions for inclusive education and teacher performance. Its main conclusions suggest that effectively the agreed changes move clearly in this direction, although with shortcomings that in the future may be dealt with or to the contrary may affect progress as intended.

2 The Ideological Policy Context before the Reforms

The economic features of neo-liberalism marked the overriding ideology behind Chilean educational development during the dictatorship period (Bellei, 2015). These features included a market-driven education system linking quality and results to freedom in the opening and running of schools, school choice on the part of parents as well as a competitive funding system of vouchers based on numbers of students in attendance during school time (Friedman, M., & R., 1980). In this creed, the role of government education authorities was limited in general to the establishment of the school system's operation rules, the setting of curriculum frames and the monitoring of educational learning results through measurement instruments. This ideology supported two types of state-funded schools: public schools managed by municipalities and privately owned subsidized schools (including for-profit and religious schools). The system also included a small number of entirely private schools. Both private-subsidized, as well as private schools, were able to select students based on varied family and student characteristics, not so the municipal public schools except for a few academically selective ones.

The dictatorship severally altered teachers' working conditions, which removed them from the regulatory statute enacted in 1969. That one covered all public servants and had secured for teachers what were then satisfactory working conditions. The statute provided for teacher contracts with a teaching/

non-teaching ratio of 65/35 and a salary system that allowed for a 140% increase over their initial remuneration by the time they reached 27 years of service.

With the transfer of public schools to municipal administration in 1981 the provisions of the statute were ignored (Guzman, 2014), salaries became insufficient and unwarranted teacher dismissals occurred in the mid-eighties (Lomnitz & Melnick, 1998). Besides affecting the working conditions of teachers, the dictatorship was also insensitive to the institutional conditions required for good quality initial teacher preparation regarding downgrading many of the programs that had been part of the University of Chile to tertiary non-university status (Ormeño et al., 1996 in Ávalos, 2002).

3 Post-Dictatorship Policy Evolution within the Education Market System

With the advent of democracy in 1990 and throughout the following two decades there has been an evident policy tension in Chile between the need to correct the effects of neo-liberal policies on educational inequities while maintaining distinct features of the market-school system, a situation observed with different intensity in other school systems (Rizvi & Lingard, 2010; Ávalos & Razquin, 2017). On the one hand, during the 1990s there were interesting school-based programs designed to improve equity in educational processes (Bellei & Vanni, 2015, García-Huidobro & Sotomayor, 2003), structural reforms such as lengthening of the school day aimed at providing more learning time and broader education opportunities as well as curriculum reforms (Cox, 2003). On the other hand, the government maintained the voucher system of funding as was also student selection in privately managed subsidized schools. In the early nineties, these schools were allowed to charge extra fees subject to parental agreement. Taken together these measures contributed to private funded schools operating under more favorable conditions to produce learning results as measured by standardized tests, and to an increasing loss of students on the part of the municipal school system reaching a low of around 35% in 2015.

As far as teachers working conditions to redress some of their deteriorated conditions, the democratically elected government enacted in 1991 a new teachers' statute that improved over existing conditions but not to the level teachers had enjoyed under the 1969 public servants' statute. The government also funded a sizeable five-year program to improve the functioning and quality of teacher education programs operating between 1997 to 2002 (Ávalos, 2002, 2005). However, later authorities missed dealing with the increase of low quality private teacher preparation programs from 2004 onwards, leaving these to develop under market forces until the situation became unacceptable towards the end of the decade (Cox, Meckes, & Bascopé, 2010). To correct this and resorting to new public management principles, the government opted for external quality control via a voluntary test for new teachers and program accreditation together with some support for teacher education quality improvement based on competitive funding and measurable outcomes (Ávalos, 2015).

4 The Pursuit of Quality through "New Public Management" Evaluation Policies

Throughout the first decade of this century, Chilean educational authorities became increasingly concerned that education quality and measurable educational results were below expectations in the light of international tests such as TIMSS and PISA, despite educational policies attempting to improve on this (Cox, 2003). Thus, without substantially altering the market and voucher system expressed in school competition for students, different governments sought to increase their "auditor" role (Charlton in Biesta, 2014) in line with "new public management" policy principles (Solbrekke & Sugrue, 2014; Sisto & Fardella, 2014; Falabella, 2015; Rizvi & Lingard, 2010; Ball, 2003). In their pursuit for improved education results, Chilean educational authorities emphasized the monitoring of learning through an enormous increase of national standardized tests (reaching up to 15) as well as through participation in international measurements led by the OECD, the International Association for Educational Achievement (IEA) and by UNESCO. Schools were publicly ranked based on average test scores, and rankings were made known to parents to orient their school choice. More recently, chronically low-performing schools have been subjected to sanctions including their closure (Bellei & Vanni, 2015).

Schools have been susceptible to the pressures implied by external standardized evaluations. According to a recent survey, 97% of school principals located in the city of Santiago reported applying assessments to train their students for the standardized tests labeled as SIMCE (System for the Measurement of Education Quality and Equity). Another 80% of principals reported altering classroom assessments to resemble the SIMCE test and the use of other forms of SIMCE test preparation such as allocating extra teaching time to those subjects evaluated by the test (Manzi et al., 2014). Research on school improvement processes has documented the effect of such practices in significantly increasing school competitiveness through improved test performance, but characterized such improvement as spurious, given the narrowing of the curriculum and pedagogical practices in pro of test preparation and the raising of scores (Bellei et al., 2016). Thus, in reality, Chilean schools have been subject to a double market-oriented and test-based accountability system, which strongly determines their school practices.

Additionally, there has been a multiplication of different types of standards' statements: for teachers, for principals and for every specialization in teacher education programs coupled with evaluations to measure achievement of these standards by teachers and prospective teachers. Teachers have been made accountable through a combination of performance evaluation procedures together with a system of economic incentives.

The most evident results of this market-oriented education system inspired in neo-liberalism and "new public management" have been to maintain a highly unequal education system with schools segregated by social class (Valenzuela, Bellei, & de los Ríos, 2014), without there being satisfactory learning results as measured by international assessments. Particularly, the proportion of "resilient" students belonging to the bottom quarter of the population concerning economic, social and cultural status who perform in the top quarter of PISA tests is well below the OECD average (OECD, 2016).

The unexpected outburst of student protests in 2006 and 2011 (Bellei & Vanni, 2015) forcefully brought out the frustration of educational users regarding the system of education to which they had access. Secondary students shouted against inequities in publicly funded education within and between types of schools (public and private). Higher education students protested about the system of bank loans to finance their studies and its impact on long-term harsh repayment costs. Teachers complained, and civil society took on the defense of teachers (El Plan Maestro, 2015) calling for improvements in their working conditions and well-being, these considered to be of increasing importance in international organizations' statements and studies (MacBeath, 2012).

Public awareness and concern together with clear evidence of an education system not working regarding equity and social justice underpinned the introduction of radical structural reforms by the government of president Michelle Bachelet (2014–2018). These reforms have been part of an ambitious program of institutional and policy change that also included tax reform and plans for a new constitution replacing the 1980 Constitution imposed by the dictatorship government.

The educational reforms cover both the school system and higher education. Their explicit objectives have been to alter the subsidiary state framework restricted to the promotion of markets by introducing a new framework in which the state actively guarantees and provides universal social rights. Two of these reforms attempt to bring principles of equity and social justice into the publicly funded education system while a third one seeks to raise the professional status and working conditions of teachers. In the rest of the chapter, we deal with these reforms, refer to the policy debates around them, including the difficulties faced for their approval and ask about the extent to which they move away from the inherited neo-liberal market and the new public management ideologies.

5 Two Policies Aimed at Reducing Market Dynamics in Education

5.1 *Inclusion Law*

The first pillar of the Chilean educational reform is the so-called Inclusion Law (Ley 20.845, 2015), comprising a highly complex set of regulations designed to diminish the market practices in the education system referred to above. It affects the subsidized private schools primarily and in particular the profit-making and fee-charging schools as well as those that select by family origins and prior education results. During its parliamentary discussions in 2014, the Law triggered a highly polarized political debate; it passed in 2015 after a constitutional review requested by right-wing parliamentarians. Below we deal with the main components of the Inclusion Law.

5.2 *End to Public Funding of For-Profit Schools*

For-profit subsidized schools expanded dramatically in Chile reaching an impressive 86% of all publicly funded private schools. Contrary to what appeared as an advantage, evidence was showing that for-profit schools did not have a higher academic performance compared to non-for-profit private schools or public schools (Elacqua et al., 2011; Zubizarreta, Paredes, & Rosenbaum, 2014; Contreras et al., 2011). There was evidence that for-profit schools did not offer a more diverse curriculum, and that instead, they allocated less financial resources to critical educational inputs such as teacher salaries. Furthermore, according to official estimates, for-profit educational providers were having annual revenues of at least US $400 million.

Given the above-described situation and to guarantee that public resources allocated to the education sector be in fact used to expand and improve educational services, the Inclusion Law requires all private educational providers receiving public funding to be non-profit organizations. To avoid the practice of "self-renting" of school premises, a well-known subterfuge used by for-profit providers to increase their revenue, the Law requires providers to be owners of the school buildings, although with some regulated exceptions. Similarly, the reform prohibits the purchasing of services, inputs and technical support from companies related to the school's owner. The Inclusion Law defines and lists the type of expenses in which schools may incur restricting these only to "educationally oriented" ones such as salaries for the school administration and prohibits the diversion of resources to non-educational ends. Finally, as there were no rules in Chile to regulate either the number or location of publicly funded schools, making it difficult for the government to manage under or oversupply of schools in specific areas, the Law gives the Ministry of Education some authority to stop the opening of new private-subsidized schools in locations where these are not needed (Ley 20.845, 2015).

Ending the public funding of for-profit schools would noticeably alter the composition of private providers in Chilean education and eventually reduce the private sector's share in school provisions. Thus, the policy was strongly resisted by private school-owner organizations during parliamentary discussions. Their principal argument was a pragmatic one. They argued that for-profit providers have control of such a sizeable proportion of the school system that it would be harmful if such schools move away. The private-owner organizations also threatened the government that in the event of the approval of the reforms they would close schools or convert them into entirely private ones. Such would lead to dramatic tuition increases severely jeopardizing the government's capacity in several cities to guarantee the right to education. In other words, the strong power and autonomy of private education providers, a group that ironically had been able to grow, be promoted and funded through state policies, could end up weakening improvement of the procedures that had provided such support.

Private providers specifically resisted the prohibition to rent school buildings forcing the government to compromise on this matter and to allocate additional state support for the purchase of buildings. That was not new as in the past private providers, including for-profit organizations, had been able to buy school buildings with public money. For-profit and non-profit private providers also resisted the limitations imposed on the use of public funds to only "educationally oriented" expenses, arguing that this would constrain creativity, reduce efficiency and limit the autonomy of private schools. Such, in turn, led to a very complex debate about the public/private nature of the school voucher system. Finally, right-wing parties rejected the idea of regulating the opening of new schools in specific locations, arguing that a key tool of market principles is to have maximum freedom to open and close schools. Given these different forms of opposition occurring during the parliamentary discussion, the approved law was in the end significantly less strict in these matters than in the government's original proposal.

6 Guaranteeing the Universal Right to Free Compulsory Education

At the time of legislative discussions on the Inclusion Law, more than 70% of students enrolled in publicly funded private schools were in schools that also charged tuition, the total cost amounting to about US$500 million each year. This "shared funding" system contributed both to student discrimination based on fee-paying capacity and to the existing high socioeconomic school segregation of Chilean education (Valenzuela, Bellei, & De Los Ríos, 2014; Valenzuela, Villalobos, & Gómez, 2013; Roje, 2014). Moreover, in spite of these extra resources at their disposal, there was no consistent evidence that fee-charging private subsidized schools were any more effective than municipal public ones regarding learning results (Valín, 2011; Mizala & Torche, 2012; Paredes et al., 2013; Kutscher, 2013; Saavedra, 2013). Thus, President Bachelet's government concluded that fee-charges by private subsidized schools were inequitable and incoherent with the State's duty to guarantee the right to free compulsory primary and secondary education.

Interestingly and somewhat paradoxically, the government decided to use the voucher mechanism to the stop fee-paying in private subsidized schools, although with some significant changes. Thus, it increased the subsidy for non-fee-charging schools employing a free-education voucher and a designed a new "middle income" voucher for students enrolled in fee-charging subsidized schools willing to become non-fee ones (Ley 20.845, 2015). The rationale was that this "middle income" voucher would be a sufficiently attractive incentive persuading private providers to switch to free education. Indeed, this has been happening. It is estimated that towards the end of the second year of the Law's implementation, about 90% of publicly funded students will be attending free schools, although further increases will depend on the availability of resources to increase the school voucher. In fact, the situation has been more complex when it comes to subsidized schools charging the highest allowed level of fees. Although initially, the Government had proposed a five-year fixed schedule to turn these schools into non-fee-paying ones, the Parlament rejected such proposal on the basis that it would harm the schools. Thus, will take a decade for the government to compensate such schools for loss of revenue and turn them into non-fee-paying schools.

The defenders of the status quo also used other arguments against the suppression of fee-paying private schools. The original rationale in the early 1990s for allowing the payment of fees was that it would serve to raise student performance. However, this has not been the case and therefore could not continue as a valid reason for opposing changes in the financing of private subsidized schools. Thus, opponents of suppression of fees had to change their arguments and so turned to ethical and political debates, particularly to education justice principles. They argued that the reform should not be discussed using public schools as a frame of reference but that the benchmark should be the elite private schools, instead. It would only be fair to provide middle-class parents with the opportunity to select schools with an education program that better approximated what elite schools offer, and not with just the alternative of public municipal schools. According to this rationale, additional fee-paying would be an instrument of social justice reducing the gap between middle-class students and those attending private non-subsidized schools. Resulting inequities in resource allocation within the publicly funded sector would thus be only a minor side effect. Additionally, opponents contended that there were other ways of reducing school segregation such as reinforcing scholarship programs for poorer students who attend fee-charging schools and increasing the low-income students' voucher to make it more attractive to private providers. This latter voucher system was embedded in policy in place since 2008 known as the Preferential School Voucher Program supporting low-income students attending subsidized schools (Raczynski, Muñoz, Weinstein, & Pascual, 2013).

Ending the payment of extra fees (or co-payment) in private subsidized schools also faced stiff opposition from parents and opinion leaders who argued that self-segregation via school choice should not be the privilege of elite families only, but also a right of middle-income families. From this point of view, state funding should not alter the nature of the relationship between families and educational providers, expressed through the freedom to enter into contracts and implement price discrimination. On the contrary, the state voucher should represent a form of public support for non-elite families guaranteeing their freedom of school choice. Thus, for example, one of the parents' organizations openly criticized the government's attempt to promote social integration in middle-class schools, while concurrently tolerating upper-class family self-segregation in elite schools. Another Catholic organization of private school owner maintained that families choose their schools because they look for safety, discipline control, lack of teacher or students' strikes as well as of drugs, all conditions presumably not found in public schools. The implication of these arguments being that the payment of extra-fees supports the right of middle-income families to select a "better" school environment for their children.

7 Prohibiting Discrimination Practices during Admission and Schooling Processes

Chilean schools (including those publicly funded) have been extensively applying student selection and expulsion procedures, which UNESCO and UNICEF consider as discriminatory and potentially affecting the right to education. Thus, for example, before admitting new students, schools test their potential performance and do so with as young as four-years-old children. Schools also interview and exclude families for economic, social or cultural reasons, including religion. Since the beginning of the 2000s, different governments have attempted to regulate these practices. In fact, the General Education Law, passed in 2008, prohibits discriminatory selection up to grade 6. Nevertheless, available evidence shows that selection practices in 1st to 6th year are still widespread in Chilean schools (Carrasco et al., 2014; Godoy, Salazar, & Treviño, 2014). These practices which occur more commonly in private schools have an additional social and academic school segregation factor. While selection practices could be considered as inconsistent with market principles in that they limit the legal right of families to select the school of their choice, they also provide schools with a spurious advantage through "artificially" raising their students' performance in national achievement tests which are used to rank schools and allocate incentives and sanctions (Bellei, 2009; Contreras, Sepúlveda, & Bustos, 2010). Positive student results in tests also serve to increase the social and academic prestige of schools, this being a critical dimension of market-oriented educational systems.

The Inclusion Law stops discrimination in all primary and secondary school admission procedures by prohibiting the use of any student assessment and parental interview for selection purposes. It establishes that academic requirements or family characteristics will not be a base for admission. The Law recognized two exceptions, both from 7th grade on artistic schools which are allowed to evaluate artistic competences of applicants; and traditional academically selective public high schools recognized by the Ministry of Education, which may select up to 30% of applicants who performed at the higher 20% of their respective primary schools.

To facilitate a non-discriminatory selection process, the Government has enacted a publicly regulated School Admission System. The system requires parents to bid for schools of their choice in ranked order using an official online portal and in turn requires schools to admit all applicants subject to availability of places. In cases of over-demand, schools must implement a random assignment system, giving priority to siblings, low SES families, and children of the school's employees, including teachers. In other words, schools no longer will have control over their admission processes. Also, with some regulated exceptions, the Law prohibits the dismissal of students by low academic performance or disciplinary problems (Ley 20.845, 2015). Broadly, the reform has significantly raised the normative standards protecting the right to education, especially in its non-discriminatory dimensions.

Opponents to the reform have disagreed with the above interpretation. Mostly, they defend an educational philosophy that values the internal homogeneity of school communities. They understand homogeneity as justifying "specialized schools" concerning religion, ethnicity, cultural traditions, academic performance, socioeconomic status, curricular orientation, and so on. Equally, diversity and pluralism are taken to mean maximum freedom to exclude those students and families considered to be incompatible with the school's mission. According to Chilean private school organizations, removing such exclusionary power puts the schools' identity and educational objectives at risk as it hides these traits from families who wish to know about the schools they select for their children within the educational market.

Those who favor selection sidestep the fact that the different private school projects use public funds. In their view, the State does not subsidize schools but parents, giving them the right to select the schools of their preference. That is why they see the voucher as a vital piece of the system. It facilitates the encounter of education supply and demand with almost no State intervention. In selecting each other schools and parents increase their complementarities and—as the argument goes—do so in pro of the education of their children. If at all, diversity is valued between and not within schools. Students and families, who do not find their place in such a market, have the public schools as their default alternative.

Seen from these views of inclusion reform, the paradigmatic definition of public education as open to everyone turns out to be an anomaly depriving its schools of identity and forcing them to compete with an enormous handicap in the educational market.

7.1 *New Public Education: Priority to Public Schools*

The market-oriented institutional framework that prevailed in Chilean education since the early 1980s promoted privatizations not only concerning support for private schools but also through forcing public schools to operate through a form of "endogenous privatization" (Ball & Youdell, 2008). Such was accomplished through the transfer of public-school administration to municipalities, leaving schools open to competition within local markets under a Ministry of Education whose role was limited to implementing an "equal treatment" policy for all public and private schools (Bellei & Vanni, 2015). Coherently, the fact that the public education systematically reduced its "market share" from almost 90% at the beginning of the 1980s to less than 40% currently was not considered as a policy concern. Officials did not see it as a problem, but merely as the result of market preferences. That was the doctrine that President Bachelet's government attempted to change through the creation of a new public education system. After a very contentious legislative process the law regulating this system, known as the New Public Education Law, was finally passed at the end of 2017 (Ley 21.040, 2017).

The most relevant change introduced by this policy was to end the "municipal" administration of public schools. A new local government system is replacing it materialized in a network of Local Educational Services (LES). Each LES will manage all preschool, primary and secondary public schools located in an area larger than that of municipalities. Thus, 70 Local Services will replace the current 350 or so municipalities. The new system's rationale is to use advantages of scale to ensure enough financial and professional resources to make for a better educational administration. As autonomous entities, the LES's will be able to manage public schools in a decentralized way. They will have an Advisory Local Board of Education made up of teachers, school employees, parents, students, and academics. Besides this Advisory Board, there will be a Local Executive Board, composed of representatives of the Regional Government, municipalities and parents. The LES's will provide professional support to public schools in all relevant matters (pedagogical, curricular, and management), promote the development of school improvement plans, and oversee the functioning of the schools under their jurisdiction. An Executive Director and highly professional staff will manage the LES's utilizing a complex set of management instruments. These will be used to coordinate school improvement plans, local educational plans, and public education national policies, as well as establish objectives and performance targets for each school level (Ley 21.040, 2017).

The Law also creates a National Office of Public Education, which must design an 8-year National Strategy for Public Education. To orient both the national strategy of public education and the LES's plans, the Law explicitly defines a set of principles for public school. These principles include a broad definition of education quality, continuous improvement, national coverage and non-discrimination, equity and equal opportunity, collaboration and network organization, citizenship education and inclusiveness, local and community participation. It is important to note that the Law explicitly indicates the mandated responsibility of local and national public education authorities to guarantee proper coverage of public schools in their territories and set goals for their increase if needed. Additionally, the new LES's will be funded directly by the national state through a specific and particular public education budget, in addition to the regular student-level voucher (Ley 21.040, 2017). There will also be a new Fund to support public schools in their transition to the new system.

Finally, the law reinforces the roles of school principals and school's teachers' councils, giving them more authority over curricular and pedagogical matters, as well as the development of school improvement plans. Specific management instruments have been developed to promote collaboration among schools employing regional networks, and public-school quality standards have been defined such as a maximum class size of 35 students which is below the current size of 45 (Ley 21.040, 2017).

Broadly, the New Public Education system establishes an institutional framework, new intermediate, and national level organizations specialized in educational management and policies, and provides a set of principles, goals, management and funding instruments, all of which will be specific to the public education sector. That represents a sharp departure from the previous situation described above. In fact, aware of the scope of this policy change, its opponents have firmly rejected the idea of giving any priority to public schools such as extra funds in addition to the voucher and refused to recognize any difference between public and private schools such as might be their defining principles and objectives. Opponents have also opposed the notion of an intermediary level of administration and proposed instead a radical decentralization of schools anchored on the concept of "school-based management."

8 Teachers and Teacher Preparation: Policy Response to National Concerns

The 1991 Teachers Statute had regulated employment conditions in the public municipal system and to some extent in the private subsidized schools. There was also an increase of teacher salaries from the early nineties onward designed to redress their very deteriorated condition, though not to the level they had enjoyed before their removal from the public servants' statute during the military dictatorship. As mentioned earlier, in the nineties teacher professional development needs were addressed through school improvement programs, and the preparation of new teachers through targeted support to 17 university teacher education institutions (Ávalos, 2005). Moving into the 2000s new concerns about the effectiveness of the education system in the light of standardized test results led to a shift of emphasis from teacher localized support measures to policies focused on quality control and incentives. Thus, after long and complex discussions with the teachers' union (Ávalos & Assael, 2007), in 2002 a compulsory performance evaluation system for municipal public teachers was put in place, involving mainly the submission of portfolio evidence. This evaluation also included salary bonuses for teachers who voluntarily took additional content-knowledge tests. Later in the decade, teacher education improvement was targeted through compulsory accreditation and a curriculum knowledge test administered on a voluntary basis to new teachers as they exited their preparation programs.

Despite the enactment of the above policies in the late 2000s, diverse actors continued to voice their dissatisfaction with teacher performance, while also recognizing that school and learning results' improvement depends on good quality teachers. Policy documents and media clippings repeated the well-known "teachers matter" mantra (OECD, 2005; Mourshed, Chijioke, & Barber, 2010). On the other side of the fence, teachers expressed strong dissatisfaction with their working conditions and the lack of time derived from their high teaching versus non-teaching hours ratio which was well above that of OECD's average (OECD, 2014). They strongly resented unfair teacher bashing for disappointing learning results as measured by the many standardized tests administered during the school year. They were equally unhappy with the teacher evaluation system mainly on account of the portion of their scarce time needed to prepare the necessary portfolio evidence (Ávalos, 2013; Centro UC Políticas Públicas/Elige Educar, 2015, 2016). There was a need for teacher policy that moved beyond the accountability and incentives approach that had been dominant in the 2000s and towards a comprehensive teacher policy. To carry out such a reform became part of the mandate by which Michele Bachelet was elected president of Chile in 2014.

8.1 *Key Teacher-Related Issues Requiring Policy Changes*

A four-month long set of discussions by different civil society groups (academics, teachers, students, union leaders, NGOs, school managers, churches) led to a set of recommendations for government action (El Plan Maestro, 2015). At the basis of these recommendations was recognition of the professional status of teachers as marked by solid knowledge, capacities and commitment, all of which should be acquired through high quality initial preparation and relevant professional development opportunities. Teachers, it was said, perform at their best in appropriate working conditions embedded in a well-structured and funded teaching career, with adequate distribution of teaching/non-teaching contractual time and free-of-charge opportunities for professional development. This, however, was not exactly operant in 2015 as shown below.

a) Teacher initial and professional development opportunities. Despite the fact that all pre-service teacher education in Chile is university-based, requirements for entry into its programs differed across institutions and were lower than those required for other similar university careers. For example, there was evidence of lower quality in the preparation of pre-school teachers as compared to other specializations (Fallabella & Rojas, 2009) and of school practicum experiences leading to new teacher classroom difficulties (Cisternas, 2016). While a considerable proportion of teachers questioned in different surveys (Ávalos, 2013; EduGlobal, 2016) indicated that they take in-service courses, they also said they were doing so at their own cost. New teachers were not supported in any way, either by formal induction and mentorship and/or by reduced teaching time.

b) Workload. The teacher yearly statutory working time in public institutions, the ratio of teaching/non-teaching time and the primary and secondary student/teacher ratios on average were considerably higher than in OECD countries (OECD, 2017). The average class size at 30 was also higher compared to the OECD's average of 15/16.

c) Contractual conditions and salary schemes circa 2015. The full-time contract of a Chilean teacher was for 44 chronological hours a week, though on average teachers were contracted for 30 hours or less (Valenzuela, 2013). Chilean teacher "basic remuneration" increased with years of experience, evidence of in-service courses taken, work in difficult contexts and school leadership responsibilities. However, after 15 years of service, the proportion of salary increase was lower in relation to the average OECD salary increase (OECD, 2017). Compared to full time/full-year workers with similar preparation, teacher salaries were also lower than in OECD countries (OECD, 2017). Besides the established criteria for salary increases, any other salary improvement for Chilean teachers was linked to incentives based on voluntary performance evaluation or school results in standardized achievement tests.

d) Teacher attrition and turnover. There was evidence that teachers with five or less years of service had been leaving the profession at rates of around 40% over a ten-year period (Ávalos & Valenzuela, 2016). New teacher school turnover after the first year of teaching was also high, showing an increase from 33% to 74% over a six-year period and higher in schools with disadvantaged populations (Carrasco, Godoy, & Rivera, 2017).

e) Accountability and testing pressures. Over time the Chilean system of education had been administering around 15 different census-based standardized tests (reduced to 8/9 as of 2016), besides others sample-based tests (Agencia de la Calidad de la Educación, 2016). Added to this was participation in international studies such as TIMSS, PISA, and in UNESCO's Latin American evaluation system. This testing climate with its pressures to increase school performance had become a cause of stress and malaise for teachers and head-teachers, even though experienced differently depending on the type of school and school leadership (Falabella, 2016). In this context, the Chilean teachers' union had criticized both the multiplication of tests and its covert use as an instrument for school and teacher accountability (Docencia, 2009).

f) Teacher performance evaluation. As noted in the OECD's evaluation of the system (OECD, 2013), municipal teachers resented the time it took them to produce the required documents such as the portfolio given its narrow directives. On the other hand, they appreciated that student results were not part of the evaluation criteria, and that school authorities had a minor role in their assessment. although this latter view seems to be changing. In fact, according to a recent teacher survey (Centro Políticas Públicas/Elige Educar, 2015) teachers now prefer to be assessed by their head-teacher or by local authorities rather than national ones. They also prefer that the system be centered on observation of their classroom practices, evidence of school-based collaboration and of professional development activities.

8.2 *The Teacher Professional Development Law and Policy*

In order to deal with the depressed conditions of teachers the Parliament passed a new teacher-centered law on 1 April 2016 (Ley 20.903), after almost two years of discussion by an ad-hoc task force in the Ministry of Education, input from a national consultation process as well as from other sources (El Plan Maestro, 2015). Probably, the critical contribution of the law is to establish a teachers' career ladder with stages and progression criteria, including salaries and performance evaluation. The Law decrees conditions for initial teacher education, creates induction and mentorship for new teachers and recognizes the right to free-of-charge professional development opportunities. The Law moves beyond earlier legislation in that it covers all teachers in subsidized schools (public and private), all school levels including nurseries and all teacher specializations, and is to be implemented gradually from 2017 to 2025. We describe below its main features.

Quality assurance and control over teacher education. The Law raises gradually (2017 to 2023) the university entry examination scores and the secondary school grade averages required for admission into teacher education programs. With the aim of increasing the quality of teachers' education, all universities will have to have their teacher education programs accredited by the external responsible agency and monitor their students' first skills through a diagnostic test. Besides, an external diagnostic test for future teachers is to be administered a year before they graduate. The bases for these examinations will be standards developed by the Ministry of Education. Institutions should use examination results to monitor and improve the quality of their programs as well as the performance of the examined student teachers. However, results must be publicly available due to requirements of a "transparency" law passed in 2010. That may foreshadow public comparisons among teacher education programs and competition for future teacher recruits, with unknown consequences.

Support for new teachers. The Law establishes to gradually implement a system of induction and mentoring over five years. New teachers, with full-time contracts in a school, will have 6 to 8 hours per week time during their first or second year of teaching and will be assisted by mentors especially prepared by the Ministry of Education. High performing schools may establish their induction procedures subject to review by the Ministry of Education.

Teacher career and progression stages. The main innovation of the Law is a teaching career with five stages covering 12 or more years of active teaching. The first three stages are labeled as "beginning," "early," and "advanced" and progress through them is subject to performance evaluation. To remain in teaching all teachers must advance through these three stages. The next two stages are voluntary and referred to as "expert 1" and "expert 2." In line with the new career requirements, the Law sets out the main changes to the existing teacher performance evaluation system. The first compulsory evaluation takes place after four years of service allowing teachers to move from the "beginning" stage of their career to the next "early" one. After eight years of service, teachers must again be evaluated to move to the "advanced" stage. Teachers who wish to continue to the next two steps may do so voluntarily on the basis also of performance evaluation. As for the focus of the assessments, the first one includes content and pedagogic knowledge component and is taken only once if teachers do well on it. Besides this, as in the former evaluation system, teacher performance assessment includes a teacher-prepared portfolio providing evidence of their classroom teaching activities and additional evidence of (a) collaborative work with other teachers and parents, leadership and cooperation; (b) development of curricular contents and materials, pedagogic innovations and research; and (c) relevant professional development evidence. The criteria for teacher evaluation also continue to be the Framework of Good Teaching (see http://www.cpeip.cl/marco-para-la-buena-ensenanza) used in the previous system but improved concerning its criteria descriptions and rubrics. Teachers are to have access to the criteria upon which they are assessed and placed in one of four categories. Unsatisfactory performing teachers will have two opportunities to improve their results through relevant professional development. If they do not improve after this, they may not continue to teach in the subsidized education system.

Working conditions. The main improvement in teaching conditions set out by the Law is the raising of the non-teaching hours component of contractual time. It does so in two stages: in 2017 from 25% to 30% and in 2019 to 35% of the contractual time. The Law also rules that school authorities should respect non-teaching time not used to cover for other teachers or to perform duties such as lunch or recreation supervision. Concerning salaries, the starting monthly salary is improved (in US$ 2016) from US$856 to US$1201, with increases at each stage of the career of up to US$2944 per month for teachers in the fifth stage of their career. Serving teachers incorporated into the new career system in 2017 gained a 30% salary improvement. The Law also encourages teachers to work in schools with disadvantaged student populations by raising their non-teaching hours of contractual time and by salary increases of up to 10% for teachers in schools with around 80% of disadvantaged students.

School-focused professional development. The Law recognizes and supports the right of teachers to non-paid-for professional development through courses and activities organized by the Ministry of Education and Local Educational Authorities as well as school-based ones. Schools are to set up plans for their teacher professional development after consultation regarding needs. They are also encouraged to form collaborative and improvement network alliances with other schools. Besides the apparent aim of improving knowledge and practices, the Law explicitly stresses the need for a focus on demands of inclusive classrooms as well as the development of reflective capacities and teacher collaboration.

9 How Much of Reform Does the New Teacher Policy Represent?

Contrary to what occurred regarding the laws of Inclusion and Public Education analyzed in the first part of this article, there was ample civic agreement that the conditions of teachers needed improvement. Thus, there were many discussions and suggestions provided by educators, the teachers' union, and others during the legislative talks. Their effect was to alter substantially the first version of the Law sent to parliament (Ley 20.903, 2016). The core of discussions and changes focused on the degree to which the Law reflected principles of new public management ideology and accountability (firm ministerial control over teachers and teacher education performance) or came close to recognizing the professional character of teaching and teachers as professionals and able to manage the quality of their performance. The second area of concern was the "universality" that provisions of the Law would have concerning covering all kinds of teachers in publicly subsidized schools. A third area and an essential one was the degree to which the Law effectively provided for improved working conditions from entry to retirement.

The first version of the Law sent to parliament in 2015 seemed to endorse the role of the State as a "quality control agent" rather than as a facilitator of teacher development and professionalism. That was symbolically expressed in the use of the word "certification" as defining the nature of progress through the career stages. The teachers' union and others strongly opposed the use of this concept as it was considered to validate the notion of "quality control" and to be indicative of the role that external narrow performance evaluations might have in determining teacher progress through their career. The final version of the Law removed such a word and labeled the evaluation process as the "system of recognition of teacher professional development." The concept of teacher progress was "softened" regarding its requirements, such as establishing that the content-knowledge test would only have to be taken once throughout a teacher's career if performance at the time was acceptable. Removing the word "certification" or "certified" thus became a symbol of lessening the performative (Ball, 2003; Rufinelli, 2016) orientation of the proposed career stages and its focus on accountability, while strengthening its rationale as a formative instrument for teacher motivation and improvement.

The second area of tension evident during and after discussions of the Law was the extent to which the new career would be universal covering all teachers in the publicly subsidized system and the pace at which this would occur. Before the Law, teachers in the public municipal system had operated under different regulations from those in the private subsidized one and were the only teachers subjected to performance evaluation. As far as the teachers' union was concerned it was imperative that the new Law cover all teachers in publicly subsidized schools including the private ones. Also, it should include not just teachers in the school system (including kindergarten), but those working in pre-school and nurseries as well. After discussions and changes as well as consideration of available resources, the Law finally settled on a three-stage process of joining the career system. All new teachers and in-service ones in municipal public schools would be required to join the network as of 2017 although those with ten or fewer years for retirement could do so on a voluntary basis. Teachers in private subsidized schools would enter the system gradually from 2018 subject to their schools deciding to do so until becoming mandatory in 2026. The process of joining the career for early childhood and nursery teachers, in turn, was delayed until 2020 and made compulsory by 2025. These differences were a subject of concern especially in the case of nursery teachers, as was also the case of School Assistants who perform various tasks in schools but not considered in the career system.

Not least significant in the new Law were improvements in teachers' working conditions, mainly salaries, time and class size. As far as salaries are concerned the Law improves a beginning teachers' salary substantially in the hope of making the career more attractive to school leavers, though increases occur at a flatter rate across subsequent stages. It also provides extra salary bonuses for teachers working with disadvantaged school populations. Nevertheless, salary issues were not the primary concern of teachers but the availability of paid time to carry out non-classroom teaching responsibilities, which as noted above is substantially lower for Chilean teachers than for example the OECD average (OECD, 2014). After two sets of discussions, the Law provides for a progressive increase in non-teaching hours reaching 35 hours in 2019 and stipulates a ratio of 60/40 teaching/non-teaching hours for teachers working in schools with highly disadvantaged populations. An essential part of the Law in this respect was the ruling that non-teaching time must be respected by school authorities who should ensure that teachers are not obligated to use such time for non-professional matters such as covering for other teachers or supervising recreation time.

Finally, regarding working conditions, there were two matters not addressed by the Law. The first one refers to the maximum class size (currently 45). The Teacher's Law does not address the issue of class size at all, although the Public Education Law does set out a maximum of 35 students per class but only for public school teachers. That leaves teachers in private subsidized schools without any ruling regarding their maximum class size, The other important matter not addressed by the Teachers' Law are conditions for retirement. Until the passing of the Law teachers' pensions had been extremely low due to the system under which they had been working as well as to a large salary debt owed to them. That is because the military dictatorship transferred them to municipality administration. This situation kept many teachers from retiring on time (60 years for women and 65 for men). The reasons provided for the Law's silence regarding teacher retirement beyond the mandatory age is that any satisfactory decision would be extremely costly for the government. The Teachers' Union negatively assessed this situation (Docencia, 2014).

All in all, how does the new teacher career system compare to those in place in other parts of the world, as well as in Latin America? A recent exploratory study on diverse teacher career systems (Creehan, 2016) provides an overview of existing teacher career models and evaluation systems, ranging from the single salary schedule to comprehensive career ladder systems found in some fifteen countries around the world. Career ladders may be based on performance where progress depends on increased assessed competence and rewards include salary increases. Ladders may also reward the taking on of non-classroom educator roles such as new teacher mentor, curriculum development or professional development facilitator. In Chile, its career ladder is based both on demonstrated and assessed performance (tests, portfolios) as well as evidence of growth through professional development in school contexts. It is, however, more anchored on externally evaluated performance than on extensive evidence of knowledge and skills as applied in schools and classrooms, although this may change as its implementation moves on and sufficient experience is gathered. As far as similar models at work in Latin American countries those that might closely resemble the new Chilean career are the ones in Peru, Ecuador and México (Cuenca, 2015).

10 Conclusions

We began this chapter by asking whether, given its current reforms, Chilean education is departing from being a market-oriented system subject to new public management forms of quality control. The answer to this question is not a straightforward one. If one attends to official descriptions of the reforms and views of its active supporters along with the persistent defensive opposition of adherents to market principles, it might be easy to conclude that Chile has effectively begun a process of dismantling the existing system. Nevertheless, a closer analysis of what is changing and will change in the future provides a more balanced picture of the situation.

The key components of the market-driven education system will continue to play a strong role in Chile (Bellei, 2015). Given retention of the voucher system of financing public and private schools, the importance of student numbers and parental school choice will probably remain. Schools will continue to compete for family preferences and given the significant rise in the value of the voucher such competition may even increase beyond its current status. The state will continue to fund private schools with added support for the purchasing of school buildings. In the case of public schools, since the voucher will now represent a lower proportion of total public education funding, the incentive to compete for students may decrease, and it is possible that a horizontal network of cooperation among schools may serve to balance competitive pressures. Also, ending some of the unfair advantages of private over public schools such as student selection and additional fee-paying should diminish the push for further privatization as well as strong public schools. Private schools as well as public ones will have to conform to reform requirements and will have common regulations to follow concerning teacher working conditions and uses of public money. In other words, if successful, the current reforms will not put an end to the market-oriented educational system in Chile but will have removed some of its more radical features and diminished the relevance of market dynamics within Chilean education.

On the side of education quality and the role of teachers in supporting children and young people to learn in public and private subsidized schools, improvement of teacher working conditions and the stimulus provided by a new career system should be an important factor in favor of such goals. Nevertheless, teachers and the system will continue under pressure to compete for results, given the persistence of the critical elements of the audit state and public management system that have remained mostly unchanged. Open communication of test results and ranking of schools, as well as of teacher education institutions will persist, despite the discourse around the reform to lessen its effects or drastically reduce the impact of external testing. This, because some policymakers and educational experts see it as a necessary tool to improve standards for a low performing country with strong school autonomy, and believe testing is good insurance for school discipline and productivity. In fact, there were opponents to the Inclusion, and New Public Education Laws who argued that their clauses were not necessary as the only relevant consideration should be not whether a school is free, public or private, with or without profit motives, but whether it satisfies test-based standards. Whatever the position is, it is probable that those who believe in improvement through competition and ranking will make use of rulings in the Transparency Law (Ley 20.285) to push for publication of school results, ranking of schools and consequent teacher praising and blaming, even though the latest report on standardized testing in Chile counsels against this (Equipo de Tarea, 2015). Thus, specific forms of competition in line with market principles may persist among schools and teacher education institutions.

There are many critical challenges the reform will face to succeed. First, implementation of the highly complex institutional changes will demand policy priority, resources and sustained efforts from the Ministry of Education. Since the current Chilean government that came into power in March 2018 is led by the political coalition that opposed vital components of the Inclusion and New Public Education laws, the implementation process may bring about uncertain deviations. Undoubtedly there will be a push from sectors close to the private subsidized schools for the new government to alter vital elements in the school reforms such as non-selection of students and lessened parental school choice.

Second, successful implementation of the reforms will require strong professional and institutional capacities at school, local and national levels. At the school level, teachers need to increase their skills to work with a more diverse student population implementing pedagogies and creating school cultures that not only respect but also value this diversity. The support provided by the Teacher Professional Development Law to school-based teacher collaboration should stimulate the development of new ways to work with students of diverse capacities and background. Induction provisions for new teachers should also target the development of capabilities to enact inclusive practices.

Teacher education institutions will have to improve the preparation of teachers for educating in inclusive classrooms, something currently lacking as often noted by practicing young teachers (Cisternas, 2016). At the local level, planners must design useful projects to expand and renovate public schools, and local level professional development activities should focus on needed and relevant administrative and teaching requirements for schools and classrooms as well on inclusive teaching practices. Local school networks should also be part of the effort. At national level (including academic institutions), the design of the new institutions charged with public education will have to be completed, providing them with strong planning and monitoring devices, assistance to identify and tackle the challenges faced and support to experiment with suitable solutions. None of these tasks (and they are just a short list of examples) have been part of the existent system, so there will be a need for much learning and correction of poor practices.

Finally, the ultimate success of the reform depends on its capacity to develop a new social understanding of the educational system, which includes the role of teachers and schools. Given that market and new public management, principles have dominated the field for so long, is only reasonable to expect that these have strongly permeated the conventional thinking about education. That includes teachers, parents and the public at large. The social stigma attached to schools that are free, non-selective, and public prevails in diverse social groups, especially in large cities. Public accountability system based on standardized test results supports that shame which exacerbates the impact of socio-economic differences on learning.

As Chilean education moves towards a reformed public and private subsidized system of schools, teacher education, school and parent communities, local education administration and national authorities need to develop a growing understanding that its principles of non-discrimination, equity and respect can also provide security, build discipline and promote learning in educationally satisfactory ways. The legislative corpus and the improved teaching conditions and teaching career that sustain the reforms discussed in this chapter, provide the context for this new and needed social understanding that should bring Chilean education closer to inclusiveness as well as to quality.

Acknowledgment

The authors gratefully acknowledge the Basal Fund for Centers of Excellence, Project FB0003 from the Associative Research Program of CONICYT, Chile.

References

Agencia de la Calidad de la Educación. (2016). *Cuenta Pública 2015*. Santiago: Agencia de la Calidad de la Educación. Retrieved February 22, 2018, from http://www.agenciaeducacion.cl/multimedia/cuenta-publica-2015/

Avalos, B. (2002). *Profesores para Chile. Historia de un Proyecto*. Santiago: Ministerio de Educación.

Avalos, B. (2005). How to affect the quality of teacher education: A four-year policy driven project implemented at university level. In P. M. Denicolo & M. Kompf (Eds.), *Connecting policy and practice. Challenges for teaching and learning in schools and universities* (pp. 39–43). London: Routledge.

Avalos, B. (2013). El trabajo docente. In B. Avalos (Ed.), *Héroes o villanos: La profesión docente en Chile*. Santiago, Chile: Editorial Universitaria.

Avalos, B. (2015). Chile: Effectiveness of teacher education. In S. Schwartzman (Ed.), *Education in South America* (pp. 201–220). London: Bloomsbury.

Avalos, B. (2017). Teacher evaluation in Chile: Highlights and complexities in 13 years of experience. *Teachers and Teaching*. Retrieved from http://www.tandfonline.com/doi/full/10.1080/13540602.2017.1388228

Avalos, B., & Assael, J. (2007). Moving from resistance to agreement: The case of the Chilean teacher performance evaluation. *International Journal of Educational Research, 45*(4–5), 254–266.

Avalos, B., & Razquin, P. (2017). The role of policy as a shaping influence on teacher education and teacher educators: Neo-liberalism and its forms. In J. Clandinin & J. Husu (Eds.), *The Sage handbook of research on teacher education* (pp. 1117–1132). Los Angeles, CA: Sage.

Avalos, B., & Valenzuela, J. P. (2016). Education for all: Attrition and retention of new teachers. *International Journal of Educational Development, 49*, 279–290.

Ball, S. J. (2003). The teachers' soul and the terrors of performativity. *Journal of Education Policy, 18*(2), 215–228.

Ball, S. J., & Youdell, D. (2008). *Hidden Privatisation in public education.* Brussels: Education International.

Bellei, C. (2009). The public-private- school controversy in Chile. In R. Chakrabarti & P. E. Peterson (Eds.), *School choice International. Exploring public-private partnerships* (pp. 165–192). The MIT Press.

Bellei, C. (2015). *El gran experimento: Mercado y privatización de la educación chilena.* Santiago: LOM.

Bellei, C. (2016). Dificultades y resistencias de una reforma para des-mercantilizar la educación. *RASE: Revista de la Asociación de Sociología de la Educación, 9*(2), 232–247.

Bellei, C., & Vanni, X. (2015). The evolution of educational policy, 1980–2014. In S. Schwartzman (Ed.), *Education in South America* (pp. 179–200). London: Bloomsbury.

Bellei, C., Vanni, X., Valenzuela, J. P., & Contreras, D. (2016). School improvement trajectories: An empirical typology. *School Effectiveness and School Improvement, 27*(3), 275–292.

Biesta, G. (2014). ¿Medir lo que valoramos o valorar lo que medimos? Globalización, responsabilidad y la noción de propósito de la educación. *Pensamiento Educativo, 51*(1), 46–57.

Carrasco, A. (2015). Revisitando el debate sobre la Ley de Inclusión. In Ignacio Sánchez (Ed.), *Ideas en Educación: reflexiones y propuestas desde la UC* (pp. 211–244). Santiago: Ediciones UC.

Carrasco, A., Bogolasky, F., Flores, C., Gutiérrez, G., & San Martín, E. (2014). *'Selección escolar' de estudiantes y desigualdad educacional en Chile: ¿Qué tan coactiva es la regulación que la prohíbe?* (Proyecto FONIDE Nº 711286). Santiago: Ministerio de Educación. Retrieved March 4, 2018, from https://centroestudios.mineduc.cl/wp-content/uploads/sites/100/2017/07/Informe-Final-F711286-Carrasco.pdf

Carrasco, D., Godoy, M. I., & Rivera M. (2017). Rotación de profesores en Chile: Quiénes son y cuál es el contexto de quienes dejan su primer trabajo. *Midevidencia, 11*. Retrieved February 6, 2018, from http://www.mideuc.cl/wp-content/uploads/2016/MidEvidencias-N11.pdf

Centro UC Políticas Públicas/Elige Educar. (2015). *Voces docentes: Encuesta de opinion de profesores de aula en Chile*. Retrieved February 6, 2018, from http://politicaspublicas.uc.cl/wp-content/uploads/2015/11/Encuesta-Voces-Docentes.pdf

Centro UC Políticas Públicas/Elige Educar. (2016). *Encuesta voces docentes. Parte II: Condiciones y cultura escolar en la labor docente*. Retrieved February 7, 2018, from http://www.eligeeducar.cl/wp-content/uploads/2017/05/F_voces_docentesII_2017-2.pdf

Cisternas, T. (2016). Profesores principiantes de Educación Básica: Dificultades de la enseñanza en contextos escolares diversos. *Estudios Pedagógicos, 42*(4). http://dx.doi.org/10.4067/S0718-07052016000500003

Colegio de Profesores de Chile. (2012). *Carrera profesional docente de calidad hoy*. Santiago: Directorio Nacional Colegio de Profesores de Chile. (unpublished manuscript)

Colegio de Profesores de Chile A.G. (n.d.). *Propuesta de Carrera Profesional Docente*. Retrieved March 1, 2018, from http://www.colegiodeprofesores.cl/images/carreraprofesional/carreradocentefinal.pdf

Contreras, D., Hojman, D., Huneeus, F., & Landerretche, O. (2011). El lucro en la educación escolar. Evidencias y desafíos regulatorios. *Trabajos de Investigación en Políticas Públicas, 10*. Retrieved March 4, 2018, from http://repositorio.uchile.cl/handle/2250/143897

Contreras, D., Sepúlveda, P., & Bustos, S. (2010). When schools are the ones that choose: The effects of screening in Chile. *Social Science Quarterly, 91*(5), 1350–1368.

Cox, C. (2003). Políticas educacionales en las últimas dos décadas del siglo XX. In C. Cox (Ed.), *Políticas educacionales en el cambio del siglo: La reforma del sistema escolar en Chile* (pp. 19–113). Santiago: Editorial Universitaria.

Cox, C., Meckes, L., & Bascopé, M. (2010). La institucionalidad formadora de profesores en Chile: Velocidad del mercado y parsimonia de las políticas. *Pensamiento Educativo, 46–47*, 205–245.

Crehan, L. (2016). *Exploring the impact of career models on teacher motivation.* Paris: IIEP. Retrieved March 3, 2018, from http://unesdoc.unesco.org/images/0024/002462/246252e.pdf

Cuenca, R. (2015). *Las carreras docentes en América Latina. La acción meritocrática para el desarrollo professional.* Estrategia Regional sobre Docentes. Santiago: OREALC/UNESCO. Retrieved March 3, 2018, from http://unesdoc.unesco.org/images/0024/002440/244074s.pdf

Docencia. (2009). Estandarización educativa en Chile: Un peligroso hábito. *Revista Docencia, 38,* agosto. Retrieved February 6, 2018, from http://www.revistadocencia.cl/new/wp-content/pdf/20100730184208.pdf

Docencia. (2014). Jubilación docente o la pobreza ilustrada: Un desafío para la carrera professional. *Revista Docencia, 54,* diciembre. Retrieved March 3, 2018, from http://www.revistadocencia.cl/new/wp-content/pdf/20141126235434.pdf

EduGlobal. (2016). *Tercer Censo Docente Formación Continua.* Retrieved from http://www.eduglobal.cl/2016/12/13/resultados-tercer-censo-docente-formacion-continua-2016/

Elacqua, G., Contreras, D., Salazar, F., & Santos, H. (2011). The effectiveness of private school franchises in Chile's national voucher program. *School Effectiveness and School Improvement, 22*(3), 237–263.

El Plan Maestro. (2015). *Propuestas Participativas para una nueva profesión docente.* Santiago: Ril Editores.

Equipo de Tarea para la Revisión del SIMCE. (2015). *Hacia un sistema completo y equilibrado de evaluación de los aprendizajes en Chile.* Informe Equipo de Tarea para la Revisión del SIMCE, Ministerio de Educación, Santiago, Chile. Retrieved March 4, 2018, from https://www.mineduc.cl/wp-content/uploads/sites/19/2015/11/Informe-Equipo-de-Tarea-Revisi%C3%B3n-Simce.pdf

Falabella, A. (2014). The performing school: The effects of market and accountability policies. *Education Policy Analysis Archives, 22*(70). Retrieved February 7, from https://epaa.asu.edu/ojs/article/view/1315

Falabella, A. (2015). El mercado escolar en Chile y el surgimiento de la nueva gestión pública: El tejido de la politica entre la dictadura neoliberal y los gobiernos de la centroizquierda (1979 a 2009). *Educação & Sociedade, 36*(132), 699–722.

Falabella, A., & Rojas, M. T. (2009). Tensiones, debilidades y fortalezas en la formación de educadores de párvulos en Chile. Un estudio de casos. *Revista Diálogos Educativos, 18.*

Retrieved February 6, 2018, from https://dialnet.unirioja.es/servlet/articulo?codigo=3158974

Friedman, M., & R. (1980). *Free to choose*. New York, NY: Harcourt Brace.

Furlong, J. (2013). Globalisation, Neo-Liberalism and the reform of teacher education in England. *Educational Forum, 77*(1), 28–50.

García-Huidobro, J. E., & Sotomayor, C. (2003). La centralidad de la escuela en la política educativa de los años noventa. In C. Cox (Ed.), *Políticas educacionales en el cambio de siglo* (pp. 253–316). Santiago: Editorial Universitaria.

Godoy, F., Salazar, F., & Treviño, E. (2014). *Prácticas de selección en el sistema escolar chileno: Requisitos de postulación y vacíos legales*. CPCE – Informes para la Política Educativa nº 1.

Guzmán, I. (2014). Reflexiones sobre la carrera professional docente: La confianza y la valoración del actor colectivo. *Docencia, 54*, 26–34. Retrieved February 22, 2018, from http://www.revistadocencia.cl/new/wp-content/pdf/20141126234927.pdf

ILO/UNESCO. (2016). *ILO/UNESCO recommendation concerning the status of teachers (1966) & UNESCO recommendation concerning the status of higher education personnel (1997)*. Geneva: International Labour Organization.

Kutscher, M. (2013). *Efectos del financiamiento compartido sobre habilidades cognitivas y no cognitivas* (Unpublished master's thesis). P. Universidad Católica de Chile, Santiago.

Ley 20.285. (2008). *Ley de Transparencia de la Función Pública y de Acceso a la Información de la Administración del Estado*. Retrieved March 4, 2018, https://www.leychile.cl/Navegar?idNorma=276363

Ley 20.845. (2015). *De Inclusión Escolar que Regula la Admisión de los y las Estudiantes, Elimina el Financiamiento Compartido y Prohibe el Lucro en lo Establecimientos que Reciben Aportes del Estado*. Santiago: Ministerio de Educación.

Ley 20.903. (2016). *Crea el Sistema de Desarrollo Profesional Docente y Modifica Otras Normas*. Santiago: Ministerio de Educación de Chile.

Ley 21.040. (2017). *Crea el Sistema de Educación Pública*. Santiago: Diario Oficial de la República de Chile.

Lingward, B., & Rawolle, S. (2010). Globalization and the rescaling of educational politics and practice. In M. A. Larsen (Ed.), *New thinking in comparative education* (pp. 33–52). Rotterdam, The Netherlands: Sense Publishers.

Lomnitz, L. A., & Melnick, A. (1998). *Neoliberalismo y clase media: El caso de los profesores de Chile*. Santiago: DIBAM.

MacBeath, J. (2012). *Future of the teaching profession*. Cambridge: Leadership for Learning, The Cambridge Network.

Manzi, J., Bogolasky, F., Gutiérrez, G., Grau, V., & Volante, P. (2014). *Análisis sobre valoraciones, comprensión y uso del SIMCE por parte de directores escolares de establecimientos subvencionados*. Proyecto FONIDE Nº 11269. Santiago: Ministerio de

Educación. Retrieved March 4, 2018, from http://politicaspublicas.uc.cl/publicacion/analisis-sobre-valoraciones-comprension-y-uso-del-simce-por-parte-de-directores-escolares-de-establecimientos-subvencionados/

Mizala, A., & Torche, F. (2012). Bringing the schools back in: The stratification of educational achievement in the Chilean voucher system. *International Journal of Educational Development, 32*, 132–144.

Mourshed, M., Chijioke, C., & Barber, M. (2010). *How the World's most improved school systems keep getting better*. McKinsey & Co.

OECD. (2005). *Teachers matter: Attracting, developing and retaining effective teachers*. Paris: OECD.

OECD. (2013). *OECD reviews of evaluation and assessment in education: Teacher evaluation in Chile*. Paris: OECD.

OECD. (2014). *TALIS 2013 results: An international perspective on teaching and learning*. Paris: TALIS, OECD Publishing.

OECD. (2016). *PISA 2015 results: Excellence and equity in education* (Vol. I). Paris: OECD.

OECD. (2017). *Education at a glance 2017: OECD indicators*. Paris: OECD Publishing. http://dx.doi.org/10.1787/eag-2017-en

Paredes, R., Volante, P., Zubizarreta, J. R., & Opazo, M. (2013). Financiamiento compartido en la educación subvencionada chilena. In *Propuestas para Chile 2013*. Santiago: P. Universidad Católica de Chile. Retrieved March 4, 2018, https://politicaspublicas.uc.cl/publicacion/concurso-de-politicas-publicas-2/propuestas-para-chile-2013/propuestas-para-chile-2013-capitulo-ii-financiamiento-compartido-en-la-educacion-subvencionada-chilena/

Raczynski, D., Muñoz, G., Weinstein, J., & Pascual, J. (2013). Subvención Escolar Preferencial (SEP) en Chile: Un intento por equilibrar la macro y micro política escolar. *Revista Iberoamericana sobre Calidad, Eficacia y Cambio en Educación, 11*(2). Retrieved February 25, 2018, from http://www.redalyc.org/html/551/55127024008/index.html

Rizvi, F., & Lingvard, B. (2010). *Globalizing education policy*. Abingdon: Routledge.

Roje, P. (2014). *Segregación escolar por nivel socioeconómico (NSE) y su relación con las políticas educacionales en Chile: El caso del Financiamiento Compartido (FC) y la Subvención Escolar Preferencial (SEP)*. Tesis para optar al grado de Magíster en Economía, Universidad de Chile.

Rufinelli, A. (2016). Ley de desarrollo professional docente en Chile: De la precarización sistemátivas a los logros, avances y desafíos pendientes para la profesionalización. *Estudios Pedagógicos, 4*, 261–279.

Saavedra, T. (2013). *Efecto del financiamiento compartido sobre el rendimiento escolar* (Unpublished master's thesis). University of Chile.

Sisto, V., & Fardella, C. (2014). El eclipse del profesionalismo en la era de la rendición de cuentas: Modelando docentes en el contexto del nuevo management público. *Cadernos de Educação, 49*, 3–23.

Sleeter, C. (2008). Preparing White teachers for diverse students. In M. Cochran-Smith, S. Feiman-Nemser, D. J. McIntyre, & K. E. Demers (Eds.), *Handbook of research on teacher education: Enduring questionsin changing contexts* (3rd ed., pp. 559–582). New York, NY: Routledge, Taylor & Francis, and Association of Teacher Education.

Solbrekke, T. D., & Sugrue, C. (2014). Professional accreditation of initial teacher education programmes: Teacher educators' strategies- between 'accountability' and 'professional responsibility.' *Teaching and Teacher Education, 37*, 11–20.

Valenzuela, J. P., Bellei, C., & De Los Ríos, D. (2014). Socioeconomic school segregation in a market-oriented educational system. The case of Chile. *Journal of Education Policy, 29*(2), 217–241.

Valenzuela, J. P., Villalobos, C., & Gómez, G. (2013). ¿Segregación y polarización en el sistema educacional chileno: ¿Qué ha sucedido con los grupos medios? (Espacio Público: Documento de Referencia Nº 3). Retrieved March 4, 2018, https://www.espaciopublico.cl/segregacion-y-polarizacion-en-el-sistema-escolar-chileno-y-recientes-tendencias-que-ha-sucedido-con-los-grupos-medios

Valín, A. (2011). *Financiamiento compartido y desempeño escolar en Chile* (Unpublished master's thesis). Catholic University of Chile.

Zeichner, K. (2010). Competition, economic rationalization, increased surveillance and attacks on diversity: Neo-liberalism and the transformation of teacher education in the US. *Teaching and Teacher Education, 26*, 1544–1552.

Zubizarreta, J., Paredes, R., & Rosenbaum, P. (2014). Matching for balance pairing for heterogeneity in an observational study of the effectiveness of for-profit and non-profit high schools in Chile. *The Annals of Applied Statistics, 8*(1), 204–231.

CHAPTER 3

The Difficult Process in Chile: Redefining the Rules of the Game for Subsidized Private Education

Gonzalo Muñoz Stuardo and José Weinstein Cayuela

Abstract

The purpose of this article is to describe and analyze the origin of the 'Inclusion Law' and the first steps of its implementation, a vital component of the educational reform in Chile since 2014. It has modified the relationship of the state to private instruction, establishing free education in all schools, ending discrimination in student selection, as well as terminating profits (lucro) from schools receiving public resources. Within this framework, this article first describes the context of the development of this law. Second, it systematizes the evidence (scarce but illustrative) that is available about the first steps of its implementation. And third, explores the challenges facing this policy and the necessary support to improve Chilean educational quality and equity. From comparative and normative perspectives this analysis shows that the Inclusion Law helps in three areas—treating quality education as a right for all; eliminating the differences that played against public school; and potentially decreasing socio-educational segregation. The principal challenges facing this legislation in the coming years is the capacity to consolidate it as policy and above all to transform it—through the social action of educational communities—into an opportunity for more and better learning in Chilean educational schools.

1 Introduction

Chilean education, toward the beginning of the last decade, entered a phase of stagnation regarding its learning results (based on internationally comparable standard tests and the consolidation of inequality levels. In spite of the dynamism and fundamental progress achieved by the country since the return of democracy, of which the expansion of open educational opportunities for the population has been particularly notable (Weinstein & Muñoz, 2009; OECD, 2017), there continues to be a majority view that is dissatisfied with the educational situation in Chile (CEP, 2015).[1] That has translated into social

 | DOI: 10.1163/9789004413375_004

movements that have demanded structural reforms in general education and that has had a direct impact on the public education agenda.[2] These public demands are consistent with the objective evidence of the country's educational situation. For a while it was possible to show undeniable advances, (educational coverage of mandatory grades, educational and financial resources for schools, teachers' working conditions), both learning results and inequality levels are clear and irrefutable deficits of the Chilean educational system at the dawn of the XXI century. This critical view of the educational system is also an expression of the broadening expectations of the public that wants more from a system than expanding opportunities for access and its functions since the 1990s. So too, this discontent and public mobilization reflect the relative gains achieved by the educational system (Weinstein & Muñoz, 2009).

The debate in Chile concerning the principal factors that are behind the performance of the educational system is entering into a phase where improvement is much more complicated and challenging. Such a move is illustrated, for example, by the stagnation of the learning results obtained in the most recent national and comparative tests following an improvement in the previous decade (OECD, 2017), and which has given rise to many different explanations. Some studies and research have shown how these variables are related to the capacity of the various actors, principally teachers and principals, while others have emphasized institutional factors which also influence educational results and procedures (Cox, 2003; Bellei et al., 2008; Weinstein & Muñoz, 2009; Martinic & Elacqua, 2010; Verdejo, 2013). In this scenario, for which there is copious evidence, the educational system is configured to function like a quasi-market, and that has created the conditions for one of the world's most extensive privatization processes but has not affected the quality or equity of the Chilean school system positively. The Chilean case has international relevance, it is a paradigm of privatization and market.[3] It has used practically all the policy tools of this proposal for more than three decades and at a systemic level.[4] It is also one of the few systems in the world in which the private sector covers the majority of enrollment (OECD, 2004; Bellei, 2015; Verger, Bonal, & Zancajo, 2016). But it is a pristine example of the limitations of this policy focus and which had required the critical stakeholders in the education system to reconsider modifications to current rules and procedures.

With this panorama in 2014, Chile initiated a process of school reform that was possible thanks to a combination of factors. First, the pressure from the social movements for education change that called for structural reform of the educational system to guarantee the right to quality education. Second, the formation of a robust political majority that supported the program of President Bachelet 's government in the 2013 presidential election and which was joined by a preponderance of the New Majority (an unprecedented coalition of the Center-Left ranging from the Christian Democratic to Communist parties and that controlled Congress between 2014 to 2018). And fourth, the accumulation of evidence and proposals from the academic and social worlds that facilitated discussion about the reforms—their speed and design—for legislative approval.

The educational reform of 2014–2018 consisted of three fundamental changes for general or school education. Chief, the Inclusion Law (the focus of this article). Next, the creation of a new institutional framework that strengthens public education, known as 'de-municipalization.'[5] And the organization of a new teacher training policy (that established an improved level for employment conditions and a professional career for teachers, funded by the State).[6] These reforms were discussed with the promise of making education 'a social right' where all citizens have the right to participate in and continue their education without cost or discrimination, to slowly eliminate rules more appropriate to the market (Government Program, 2014; Programa de Gobierno Bachelet, 2014), and that inevitably redefined the private sector's role in education.

This work analyzes the first step in the reform of the Chilean school system, the Inclusion Law, and its recent development in depth. The first section describes the educational context in which this law originated and justified its creation. Second, the article describes the complicated discussions that molded the regulations together with the many pushbacks that yet had to be overcome, as well as explaining the reform's final content. The third section looks at the first steps of its implementation and some preliminary results. Finally, the article closes with a reflection on the challenges that the Inclusion Law opens for Chilean education in the medium and short terms and the lessons that this reform offers to other similar processes in Latin America.

2 The Inclusion Law: The End of Three Anomalies in the Chilean School System

The Inclusion Law, approved in January 2015, has the objective of modifying three central features of the way that the school system functions in Chile. First, it ends making profits in general education (primary and secondary), from public funds. Second, it ensures that there is a school system that is completely free for children (by eliminating co-payments from families, widely used until now in Chile). And third, it ends the practices of selection and discrimination (academic and other) that have been practiced by part of the education system. Given the effect that structural measures like this will have on social diversity and teaching in schools, the preliminary draft of the law was called 'the Inclusion Law' and became, symbolically and educationally, the first step in the overall educational reform legislated anπd implemented between 2014–2018. Table 3.1 explains each of the three elements of the Chilean school system that are in the process of reform.

The evidence available about the relevance and effects of the three dimensions on the Chilean school system shows that in for profit schools, the Ministry of Education calculates that around US$ 500 million annually of public funds were not invested in directly into education and this 'surplus' was converted as an economic gain for school owners or administrators (Mineduc, 2014). That amounts to around 8% of all public resources transferred as school subsidies in 2013.[7] As shown in Table 3.2, before the Inclusion law there were approximately 4,500 educational establishments classified under the legal rubric that allows profits; that is around 70% of private schools receiving public funds and 40% of all existing educational centers. Concerning the school population, for-profit schools account for 38% of the total school population in Chile, that is around 1.3 million students. This penetration of for-profit schools has no equal internationally (Elacqua et al., 2011; Bellei, 2015).

Regarding the impact of for-profit schools, the evidence demonstrates that the profit impulse does not translate into favorable results for the students and their families. In spite of the explosion in the number of these schools, these schools do not achieve better effectiveness levels. Considering, for example, SIMCE test results when compared to non-profit schools (Elacqua, 2011; Contreras et al., 2011; Chumacero & Paredes, 2008; Elacqua et al., 2014; Zubizarreta et al., 2014).[8] Neither has the incentive of profits given rise to a greater diversity of educational projects or plans which was another of the arguments used to defend its existence (Elacqua & Montt, 2012). Further, for-profit schools contracted, on average, younger, less experienced and specialized teachers, and for shorter days, which implies that by 2010 only around 60% of those schools have been incorporated into the Complete School Day program as against 85% of non-profit schools (Elacqua et al., 2011).[9]

In the case of co-payments (or shared funding), the official 2014 figures show that around 70% of students attending private subsidized schools are subject to some payment, which amounts to about 40% of total national enrollment.[10] Although these payments vary by school and internally by the student in the same year, the average monthly charge reached US$35 per student (as of March 2014). These family contributions also expanded the opportunities for profits in the system, for almost two-thirds of the schools that apply co-payment constituted as for-profit establishments. As can be seen in the following chart, the reality of co-payment, including its co-existence with a Preferential Pupil

TABLE 3.1 Characteristics of profits, copayment and selection in Chile until 2014

	Origin and justification	How does it function?
Profits (*Lucro*)	Since the beginning of the XX century Chilean legislation has allowed for the delivery of student subsidies to private education. However, the military dictatorship (1973–1990), established a system of financial equivalence for public and private (vouchers per student) schools with no restrictions as to the use of public resources. This funding policy, together with few requirements for the provision of educational services, became the incentive for the incorporation of the private sector into the educational system from the 1980s (in the first two decades following the return of democracy, 1990–2010, around 2,000 private subsidized schools were created in Chile of which more than 80% were for profit), which contributed to an expansion of supply and greater coverage of primary and secondary education.	The owners (*sostenedores*) of private establishments had no obligation to deliver all funds from subsidies to the educational process and so were able to make a profit from the difference. This profit could also be supplemented with family co-payments that were not subject to a legal framework that guaranteed their exclusive use for educational ends. Prior to the Inclusion Law profits could be made from both family contributions and State subsidies. In Chile there are around 4,800 private educational administrators financed by the State (MINEDUC, 2016). The great majority administer only one educational establishment.

(*cont.*)

TABLE 3.1 Characteristics of profits, copayment and selection in Chile until 2014 (*cont.*)

	Origin and justification	How does it function?
Co-payment (*Copago*)	In 1994 the possibility was introduced for primary and secondary private schools (and secondary public schools) to charge for educational services and which parents were required to pay. The principal arguments to justify the legislation were the need for greater resources for the functioning of the educational system and to create a greater bond with parents and families.	A co-payment is a monthly amount that families have to pay to school owners as a condition for remaining in the school. The norm sets a payment ceiling (which today is around US$ 120 per month per student) and a progressive discount with the subsidy depending on the payment range of families. From 2005 all establishments that receive public finance have to incorporate 15% of students free of this payment. From 2008 the average was expanded to the 40% of the most vulnerable students in the country and for which a special subsidy was created, the Preferential Pupil Subsidy, (*Subvención Escolar Preferencial,* SEP), and which also brought free education to these students.

(*cont.*)

TABLE 3.1 Characteristics of profits, copayment and selection in Chile until 2014 (*cont.*)

	Origin and justification	How does it function?
Selection	Similar to profits, Chilean educational legislation did not contain, until 2009, an explicit regulation about admission procedures for primary and secondary schools. This, coupled with co-payment, encouraged some owners to introduce different selection procedures to form their annual enrollment. The General Education Law (*Ley General de Educación,* 2009) established a normative framework that attempts to avoid some discriminatory admission practices (such as requiring pupil's socioeconomic data) but only for primary education, leaving the door open for families which adhered to the 'educational project' of the school.	State financed educational establishments have to develop a transparent admissions process and which respects the dignity of families. Within this framework, the schools manage a selection process with the final decision being that of the owner who then 'accepts' a specific list of students. The majority of private schools apply admission tests, hold family interviews, request religious antecedents (in the case of church schools) among other procedures. In the case of secondary education, the educational establishments can consider a student's past performance (qualifications) practices principally used by public secondary schools known as 'emblematic' (*emblemáticos*) for their academic demands and selection. Selection combines synergistically with co-payment for it acts as a first filter for admission to the school.

TABLE 3.2 For-profit establishments and enrollment, prior to the Inclusion Law

Administrative type	Number of schools according to type of owner									
	NPS (Schools)		FPS (Schools)		NPS (Enrolment)		FPS (Enrolment)		Total	
	N	%	N	%	N	%	N	%	Schools	Enrolment
Municipal	5,331	100.0%	0	0.0%	1,304,000	100.0%	0	0.0%	5,331	1,304,634
Private with public subsidies	1,646	27.1%	4,419	72.9%	709,790	37%	1,209,602	63.0%	6,065	1,919,392
Private—no subsidies	310	52.1%	283	47.6%	135,158	50.0%	133,531	49.4%	595	270,491
Delegated Administration	70	100.0%	0	0.0%	46,802	100.0%	0	0.0%	70	46,802
Total	7,357	61.0%	4,702	39.0%	2,196,384	62.1%	1,343,133	37.9%	12,061	3,541,319

NPS: Non-Profit Schools; FPS: For-Profit schools

SOURCE: BASED ON THE DIRECTORY OF OWNERS AND ESTABLISHMENTS, MINEDUC (2014).

Subsidy (Subvención Escolar Preferencial),[11] translates into a regressive and unfair finance system, above all for students at average socio-economic levels.

The evidence in Chile about the effects of co-payments on socio-economic segregation in the school system is overwhelming (Gallegos & Hernando, 2009; Flores & Carrasco, 2013; Valenzuela, Bellei, & De Los Ríos, 2014; Valenzuela, Villalobos, & Gómez, 2013; Roje, 2014). After functioning for twenty years, co-payment funding has not contributed to educational quality—instead, it increases segregation in Chilean education. This segmentation is to be found within private education but also in the gap between private and public school, with the latter experiencing a growing concentration of the most socially disadvantaged students. In 2014, 50% of students identified as socio-economic priorities studied in public education even though this modality amounted to less than 40% of all students. Similar to 'profits' there is no evidence that schools using co-payment have a better academic performance (Mizala & Torche, 2012; Paredes et al., 2013; Kutscher, 2013).

Since 2009 Chilean legislation has prohibited any discrimination in admission or access up to sixth primary grade; however, the evidence available for 2014 indicates that selection continues to be an extensive practice. These are principally through family interviews (to decide according to their 'closeness' to the school's educational project) and entrance tests (standardized or in other forms, above all for children at the primary infant level). While some national studies confirmed that there is a positive evaluation of the selection process by families and proxies (Canales et al., 2016; CEP, 2014), it is clear that selection has increased segregation (García Huidobro & Corvalán, 2009; Villalobos & Valenzuela, 2012; Carrasco et al., 2014). Above all, it has impeded

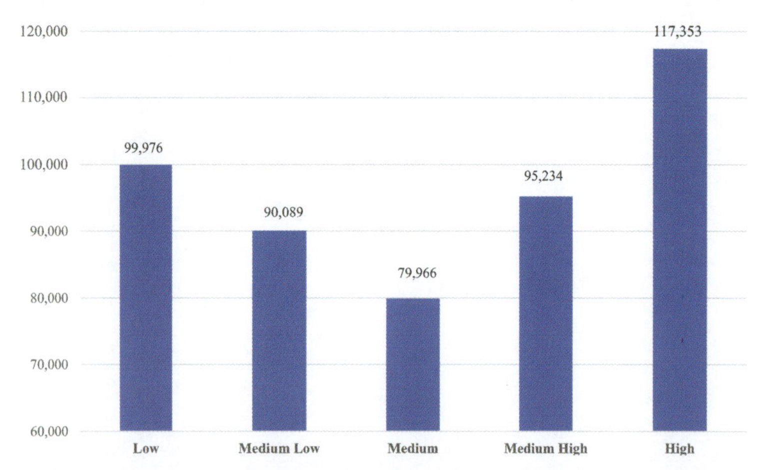

FIGURE 3.1 Average student expenditure by income quintile considering state subsidies and family co-payments: 2013 Chilean pesos (from Ministry of Education, 2014)

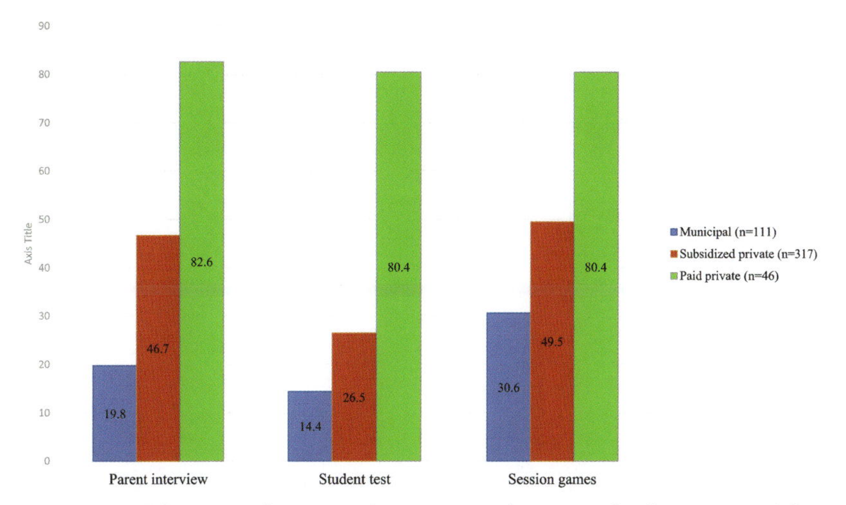

FIGURE 3.2 Selection mechanisms at pre-primary and primary schools current in Chile prior to the Inclusion Law by type of school (from Carrasco et al., 2014)

the exercise of one of the fundamental rights of Chilean education norms: the free choice by families (that naturally collides with the selection made by the school or its owner).

The prevalence of these selection practices is even more general, as well as being completely legal, between grades seventh and twelfth (Carrasco et al., 2014; Godoy, Salazar, & Treviño, 2014). This also has to do with the practice, already settled by an essential group of public schools, [secondary educational centers called 'emblematic' (emblemáticos) for their long and recognized history that has selected their students according to their prior academic performance and admission test results], a practice followed in other school systems (Dupriez, 2010). Some researchers have asserted that the educational effectiveness of these schools (around 50 nationally) is mainly due to the selection of students with better prior skills (González & Valenzuela, 2016).

> In sum, the Inclusion Law is, first, a response to an accumulation of evidence that overwhelmingly showed that these features (profits, selection, co-payment) produced adverse effects for the education system as well as not being shared by the educational policies of countries that now possess better educational indicators. The technical evidence complemented the intense political and social pressure to move to education with the right to quality of all social sectors (incompatible with co-payment and selection) together with greater regulation of the supply of private schooling—at least that sector financed by the State. It is these factors—with abundant evidence and pressure from different social and

educational actors to regulate (but not eliminate) the education market that set the stage for what was to be the first step of the Bachelet government's educational reform.[12]

3 The Inclusion Law: Process and Results

3.1 *The First Proposal*

In May 2014 the administration of President Bachelet sent Congress the first version of the Inclusion Law. To end profits, the project established the obligation for all educational administrations to be constituted as non-profit entities (thus ensuring that all resources had to be reinvested in the educational process). It also regulated the operations and expenditures that owners would be able to undertake (to guarantee these expenditures for 'educational objectives') and to propose that educational administrators own the buildings in which the establishment operated (to avoid 'auto-rental' [auto arriendo.]).[13] The aim was to ensure that the educational project was sustainable.[14] The first version of the law set two years for all institutions to change to non-profits and twelve years to acquire buildings and infrastructure.

To advance toward free education, the project prohibited any type of compulsory payment for families with children that attended schools financed by the state while at the same time it established a gradual increase in the value of the pupil subsidy (monthly payment transferred by the state to educational owners), replacing in this way—progressively—the contribution made by families to private education and increasing the state contribution to public schools that would continue to be free. The government proposed that establishments joined this new scheme voluntarily within ten years to implement that process. To this end, two new subsidies were created: a special subsidy for free schools and another preferential subsidy that was called "expanded."[15]

The Bachelet government's project proposed a general regulation for the admission process in all state-subsidized establishments, both private and public schools prohibiting inquiries about the family's socio-economic background and a student's previous academic performance when applying to an educational center to eliminate access selection and discrimination.[16] The projected law proposed the creation of a unique admission system, that would permit all families—in person or by e-mail—to apply for all their preferred schools. It was a way to safeguard compliance with this general regulation. A random system would resolve the cases of highest demand for the places available, by guaranteeing in the first-place siblings, the sons and daughters of school officials and vulnerable students proportionally not less than 15%

of enrollment. The proposed law suggested a unique system for traditional or emblematic schools (that historically had applied academic selection procedures) by allowing them to fill up to 20% of their enrollment with students of better performance than their original schools and setting a more extended transition period compared to the rest of the system.[17] Finally, the bill also proposed a new regulation for the resolution of conflicts and potential dismissals in educational centers, setting strict standards of procedure, establishing the obligation of having psychosocial support plans for students at risk, and increasing the sanctions for cases of arbitrary discrimination by school managers and their owners.

3.2 *Discussion and Resistance to the Law*

The government suggested a process of gradual implementation for each of these reforms, with the purpose of easing changes to the school system in the best possible way. However, the magnitude of the changes together with higher expectations (and preoccupations) of the different stakeholders about the effects of this project rapidly generated varied reactions which were reinforced by a complicated political-social context for the approval of the law. The debate about the new law was constant news in the communication media with continuous pronouncements about it by different social and political stakeholders.

Concerning the end of profits, the major criticisms and controversies had to do with new obligations for owners. A point of contention was the sanction on benefit making but above all the requirement to become the owners of their school property and infrastructure and to dedicate public resources exclusively to educational activities. The owners themselves, led and represented by The Federation of Private Education Institutions (Federación de Instituciones de Educación Particular, FIDE) and Private Schools of Chile (Colegios Particulares de Chile, CONACEP), their two most essential associations, publicly resisted the proposed law and threatened a massive school closure.[18] Given that middle class Chilean families, for various motives, had made their choices and associated private education with more significant opportunities for mobility (Canales et al., 2016) the threat of closure and opposition from school proprietors reflected an essential proportion of the parents and guardians of the subsidized private sector, who interpreted the reform as risking and reducing their educational options.[19] That also made possible a strong positioning of the nascent Confederation of Parents of Private Education (Confepa) which criticized the reform and defended subsidized private education.[20]

The end of co-payment and selection were also the object of criticism. While the replacement of shared funding was received as good news by the majority of owners (given that they were being guaranteed a more stable income flow, for co-payment has always involved high delinquency rates) some parents and proxies interpreted this change as a setback for the opportunity to choose and support education. The Confepa claimed it was a restriction on the freedom of parents, arguing that the law was usurping the "right to pay for the education of your children" (El Mercurio, 2015).[21] A different argument against the end of co-payment, from socio-educational actors close to the political center-left, was that it demonstrated the definitive weakness of public education, as private subsidized education, now free, would massively attract families currently in the public system.

Regarding selection, the principal point of conflict was the rejection—by some political and educational groups—of admission with academic criteria which is practiced by the 'emblematic' schools, which led a variety of actors, including some defenders of public education to join in criticizing the law.[22] The creation of a centralized admission system with random choice caused a wave of criticism by people and institutions that registered their lack of confidence in such a system. Some critics caricatured it as a "tombola," using the argument that it would not be the families themselves that make the final decision of where their children would study (regardless that this was precisely how the system functioned before the Inclusion Law).

The vast majority of the educational actors directly involved in the Inclusion Law resisted this change (El Mercurio, 2015), so the reform and the project, in particular, were left—as the legislative process continued—without relevant political or social support. Nor was there strong backing from the student movement, the teachers' union or the academic world, preferring to distance themselves and privilege criticism over the advances or the other positive aspects of the project. On the other hand, the media played a fundamental role in increasing the sensation of threat or "crisis" and encourage confrontation between actors rather than provide quality information about the bill and its implications (Cabalín & Antezana, 2016).

These complications in the public reception of this legal initiative increased by weak political management (the government failed to unite the ruling coalition around the proposed reform), and communication of the reform process (the government had severe difficulties in publicizing the objectives and implications of the law).[23] All this translated into low public support. According to an opinion survey research, by the second half of 2014, during the discussion of the Inclusion Law, a majority of citizens disapproved of the educational reform (Cadem, 2014; CEP, 2014). As shown in Table 3.3, this general disapproval was for each of the components under discussion.

TABLE 3.3 CEP survey results about educational reform (August 2014)

When asked "Do you believe that it is a good idea that parents complement the educational subsidy granted by the State with co-payments (paying attendance and/or tuition) to improve your children's education? Or do you believe that it should be banned?" The first question, supporting co-payment, was approved by 52%t while 37% rejected it with the second question.
When asked about their attitude about the perception that schools are making profits, their answer to the question "How does it appear to you that private subsided schools, as well as delivering education, generate profits for their owners?" 49% agreed providing that the schools were of high quality and inform parents; against 42% that disagreed.
Regarding the section on selection processes, one question was "Do you agree or disagree that schools of excellence, such as the *Instituto Nacional* select their students by admission test?" 54% agreed that such schools use this test while 39% did not.

SOURCE: BASED ON DATA FROM AT WWW.CEPCHILE.CL

Beyond the natural opposition exercised by those who saw their educational and economic interests affected (as happened in this case with owners), it is essential to note that the most challenging resistance to this law was society itself. More precisely of its middle segments, who want to differentiate themselves through the educational subsystem they access and who are far from seeing inclusion as the central focus of educational policies. Reforms based on equal opportunities find the social and cultural foundations of segregation (especially in highly unequal societies) reasonable. That is a significant limitation to reforms encouraging equity.

3.3 *The Final Outcome*

In spite of all these difficulties, in January 2015 and then with adjustments and negotiations—which took eight months—Congress approved the Law 20.845 which regulated student admissions, eliminated shared funding and prohibited profits in those educational establishments that receive contributions from the state. The government finally processed various technical and political criticisms made by different actors and transformed them into changes that made their endorsement viable, keeping the central ideas of this reform. The parties resolved their differences partly by making the changes more gradual (for each of them longer terms and transitions were considered), and also, with greater public investment to ensure that educational projects were not affected by the lack of resources (which caused the approved plan to imply a fiscal cost of more than 1,300 million dollars a year).

Table 3.4 synthesizes the contents of the final version of the Inclusion law as well as the time periods established for each of its components.

In summary, after a brief period and without introducing substantial changes into its original design, the government won approval thanks to its legislative majority. The Inclusion Law ended profit-making, co-payment and selection in Chilean private subsidized education. This political triumph was marred, however, by attitudes critical of reform by the majority of the public, particularly the middle class (which in recent decades have primarily opted for private subsidized education) and who feel threatened rather than benefitting from this new initiative.

4 First Steps toward Implementation: More Lights than Shadows

Although the law has only been in force since March 2016, and even though several of its provisions are applied gradually, it is possible to make a first tentative evaluation of the primary results.

As general background, two systemic effects prophesied by the law's critics have not occurred; namely, there has been no significant closure of private subsidized schools and nor has there been a massive transfer of municipal school pupils to private subsidized schools. The number of private establishments that have ceased their activities over the last two years is no different from that before the law (that is between 100 to 150 schools annually). On the other hand, schools that changed from private subsidized to entirely private schools were 108, with no more than 2% of total enrollment. Most of these, as might be expected, charged the highest co-payment to families (between US$ 90 and US$120 per month) and had for-profit owners.

Concerning the transfer of students from the municipal to the private subsidized sector, the data show that this 'exodus' is less than in previous years; over the last three years (2015–2017) this has amounted to 1% annually, while in past years it reached between 2.5 and 3.0%. This figure is doubly positive for in 2015 many teaching activities were paralyzed in public schools which usually triggered an increase in families abandoning municipal establishments for those in the private sector (Navarro & Gysling, 2017).

The application of the Law about the change from privately owned subsidized for-profit schools to non-profit foundations has evolved gradually. As of January 2, 2018, the private owners of the 5,501 private establishments

TABLE 3.4 Definitive content of the Inclusion Law

	What the law establishes	Application by time
End of profits	All owners to be constituted as non-profit legal entities (5,500 schools)	December 31, 2017 set as end of the transition period. From 2018 all owners will work as non-profit entities.
	All owners are obliged to acquire building and infrastructure with exceptions for those who cannot meet this requirement, (regulated rental, loans)	The deadline is fixed as three years following the change to a non-profit entity (during which time the decision can be made to buy, rent with regulation, or loan). There is a special six-year regulatory regime for establishments with less than 400 students.
	Items for investment from resources from subsidies explicitly listed with a new inspection regime for their use under the Superintendence of School Education (*Superintendencia de Educación Escolar*).	Applied from the beginning of the school year 2016
End of co-payment	Copayment was abolished as alternative finance for educational establishments. By 2018 it is estimated that 90% of the enrollment in general education will be free. The schools receive new funds (subsidies for free education and expanded preferential subsidies) as they voluntarily join free education (the decision of the owner).	Co-payments will decline gradually as schools move to free education replacing private for public resources. The maximum amount contributed by a family is frozen during the transition. The implementation of free education (and transfers to the new subsidies) began in 2015.

(*cont.*)

TABLE 3.4 Definitive content of the Inclusion Law (*cont.*)

	What the law establishes	Application by time
End of selection	The Law establishes that owners of schools funded by the State cannot use selection procedures and should make their admissions procedures consistent with the law.	Application began in 2016
	A single admission system will begin to govern all educational centers financed by the State (with some exceptions, such as special education or centers of high academic demand)	The application began in one region in 2016 to which were added 4 regions in 2017. The remaining regions (10) will join the system in 2018. Schools with high academic demand can opt for an additional 5 years transition to completely end selection.
	Regulation of processes of expulsion and management of diversity in school (students' preferential right to remain in school)	Application began in 2016 for all educational establishments.

(representing 97% of all subsidized schools and 98% of enrollments), had begun or already completed the transfer process to a non-profit legal entity. It was only a small minority that decided to close their doors or become independent private schools. The vast majority has transferred to the new system.[24]

Copayments have been reduced gradually, by replacing cash from families with public funds. In 2018 around 72% of the enrollment in private subsidized schools made no payment, implying that 40% of the schools that had previously levied families before the Inclusion Law, no longer did so. If one unpacks the schools that continued with co-payment—with an enrollment of 500 thousand students—then most of them have a family contribution that is relatively high; two-thirds of these students contribute more than US$ 40 per month each to their schools. In 2018 more than 3.2 million students, that is 84% of the enrollment financed by the state, attended schools under the non-profit regime.

The new admission system can show the results of the two completed cycles between 2017 and 2018.In the last year, five of the fifteen regions of Chile participated in the new system, four for the first time (Tarapacá, Coquimbo, O'Higgins and Los Lagos) only for first-year students entered the establishment (that is pre-school, kinder, first 1st and 7th grades and 1st secondary). The region which applied the new admission procedures for the second time (Magallanes), embraced the new rules at all levels (that is from pre-kinder to 4th grade secondary). The general results show that the majority of the students remained in the establishments that they had registered as their preferences. Thus, 93.3% of the 81,243 applicants entered to schools preferred by their parents. And 58% of the children were directly exposed to their first chosen option. Alternatively, another way of looking at this data is that only 0.3% of the students had no choice (or did not exercise that choice) and were merely "assigned" to a school by the admission system, which in any case ought to be the nearest available to their home and not listed as "insufficient" by the Quality Agency.[25]

In the Austral region of Magallanes, which began the gradual application of the new admission system, it has been possible to draw additional conclusions. If one compares the results of the first year of the new admission system in Magallanes to that of New York, with a more extended implementation period, the results are very similar and even somewhat higher in the Chilean case (Mineduc, 2017), as can be seen in Table 3.5. Two behavioral patterns of families appear to challenge how the new system is functioning. First, some families only apply to a few high demand establishments, not making "low risk" applications, which harm their chances of obtaining their preferences. Second, there is a tendency by some families to show impatience with the waiting lists by resorting to other options than those that they had initially marked.

The other relevant area to understand is the effects on changes to co-existence and school climate produced as a result of greater inclusion. It should be recalled that the new legislation is likely to provide a more significant social mix in subsidized private schools mainly as a result of the entry of more diverse social groups (the effects of non-selection and the end of co-payments) but also because of the substantial restrictions on student relations (expulsions, not renewing enrollment). The Superintendence of Education reports there is continuity regarding complaints made, but with some minor changes; the number of complaints (around eleven thousand) was similar to 2014 and 2016 and there continue to be more complaints about private subsidized than municipal schools. However, while complaints about expulsions and the non-renewal of enrollment diminished (in the direction established by the law), those from students and parents about discrimination, psychological and physical mistreatment in schools increased. The Superintendence attributes this to "less tolerance by the school community for the violation of

TABLE 3.5 New York and Chile; comparison of the admission systems' results (Ministry of Education)

First year New York	First year Chile-Maganalles
From 90,000 admission requests, over 70% gained a place in schools from the preference list (77.7%)	From 3,580 admission requests, (a similar total in both rounds), 3,107 were placed in schools of their choice (86.6%).
7,600 students were unassigned in the first round, but admitted to schools of their choice in the second round (8.4%)	199 students who were not admitted in the first round, were admitted to a school of their choice in the second, (5.5%).
Around 8,400 students withdrew during this process (8.8%).	258 students withdrew during the process (7.8%)
More than 2, 000 remained in the same school or repeated a year.	Those continuing at their original school after both rounds were 3.7% (131)
Around 3,000 did not remain on either list and so did not participate in either round (3.3%)	84 students were assigned to a school close to home after both rounds, (2.3%)

SOURCE: ABDULKADIROGLU ET AL. (2005)

rights associated with mistreatment and discrimination by students" (Superintendence of Education, 2017).

In this short period of life of the Inclusion Law, there is also evidence about how different educational stakeholders perceive it to lend their support to the work of education centers. For example, a recent survey (Weinstein, Muñoz y Rivero, 2017) shows that the head teachers have a mixed view of the new law. For a while, they appreciated its impact on equity and equality of opportunities (less discriminatory admission system, a more equitable education system). But they do not think there has been sufficient preparation in schools to absorb the diversity of students incorporated and believe that the law will have little effect on learning quality. The principals of private subsidized schools have a more critical position than those from municipalities. Over time, however, their perceptions have become more positive (see Figure 3.3). While 59% of headteachers thought that the law would have adverse effects in 2015, by 2017 this proportion had fallen by 17% so that now a plurality of heads (43%) believed that the law would have a positive impact on their school.

Another study about school leadership, in two regions (Rojas et al., 2017) confirmed the generally favorable opinion of the principles that inspired the law (including the reduction in arbitrary expulsions) while at the same time

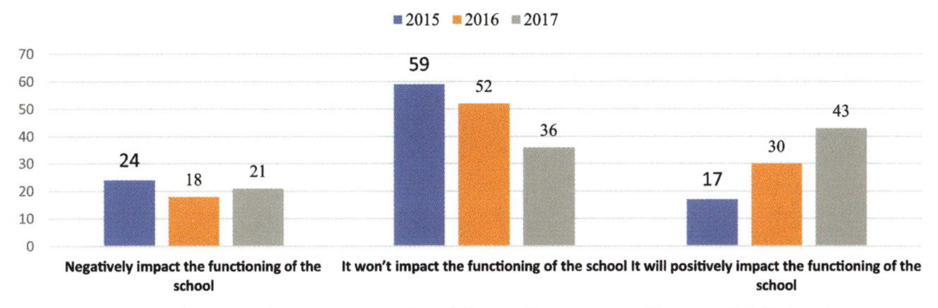

FIGURE 3.3 Evolution of perceptions about the Inclusion Law (from CEDLE, 2017)

thinking that neither free education nor the end of selection would have a high impact on the work of their school. A novel result of this study is that diversity is perceived above all by the schools' principals from a cognitive viewpoint and those of students' academic capabilities. The law is not understood to signal a greater social mix in schools. For if they foresee difficulties for the student (such as the lack of teacher preparation to work with different classes), it is not likely that the Law means a greater social mix in establishments. Rather, they conceive difficulties (such as the lack of preparation of teachers to work with different classes) as the integration of students with special educational needs. Further, they consider that inclusion could lead to tension concerning obtaining good academic results, a policy that has guided the Chilean educational policy for decades.

In summary, despite the difficulties, the Chilean school system has been adapting to these new legal regulations and which has not resulted in the adverse effects that some predicted. The figures presented here reflect a process that now faces the challenge of consolidation (in a scenario in which criticism of its design persists) and the translation of these new conditions into better procedures and educational results.

5 Discussion

The Inclusion Law is an educational policy intended to advance the right of education for all and to regulate the supply of mixed education in Chile. This reform, promoted by the government of Michelle Bachelet and supported by a new center-left political alliance, represents an inflection point in the educational reforms of post-dictatorship Chile. Over this extended two-decade period, the four governments of the Coalition of Parties for Democracy (Concertación de Partidos por la Democracia), supported policies backed by the Executive branch with such characteristics such as their gradualism and a search for consensus among the distinct educational, social and political stakeholders (Dellanoy, 2000). Thus, changes during this period concentrated on less controversial issues (Cox, 2003; Muñoz, 2013), such as the expansion of educational or school times, teacher salary increases, the modernization of the educational institutions and the curriculum, or improving conditions for socially disadvantaged pupils. In contrast to these prior changes—made under the assumption of win-win for all stakeholders—the Inclusion Law did not count on a broad consensus, nor political support because the state restricts some activities of a key stakeholder: the owners of private subsidized schools. It moves, using Corrales et al. (2009) terminology, from reforms about 'accesses to those of 'quality,' with the 'costs' of the latter falling on specific sponsors, rather than being diffused among many. Part of the difficulty facing the reforms described in this chapter concerns their controversial nature and the opposition that comes from attacking the interests and questioning the practices of a key stakeholder; and who is now is obliged by law to redefine their role and responsibilities within the educational system.

This educational reform model will be put to the test by the government that has just taken office (2018–2022), a center-right coalition, opposed from the beginning to the Inclusion Law, now in charge of guiding national education (without a legislative majority). The government of the new President, Sebastián Piñera, has the explicit objective of 'correcting' some features of the Inclusion Law, although at the point of writing no documentation has been unveiled. However, these issues will be central questions of educational policy during this period (Government Program, 2107). It is evident that managing a reform of this magnitude is likely to be conflictive; further, its negative effects on some stakeholders might complicate its sustainability. Indeed, the government has questioned other normative frameworks, which it opposed when in opposition and which were approved by the previous government. The conflictive character of the Inclusion Law and its only moderate support from a part of the education system implies that the new administration will have to choose between continuing to implement the approved regulations or modify them for the private subsidized sector if the president obtains political support to do so.

The experience of the Inclusion Law also provides lessons about how to influence the role of private education and face the undesired effects of deregulation. From the 1980s onwards, the governments increasingly privatized Chilean education services through market mechanisms, which while expanding educational coverage, did not fulfill its promise of improvement in quality and had adverse effects regarding school segregation. The Chilean experience shows that a mixed system can contribute to educational development but only if it is guided appropriately within a public regime. The end of for-profit schools, together with co-payment and selection, represent fundamental regulation issues for a state-funded educational system. Taking an historical and comparative perspective what this law achieves after various decades—indeed centuries of learning in countries with a high incidence of publicly funded private education (Holland, Belgium, Canada)—is to move the Chilean school system to a basic regulatory framework that promotes educational quality and equity (OECD, 2017). This action is both relevant and pertinent for other Latin American countries which are beginning their journey toward the greater participation of the private sector and where the discussion appears to be limited to its supposed virtues—innovation, diversity, coverage—but not those challenges and problems that come with the incorporation, massively, of private stakeholders in educational provision. An examination of the public regulation of private education from the very beginning of this process would be very advantageous, as illustrated by the Chilean Inclusion Law, for possible consequences and correction.

The construction of a "public regime," which appropriately includes private education, is not limited to the issues involving the regulations around the Inclusion Law. In fact, at the same time, Chilean legislators began to debate a new structure for the teaching profession and the new law. Finally, Congress approved the Inclusion Law in 2016 (Law No. 20.903) which established similar working conditions for teachers in public and private subsidized schools. To enhance educational quality of all schools financed by the state it is mandatory that teachers in both types of schools will be paid equal salaries and have a similar career structure and professional development opportunities. Taking this into account if the richness of the mixed provision is the complement between the public and the private, it is essential then to define the standard and differentiated conditions that must be asked of both systems for such general enrichment to occur.And it raises the question as to whether this framework of a 'public regime' should not be extended as the policy to other areas such as school leadership or technical support.

A critical issue for the reform discussed in these pages is its potential effect on the obverse of the coin—public education. In Chile, under the dictatorship, private education grew at the expense of public school, and the democratic governments that followed have proved incapable of reversing this trend (Weinstein & Muñoz, 2009; Bellei & Vanni, 2014). The provision of public education by municipalities failed, and apart from a handful of exceptions, local government has been an inefficient manager of educational services (Raczynski & Marcel, 2008). In fact, while the private subsidized sector expanded, the public sector contracted and, by accumulating the most disadvantaged students within the public system, increased socio-economic segmentation. Of course, the reform established by the Inclusion Law will not resolve the crisis in public education. Instead, a better regulated private subsidized system using public resources exclusively for education, without admission barriers (such as co-payments and selection) for different social groups could deepen this crisis if it is not matched by a clear policy to strengthen and recuperate the state sector.Here resides the importance of the law to create a new system of public education (Law 21.040) approved in 2017 which transfers school administration from municipalities to a new Local Education Service (Servicios Locales de Educación). These can manage a larger scale of the school population, not dependent on the electoral cycles for its staff and policies, to have a technical support structure, base funding for its operation, and be equipped with diverse and participatory governance bodies, such as Local Education Councils (Consejos Locales de Educación). The new public education law has a long way to go to, in fact, by 2025, complete the total transfer from the municipalities to the Local Education Services.

This point is closely related to another lesson: the sequence by which policies of this scope are discussed and legislated for it has a decisive effect on their approval and political support. President Bachelet's educational reforms, with the Inclusion Law, chose to initiate changes by regulating the private sector and 'leveling the playing field' concerning public education. That had the effect that for many stakeholders—including the center-left—the reforms were regarded with suspicion as they would have preferred the priority to have been strengthening public education. There were compelling reasons why the Inclusion Law was an unavoidable first step (due to its political complexity and because it was an inevitable step to eliminate some aspects that complicated the situation of state education).[26] Whereas if the path to change had initiated with a project to improve the public school or at least discussions held in parallel that would have resulted in enhanced political support. In any case, from here forward, one of the main challenges (and difficulties) for the next governments will be to manage the implementation of these two processes in parallel, so that strengthening of the new public education coexists with the consolidation of the mixed system and the new private subsidized sector regulation.

Finally, we emphasize the political and cultural difficulty of reforming private education services, especially when media groups participate massively in a culture permeated by neo-liberal values in which selection, the educational market and the 'right to choose' based on economic resources, are the norm. Private school choice has operated in Chile as a practice and tool for social differentiation (Carrasco et al., 2016), and for the middle class represents one of the ways by which to face the risks of relations with disadvantaged sectors. These practices seek to ensure homogeneity—not only social but moral—for this particular group of students and families while, at the same time, it is believed to act as a passport to higher educational opportunities and social mobility for their children (Canales et al., 2016). The Inclusion Law conflicts with these beliefs as it affirms that schools should be places for meeting and living together; that is social mixing is an educational value in itself. In other words, the main difficulty facing the law is neither technical nor political but cultural, since it bases education on values and styles of student coexistence that conflict with the subjectivity that predominates in Chilean society today. But how then to advance towards a culture that celebrates its diversity as a positive value for education? What kind of educational policies and experiences can change the culture that legitimizes present day socio-educational segmentation? What role does the school have in this transformation? Answers to these questions will play an essential part in shaping the challenges raised by this and other laws in favor of educational equity.

Notes

1. Chile has experienced over the last two decades two strong social and student movements that have demanded the transformation of the educational system. Secondary students led the first (2006) and the second by university students (2011). Both movements had important citizen support and have had an impact on the educational policy agenda in recent years (Muñoz, 2013; UNICEF, 2014).
2. The social movement for education in Chile has also turned its focus on higher education. This analysis concentrates exclusively on obligatory education which in the Chilean case spans kinder (per-school to fourth year secondary) with eight years assigned to primary education.
3. In the Chilean case, these market mechanisms have coexisted with a process of weakening public education, which is partly explained by the creation—at the beginning of the 1980s—with a public education system that depends on municipalities, with neither sufficient skills nor resources, and that was losing relevance owing to their disadvantages with respect to the conditions that are institutionally offered to private education.
4. Chief among these tools is the model of equivalent financing and based on competition among public and private schools (vouchers); the possibility of making money with public funds; low entry barriers for new school suppliers (proveedores) to education system and free choice by families. To the Chilean case should be added the possibility of a private school backer/promoter (sostenedor) choosing pupils and requiring a copayment from families.
5. For detailed information on this process see https://educacionpublica.Mineduc.cl/

6 For detailed information on this process see http://www.politicanacionaldocente.cl/

7 The 'school subsidy' (subvención escolar) is the amount of resources per student that the State delivers to each educational provider or owner. It is calculated as a monthly amount and depends on the attendance record of students at the school. Its value varies by educational level and modality.

8 SIMCE or the Educational Quality Measurement System (Sistema de Medición de la Calidad de la Educación) consists of a group of standardized tests administered to pupils at different levels and subjects in the Chilean school system. In practice these tests results have enormous consequences and are used as one of the principal indicators for school quality. Detailed information about SIMCE can be found at www.agenciaeducacion.cl

9 The Full School Day is a policy promoted since the second half of the 90s in Chile and consisted in ending the existence of two "shifts" of students in the same establishment, increasing school time by 30% -which involved a great investment in infrastructure, teacher salaries and student nutrition. Today in Chile the school year involves the development of approximately 1,500 teaching hours per year.

10 Legally public secondary schools (enseñanza media) can also charge families. However, in practice, only 2% of the schools at this level used co-payment and the average payment is less than US$ 4.

11 The Preferential Pupil Subsidy (Subvención Escolar Preferencial, SEP) was created in 2008 with the objective of providing additional finance to students belonging to the 40% most socio-economically disadvantaged attending both public and private schools. This policy which has undergone important changes with the Inclusion Law, requires schools and their owners to invest these additional resources in an Educational Improvement Plan (Plan de Mejoramiento Educativo, PME). For more information about SEP see Weinstein et al. (2011).

12 In effect the principal slogans and demands of the 2011 student movement, (similar to its predecessor of 2006) were "the end of profit" and "public education—free and with quality" (UNICEF, 2014).

13 By which owners used different legal entities obtained an additional profit with resources from subsidies.

14 To achieve this last point, the legal project opened an alternative with the possibility that the State buy the original educational buildings and infrastructure in those cases where the owner wished to continue to administer the center but could not acquire them.

15 The first implies an additional amount of US$ 20 per student for attending a non-profit school, while the second is an additional subsidy for students from the third- and fourth-income quintile of approximately, on average, US$ 35. The Preferential Pupil Subsidy (Subvención Escolar Preferencial, SEP) targeted at the first two quintiles increased from US$ 50 to US$ 70 on average. Using a student from the second quintile in second year primary as a reference point, the Chilean educational

system invests (only considering direct transfers to owners) approximately US$ 200 monthly per student.

16 The proposed and approved legislation also took an important step in the case of private-private schools with this law by establishing transparent and non-discriminatory admission procedures.

17 The majority of the emblematic schools begin their academic courses at the level of seventh year primary.

18 In October 2014, the President of CONACEP claimed that "at the national meeting held fifteen days ago a survey was held of the owners present and the result was that 92% claimed that they could no longer continue as private subsidized schools (under the Inclusion law)" (Radio Universidad de Chile, 2014).

19 Or become a private school, which implied a significant increase in family payments.

20 Confepa was founded in 2014, as a combined group of some opposition political actors and owners in the private subsidized sector to represent parents and proxies in the sector. Erika Muñoz, the President of CONFEPA was a member of Sebastián Piñera's Education Program Committee during 2017 and later became a candidate for deputy with the Independent Democratic Union (Unión Demócrata Independiente, UDI) a party opposed to the government and reforms of President Bachelet.

21 To this should be added the concern of families (partly shared by teachers and head teachers) for the greater socio-economic diversity of schools (owing to the progressive application of free schooling) that was and is interpreted by a segment of the population as risking quality and educational results, (Canales et al., 2016).

22 By using the argument that the existence of academically selective schools is a practice for which there is considerable international experience and that their continuation could ease social mobility in contexts of high inequality such as those of Chile.

23 To this should be added the concern of families (and also teachers and headmasters/management of the schools) for the greater socio-economic diversity of schools (owing to progressive application of free places) that was and is interpreted as a risk for the quality of the process and educational results (Canales et al., 2016).

24 This does not imply that there were not administrative difficulties in making this change in legal personality nor that all private owners have accepted the change without remorse. The main reason for the delay in moving from private ownership to a foundation, for many owners, is because of legal issues about ending infrastructure rental and complying with the requirement for their own infrastructure.In fact, special laws have been enacted that have made it possible to extend the periods in which the holders can keep the buildings of the establishments and rent, at a regulated price, at the same time that they function as non-profit foundations.

25 In Chile schools are classified by their results in standard tests (Simce) and other quality indicators that have a range of consequences and potential support. For more information on the classification see www.agenciaeducacion.cl

26 The Chilean experience clearly shows that public education has been weakened by rules of the game that bias the playing field/court against it (OECD, 2004; Bellei et al., 2010). Profits, selection, and co-payment transformed this area into a segregated space and with conditions that were more adverse than the rest of the school system, so that it was necessary to end this unsustainable situation to avoid a crisis.

References

Abdulkadiroglu A., Pathak P. A., & Roth A. E. (2005). The New York City High School match. *American Economic Review, 95*(2), 364–367.

Bellei, C., Contreras, D., & Valenzuela, J. P. (2008). *La agenda pendiente en educación: profesores, administradores y recursos: Propuesta para la nueva arquitectura de la educación chilena.* Santiago de Chile: Universidad de Chile.

Bellei, C., Contreras, D., & Valenzuela, J. P. (2010). Fortalecer la Educación Pública: Un desafío de interés nacional. In C. Bellei, D. Contreras, & J. P. Valenzuela (Eds.). *Ecos de la revolución pingüina: Avances, debates y silencios de la reforma educacional.* Santiago de Chile: Editorial Pehuén.

Bellei, C. (2015). *El gran experimento: Mercado y privatización de la educación chilena.* Santiago de Chile: LOM ediciones.

Bellei, C. (2016). Dificultades y resistencias de una reforma para des-mercantilizar la educación. *Revista de la Asociación de Sociología de la Educación, 9*(2), 232–247.

Cabalin, C., & Antezana, L. (2016). La educación en portada: la visualización de la política educacional en la prensa. *Cuadernos Info, 39*, 195–207.

CADEM. (2014). *Encuesta de opinión pública Plaza Pública CADEM.* Santiago de Chile. Revisado en www.cadem.cl

Canales, M., Bellei, C., & Orellana, V. (2016). ¿Por qué elegir una escuela privada subvencionada? Sectores medios emergentes y elección de escuela en un sistema de mercado. *Revista Estudios pedagógicos, 42*(3), 89–109.

Carrasco, A., Falabella, A., & Tironi, M. (2016). Sociologizar la construcción de preferencias: Elección escolar como práctica sociocultural. In J. Corvalán, A. Carrasco, & J. E. García Huidobro (Eds.), *Mercado escolar y oportunidad educacional: Libertad, diversidad y desigualdad.* Santiago de Chile: Ediciones UC.

Carrasco, A., Mizala, A., Contreras, D., Santos, H., Elacqua, G., Torche, F., & Valenzuela, J. (2014). Hacia un Sistema Escolar más inclusivo: Cómo reducir la segregación escolar en Chile. *Informe de Políticas Públicas Espacio Público, 3.*

CEP. (2014). *Encuesta de opinión pública.* Santiago de Chile: Centro de Estudios Públicos.

CEP. (2015). *Encuesta de opinión pública.* Santiago de Chile: Centro de Estudios Públicos.

Chumacero, R., & Paredes, R. (2008). *Should for-profit schools be banned?* (MPRA Paper). Santiago de Chile.

Contreras, D., Hojman, D., Huneeus, F., & Landerretche, Ó. (2011). *El lucro en la educación escolar. Evidencia y desafíos regulatorios* (Working Paper). Universidad de Chile. Santiago de Chile. Tra

Corrales, J., Roldán, M. B., & Garchet, P. M. (1999). *Aspectos políticos en la implementación de las reformas educativas*. Santiago de Chile: PREAL.

Cox, C. (2003). *Políticas educacionales en el cambio de siglo: La reforma del sistema escolar de Chile*. Santiago de Chile: Editorial Universitaria.

Delannoy, F. (2000). *Educational Reforms in Chile, 1980–1998: A lesson in pragmatism*. USA: The World Bank.

Dupriez, V. (2010). *Methods of grouping learners at school*. Paris: UNESCO.

Elacqua, G., Martínez, M., & Santos, H. (2011). *Lucro y educación escolar* (Working Paper). Universidad Diego Portales. Santiago de Chile.

Elacqua, G., Montt, P., & Santos, H. (2012). *Financiamiento compartido en Chile: Antecedentes, evidencia y recomendaciones* (Working Paper). Santiago de Chile: Universidad Diego Portales.

Flores, C., & Carrasco, A. (2013). *Preferencias, libertad de elección y segregación escolar* (Working Paper). Santiago de Chile: Espacio Público.

Gallego, F., & Hernando, A. (2009). *School choice in Chile: Looking at the demand side* (Working Paper). Santiago de Chile.

García-Huidobro, J. E., & Corvalán, J. (2009). *Obstáculos para el logro de una educación democrática inclusiva* (Working Paper). Santiago de Chile: Universidad Alberto Hurtado.

Godoy, F., Salazar, F., & Treviño, E. (2014). *Prácticas de selección en el sistema escolar chileno: requisitos de postulación y vacíos legales* (Working Paper). Santiago de Chile: Universidad Diego Portales.

González, C. A., & Valenzuela, J. P. (2016). *Efectividad de los liceos públicos de excelencia en Chile* (Working Paper). Santiago de Chile: Centro de Investigación Avanzada en Educación, Universidad de Chile.

Kutscher, M. (2013). *Efecto del financiamiento compartido sobre habilidades cognitivas y no cognitivas* (Unpublished master's thesis). Universidad de Chile, Santiago de Chile.

Marcel, M., & Raczynski, D. (Eds.). (2009). *La asignatura pendiente: claves para la revalidación de la educación pública de gestión local en Chile*. Santiago de Chile: Uqbar.

Martínez, J., & Palacios, M. (1996). *Informe sobre la docencia*. Santiago de Chile: Ediciones SUR.

Martinic, S., & Elacqua, G. (2010). *¿Fin de ciclo?: Cambios en la gobernanza del sistema educativo*. Santiago de Chile: UNESCO.

MINEDUC. (2017). *Estadísticas de la Educación 2016*. Santiago de Chile: Ministerio de Educación.

Mizala, A., & Torche, F. (2012). Bringing the schools back in: The stratification of educational achievement in the Chilean voucher system. *International Journal of Educational Development, 32*(1), 132–144.

Muñoz, G. (2013). Claves de una nueva reforma ducacional para el Chile que viene. In G. Muñoz et al. (Eds.), *Es la educación, estúpido*. Santiago de Chile: Editorial Ariel.

Navarro, L., & Gysling, J. (2017). Educación general en el gobierno de Michelle Bachelet: avances y rezagos. In P. Díaz, A. Rodríguez, & A. Varas (Eds.), *Bachelet II. El difícil camino hacia un Estado democrático social de derechos*. Santiago de Chile: BPE.

OECD. (2004). *Revisión de Políticas Nacionales en Educación*. Paris: OECD.

OECD. (2017). *Revisión de Políticas Nacionales en Educación*. Paris: OECD.

Paredes, R., Volante, P., Zubizarreta, J. R., & Opazo, M. (2013). *Financiamiento compartido en la educación subvencionada chilena* (Working Paper). Santiago de Chile: Universidad Católica de Chile.

Roje, P. (2014). *Segregación escolar por nivel socioeconómico (NSE) y su relación con las políticas educacionales en Chile: el caso del financiamiento compartido (FC) y la subvención escolar preferencial (SEP)* (Thesis, MA in Economics). Universidad de Chile, Santiago de Chile.

Superintendencia de Educación Escolar. (2017). *Informe de Denuncias 2016*. Santiago de Chile: Superintendencia de Educación Escolar.

Valenzuela, J. P., Bellei, C., & Ríos, D. D. L. (2014). Socioeconomic school segregation in a market-oriented educational system: The case of Chile. *Journal of Education Policy, 29*(2), 217–241.

Verdejo, M. I. P. (2013). *Las políticas escolares de la concertación durante la transición democrática*. Santiago de Chile: Ediciones Universidad Diego Portales.

Verger, A., Bonal, X., & Zancajo, A. (2016). Recontextualización de políticas y (cuasi) mercados educativos. Un análisis de las dinámicas de demanda y oferta escolar en Chile. *Education Policy Analysis Archives, 24*.

Villalobos, C., & Valenzuela, J. P. (2012). Polarización y cohesión social del sistema escolar chileno. *Revista de Análisis Económico, 27*(2), 145–172.

Weinstein, J., & Muñoz, G. (2009). Calidad para todos: La reforma educacional en el punto de quiebre. In Bascuñán et al. (Eds.) *Más acá de los sueños, más allá de lo posible: La Concertación en Chile*. Santiago de Chile: LOM Ediciones.

Weinstein, J., Muñoz, G., & Rivero, R. (2018). Los directivos escolares como informantes cualificados de las políticas educativas: Sus opiniones bajo el gobierno de Michelle Bachelet en Chile (2014–2017). *Revista Iberoamericana sobre Calidad, Eficacia y Cambio en Educación, 16*(3), 5–27.

Zubizarreta, J. R., Paredes, R. D., & Rosenbaum, P. R. (2014). Matching for balance, pairing for heterogeneity in an observational study of the effectiveness of for-profit and not-for-profit high schools in Chile. *The Annals of Applied Statistics, 8*(1), 204–231.

CHAPTER 4

Education Reform in Brazil: Multicultural Reflections

Ana Ivenicki

Abstract

The present chapter aims to discuss one of the most recent documents of education reform in Brazil, namely one that affects primary school curriculum, with implications for teacher education institutions—the *Base Nacional Comum Curricular*—Brazilian National Curricular Guidelines for Primary Education, approved in 2017 and homologated by the Presidency of Brazil. The aim of the chapter is not to delve into the curricular guidelines themselves, but rather to discuss the perceptions gleaned from the analysis made by the National Council of Education (Brazil, Conselho Nacional de Educação, CNE, Parecer sobre a Base Nacional Comum Curricular, 2017). It is also to argue on reactions expressed by counselors that revealed their judgments. Lastly, it considers the opinions gathered in emails and manifestoes by the National Association of Post Graduate Studies (ANPEd), as well as in Brazilian newspapers about the subject. It argues that a multicultural approach should contribute to link the search for excellence to social inclusion and to the development of citizens that value diversity and have a clear stand against prejudices on the lines of race, gender, ethnicity, and other identity markers. It posits that educational reforms in Brazil should gears to challenge educational inequality and to promote the inclusion of marginalized groups. It also analyses the extent to which the state has been subject to disparate forces that impinge on the present curricular reform.

1 Introduction

Education reforms have been at the center of debates in Brazil and elsewhere. The present study argues that a multicultural approach should contribute to link the search for excellence to social inclusion and to the development of citizens who value diversity and have a clear stand against prejudices on the lines of race, gender, ethnicity, and other identity markers. It posits that educational

 | DOI: 10.1163/9789004413375_005

reforms in Brazil should prepare to challenge educational inequality and to promote the inclusion of marginalized groups.

To develop the argument, this chapter will mainly focus on the most recent curricular reform on Primary Education as stated in the National Common Curricular Foundation (Brazil, Base Nacional Comum Curricular, preliminary document, 2017), from now on being referred to as BNCC, recently approved by the National Council of Education and homologated by the President of the Republic in December 2017.

The objectives of the chapter are: to discuss the extent to which multicultural concerns have (or have not) been present in that document, as assembled from the narrative of the review that approved the BNCC, as well as from opinions of the counselors who were against its approval. Also, the judgments expressed in Brazilian newspapers, in newsletters and manifestoes issued by one of the essential educational associations in Brazil, the Post-Graduate Brazilian Research Association (Associação Nacional de Pós-Graduação e Pesquisa em Educação, ANPED) during 2017 are discussed. The aim is to gauge challenges and possible ways ahead towards educational reforms geared towards combatting prejudices and promoting social inclusion.

Results of the analysis pinpoint how monoculture and multicultural pressures impinge on the proposed curriculum reforms within a turbulent political Brazilian scenario. It shows that multicultural tensions in educational reform may reflect how Brazilian state, arguably, is perceived as a mediating force that is in itself multicultural, hybrid, informed by a correlation of forces and pressures of grassroots agency and disparate worldviews within particular political and economic contexts.

The relevance of the study comes insofar as Brazil, standing as the biggest country in Latin America with a young democracy since 1985, has been dealing with educational reforms aimed at raising the performance of its population and, at the same time, promoting social and cultural inclusion. In addition to the complexities of the impacts of a contemporary Brazilian political scenario, that analysis is relevant comparatively in that it may shed light on the challenges of educational reforms in the context of Latin America and other increasingly multicultural countries.

2 Multicultural Thinking and Its Relevance for Policy Reforms in Brazil

Cultural diversity related to plural ethnic, racial, gender and other identities has been increasingly brought to attention all over the world, particularly in the context of global migrations. Brazilian multicultural society and its efforts to articulate it to educational reforms may be essential to discuss multicultural thinking, which advocates the need to value the diversity of identities. The purpose of those educational reforms is to foster the inclusion of marginalized groups and promote an equalitarian society that shuns prejudices and takes plurality on the lines of gender, ethnicity, race, language and other identity markers as assets rather than liabilities (Ivenicki, 2015; Warren & Canen, 2012).

However, scholarship in multicultural education has also pointed to the complex nature of multicultural thinking, as well as its affordances and challenges. Moland (2015), for example, makes the case that multicultural education should consider the local contextual ecologies where it is embraced, particularly in educational contexts bereft by inequalities, so that it does not exacerbate divisiveness instead of promoting unity and tolerance. In the same vein, Aman (2017) contends that intercultural thinking (which the mentioned author prefers to multiculturalism, in that it would be less descriptive of plurality and more akin to relations among plural identities) is highly dependent on where and who articulate them. He claims that power relations should be acknowledged when discussing it in postcolonial perspectives. That is because even though a general view of tolerance and acceptance of diversity may be accepted, it is not certain how they do translate into particular contexts ridden by conflicts. To apply multicultural thinking becomes more challenging and nuanced.

In fact, scholarship in multicultural thinking has taken on board postcolonial and de-colonial approaches, challenging more liberal approaches that align it with the celebration of cultures. In opposition to that perceived "touristic multiculturalism," the post-colonial and de-colonial perspectives aim to challenge the colonial nature of cultural hegemony. It posits the need to put colonized and oppressed identities' cultures at the center of educational reform, including the need to view immigrants and refugees as part of those multicultural sensitivities (Canen, 2011).

That way, postcolonialism and de-colonialism have brought to the scene the importance of both problematizing the unexamined recognition of hegemonic, colonial paradigms, as well as embedding educational reform with local, contextual and oppressed groups' cultures and strategies that allow for engagement, identity-seeking, and liberation from colonial oppression. Particularly in the global south, those perspectives have problematized the annihilation of indigenous identities. They enforce the crucial role of educational reforms in addressing injustices and valuing local identities and cultures in critical multicultural pedagogies.

On the other hand, as rightly pointed out by Park (2017), the dangers of de-colonial and postcolonial approaches come insofar as they may end up rearticulating binary strategies that freeze "I" and "the other," "western and non-western knowledge" and so forth. The referred author calls for caution so that knowledge transfer in post-colonial and de-colonial approaches should prevent them to fall into the trap of essentializing a "western identity" as opposed to an "eastern identity," thus to shun the idea of new subaltern identities that fail to recognize the complexity of identity formation and knowledge production.

I argue that a multicultural perspective that takes hybridity as its core category may help overcome essentialization of binary approaches to diversity, therefore potentially contributing to analyzing educational reform in ways that may help understand why contradictory policy goals emerge in particular contexts (Tarlau, 2017). I contend that a multicultural country such as Brazil, which has been trying to articulate excellence and multicultural concerns in its proposals, could be a relevant case study comparatively as related to discourses that embed educational reforms.

Hybridity refers here to two dimensions of identity formation, namely ways in which identities perform in a complex of markers that intersect and interplay with one another, being akin to what scholars denominate as intersectionality. Therefore, it challenges essentialization and highlights intersectional cultural identities on the lines of gender, race, ethnicity and so forth. Hybridity also refers here to ways in which actors locally transform globally or nationally to present discourses and narratives in educational reform proposals in different local contexts, recontextualizing and reinterpreting them in other frames of reference.

Tarlau (2017) argues that it is critical to gauge explicit or implicit theories of the state when dealing with global educational policy transfer. In those ways, analysts are stretched to analyze the impacts of civil society groups, grassroots and pressure collective actors in shaping the state forces that impact educational reform in multicultural countries such as Brazil. Carnoy et al. (2017) illustrate how local, municipal and state spheres in Brazil may produce different educational results depending on variables that are locally situated.

The Brazilian state may arguably be perceived as a mediating force that is in itself multicultural, hybrid, informed by a correlation of forces and pressures of grassroots agency and disparate worldviews of diverse groups. These include highly conservative ones within particular political and economic perspectives.

That view embeds the present analysis of the documents of educational reform in Brazil, mainly focusing on the text issued by the Brazilian National Council of Education. That is a consultative body linked to the Ministry of Education and charged with the responsibility of recommending educational policies and reforms, which approved the BNCC's Guidelines in December 2017

(Brazil, CNE, 2017). The present chapter examines the extent to which multicultural concerns have (or have not) been present in that document, as gleaned from the narrative of the review of the Brazilian National Council of Education that approved it, as well as from opinions of the counselors of that body who expressed differing views concerning that issue. The chapter will also draw on appraisals expressed in Brazilian newspapers and newsletters and manifestoes issued by one of the essential educational associations in Brazil, the Post-Graduate Brazilian Research Association (Associação Nacional de Pós-Graduação e Pesquisa em Educação, ANPED) during the year of 2017 (ANPEd, 2017). It will gauge challenges and possible ways ahead towards educational reforms geared to combatting prejudices and promoting social inclusion.

3 The Base Nacional Comum Curricular and Multicultural Issues

Brazil is a country of around 207 million people: 47.51% of whites; 7.52% of African descent, 1.10% of Asian ancestry; 43.42% mixed race people; 0.43% of indigenous groups, and 0.02% that opted not to declare their ethnicity (Brazil, IBGE, 2017). It is, therefore, a multicultural country, in which indigenous groups were already in its territory before the Portuguese came in 1500 and brought with them colonial values and an imperial worldview. Indigenous peoples were affected by colonialism, and are now composed of around 200 ethnicities, with their own cultures and languages.

Also, as described by Warren and Canen (2012), forced immigration of African peoples was undertaken for slavery purposes in the 19th century, which ended in 1888, leaving most afrobrazilian people in poverty since then. Apart from those, European and Japanese populations, among others, came to Brazil in the 20th century. Some were searching for new economic opportunities, others fleeing from wars and persecutions. At the outset of the 21st century, due to its economic boom (having somewhat declined in the last years), a wave of immigrants from Syria, African and South American countries have also come to Brazil.

In political terms, Brazil is a federal country, in which central governing authority shares its power (including that of issuing educational policies) with territorial units. Those "are bound together by a constitution that spells out the rights and obligations of the constituent members" (Carnoy et al., 2017, p. 727), since 1822, when Brazil achieved independence from Portugal. In the aftermath of the demise of military dictatorship, the Federal Congress issued a new constitution, in 1985. Regarding education, the Conselho Nacional de Educação—the National Council of Education (CNE) composed of 24 members, half of them chosen by educational associations which send lists of names to the Ministry of Education, responsible for the final choice. The President of the Republic appoints the other half. This board has the mission to review educational projects and reforms and help the Ministry of Education to make decisions.

From the 1990s onwards, Brazil has started to get aligned with educational policies aimed at comparing standards and performance of students in a global perspective, focusing on national curricular guidelines and general quantitative data for assessment of students and educational institutions, in the context of the growth of influence of transnational agencies.

However, the impact of the Brazilian educator Paulo Freire has not waned: he continues being the inspiration of multicultural thinking. As argued elsewhere (Canen, 2012; Ivenicki, 2015), in Brazil adult education has still been associated to compensatory education for those above the age of 14 years old who have not had the opportunity to develop their studies regularly. It is a way to address the persistently high rate of adult illiteracy among the country's disadvantaged groups. That became a responsibility of the state since the Federal Constitution of 1988; it is named Popular Education. Concerning the language of instruction in Indigenous education, the Ministry of Education regulated it, clarifying the importance of preserving mother tongue and indigenous cultures within that scope in bilingual and multicultural approaches.

Likewise, educational policies since 1988 emphasize the need to educate in anti-racist, multicultural perspectives. In 1998, the Parâmetros Curriculares Nacionais (the National Curricular Guidelines) (Brazil, 1998) presented education for diversity as one of the curricular themes to embed all the others, stressing the importance of imbuing syllabuses with anti-racist and anti-discriminatory perspectives. Those guidelines were also accompanied by pedagogical materials that suggested how to incorporate such approaches into school activities. Similarly, the Law 11645/2008 (Brazil, 2008) instituted the mandatory teaching of African and Indigenous cultures in schools, to develop the appreciation of diversity and the shunning of racism within the curriculum. Even though the Parâmetros Curriculares Nacionais (Brazil, 1998) were thought to embody a National Base for Curriculum in Brazil, the National Council of Education thought otherwise and began discussions about curricular guidelines. The aim was to build a National Base for Curriculum in Brazil, boosted after the Brazilian National Plan for Education of 2014. It delineates the goals and strategies for the development of education in the country up to 2014.

As claimed elsewhere (Ivenicki, 2015), Freire's concerns that education should build on marginalized and oppressed adult identities' cultural life histories and perspectives opened the way towards thinking of the plural, hybrid intersectional cultural identities. Especially for those that have been subject to colonial oppression, the aim is to enfranchize them in multicultural, de-colonial and postcolonial approaches to education and curriculum in Brazil. Therefore, when analyzing educational reforms in this country, hybridization of global and local/multicultural influences should arguably be borne in mind. More recently, as suggested elsewhere (Ivenicki, 2015), the "Plano Nacional de Educação"—National Plan for Education 2014–2024, which make explicit the goals for Brazilian education for those ten years, provides some further evidence for that argument. For example, while some parts of that record stress the importance of providing resources that allow situating education positively in the global, technological world, others highlight multicultural concerns related to the centrality of opening universities to more culturally, ethnically and racially diverse and marginalized groups, through programs that present quotas for blacks and indigenous population and other incentives to give voice and presence to rural people and ethnic/racial disenfranchised identities.

From the above, it seems to be clear that multicultural perspectives have been present in educational reforms in Brazil in the last years, even though being articulated to more universal, technologically driven ideas in the field. In that context, I turn now to the analysis of the most recent document of education reform in Brazil, namely one that affects primary school curriculum, with implications for teacher education higher education institutions—the BNCC. The report expresses ten general competencies that should embed the specific areas of study and syllabi. Among them are the valuing of diversity, democracy, and inclusion, particularly concerning the plural black and indigenous collective identities of Brazil, showing a continuation of those multicultural and anti-racist concerns pinpointed in previous educational reforms. At the same time, it stresses the importance of preparing students for the labor market, again evidencing the effort to articulate local, anti-racist concerns with more global curricular scopes in its objectives.

The aim of the present chapter is not to delve into the curricular guidelines, but rather to discuss the perceptions gleaned from the analysis made by the National Council of Education (Brazil, Conselho Nacional de Educação, CNE, Parecer sobre a Base Nacional Comum Curricular, 2017). Another goal is to examine appraisals expressed by educational actors such as the National Association of Post Graduate Studies (ANPED).

The first issue that has been at the center of contentions was the existence of the document itself. Although the elaboration of the plan was an object of strife in 2015, its final draft raised further criticisms from the academic community in 2017. As claimed by the ANPED newsletter of December 5, 2017, that association, as well as other ones, issued a bid to the National Council of Education asking them to suspend the voting on the BNCC. They claimed that even though there was a consultation amongst the research community concerning the drafts of the curricular report, the contributions were allegedly not taken into account in the last final version of that text.

However, the voting took place at the end of December, and the BNCC was approved by the counselors, except for two, who manifested their views (to be analyzed later). The President of the Republic homologated it on December 20, 2017, and now it is a remarkable record that concerns the curriculum of all schools in Brazil.

At the time of its homologation, the Minister of Education employed a multicultural terminology to say that the BNCC was an edge breaking curricular document that should 'guarantee that Brazil will be among the foremost nations of the world in educational terms. While it also ensures that children of needy families and that of the middle class should have the same "educational treatment" (Minister of Education Mendonça Filho, as reported by Clarissa Pains, Leticia Fernandes e Patricia Cagni, O Globo, 21/12/2017, p. 30). They went on to say that

> We did not stay only in the discourse. We did not get involved in a sterile debate. The BNCC is plural, as it respects the differences and human rights. It is the fruit of a collective construction. It is not perfect, but we tried to make it embody the identity of a Brazil that is ample and diverse.

However, as opposed to that supposedly multicultural statement, the ANPED manifesto argues that the fact of having a national curricular document would be detrimental to cultural diversity in Brazil, by imposing a homogenized national model for a plural country. The critique also mentioned that the composite construction of the document was not as collective as it should have been. The criticism of the absence of a multicultural framework was evident in the following excerpts from the manifestoes produced by the referred association, the first in 2015, the second in 2017:

> The creation of the BNCC does not contemplate the dimensions of the diversity in the Brazilian education. Therefore, there is a severe risk of ruining all the educational and environmental policy in our country [...] The associates of the ANPED confirm their position contrary to the BNCC, due both to its methodology of elaboration and to the obvious

> implications in the processes of evaluation of learning. The homogenization of curriculum and teacher education; and the menace it represents to schools' autonomy. (ANPED motion 12, cited in ANPED, 2017, p. 1)

> There are critical elements in our critique of the BNCC, among which [...] the homogenization of curriculum guidelines and the implications for teacher education and the schools' autonomy that become fragile in the context of the high centralization that the BNCC represents in school education (...). The ANPED is highly concerned with that centralized and homogenized model. (ANPED manifesto, December 2017, p. 9)

To answer to those critiques, the Minister of Education elaborated a discourse in the news reports. Also, the narrative of the document issued by the National Council of Education that approved the BNCC (Brazil, CNE, 2017) takes pains to show that the existence of a standard national curriculum is something historical, present in the Brazilian legislation, including the Federal Constitution (1988). On the other hand, it reinforces that besides an everyday curricular basis, the BNCC makes room for a diversified curriculum part that considers regional and local cultures and worldviews (p. 21), hinting at a multicultural approach to curriculum. Also, critical multiculturalism was present when the National Council of Education pinpoints that the BNCC expresses the centrality of curriculum that deconstructs prejudices and intolerance, fostering acceptance and recognition of differences. It goes on to stress that the BNCC also valued the plurality of languages, including those of deaf people, from an inclusive perspective.

However, the ANPED manifesto did not perceive that multicultural perspective which contends that:

> The BNCC expresses recognition of the Brazilian society as multicultural to enhance the considering of difference ... However, that presents it in a liberal multicultural tone, which means that political actions recognize the differences but emphasize them only in private contexts. The ANPED perceived in this version of the report that there is a common universalized and homogenized base. Only at the regional levels is the contextual cultural and social, localized diversity perceived as necessary for the diversified part of the curriculum ... Even though those differences may be present in local curricular constructions, the hegemonic power of the national, the established 'universal' curricular dimension is continuously reinforced by evaluation policies. ANPED argued that pedagogical

> materials distributed to schools and teacher education courses should positively promote the hierarchizing of knowledge. Thus, legitimizing the homogenization of a national curriculum to the detriment of the local, diversified curricular part of the proposal ... Therefore, the BNCC represents an instrument that aims to silence, marginalize and exclude. Apparently, under the guise of inclusion, it establishes very rigid and strict criteria and learning sequences, which are to be reinforced by evaluation instruments that will translate relative and decontextualized numbers related to quality in education. (ANPED manifesto, December 2017, p. 14)

In that perspective defended by the ANPED, the discourse of the document is detrimental to postcolonial and de-colonial multiculturalism, in that it will end up creating a disqualifying view of differences as embedded in the normative materials and large, homogenized evaluation processes of schools.

On the other hand, one perceives the hybridization of those liberal, apparent multicultural concerns with more global perspectives when the narrative of the referred National Council of Education document (Brazil, CNE, 2017) goes on to say that the BNCC ensures the acquisition of learning in levels compatible with the contemporary needs: that is, to participate entirely in the local and global society, by considering the links with the countries in Latin America and the Caribbean. Such a sentence seems to point to the influence of a decolonized multicultural perspective, linking the local multicultural Brazilian scenario with the decolonized perspective that highlights the Global South and challenges the North hegemony. However, such a view may fall into the trap rightly pointed by Park (2017) of reinforcing an essentialized dichotomic view that freezes north and south, ignoring processes of hybridization in knowledge production and in the curriculum itself.

Furthermore, such an apparent multicultural de-colonial perspective does not seem to be present in the rest of the document. There appears no mention about the change made to the initial idea of contents for the History syllabus, which dealt with indigenous and Afro-Brazilian populations' histories and cultures to the benefit of more conservative, universalized views of a Western Northern Hemisphere historical approach to human development. That view is highly centralized around cultures and worldviews expressed by European historical perspectives.

In fact, controversies generated by a first multicultural de-colonial version of the History curriculum within the BNCC could also be felt concerning gender identities, as can be noted in the following excerpt, where the Brazilian National Council of Education (Brazil, CNE, 2017) justifies the absence of the gender issue in its final version:

> Gender has been the object of many public discussions of the BNCC. Therefore, the National Council of Education will leave it for the future, even though it recognizes the importance of that theme so as to provide the development of values and attitudes of respect, tolerance to diversity, pluralism and individual liberties, combatting any form of prejudice and violence. (Brazil, CNE, Parecer sobre BNCC, 2017, p. 30)

As can be distinguished in the above quotation, the most controversial issue has been the gender identity in the discussions about the BNCC. As opposed to critical, de-colonial multiculturalism, the point of the diversity of gender fueled strong reactions from conservative groups in Brazil, which had a direct impact on the last version of the BNCC, where gender identity and its articulation to curriculum guidelines wholly disappeared.

Some excerpts from the discourses of the two counselors of the Brazilian National Council of Education that were for and against the approval of the BNCC, as well as the perceptions from the academic community as gleaned in the ANPED manifesto give a snapshot of those controversies:

> I herewith declare my vote contrary to the Review referring to the BNCC [...] because I believe it breaks the unity of basic education by presenting only primary education curriculum and by practically ignoring schooling for young and adult people. Also, it does not touch on the specificity of rural education, and it does not respect the principle of pluralism .... (Brazil, CNE, 2017, p. 43)

> I at this moment declare my vote in favor of the Review referring to the BNCC ... However; I wish to announce my restrictions to it, namely: the BNCC has not included the secondary education. It focuses only on primary and child education, being detrimental to a holistic vision of basic education. Also, it has excluded references to gender and sexual orientation, because the Ministry of Education and the majority of the members of the National Council of Education (CNE) ended up giving up to the pressures of fundamentalist and ultraconservative groups that were against the inclusion of those themes in the BNCC. (Brazil, CNE, 2017, p. 45)

> The disappearance of any mention of the issue of gender identity and sexual orientation from the final text of the BNCC evidences its opposition to the idea of respect to diversity. That also shows the level of concessions and compromises that the Ministry of Education had to undertake

> to please conservative segments in Brazil … Because of those concerns, the ANPEd manifests its understanding that education is a commitment to the public sphere, as well as with the common good and with cultural diversity … Aspects that were not taken into account by the curricular document handed by the Ministry of Education for appreciation by the National Council of Education. (ANPED, manifesto concerning the BNCC, December 2017, p. 15)

As can be noted from the above excerpts, multicultural issues, their meaning and the theme of diversity, particularly of gender identity, were at the forefront of the polarization of discourses. All actors involved in the construction of the curricular guidelines participated, from the Minister of Education to the Counselors of the Brazilian National Council and the academic community as expressed in the manifestoes from the ANPED. Concerning adult education, the fact that the report stressed curriculum for primary education without explicitly addressing that significant level of schooling gave a motive for other criticism, mainly concerning the importance of literacy and numeracy acquisition for adults and the contributions of Paulo Freire for that area of education. It seems indeed that the curriculum reform document should benefit from making such a theme amongst the priorities in the BNCC. Also, concerning secondary school, it should be pointed out that in March 2018, the government sent to the National Council of Education a draft with the proposal for the Curricular Base for Secondary Schooling, which had not been analyzed by that Council at the time of writing this chapter. Rather than viewing identity building as hybrid and intersectional, the record and the Minister's words—as gleaned earlier in the excerpt from the newspaper—seem to evidence a kind of liberal multiculturalism that values diversity in abstract terms. That reinforces essentialization of identities and the silence of gender issues in the school curriculum. Such a perspective is present within the context of the ten general competencies explained in the BCNN in its presentation, as commented on before, in which the focus was on the collective Black and indigenous plural identities' cultures rather than on the challenge of racism.

Apart from that, the excerpts also show a broader view of the state and its influence on educational reforms, particularly concerning the extent to which multicultural sensitivities are (or are not) section of them. It is important to note that Brazil has been under economic and political tensions mainly from 2016 onwards when issues affecting elected presidents and past presidents came to the forefront. The vice-president assumed the presidency, seeking out the necessary popular and academic support, with implications for the forces that fight for influence on policies, including educational ones.

As gleaned from the discourses of the CNE counsellors and those from the ANPED, it seems to be clear that conservative groups of society were strong enough to alter the initial drafts of the BNCC and extirpate de-colonial multiculturalism from the proposal, eliminating from any curricular consideration hybrid/intersection of markers of identity, particularly gender identity and sexual orientation.

The argument seems correct that Brazilian state is a mediating force that is in itself multicultural, hybrid, informed by a correlation of forces and pressures of grassroots agencies and disparate worldviews of plural groups within particular political and economic contexts. Making concessions to groups, conservative ones in the present case, end up impinging on the curriculum guidelines, showing once more that curriculum and educational reforms, in general, are far from neutral, embodying power struggles around their meaning and development.

As Brazil starts the year of 2018 with national elections for president and state governors, it may be worthy to wait for further developments in educational reforms. In any case, it is clear that curriculum guidelines have to have compliance with the foremost educational actors to come to life: the teachers. It remains to be seen the extent to which they will feel competent and, most of all, empowered to develop those curriculum guidelines. It is feasible that they will strive for resistances contending for further local multicultural curricular hybridizations which may consider the need to understand plural identities as a hybrid, intersectional, to raise future generations into the values of tolerance and the challenge of prejudices, racisms, and other discriminations.

4 Conclusions

The National Brazilian Curricular Guidelines (Brazil, 2017) is a document that represents a relevant part of educational reform in Brazil. It comes as a continuation of previous educational policies geared toward valuing cultural diversity and, at the same time, preparing for students for market and work environments. In the present chapter, I argue that the BNCC embodies the contradictions and the tensions between multicultural de-colonial perspectives geared towards combatting prejudices and valuing hybrid identities, and conservative forces in favor of universalized, genderless approaches. Those traditional powers shun the possibility of imbuing curriculum with discussions related to tolerance and the challenge of stereotypes, and which reinforce education and its evaluation in more universalistic criteria.

The controversies related to de-colonial approaches in curriculum content, as illustrated in the History syllabus, as well as the initial presentation and then the complete absence of gender identities in the report produced by the National Council of Education, seems to reinforce the tensions between conservative movements and those more multicultural sensitive ones. The controversies are amplified in the scenario of a temporary government that has to mediate pressures to gain the necessary support to implement educational reforms in the Brazilian contemporary political context. The multicultural de-colonial perspective has only superficially made its inroads in educational reform. As it stands now, the conservative forces won the curriculum battle.

The perceptions and discussions as harvested in the record issued by the National Council of Education, the emails, and manifestoes by the ANPED and the extracts from Brazilian newspapers related to the subject, seem to reinforce the argument that the state is in itself a hybrid, multicultural entity. It acts within the context of power relations which impinge on the final narratives of the reforms. The case of Brazil is relevant comparatively, in that it is a multicultural country that has arguably produced curriculum accounts that value its diversity and instill in the future generations the need to combat any form of violence against plural identities, including the gender ones.

A multicultural perspective that views hybridity as a lens to analyze both the production and the product of educational reform in Brazil as argued in the present study helps to understand how contradicting forces with diverse cultural and ideological views impact on how educational policy narratives and discourses have been produced and perceived in the Brazilian context. A picture of the production of educational reform texts as the result of multicultural, conflicting cultural views and identities within the state apparatus may also enrich the sight of such policies, as well as its challenges and affordances.

References

Aman, R. (2017). Colonial differences in intercultural education: On interculturality in the Ades and the decolonization of intercultural dialogue. *Comparative Education Review, 61*, 103–120.

ANPED—Associação Nacional de Pós-Graduação e Pesquisa em Educação. (2017). Nota ANPEd | A proposta de BNCC do ensino médio: alguns pontos para o debate. Retrieved from http://www.anped.org.br/news/nota-anped-proposta-de-bncc-do-ensino-medio-alguns-pontos-para-o-debate

Brazil, Conselho Nacional de Educação (CNE), Ministério da Educação- Ministry of Education (MEC). (2017). *Parecer Homologado sobre a Base Nacional Comum*

Curricular (BNCC) (Portaria n° 1.570, Section 1, p. 146). Retrieved from http://portal.mec.gov.br/index.php?option=com_docman&view=download&alias=78631-pcp015-17-pdf&category_slug=dezembro-2017-pdf&Itemid=30192

Brazil, Instituto de Geografia e Estatística Aplicada (IBGE). (2017). *População.* Retrieved from https://www.ibge.gov.br

Brazil, Ministry of Education. (1998). *Parâmetros Curriculares Nacionais.* Retrieved from http://portal.mec.gov.br/seb/arquivos/pdf/livro01.pdf

Brazil, Presidency of Republic. (2008). *Law 11645/2008.* Retrieved from http://www.planalto.gov.br/ccivil_03/_ato2007-2010/2008/lei/l11645.htm

Canen, A. (2011). Boosting Immigrant Student Identities in Brazilian Schools: Towards a multicultural framework for teacher education. In S. Vandeyar (Ed.), *Hyphenated Selves: Immigrant identities within education contexts* (pp. 149–164). Amsterdam: Savusa/Rozenberg/UNISA Press.

Canen, A. (2012). Brazil; Lifelong learning and the role of University in Brazil: Some reflections. In M. Slowey & H. Schuetze (Eds.), *Global perspectives on higher education and lifelong learners* (pp. 266–278). London: Routledge.

Carnoy, M., Marotta, L., Louzano, P., Khavenson, T., Guimarães, F. R. F., & Carnauba, F. (2017), Intranational comparative education: What state differences in student achievement can teach us about improving education? The case of Brazil. *Comparative Education Review, 61*(4), 726–759.

Ivenicki, A. (2015). Adult education and cultural diversity in Brazil: National policies and contributions of higher education. In M. Milana & T. Nesbit (Eds.), *Global perspectives on adult education and learning policy* (pp. 60–72). New York, NY: Palgrave MacMillan.

Moland, N. A. (2015). Can multiculturalism be exported? Dilemmas of diversity in Nigeria's Sesame Square. *Comparative Education Review, 59*(1), 1–23.

Park, J. (2017). Knowledge production with Asia-Centric research methodology. *Comparative Education Review, 61*(4), 760–779.

Tarlau, R. (2017). State theory, grassroots agency and global policy transfer: The life and death of Colombia's Escuela Nueva in Brazil (1997–2012). *Comparative Education Review, 61*(4), 675–700.

Warren, J., & Canen, A. (2012). Racial diversity and education in Brazil. In J. A. Banks (Ed.), *Encyclopedia of diversity in education* (Vol. 1, pp. 262–265). Washington, DC: Sage Reference.

CHAPTER 5

Endurance and Absences in Peru's Reform: The Challenge of Second-Order Reforms in the Core of Educational Practice

María Balarin and María Fernanda Rodríguez

> Economics is at heart a narrative art, a frame across which data points are woven into stories about how the world should work.
>
> NATHAN HELLER, "Take the money and run," 2018

Abstract

Through a discussion of the three last decades of education policymaking in Peru, the argument of this chapter is that most education reform efforts have focused on bringing about first-order changes that seek to improve the efficiency and effectiveness of what is done by schools. While improvements have been attained, constant changes in ministerial teams and policy orientations have made it difficult to achieve such first-order changes and there is evidence that many of the problems that were identified and began to be addressed three decades ago still dominate the education policy agenda. In this context, the chapter argues that much needed second-order pedagogical reforms that seek to bring about fundamental changes in the core of educational practice have been constantly postponed.

1 Introduction

Since the early nineties, after a decade of mounting internal violence and hyperinflation which led to the almost total collapse of the state, there has been an urgency to reform Peruvian education. In 1992, a General Diagnosis of the Education System painted a bleak picture (Ministerio de Educación del Perú, 1992). While access to education, especially at the primary level, had widened,

 | DOI: 10.1163/9789004413375_006

this had happened without any concomitant increase in the national budget for education. On the contrary, since the 1950s, when public investment in education peaked, public funding had been steadily diminishing. Educational democratization regarding access thus came together with a pauperization of the public education system. In 1991, yearly per pupil investment was as low as US dollars 162 (Saavedra & Suárez, 2002), teachers' salaries were less than US dollars 155 per month (both below the level reached in 1950), school infrastructure was critically weak and insufficient, and schools received no materials to work with (Bing Wu, 2001).[1]

During the almost thirty years that have followed the moment of public consciousness about the crisis of education that the 1992 Diagnosis represents, the Peruvian education system has been subjected to a series of both comprehensive and partial reform attempts, marked by radical discontinuities in both the goals and teams leading reforms.

In the following pages, we briefly recount the last three decades of attempts at reforming Peruvian public education. We propose that most efforts have focused on bringing about first-order changes which focus on improving the efficiency and effectiveness of what is done by schools; and show that there have been significant limitations for promoting necessary second-order changes at the core of educational practice (Cuban, 1990).

We show the difficulty of promoting second-order changes amidst an education policy arena that is prone to constant discontinuity in the definition of broad policy discourses and goals, and where the meaning of such discourses and goals has gone from being highly idiosyncratic to being narrowly technocratic, making the definition and pursuit of second-order reform goals almost impossible. In recent years, as a more technocratic style of policymaking has taken hold of the public sector and the Ministry of Education (MoE) in particular, educational quality has become narrowly equated to improvements in maths and language learning achievement as measured by standardized tests, making it difficult for policymakers to commit to expensive long-term goals linked to the promotion of fundamental changes in school practices. We make this argument through an analysis of recent attempts at introducing pedagogical reforms in Peru.

2 Crisis, Change and Continuity in the Past Three Decades of Peruvian Public Education

The history of Peruvian education policies since the 1990s exemplifies the complex challenges of bringing about sustainable change in education. The first reform attempts came soon after the aforementioned 1992 Diagnosis. Early in the decade, the government lead by President Alberto Fujimori (1990–2000) attempted to bring in system governance reforms that introduced market mechanisms into the public education sector (choice, school autonomy, and demand-led funding). The government soon abandoned such reforms because of strong opposition from organized groups that questioned their privatizing aims (Arregui, 1994). During the second half of that decade, reform efforts appeared under the World Bank funded Primary Education Improvement Program (MECEP), a comprehensive reform package that sought to improve infrastructure, governance, educational quality and the education system's capacity to monitor its improvements through standardized testing and statistical data. While there were no more attempts at introducing market mechanisms in public education, the passing of a law that liberalized for-profit private investment in education led to a massive growth of the private education market that slowly embedded choice in families' educational decisions (Balarin, 2015; Balarin, Kitmang, Ñopo, & Rodríguez, 2018; Cuenca, 2013; Sanz, 2014).

In 2000, after winning an unconstitutional re-election, evidence of deep corruption led to President Fujimori's demise. His successor, Valentín Paniagua (2000–2001), declared there was a need to reform the education system, to make it more attuned to the country's evident democratic deficit. The government conducted a national consultation, and its diagnosis was more or less the same as that of the early nineties. A decade of massive spending through international loans had led to little change.

The following government, led by Alejandro Toledo (2001–2006), passed a new General Law of Education which drew inspiration from the National Consultation Process. It had a strong emphasis on democratizing and decentralizing a highly-centralized education system. In 2003, evidence of Peru's low results in the PISA Tests led then Minister Carlos Malpica to declare the education system in a "state of emergency" and to propose a sectoral Emergency Plan to improve the quality of schooling. The necessary funds to implement the Plan never materialized. Adding to this, constant ministerial changes, led to equally ceaseless changes in policy orientations and little progress concerning actual improvements in the quality of public schooling.

A subsequent government, led by Alan García (2006–2011), declared its adhesion to the General Law of Education and to the National Education Plan (NEP) that was prepared by the National Council for Education, a recently formed institution that was meant to set the primary goals for the national education system. García's government, however, took a different direction to the one he embraced in discourse and to the one the Law and the NEP mandated. The MoE made a U-turn in decentralization efforts and focused on a small number of policies which yielded few sustainable results, later questioned because of the quality of their public spending.

In 2011, the following government, led by Ollanta Humala (2011–2016), began with a serious reform effort. Its first education minister, Patricia Salas, sought to define a more explicit reform agenda, aligned to the goals set in the General Law of Education and the National Education Plan. Education policies thus acquired a strong focus on decentralization and on strengthening administrative and pedagogical leadership capacities at the local and regional levels. Salas' policies also had a solid commitment to equity, through an emphasis on closing the rural-urban quality gap in education. The central reform package passed during her term in office, was a significant reform in the law that governs the teaching profession, making it more meritocratic. This change led to a protracted strike which cost Salas the post.

Political and social actors criticized Salas for not achieving quick results regarding pupil achievement in early primary national assessments. Her successor, Jaime Saavedra, entered office with a strong reformist commitment and a promise to yield more rapid improvements in educational results measured through standardized tests. To do so, he prioritized school infrastructure, the promotion of pedagogical programs, improvements in institutional governance, the reform of the teaching profession along meritocratic lines, and a reform of the higher education system. His running also inaugurated a more evidence-based and data-driven approach to policymaking. Saavedra was ousted by a Congress permeated with sturdy interests, mainly linked to private universities that opposed the MoE's Higher Education Reform. The same Congress ousted Saavedra's successor, Marilu Martens, who was following on his reform proposals, this time adding support towards the inclusion of a gender perspective in the National Curriculum, which gave rise to a highly conservative and highly organized opposition, led mainly by neo-Pentecostal evangelical groups.

The radical discontinuity in policy making, which expresses itself not only in the constant changes in policy teams (23 Ministers in 28 years) but also in the frequent renewal of policy orientations, has translated into a kind of stasis in the educational policy agenda.

In the almost thirty years since the first evidence came out showing the degree of the crisis of Peruvian education, improvements have been slow. Peru, it is true, has taken remarkable strides in improving the learning achievements of those who were most lagging behind, and it has done so in a context in which access to education grew (enrolment in primary schooling is now universal, and at the secondary level reaches 86% of the school-age population). The country has also made significant improvements in reducing drop-out and repetition rates (which, respectively, moved from 18.68% to 10.4% and from 30% to 3% in between the early 1990s and 2017).[2] According to PISA 2015 results, Peru is the

Latin American country which has most improved its educational outcomes in comparison to the 2012 test (Rivas, 2015). The Census Student Assessment (ECE by its acronym in Spanish) registered similar improvements.[3] While in 2012, 49% of students were in the lowest level of achievement, by 2018, only 28.6% of students are that level. Between those same years, the proportion of students who reached the highest 'satisfactory' level in the tests almost tripled, going from 12.8% to 34.1%.[4]

These improvements notwithstanding, after thirty years of partial and discontinuous reform attempts, Peruvian teachers are still some of the worst paid in the region (Díaz & Ñopo, 2016); the educational infrastructure gap is massive (Glave, 2015), and inequality remains a critical issue. Almost one out of every two young people among the country's poorest drop-out of school or does complete their schooling in time; repetition rates in public schools are eight times higher than those of private schools (Guadalupe, León, Rodríguez, & Vargas, 2017, pp. 186–198). Moreover, although improvements are visible in the primary education level little has changed at the secondary level, where learning results remain alarmingly low.[5]

Moreover, in the past thirty years, socioeconomic school segregation has deepened. Recent research shows that Peru's education system has become the most socio-economically segregated in the region (Rivas, 2015) and that the school system is now much more unequal than the country's society as a whole (Benavides, León, & Etesse, 2014). Research suggests that such a move may be a consequence of the naturalization of choice in a context in which the MoE promoted the growth of private schooling, enabling many families to opt out of public services and to move to a highly unregulated education market, where quality and results stratified along price lines (Balarin & Escudero, 2018).

These last two decades of Peruvian educational policies are reviewed in a recent book on *The State of Education in Peru* (Guadalupe et al., 2017), where the authors find an impressive degree of continuity in the problems that make up the education policy agenda. The authors suggest that, while policy ideas have evolved, the issues of today's reforms are to a large extent the same ones that were raised at the beginning of the 90s in the General Diagnosis of Peruvian Education.

3 Second-Order Reforms to Change the Core of Educational Practice

The distinction between first- and second-order changes is valuable to analyze education reforms. Cuban (1990, p. 73) describes first-order changes as those that: "try to make what exists more efficient and more effective, without disturbing organizational features, without substantially altering the ways in which adults and children perform their roles."

In comparison, second-order changes seek to alter the fundamental arrangements of schools and school systems:

> they reflect major dissatisfactions with present arrangements... [and] introduce new goals, structures, and roles that transform familiar ways of doing things into new ways of solving problems ... reforms [that] seek to alter existing authority, roles and uses of time and space. (p. 73)

Some of the literature on school reform casts first-order reforms in a somewhat more negative light, as cosmetic or superficial changes, while second-order changes are portrayed as those that bring meaningful reform to schools, altering philosophical understandings about the nature of teaching and learning (Goodman, 1995). According to Fouts (2003):

> One of the reasons schools remain unchanged is that the reforms or changes [may] have been superficial in nature and/or arbitrary in their adoption. Teachers and schools often [go] through the motions of adopting the new practices, but the changes [are] neither deep nor long-lasting. In other words, the outward manifestations of the changes [are] present, but the ideas or philosophy behind the changes [are] either not understood, misunderstood, or rejected. Consequently, any substantive change in the classroom experience or school culture failed to take root (...) The illusion of change is created through a variety of activities, but the qualitative experience for students in the classroom remains unchanged when the ideas driving daily practice remain unchanged. (p. 20)

The continuity of effectiveness and efficiency problems in Peruvian education (i.e., infrastructure and teaching quality) shown above suggests that first-order reforms have moved at a plodding pace. Second-order changes, moreover, have been even more difficult to achieve. Since the 1990s, Peru has made various attempts at introducing second-order reforms in the education system. These have included a broad change in pedagogy, from traditional instructional practices that were focused on memory and rote learning and in which students were only passively involved (and therefore often uninterested) in their own learning process, to new more active and participative instructional practices (Hunt, 2001). Also, a curricular reform that moved from a very prescriptive content-based curriculum to a more open outcomes-based curriculum that focused on the development of broad competencies (rather than on the acquisition of specific knowledge) (Ferrer, Valverde, & Esquivel Alfaro, 1999). Plus, a decentralizing reform of the education system's governance (Ministerio de Educación del Perú, 1992, 2012). Moreover, finally, a change of the teaching profession that has sought to make it more meritocratic. While all these reforms exist on paper (i.e., in-laws and documents), bringing about changes in both the system's governance and in school practices remains an elusive goal.

A recent study conducted in urban public schools in Peru (González, Eguren, & Belaúnde, 2017) suggests that some of the most fundamental problems in school practices that were found in the early 1990s are still prevalent today. In 1993, the General Diagnosis of Peruvian Education showed there were severe problems in classroom practices (Ministerio de Educación del Perú, 1992). The latter, it was revealed, followed a very traditional top-down model, centered the transmission and memorization of specific content, without students getting opportunities for problem-solving, reflection or critical thinking; and students received little or no formative feedback through school assessments. By 2017, Gonzales et al. show that while some positive changes have occurred regarding teacher-pupil interactions (specifically a reduction in physical and verbal violence from teachers towards students), teachers' instructional practices are still insufficient. Classes are still mostly organized around curricular content dealing in a very superficial manner, mainly using question-answer strategies that point towards a pre-specified and precise answer, rather than to generate ideas and thinking, and without providing students adequate feedback, nor opportunities to analyze, create or criticize ideas (p. 33). Some other studies have also shown the insufficient opportunities for learning that Peruvian students get in schools (Cueto, León, Ramírez, & Azañedo, 2006; Cueto, León, Ramírez, & Guerrero, 2016).

One explanation for the slow pace of change in school practices may point to the shallow starting point from which reforms began. As discussed by Hunt, one of the main difficulties that the MoE's administration faced in the 1990s when the first attempts at instructional change started, was that:

> many teachers ... knew virtually nothing about teaching. It was not that they were good but old-fashioned teachers; the problem was that most of them were unfamiliar with traditional teaching methods. They did not know how to arrange a classroom, how to plan a lesson or sequence of lessons, how to plan a day or a week. They knew next to nothing about evaluation and did not know how to diagnose students' needs and provide instruction to small groups for reinforcement of needed skills. (Hunt, 2001, p. 9)

Another explanation, however, would point to the lack of a consolidated and communicable policy discourse as to what processes are linked to educational quality and what desirable school and classroom practice should look like; as well as a lack of financial and political support for the implementation of policies which seek to bring about change in the core of educational processes. By this, we mean, following Elmore (1996), changes in the way in which:

> [...] teachers understand the nature of knowledge and the student's role in learning, and how these ideas about knowledge and learning are manifested in teaching and classwork. The "core" also includes structural arrangements of schools, such as the physical layout of classrooms, student grouping practices, teachers' responsibilities for groups of students, and relations among teachers in their work with students, as well as processes for assessing student learning and communicating it to students, teachers, parents, administrators and other interested parties. (p. 2)

The pedagogical core is, in other words, what is fundamental to any educational process. The literature suggests that in order to change the core, reforms need to consider the whole school as the unit of change and should include all the actors that compose the school community, instead of targeting specific processes or actors within schools (Smith, 2015). Referring to reform processes in the United States, Elmore criticizes that institutional changes have not touched the pedagogical core but have modified it only tangentially. As an example, he explains the constant changes in the organization of the school schedule, accompanied by changes in the distribution of curricular content and in the extension or reduction of pedagogical time. Although these modifications have an impact on the way in which learning develops or in the time that teachers have to generate content, they do not explicitly connect to fundamental changes in the way in which knowledge is acquired and is understood, nor on teachers' and students' roles in this process (Elmore, 1996, p. 3).

In Peru, both first- and second-order reforms have been prone to essential discontinuities and U-turns between ministerial administrations. This has slowed down the pace of implementation, often impacting on the definition and communication of policy goals and generating confusion among teachers and school administrators. No reforms have suffered more than those that have sought to alter the core of educational practice in schools.

While changes in the educational core may be hard to bring about, this does not mean that schools do not experience constant change involving pedagogical elements. In fact, schools are always changing: they modify evaluation methods, they change teachers' tools, they adopt new curricula or create new mechanisms of educational management (Elmore, 1996, p. 5). However, very often, such changes do not reflect more fundamental shifts in the way in which learning occurs or in the way schools produce knowledge.

The literature on school change suggests that in order for reforms of the pedagogical core to work and bring about long-lasting effects, change needs to be systemic (involving all administrative levels) and needs to treat the whole school as the unit of amendment (rather than focusing on changing individuals, such as headteachers or teachers). Transformations in the educational core need to involve government officials at the highest administrative levels, as well as *meso* and local level executive officials and other actors in non-governmental organizations that seek to influence educational practice. As analyzed in the literature on policy implementation, educational policies and programs will not be successful if the actors at local and school levels, including parents, fail to commit to change, and if the reforms do not allow for some degree of contextualization and some margin of decision making for local actors to adapt proposals to their local context (Hill & Hupe, 2014).

Comprehensive second-order reforms take time; one should not underestimate the effects that they can have on schools and the educational community. Such reforms, therefore, need to have an adjustment period, which officials not always take into consideration in the rush of policy implementation and the political pressure for quick results in learning achievement.

Second-order reforms also need to devise adequate scaling up strategies. Without them, they cannot achieve sustainability and long-term impact (Fullan & Miles, 1992; Hopkins, Harris, Stoll, & Mackay, 2010). As Hopkins et al. suggest: "system transformation depends on excellent practice being developed, shared, demonstrated and adopted across and between schools" (Hopkins et al., 2010, p. 16). Once again, this requires time and the commitment of considerable financial resources.

4 Tinkering with the Core of Educational Practice in Peruvian Public Schools

Since the early 1990s, there have been two partial attempts at generating changes in the core of educational practice, but only one qualifies as a reform.

As mentioned, the General Diagnosis of Peruvian Education conducted in 1993 suggested significant problems in the quality of school and classroom practices. One of the main components of the World Bank and International Development Bank funded Primary Education Quality Improvement Programme

(MECEP)—which articulated the reform efforts—was the improvement of "educational quality." This component focused on the revision of curricula, the development, and provision of school texts and materials and in-service teacher training. All of these policy initiatives joined around the idea of introducing a significant change in the core of educational practice. Their aim was to move the system from a traditional approach to teaching and learning which focused on memorization and facts, and in which teachers were at the center of classroom practice to a more active approach to teaching and learning, in which students could actively participate in the learning process, and which would enable them to develop capacities for critical thinking and problem resolution (Hunt, 2001). Improving quality, therefore, meant changing the educational core.

However, changing the core was a hard task to sell. Hunt discusses how government funds that were meant to complement financial support from foreign sources never materialized, and administrative support for the quality component of MECEP—the part aimed at the core—waned over time as the government emphasized more politically capitalizable goals such as infrastructure (which gathered 60% of all the Program budget). Adding to this, the teacher training program (PLANCAD), which was the centerpiece of change, faced the challenge of promoting the variations mentioned above among a teacher workforce that was barely prepared to perform the most basic tasks expected of the profession; and it had to do so with fewer resources than expected.

The training program was a feat. It reached almost ninety thousand teachers from first to sixth grades. It did so, however, in extensive training sessions that were outsourced to local providers of varying quality. Teachers often changed schools, and many had to work with principals and families who were unacquainted with (and unsupportive of) proposed changes. In time, innovations promoted by the training program were hard to sustain (Hunt, 2001).

When president Fujimori renounced (by fax from Japan), having 'won' an unconstitutional third term in office through rigged elections and after visual evidence of deep corruption at the center of his government was leaked to the press, education reform was, once again, at the center of political discourse. The interim president, Valentín Paniagua, emphasized new reforms to democratize institutional governance through decentralization and participatory mechanisms, to inhibit the cooptation of educational investment for political purposes. A nation-wide consultation set the basis for the development of a new General Law of Education, as well as for the creation of the National Council for Education. That Council was charged with the development of the National Education Project that set the primary goals and guided policies with a long-term vision.

During the first decade of the millennium, policy discourses were surprisingly silent about the importance of reforming the core of educational practice. During this time, the notion of educational quality became increasingly focused on achievement results. In the 1990s, another one of MECEP's components focused on developing a system for measuring student achievement. That was to become one of the most sustained policies over the following decades. Though Fujimori's government was averse to publishing national assessment results which showed the dire state of student achievement, later governments made yearly national standardized tests in the second grade of primary school a central feature of policy decision-making. Until 2015, annual test results showed little progress.

It was not until the period 2011–2016, during the government of Ollanta Humala, that an emphasis on bringing about changes to the core of educational practice would again acquire a central space in education reform discourses. Although with different approaches to change, both of the ministers in this term Patricia Salas (2011–2013) and Jaime Saavedra (2013–2016) in the MoE, proposed a reform agenda that brought changes in the pedagogical core to the center of education reform plans.

Salas, a sociologist, took office as Minister of Education in 2011 with a strong focus on education reform. In the 2012 MoE's institutional memory, she stated that:

> ... it is imperative to shift the axis of national educational debates and concerns towards learning, instead of continuing to focus solely on educational infrastructure or teacher training problems, as has been customary in the country. Moving forward in this process requires important changes in the education system, a great transformation .... (Ministerio de Educación del Perú, 2012, p. 11)

As suggested in the quote, Salas placed a strong emphasis on a second-order reform. This led her to develop a series of policies focused on changing systemic problems such as the precarity of the teaching profession and of teachers' working conditions, the improvement of the ministerial administration in central, local and regional levels, an accent on closing the rural-urban quality gap in education and a curricular and pedagogical reform.

The significant reform of this period took place in 2012, when the MoE introduced a Law Reforming the Teaching Career (Ley de Reforma Magisterial) which made advancements in the teaching profession meritocratic and based on compulsory evaluations of teachers' performance; the Law also introduced an increase in teachers' salaries and the possibility of promotion and career advancement through public tenders. To accompany and promote desired changes in teaching practices, the MoE designed and began the implementation of a series of pedagogical support programs for teachers. They included training and one-to-one tutoring (known as "acompañamiento pedagógico") and developed a Framework for Teaching Practice (Marco del Buen Desempeño Docente) which defined the professional characteristics, knowledge and pedagogical skills expected from teachers throughout the stages of their career. This document would guide the MoE's teacher's training, evaluation and recognition policies (Ministerio de Educación del Perú, 2012).

The passing of the new teachers' Law led to a protracted strike that cost Salas the post. In Congress, the opposition questioned her alleged incapacity for managing the crisis that the strike had brought about. In the end, however, the new Law remained. In 2013, Salas had attempted to reform the National Curriculum, but this task was left unfinished. She left the office that same year.

Continuing this effort, the economist Jaime Saavedra entered office with a robust reformist commitment and a promise to yield more rapid improvements in educational results measured through standardized tests. Saavedra prioritized the pedagogical programs in his reform agenda, which also included increases in school infrastructure, school management, and the teaching profession. The objective was to seek a systemic reform, which would later include changes in higher education and a more evidence-based and data-driven approach to policymaking. In matters of curricular and teachers' policy, Saavedra was more aggressive than his predecessor, and implemented the curricular reform that had been left unfinished (which then backfired on his successor) and managed to obtain the National Teachers' Union support for the new Law.

The MoE's prioritized programs for the period (or interventions) included so-called Pedagogical Support Programs for all levels and modalities of basic education.[6] Even though they were not publicized as reform by Saavedra nor by the media, such options sought to bring about changes in the pedagogical core of educational practice by promoting a series of integrated processes that had schools as their primary unit of change. Such a focus on school-level changes meant a shift in the MoE's approach to policy-making, from an emphasis on separate interventions or "magic-bullets" (Smith, 2015) to a commitment for more complex interventions that sought to bring about changes in all of the inside dimensions of school practice.

The most comprehensive of the pedagogical programs was Soporte Pedagógico Urbano (SPU), directed to urban primary schools. The program included four integrated lines of action: (1) The strengthening of school management teams and teaching practices. (2) A school reinforcement program for children lagging behind. (3) The timely provision of materials and educational resources. (4) School management aimed at strengthening institutional administration capacities for pedagogical leadership and for working with families and other relevant actors in the schools' close community.

Even though the program did not propose a significant change in school pedagogy, it followed the previous reform's focus on promoting more active and engaging teaching practices and also sought to improve teachers' capacities for planning their lessons and assessing their students' progress. The plan provided teachers not only with training workshops (which took place twice in the school year), but also with one to one in-classroom pedagogical tutoring, which focused on providing teachers with basic teaching strategies and tools, and to promote self-critical analysis and reflection on instruction practices.

While there was scope for improvement, SPU's proposals and its focus on promoting school-level changes and including one-to-one tutoring for teachers were very much in line with what the literature suggests are suitable strategies for changing teaching practices and affecting the educational core. In 2015, two separate evaluations (Balarin, Rodriguez, & Escudero, 2016; Chinen & Bonilla, 2017) highlighted the soundness of the program's design and implementation strategy and suggested that just over a year after the start of its implementation, it was showing some positive, although reasonably still very incipient impacts in terms of student achievement in national standardized tests.

The program, however, was costly. Its implementation, as it scaled-up the whole system, meant mobilizing an entire series of new actors, like teaching tutors, support teachers for after school reinforcement lessons, local and regional coordinators; as well as investments in training workshops and expenses involved in school visits. Negotiations between the program leaders and the MoEs Strategic Planning Office, in charge of budgeting, were tense. The latter demanded short-term results, visible in improvements in the yearly national assessments. Little by little, program features deemed too expensive were cut—the number and duration of teacher training workshops, the number of school visits by teacher tutors.

In 2016 a significant government crisis generated by a Congress that opposed the Higher Education Reform promoted by Saavedra led to the ousting of the Minister. His successor was also dismissed by the same Congress, plagued by private and conservative interests which were also against the introduction of a gender perspective in the school curriculum. The new minister, Idel Vexler, re-introduced a style of policymaking that had appeared extinct: idiosyncratic, not evidence-based, not prone to public accountability, nor for justifying policy changes. The Minister fired most high and mid-level officials, including many of those in charge of the pedagogical reforms.

Throughout this time SPU and other pedagogical reform programs suffered so many changes that little of their original design remained. Early in 2017, a new government crisis led President Pedro Pablo Kuczynski to resign. His vice-president, Martin Vizcarra, took over. A new ministerial administration occupied office, and some of Saavedra's collaborators re-entered the MoE. There is as yet no clear public discourse as to the directions and goals that will guide education policies. The new minister, a young technocrat, seems focused on administering what already exists. Informal talk is of the dismissal of pedagogical programs because of their cost and little impact on improving quality, understood as short-term improvements in national assessment results in language and math.

5 The Difficulty of Gathering Political Support for Changes in the Core of Educational Practice

Bringing about second-order changes in education systems is always a difficult task. It requires consistent efforts, as well as political and financial commitments over time. Changing the core of educational practice is one of the most difficult challenges that education reformers face, as it implies changing teachers' and other educational actors' understanding of educational processes, of the nature of knowledge and how it is acquired, and of their own role in developing their students' capacities for acquiring and producing knowledge.

The story of the two most recent attempts at bringing about changes in the educational core of Peruvian public schools, and their dismissal, leaves us some lessons for second-order reform.

The first one may be about the difficulty to develop a convincing narrative about the need for change in educational practice and how such changes connect with improvements in quality. Education policymakers rarely have the last word on funding. On the contrary, they need to convince other politicians, with control over finance, about the soundness of their narrative for change. Moreover, they need to develop sound implementation plans with goals that are clearly defined and achievable in the short, medium and long-term.

When comparing the two attempts at reforming the heart of education practices in Peru, we find that the first one had a much clearer narrative about the changes in school and classroom processes that are needed to produce a good quality education. It promoted a focus on learning rather than teaching, more active and participatory classroom processes, less teacher control over the learning process, less emphasis on knowledge transmission and the rote learning of facts and prominence on the students' own thinking and learning to think and acquire knowledge. That reform attempt, however, did not have a clear and sound implementation and scale-up strategy. The changes to be brought about were expressions of desire, and they were very far from the realities of classrooms where teachers barely knew how to perform the most basic tasks of the profession. The different elements that composed the quality component of the 1990s' reform program were not adequately articulated; training was insufficient and the fact that it targeted teachers outside of schools meant that changes were not sustainable over time.

The 90s decade ended in political turmoil which dismissed the reforms proposed during the Fujimori government. The characteristic of the following decade was of a very erratic approach to policymaking that was marked by radical discontinuities in directions and very idiosyncratic styles of leadership in the MoE (Balarin, 2006). The focus on the need for change in the educational core had no part in policy discourses.

During those years, however, a series of changes were remaking the policy arena. As the Ministry of Finance established a results-based budgeting system, different sectors slowly pushed towards a more evidence-based and results-oriented style of policymaking. In parallel and association to that, a national assessment culture became established, and educational quality became synonymous with improvements in math and language as measured by yearly national standardized tests. The MoE turned its gaze towards the search for "magic bullets" that could bring about quick changes in those results, at the lowest possible cost. Education policy-making was becoming more technocratic, and this meant a kind of epistemological change in policymakers understanding of what policy goals are worthy to pursue. As Cuban (1990) suggests, "The judgment of whether a change is an improvement rests in the mind of the beholder" (p. 83).

While the 2011–2016 administration placed a strong emphasis on pedagogical reforms that sought to affect the core of educational practice, commitment to such reforms has waned. The cost of implementation, as well as the slow pace of changes and results brought about by reforms, was partly to justify so. The political turmoil and ministerial changes of the 2016–2018 period also had a substantial part to play. Endurance, thus, seems to be a crucial characteristic of Peru's education.

However, adding to this was, once again, the inability to construct a strong, publicly justifiable narrative about the need for change in the core of educational practice as a means to improve the quality of education. As the definition of educational quality is very narrow—it only considers tightly prescribed outcomes in standardized tests—the narrative about how to make school and classroom practices more relevant to promote the kind of capacities for deep, reflective and critical learning that students need seems to have no place in current policy discourse. Such capabilities for learning and developing knowledge are crucial if the education system is to fulfill the goals that both the economy and the country's democracy require.

Notes

1 By 1991, teachers' salary was around 500 Nuevos soles in the local currency, which meant only 17% of what it was in 1945 (Díaz & Saavedra, 2000).
2 Sources INEI—Censos Nacionales: IX de Población y IV de Vivienda 1993 and Unidad de Estadística Educativa del Ministerio de Educación del Perú (ESCALE).
3 The Census Student Assessment (ECE) is a national evaluation conducted annually by the MoE. It seeks to obtain information on the performance in Math and Reading of second-grade and fourth-grade students in primary school and second-grade students in secondary schools.
4 These changes can be partly attributed to the country's economic growth, and to the reduction of extreme poverty, which came hand in hand with an increase in the national budget for education (Rivas, 2015).
5 In 2016, the achievement of 32.3% of students attending second grade of secondary schooling was below the lowest 'starting' level of test results. Only 11,5% and 14.5% of students achieved a satisfactory level of achievement in mathematics and reading comprehension respectively (Evaluación Censal de Estudiantes 2016).
6 The MoE had 5 flagships pedagogical programs: the Pedagogical Support Programme for Urban Primary Schools (SPU), the Pedagogical Support Programme for Intercultural-bilingual Schools (SPI), the Extended School Day Programme for Urban Secondary Schools (JEC), the Pedagogical Support Programme for Rural Secondary Schools and the Pedagogical Tutoring Programme for Single-teacher and Multigrade Rural Schools (Ministerio de Educación del Perú, 2017).

References

Anderson, S., & Kumari, R. (2009). Continuous Improvement in Schools: Understanding the practice. *International Journal of Educational Development, 29*(3), 281–292.

Arregui, P. (1994). Dinámica de la transformación del sistema educativo en el Perú. *Notas para el debate, 12*, 53–95.

Balarin, M. (2006). *Radical discontinuity: A study of the role of education in the Peruvian state and of the institutions and cultures of policy making in education* (PhD in Education Policy, Education). University of Bath, Bath.

Balarin, M. (2015). *The default privatization of Peruvian education and the rise of low-fee private schools: Better or worse opportunities for the poor?* (ESP Working Paper Series, 65).

Balarin, M., & Escudero, A. (2018). The ungoverned education market and the deepening of socioeconomic school segregation in Peru. In X. Bonal & C. Bellei (Eds.), *Understanding school segregation: Patterns, causes and consequences of spatial inequalities in education*. London: Bloomsbury Academic.

Balarin, M., Kitmang, J., Ñopo, H., & Rodríguez, M. F. (2018). *Mercado privado, consecuencias públicas: Los servicios educativos de provisión privada en el Perú* (Documentos de Investigación, 89). Lima: GRADE.

Balarin, M., Rodriguez, M., & Escudero, A. (2016). *Evaluación del diseño e implementación de la intervención de Soporte Pedagógico del Ministerio de Educación del Perú*. Lima: Proyecto FORGE/GRADE.

Banerjee, A. V., Banerjee, A., & Duflo, E. (2011). *Poor economics: A radical rethinking of the way to fight global poverty*. New York, NY: Public Affairs.

Benavides, M., León, J., & Etesse, M. (2014). *Desigualdades educativas y segregación en el sistema educativo peruano: Una mirada comparativa de las pruebas PISA 2000 y 2009* (Avances de Investigación, 15). Lima: GRADE.

Chinen, M., & Bonilla, J. (2017). *Evaluación de impacto del Programa de Soporte Pedagógico del Ministerio de Educación*. Lima: GRADE.

Cuban, L. (1990). A fundamental puzzle of school reform. In A. Lieberman (Ed.), *Schools as collaborative cultures: Creating the future now* (pp. 71–77). New York, NY: The Falmer Press.

Cuenca, R. (2013). La escuela pública en Lima Metropolitana. ¿Una institución en extinción? *Revista Peruana de Investigación Educativa, 5*, 73–98.

Cueto, S., León, J., Ramírez, C., & Azañedo, S. (2006). Oportunidades de aprendizaje y rendimiento en comunicación integral de estudiantes en tercer y cuarto grado de primaria en Lima y Ayacucho. In M. Benavides (Ed.), *Los desafíos de la escolaridad en el Perú: Estudios sobre los procesos pedagógicos, los saberes previos y el rol de las familias*. Lima: GRADE.

Cueto, S., León, J., Ramírez, C., & Guerrero, G. (2016). Oportunidades de aprendizaje y rendimiento escolar en matemática y lenguaje: Resumen de tres estudios en Perú. REICE. *Revista Iberoamericana sobre Calidad, Eficacia y Cambio en Educación, 6*(1).

Díaz, H., & Saavedra, J. (2000). *La carrera de maestro: Factores institucionales, incentivos económicos y desempeño*. Banco Interamericano de Desarrollo.

Díaz, J. J., & Ñopo, H. (2016). La carrera docente en el Perú. In GRADE (Ed.), *Investigación para el desarrollo en el Perú: Once balances*. Lima.

Elmore, R. (1996). Getting to scale with good educational practice. *Harvard Educational Review, 66*(1), 1–27.

Ferrer, G., Valverde, G. A., & Esquivel Alfaro, J. M. (1999). *Aspectos del currículum prescrito en América Latina: Revisión de tendencias contemporáneas en curriculum, indicadores de logro, estándares y otros instrumentos*. Grupo de Trabajo sobre Estándares y Evaluación de GRADE y PREAL.

Fouts, J. T. (2003). *A decade of reform: A summary of research findings on classroom, school, and district effectiveness in Washington State*. Research Report.

Fullan, M., & Miles, G. (1992). Getting reform right: What works and what doesn't. *Phi Delta Kappan, 73*, 745–752.

Glave, M. (2015). *Análisis de las modalidades de inversión con participación privada de la política de infraestructura educativa*. In FORGE. Lima: GRADE.

González, N., Eguren, M., & Belaunde, C. D. (2017). *Desde el aula: Una aproximación a las prácticas pedagógicas del maestro peruano*. Lima: Instituto de Estudios Peruanos.

Goodman, J. (1995). Change without difference: School restructuring in historical perspective. *Harvard Educational Review, 65*(1), 1–5.

Guadalupe, C., León, J., Rodríguez, J., & Vargas, S. (2017). *Estado de la educación en el Perú: Análisis y perspetivas de la educación básica*. Lima: GRADE.

Heller, N. (2018, July 9 & 16). Take the money and run. *The New Yorker*.

Hill, M., & Hupe, P. (2014). *Implementing public policy: An introduction to the study of operational governance*. Los Angeles, CA: Sage.

Hopkins, D., Harris, A., Stoll, L., & Mackay, T. (2010). *School and system improvement: State of the art review*. Paper presented at the International Congress of School Effectiveness and School Improvement.

Hunt, B. (2001). *Peruvian primary education: Improvement still needed*. Paper presented at the Latin American Studies Association meetings, Washington, DC.

Ministerio de Educación del Perú. (1992). *Diagnostico general de la educación peruana* (General Diagnosis of Peruvian Education). Lima: World Bank, UNDP, GTZ, UNESCO – OREALC.

Ministerio de Educación del Perú. (2012). *Memoria Institucional 2011–2012*. Lima.

Resolución de Secretaría General Nº 008 2017-MINEDU. (2017). Retrieved from https://cdn.www.gob.pe/uploads/document/file/110933/_008-2017-MINEDU_-_18-01-2017_05_39_38_-RSG_N__008-2017-MINEDU.pdf

Rivas, A. (2015). *América Latina después de PISA: Lecciones aprendidas de la educación en siete países* (2000–2015). Lima: Fundación Cippec.

Saavedra, J., & Suárez, P. (2002). *El financiamiento de la educación pública en el Perú: El rol de las familias* (Working paper No. 38). Lima: GRADE.

Sanz, P. (2014). *'We don't need the state': A study of the habitus formation process through school choice in Peru's rising middle class* (Unpublished PhD thesis). University of Bath, Bath.

Smith, M. (2015). Systemic problems systemic solutions. In M. J. Feuer (Ed.), *Past as prologue: The national academy of education at 50: Members reflect*. National Academy of Education.

World Bank. (2001). *Peruvian education at a crossroads: Challenges and opportunities for the 21st century* (Wu, K. B., Team Leader). Washington, DC: World Bank Publications.

CHAPTER 6

The Paradox of Power in Ecuador: Governance and Education Reform (2007–2015)

Jorge Baxter

Abstract

This chapter identifies and compares competing policy stories of principal actors involved in the Ecuadorian education reform under President Rafael Correa from 2007–2015. By revealing these competing policy stories, the chapter generates insights into the political and technical aspects of education reform in a context where decades of neoliberal policies eroded the state capacity. Since the elections in 2007, President Correa has focused much of his political effort and capital on reconstituting the state's authority and capacity to not only formulate but also implement public policies. The concentration of power combined with a capacity building agenda allowed the Correa government to advance an ambitious, comprehensive education reform with substantive results in equity and quality. At the same time, the concentration of power has undermined a more inclusive and participatory approach which are essential for deepening and sustaining the reform. This chapter underscores both the limits and importance of state control over education; the inevitable conflicts and complexities associated with education reforms that focus on quality.

1 Introduction

Over the past decade, several countries in Latin America (Argentina, Chile, Brazil, Ecuador, Peru, Mexico, Colombia, Costa Rica) have attempted education reforms to enhance quality (Grindle, 2004; Minteguiaga, 2014; Bruns & Schneider, 2016). Investment in education has risen in Latin America over the past 15 years from an average of 2.4% of GDP to around 4.5% of GDP (Board, 2006). Policymakers in most countries now have access to supposed global "best practices" and technical assistance from groups such as UNESCO, UNICEF, the World Bank, and other international nongovernmental groups involved in education reform. However, despite access to knowledge, technical

 | DOI: 10.1163/9789004413375_007

assistance, and rising levels of investment, very few countries in Latin America have seen a sustainable improvement in learning outcomes.

One possible reason for this poor educational performance in Latin America may have less to do with adopting the "right" package of policies and more to do with broader governance issues. Several decades of neoliberal reforms undermined the capacity of states to implement policy reforms effectively (Rhodes, 1997). Within the education sector in many countries in Latin America, power was increasingly fragmented and dispersed among non-state actors, including international donor agencies, teacher unions, civil society organizations, and even private companies. In the case of Ecuador, this fragmentation of power went to extremes before the arrival of Rafael Correa Delgado, President of Ecuador (2007–2017).

Starting with his election in 2007, President Correa focused much of his political effort and capital on reconstituting the state's authority and capacity to not only formulate but also implement public policies. This chapter focuses on the perceived impact of this state-building program on education reform and politics and in particular, explores the following questions:

- What are the competing narratives around governance and what do these reveal about the politics of the education reform under Rafael Correa?
- What are the implications for educational change and governance theories?

This chapter is based on research conducted on the education reforms in Ecuador during the Rafael Correa Delgado administration from 2007 to 2015. The study provides insights into the complex ways in which politics shape educational policy (Schattschneider, 1935; Weir, 2006) and the work of scholars to describe new emerging forms of educational governance that mix hierarchy, market and networks (Ball & Junemann, 2012; Torfing, 2012).

2 Methods

This study uses policy narrative analysis (Stone, 2002; Roe, 1994; Hajer, 1995; Fischer, 2003; Jones et al., 2014). There are various approaches to narrative policy analysis. Stone, Hajer, and Fisher exemplify the interpretive approach while Roe and Jones et al. (2014) utilize a more structural approach. Interpretive approaches argue that the combination of language, discourse and power represent a constitutive force that acts upon the social world. Therefore, an interpretive approach is not just concerned with the explanation of reality but rather brings different perspectives to bear on an issue, thus promoting policy argumentation and deliberative democracy (Fischer, 2003; Yanow, 2014).

In the book *Science of Stories*, Jones et al. (2014) present a structural approach to what they call the Narrative Policy Framework (NPF). They describe the NPF as applying objective methodological approaches (i.e., science) to subjective social reality (i.e., policy narratives). Structuralists argue that reality consists of scientific facts, which are more stable in nature, as well as contested socially constructed concepts which are unstable and susceptible to changing and competing interpretations. From this ontological position, understanding policy implies systematically tracing "variable meanings that individuals or groups give to processes associated with public policy" (Jones et al., 2014).

According to the Narrative Policy Framework approach by Jones et al. (2014), belief systems bound these meanings, ideologies, and norms and thus are not random. Furthermore, they identify structures within narratives (characters, plots, settings) that are generalizable. From an NPF approach, universal structural elements include the setting, characters, plot, and moral of the story. The setting is mostly the background that sets up and frames the policy problem within a context. That consists of less disputed facts that provide context to the issue. It portrays such characters as heroes with the solution to a policy problem, villains as who created and caused the problem, and victims. The plot usually includes a subsequent revelation of situations moving from the beginning, middle to end. The moral of the story contains the final policy solution or lessons learned from the perspective of a particular narrative (Jones et al., 2014).

The approach taken in this study is situated within the interpretive approach to policy narrative analysis but draws on some of the more structural elements proposed by Jones et al. (2014). Rather than producing generalizable concepts, the principal aim is to generate useful insights into the politics of education change. Some of these insights may be context specific and relate to the unique historical, cultural, and political contexts in Ecuador while others may aid in understanding the dynamics behind an educational change in other settings.

The research included semi-structured interviews with 24 individual participants from within government including ministers, vice-ministers, and sub-secretaries, teachers and school directors from different areas of Ecuador, teacher union, civil society and international organization leaders.[1]

3 Governance

Governance has multiple meanings and uses, but in this study, it refers to the changing boundaries between public, private and voluntary sectors, and in particular the changing role of the state since the 1980s (Bevir & Rhodes, 2010; Rhodes, 2012). In modern societies, it is common the making of collective choices around many different types of issues, including education.

Governance theory emphasizes three main ways in which societies organize to make collective decisions: hierarchy, markets, and networks.

The welfare state of the mid 20th century epitomizes a hierarchical mode of governance. This mode of authority is state-centric, bureaucratic, top-down and focused primarily on command and control. Official laws and rules, systems of control and enforcement, and the distribution of resources guarantees to achieve compliance. Hierarchical governance has been instrumental in advancing educational development regarding the expansion of educational access for all citizens (Carnoy, Gove, & Marshall, 2007).

Since the late 1970s, a group of reform efforts that aim to increase efficiency and effectiveness within the state challenges the role of the state as a centralized, hierarchical system of planning and policymaking. Neoliberal ideology underpins these reform efforts. The core belief of neoliberals is that markets (as opposed to states and bureaucracies) are the most effective and efficient mechanisms for resolving collective problems and allocating resources, both public and private. New Public Management (NPM), underpinned by neoliberal ideology, focuses on the introduction of quasi-markets and competition into public service delivery, primarily through outsourcing of program delivery to private and civil society actors. NPM also focuses on the performance and accountability of public institutions, introducing outcome-based and user satisfaction orientation (Tolofari, 2005; Spreen, 2001).

More broadly, the application of neoliberal policies in the 1980s and 1990s (deregulation, structural adjustment, fiscal austerity, decentralization, privatization) weakened states' control over social actors and increased fragmentation in political and social arenas. An unintended consequence of neoliberal policies was the growth of social movements and third sector organizations or groups outside of government. In part, this growth can be seen as a response from social actors to defend fundamental political, civic and social rights that were under attack by neoliberal policies. On the other hand, policy networks or groups of organizations, such as lobbyist and interest groups, multiplied and grew in strength under neoliberalism as a consequence of an increasingly fragmented state and vacuum of power. During this period, scholars emphasized a new form of social organization, called network governance (Ball & Junemann, 2012; Sorenson & Torfing, 2007). Network governance refers to more organic informal and spontaneous collaboration between a large number of interdependent social organizations. Achieving compliance in network governance is through trust and affiliation. Network governance is perceived increasingly as an alternative to other forms of management to address so-called "wicked problems" that emerge in a context of increasing complexity and uncertainty (Bourgon, 2011).

Some governance scholars have argued that the increasing diffusion of political power brought about by globalization and neoliberalism did not necessarily lead to a weakening of the state but instead to a shift in how states exert their influence and control (Peters & Pierre, 1998). These scholars argued that a new "meta-governance" emerged in states that shifted from direct forms of coercion and policy instruments to "govern through governance," steering social actors in more indirect forms through regulatory powers and policy networks to develop policy agendas, co-produce and implement policy, and increase legitimacy.

All three forms of governance (hierarchy, market, network) coexist and overlap. In some cases, new ways of management are perceived to emerge. Those are termed as heterarchies, or the combination of hierarchy and networks (Ball & Junemann, 2012). We also see the emergence of the "new regulatory state," which in its polycentric and decentered nature is distinct from the "old" centered and hierarchical state (Levi-Faur & Gilad, 2004). Certain discourses associated with one form of governance may predominate during periods with essential consequences on policy. From a historical perspective, state-centric hierarchy governance discourse prevailed from the 1950s to the 1970s with the rise of the welfare state and modernization discourses. Starting in the early 1980s, emerged a market governance discourse to dominate policy and planning for the next twenty years. In the early 2000s, network governance gained in currency among policy makers and scholars. Most recently, there has been a return of attention to the importance of state-building and institutional capacity with the perceived failure of democracy promotion and development efforts in certain regions of the world such as the Middle East, Africa and Haiti for example (Collier, 2008; Fukayama, 2004).

The following sections present narratives around educational governance from different policy actors in Ecuador from 2007 to 2013. The aim is to explore and disaggregate these differences across actors by comparing competing policy narratives around the reform from top to bottom, looking both inside and out. By revealing these competing policy narratives, the study aims to generate insights into the complex interplay between governance and politics in the context of education reforms.

4 Education Governance Narratives in Ecuador during 2007–2013

Since 2007, there has been a vigorous discursive battle around national development in Ecuador, mirrored within the education sector. This battle centers on the definition of the role of the state in development, on who is involved in setting the policy agenda, and on the meanings of concepts such as governance, public, participation, and education quality.

The dominant narrative argues that it is the state's sole responsibility to recuperate the public nature of the education system and to set the policy agenda. This role requires a strong state to retake control over key policy decisions from international donors and local corporatist actors. The story told by those interviewed begins by describing the governance crises in education in Ecuador during the neoliberal period, from roughly 1980–2006. The villains in this narrative are international donors, local oligarchic elites, corrupt political parties, the teacher union and various civil society organizations. The government frames these groups as obstacles to change. In this story, they exploited the educational system to pursue their private interests to the detriment of the public interest. The heroes, in this case, are the President and a group of reformist bureaucrats who actively intervened on behalf of all citizens to wrest power from these groups and transform the state to serve the public interest and advance a citizen and education revolution.

The central counter-narrative questions a state-centric definition of governance and "public." It argues for a broader conceptualization of governance where social actors, local communities, and the state co-define the educational policy agenda, goals and strategies. This narrative points to the contradictions in Correa's rhetoric that distort the terms "citizen revolution" and "*Buen Vivir*" to mask a more neoliberal and conservative educational and political project. This counter-narrative considers Correa's approach to educational governance as technocratic, centralized, hierarchical, insular and exclusionary.

4.1 *The Setting: The Long Neoliberal Night*

According to nearly all of those interviewed for this study, particularly Ministers and high-level officials in the Correa administration, the story begins with the period before Correa, from the 1980s through 2006 and during the so-called "long neoliberal night." Neoliberal policies including fiscal austerity and structural adjustment did not lead to a more efficient and better run state, more productive markets, or better social policy outcomes. On the contrary, neoliberal policies were perceived to contribute to political instability and social unrest, undermining the state's authority and capacity to manage reforms and ultimately leading to declines in social welfare outcomes.

Under the neoliberal regime, social sectors including education and health were the hardest hit. Despite the rhetoric on the need to enhance the quality of education, education spending as a percentage of government expenditure dropped by almost 50% between 1980 and 1990 (Luna Tamayo, 2014). That occurred regardless of the speechmaking on the need to enhance the quality of education. While the educational bureaucracy diminished in size, it remained hierarchical, and its capacities were severely limited. As one high-level Ministry official in the Correa administration explained:

> The Ministry was a pyramid. At the top was the Minister of Education and there was only one person below, which was the Sub Secretary of Administration and Finance. The minister's job was to go to cocktail events and say hello. The Sub Secretary's role was to pay salaries. The Ministry was so centralized that the Minister had to approve the vacations of all of the teachers in the country personally, through a document which had to be signed personally by the Minister. It was a disaster! (Ministry official, personal communication, January 23, 2013)

In addition to these structural issues, most ministry personnel lacked the qualifications and competencies required to manage reforms. The same ministry official highlighted this point:

> Similar to other places in Latin America, we did not have a meritocratic system to select qualified officials. In the case of the Ministry of Education, it was a system that paid salaries, and that is it. It was mostly just a bureaucracy. (Ministry official, personal communication, January 23, 2013)

Given the structure and composition of the bureaucracy, the Ministry focused mostly on low-level administrative functions. Political patronage exploited bureaucratic posts and other limited resources. An Interamerican Development Bank (IDB) governance evaluation around the region characterized Ecuador's bureaucracy as low in autonomy and small in capacity (Lora, 2007). Many of the primary inputs and services required to make an education system work (like salaries and materials) were lacking. According to one respondent within the Ministry leadership, teachers were sometimes not paid for months and this inevitably led to absenteeism and teacher strikes (Ministry official, personal communication, January 23, 2012).

In this scenario, effectively implementing education becomes nearly impossible. The lack of policy direction from the government created a vacuum of power increasing incentives for "advantage seeking groups" to organize and seek returns for political action, essentially creating what Cohen and Rogers (1995, p. 17) refer to as a "bargaining democracy."

4.2 *The Beneficiaries of Anarchy*

Several high-level policymakers and civil society organization leaders interviewed for this study noted the diminished institutional capacity of the

Ecuadorian government and its ministries benefited a whole host of actors outside of the state, starting with the international organizations themselves and moving down to local Non-Governmental Organizations (NGOs) and private organizations (civil society arrangement representative, personal communication, January 22, 2013). During the 1980s and 1990s, international organizations' influence over social policy grew, and, according to several Ecuadorian analysts, the educational agenda increasingly was de-linked from national and local issues and priorities (Luna Tamayo, 2014; Torres, 2006).

> Most of the agendas for the social policy were done in the United Nations offices, education in particular with UNICEF. UNESCO had less of a presence. (Civil society organization representative, personal communication, January 23, 2013)

Three big reforms funded by the World Bank and the IDB focused on decentralization and the creation of a network of schools. The premise was that these reforms would enhance the quality and the capacity of both the Ministry and teachers in schools. The programs not only failed to improve learning but contributed to increased conflicts that undermined the governance capacity of the Ministry (Whitman, 2009; Ministry official, personal communication, January 23, 2013).

The increasing influence of international organizations and donor agencies over the sector combined with growing intrusion of the Teacher's Union and NGOs in setting educational agenda and goals:

> A weak Ministry with no authority and capacity led to excessive intromissions from the Teacher's Union in administrative and bureaucratic decisions on the one hand and the other to the excessive presence of international organizations and NGOs in the definition of education policies. It is not that participation from social groups is bad, but when the Ministry does not have institutional strength and is not clear on institutional policies, then it's dangerous because each group has an opinion based on their particular interests and not necessarily the interests of the overall public. (Ex-Education Minister of Correa, personal communication, April 15, 2014)

Another Minister of Education under Correa echoed similar themes:

> There were many anarchical issues with the lack of governance in the system. Any person, any institution, even international organizations

> de facto made public policy. Without a strong ministry, anyone (NGOs, municipalities, mayors) made policy. That made the system chaotic, with a whole variety of actors supplying education with different criteria. Private education proliferated with indiscriminate growth and was privileged over public supply. (Minister, personal communication, March 2, 2013)

During this period, public education was semi-privatized and schools lacking resources charged fees for admissions, textbooks, materials, and uniforms. Inequality within the education system also grew through what appeared to be an unorganized supply of education with no common core curriculum that would allow children to gain the skills needed to be more proactive agents in their futures (Vice-Minister, personal communication, March 2, 2013).

Bermeo (2008) published a study around the time that Correa took office and assessed the situation of educational governance at the local state, municipal, and district levels. The study included input from local territorial officials and experts. The report highlights the lack of coordination and decision-making power at local levels:

> There is no articulation with the territory between schools, between levels of schooling, between local and national entities. No learning processes and exchange allow schools to learn collectively. There are no collective processes of teacher development or learning between students. To talk about the Educational system in Ecuador is an aspiration, because really what you have is profound fragmentation and atomization of educational establishments. (Bermeo, 2008, p. 11)

Many reforms in Latin America are primarily symbolic. Political leaders have little incentives to implement education reform, particularly those that deal with transforming the system. That is because of short time-horizons and also the fact that these types of reforms are complicated and usually generate conflict. As a result, every few years states adopt new legislation and long-term education plans, but nothing gets implemented.

The prevalence of symbolic policies may also have to do with weak institutions in Ecuador and other countries in Latin America. Theories on failed and fragile states argue that the lack of state penetration in social institutions leads to the inability of the state to deliver essential public goods, such as education (Migdal, 1988; Centeno, 2002). Over the past few decades in Ecuador, one can see the mutually reinforcing dynamic between symbolic policymaking and weak state capacity.

5 The Plot: Recuperating the "Public" in Education

In 2006, Correa assembled a coalition of the democratic left, the indigenous *Pachakutik* party, and socialist parties. Correa ran on an anti-neoliberal platform that prioritized reducing the burden of foreign debt, investing in social programs, political sovereignty, and regional integration with like-minded leftist governments. He vowed to launch a "citizen revolution," instituting profound economic and political reforms starting with a referendum to gain citizen approval to rewrite the constitution.

The cornerstone of Correa's political project represented an alternative model for economic and social development. The Constitution of 2008 and the National Development plan *Buen Vivir 2009–2013* articulated that alternative vision. It espouses a politics of redistribution with a strong emphasis on social inclusion, citizen participation, and diversity. It also calls for a return of the state's central planning in economic and social development.

Given the loose organization of this coalition, Correa was perceived by citizens as semi-independent from any one particular party and economic powers. When Correa took power, he faced a sizeable conservative opposition in Congress. Given Correa's combative campaign and discourse, it was almost sure that the majority in Congress held by conservatives would block any attempts at reform.

5.1 *State Autonomy*

In his first few days in office, Correa made several political moves that allowed his government, including the education minister, some autonomy, and space to govern. These actions including removing opposition groups in Congress, advancing a referendum to rewrite the constitution, creating public enterprises in strategic areas such as energy, mining and public services; reducing foreign debt; and implementing a series of legal reforms that gave his administration more control over the public agenda. The opposition labeled these steps as anti-democratic. From the government's perspective, these actions were necessary to rebalance the scales and regain power from entrenched groups that had captured the state and economy (Gallegos, 2010).

Within the education sector, Correa also worked to reconfigure power between the state and various actors, including international organizations and donors, the teachers' union, and civil society. An ex-minister of education described this as creating a broader "policy of the state":

> If I have a foundation and fix 20 schools in the neighborhood and develop a nice-looking program, then I am someone who is concerned with

> education. That isn't bad in and of itself, especially in poor societies. But when a policy of the state says, "No sir, this is a broader policy," or "No Mr. International Bank, I don't want your loans for education, I want you to invest in hydroelectric infrastructure, but I'll finance education myself," this implies a substantial shift in public policy. (Ex-Minister, personal communication April 14, 2014)

Relative state autonomy from international donor agencies, business elites, military and other social actors is a critical component of democratic governance (Bowen, 2015). This autonomy is relative because other groups and social actors that often have a vested interest in the status-quo and who attempt to block reforms that imply a redistribution of benefits always penetrate the state. However, at certain political junctures, able political leaders may regain enough political control to not only set a different policy course but to implement it.

5.2 *State Capacity*

As Correa entered into office in 2007, many of those representatives from civil society and social movements that once opposed the government found themselves in government. With them, they brought a previously socially validated educational agenda in the 10-year education plan.[2] This educational agenda was developed through a process of three years of social dialogue (prior to 2007) and was ratified by citizens during the presidential election on a special ballot.

However, after the first few years, it was evident to the Ministry that the 10-year plan had short-comings concerning its implementation and needed to be updated to align more with the new Constitution and National Development Plan. By 2009, due in part to growing critiques of the 10-year plan for progress quality, the Ministry began to turn its attention to establishing the legal basis for deepening certain aspects of the reform. This legal basis was a first required step in the state-building agenda:

> There was a complicated and very difficult process of recuperating the Ministry's authority and governance. It started with legislation and the creation of new education law. That was a real triumph! Several key elements were added to this law, like the concept of citizen participation, the concept of interculturality and the principle that education is not only a right but also as a public good. An absolute majority in the

> assembly approved the law despite their very diverse political views. That is interesting. (Minister of Education, personal communication, March 2, 2013)

The law helped to consolidate the authority, jurisdiction, and power of the State over the education sector while setting the legal parameters for reforms that address quality such as teacher recruitment and career advancement, evaluation of education, and issues related to traditional obstacles to reform such as teacher protests.

Correa and his education Minister Raul Vallejo (2007–2010) realized that they needed more than legislation and strong rhetoric to move the educational reform forward, especially when it came to advance the reform dealing with quality. His executive team focused on building the internal capacity of the Ministry to execute improvements by instituting various fundamental changes, including restructuring the Ministry, developing strategic planning capacity, and establishing recruitment criteria and performance standards.

The first step involved restructuring the actual Ministry of Education to reflect its new intention to formulate and execute policy:

> When Raul Vallejo entered, he created a Sub-secretary of Quality, then a Vice-Ministry of Education. Wow! It was a significant shift. Now we were thinking of producing and administering educational policy. (Ministry Official, personal communication, January 23, 2013)

As part of this restructuring, there was a concerted attempt to begin to develop internal capacity to generate and manage new projects:

> Recuperating governance does not only happen by passing a new law. We had to reorganize the system with a series of strategies that had an impact on a changing Ministry that just paid salaries to generate a set of projects that had a direct effect on citizen's lives in the educational sphere. (Ministry Official, personal communication, January 23, 2013)

There were internal institutional challenges and tensions in this process, particularly when it came to changing work culture and expectations within the Ministry.

> We had two groups within the Ministry. The old bureaucracy began to mix with the new administration. The old cadre was not used to the new pace of work. To be fair, many of them never had the essential resources

> to do their job, not even pencils and paper. All of a sudden, they had these things and more. Expectations changed. We were now asked to manage programs and resources and deliver results. That was a challenge for many of them. (Ministry Official, personal communication, December 22, 2012)

Correa, with a background as an economist, stressed efficiency and transparency in government. The Ministry designed and implemented a performance-based system, and the new laws established criteria and minimum requirements for the recruitment of different government officials, including teachers, school directors, supervisors and even crucial ministry officials.

In these first few years of reform, bottlenecks and implementation issues did crop up. Several high-level officials acknowledged shortcomings, but also reframed the question as a capacity gap and credited the reform for having contributed to growing expectations from society around education:

> Increasing demands and lack of prioritization are creating problems. For example, one of the primary goals of the 10-year plan is to increase investment in education to 6% of GDP from its initial level of 2%. However, it is evident that there is a lack of capacity to manage these funds. Many areas have budget surpluses at the end of the year. They haven't spent the money. (Civil Society Representative, personal communication, February 2, 2013)

Even local school officials recognized the challenges. They did, however, also expressed hope:

> In implementation there are issues. There are still lots of people who lack information. There are bottlenecks. But it is an ongoing process. With the new model to decentralize management, the flow of information should improve. At least now there is an aspiration to improve, to play a more significant role. (Rural School Director, personal communication, March 4, 2013)

State capacity to deliver public goods is an effective route to legitimacy which in turn strengthens governance. Correa understood this and attempted to restructure the state bureaucracy to focus on policy results. One key strategy concentrates on selecting capable officials for critical posts within the administration and on renewing the teaching force through an early retirement program and new recruitment and professional advancement criteria. Despite this vision to modernize the sector, Correa and his sector leaders faced obstacles in implementation not to mention increasing political resistance from teachers and social groups.

5.3 *Rhetorical Leadership*

Olson (2007) argues that rhetorical leadership and the strategic use of symbols are critical for promoting cooperation between groups. Strategic communication by the government can strengthen governance by bolstering citizen support for a policy agenda (George Washington University, February 19, 2009).

In Ecuador, public communication was a critical component of the education reform effort. Under Correa, the Ministry invested considerable resources and efforts in crafting public messaging to help build support for the policy reform agenda among general citizens. This communication, combined with Correa and his Ministers' constant use of the bully pulpit, bolstered the government despite fierce opposition from both the right and leftist interest groups and the media.

The President himself instituted several mechanisms to keep his political agenda present in the minds of citizens. Given the anti-statist stance of the mainstream private press, Correa channeled funds towards state-run television and radio and has worked to pass legislation that mandates that all channels, public and private, are obligated to provide the government with several hours a day to "inform" citizens on "progress made."

Besides, Correa instituted a "traveling cabinet." Every week, Correa and his ministers traveled to a different part of the country to meet with local citizens in round-table sessions to listen to their claims, respond, and to simply inform people of the government's agenda. The combination of these strategic communication actions aimed at shaping the narrative and bolstering support for the reforms.

5.4 *Executive Leadership*

Several of those interviewed attributed executive leadership as a critical factor for reform success. While Correa's rhetoric was fiery, it is evident that he backed it up in many cases and committed real political and financial resources towards advancing education reforms.

During stressful moments in the reform, Correa came out in public to defend the reform. The President directly organized and attended several counter-protests against those groups opposing the change. The President's reform fervor also inspired many high-level bureaucrats to believe in their political projects and to persist despite the low pay, long hours, constant political battles and opposition. Many of the high-ranking officers interviewed indeed believed this was a unique historical opportunity for Ecuador to make a significant educational change.

> We have shown that real change is possible if you have the political support. The President has been vital in this area. His strength and vision have been significant. Yesterday in his speech the President said that if he had to choose only one thing to do, he would focus on education; he would not do anything else. He has said publicly: 'If I am forced out of office because I bet on education reform then so be it.' (Minister, personal communication, March 2, 2013)

5.5 *Governance and the Limits of Participation*

Despite the initial rhetoric around a citizen revolution, Correa's top-level officials were wary of the unmediated participation of social actors given the previous decade of political turmoil. Several high-level officials in Correa's administration were keenly aware (as authorized decision-makers) of the potentially destabilizing effect that social movements could have on governance capacity. They were also sensitive that divisions in Ecuadorian society (political, economic, social, ethnic) contributed to social unrest. They had to strike a balance between recuperating the ability and authority to make decisions (for example, shifting resources from one group to another) and the need to legitimize policy decisions through participation. Here, one Minister of Education interviewed for this study explains this tension:

> I think there are limits to participation. In our societies, particularly after the destruction of the state in the neoliberal years, we conclude that society has to govern itself. That is not possible in certain moments. I consult. I compare consultations. I compare peoples' opinions. However, at a precise moment, I am responsible for making a decision. I, as a capable politician, make a decision. This decision can be criticized, but it represents the moment when you exercise what is called *rectoría* (authority and control) and good government in a positive sense. What a governor cannot do is wish for unanimity. That doesn't exist. Our decision will make some happy and will be criticized by others. Others will be indifferent. That is what I think is what is at stake. (Ex-Minister of Education, personal communication, April 15, 2013)

Some reframed critiques of lack of participation in the broader government reform agenda as the inevitable consequence of the shifts in power. Here,

Alberto Acosta, one of the original architects of Correa's initial political project explains:

> You criticize the government for lack of dialogue and consensus, but how can you have dialogue and consensus with sectors that have such different interests? In principle, I think you can have a conversation with all sectors if national interest is at stake. But to seek consensus with those who are against a process is impossible. In the context of profound and radical transformations, it is difficult to achieve consensus with those who stand to lose their privileges. Frankly, it's a waste of time. Then if the citizen revolution has a deficit, it is in citizenship. There needs to be more participation, and decisions should not be taken from a desk. (Saravia, 2009)

Furthermore, several interviewed warned of the dangers of having a naïve concept of civil society and how this might undermine reforms. Despite the democratic commitment, they were aware of the risks and pitfalls of participation:

> I assume that people who participate have good intentions and want to collaborate. But of course, this is naïve, because those who have done this for years know that the social organizing capacity of some groups is broad. They can organize to sabotage and boycott reforms. That is our social reality in the end. (Government Official, personal communication, February 23, 2015)

In a similar vein, an academic interviewed for this study highlighted the need to recognize that power and inequality penetrate all social relations and spaces. She also raised an important question, which circulated in many of the interviews with government officials, around who constitutes or claims to represent civil society:

> With all due respect, the participation of parents and the community and civil society has limits. It is as if the unrestricted involvement of civil society for some people is the broad umbrella that guarantees a public and democratic education system. But participation can't be unlimited. There are things that civil society can't ensure because civil society, just like the state, is penetrated by relations of inequality and power. Unless we think of civil society as a panacea for equality, what is the civil society? (Scholar, personal communication, March 6, 2013)

6 The Moral of the Story: Governance as "Laying Down the Train Tracks"

The moral of the story in this narrative is that successfully advancing educational reforms in contexts characterized by weak public institutions may require first and foremost recuperating the institutional authority and capacity of the state. Re-establishing the supremacy of the state over a sector may require taking power away from entrenched groups that have a hold over public institutions and addressing the distortions that participation can create for governance in contexts of inequality.

In the case of Ecuador under Correa, this implied a strategic set of top-down actions aimed at weakening the influence of international donors and agencies as well as local unions and social groups. The net result was the ability of the central government to formulate and pass universal policies. Ensuring essential compliance across the system in basic educational inputs and processes (infrastructure, salaries, core curriculum) was a fundamental stepping stone to higher-order and more complex reforms focused on quality. Correa likened the project of recuperating institutional governance as laying down the tracks so that the train can run. Here the Minister of Education captures Correa's framing:

> When a Minister of Education in France, Belgium or Japan begins his or her term, they position themselves on a system that is already working and in implementation. The difference in Ecuador is that when a Minister of Education comes in, they have to rebuild the system from zero. This minister has to put the tracks down to the train can run. (Minister paraphrasing President Rafael Correa, personal communication, March 6, 2013)

7 The Counter Narrative: Correa the "Techno-Populist"

Correa came into power through the support of a leftist coalition that included social movements, labor unions, leftist and socialist parties and intellectuals. Many of the individuals from these groups joined Correa's government, and most of these groups actively collaborated in drafting the new Constitution.

Correa's government articulated its overarching governance narrative in the new Constitution of Montecristo and the National Development Plan *Buen Vivir* 2009–2013. The plan begins with a description of the old paradigm of development and its faulty linear assumptions about progress, modernization, industrialization, and overemphasis on economic growth. This old development paradigm is to be replaced with a new humanist model of societal organization loosely based on the indigenous concept of *Sumak Kawsay*, or in Spanish translated as *Buen Vivir*.

The concept of *Buen Vivir* connotes the idea of a full life, beginning with the balance and harmony of men and women as and with themselves. A fundamental notion embedded in the re-signification of *Buen Vivir* is the satisfaction of necessities for the entire population. This notion opposed the neoliberal emphasis on economic growth and individuality and provided a conceptual argument to bring the state back to the center to recuperate public services and goods privatized under neo-liberalism.

The alternative and progressive language in the Constitution and even in the National Development Plan *Buen Vivir* broadly highlighted the possibility of a more humanist and alternative conception of education and development. However, by 2009, several groups became discouraged with what they perceived as increasing contradiction between Correa's "citizen revolution" and specific policies pursued by his administration.

7.1 *Resignifying Buen Vivir*

The concept of *Buen Vivir* was used as an overarching guiding metaphor of the Correa governance narrative to signal a shift in the development paradigm away from neoliberalism. However, critiques quickly emerged around Correa's co-option and re-signification of the indigenous term:

> Correa learning a few words in Quechua is merely a revalorization, a sort of joke, a kind of folklore, a trick. If they respected our cultural and linguistic diversity, they would have maintained the autonomy of the intercultural system of education as it was before. Their distortion of our symbols is a type of folklore that is used to convince citizens. We interpret it as the commodification of our symbols, of our intangible culture. (Indigenous Union Leader, personal communication, March 5, 2013)

Within the education sector, Correa's administration retook control over the intercultural education system under the rationale that quality in this sub-system had degenerated and adversely affected some communities over others. One of Correa's ministers interviewed in this study described the previous administration's policy of providing each community with funding to do whatever they pleased without accountability as "irresponsible." However, the reaction on the part of social movement leaders to Correa's education reform agenda was adverse:

> The intercultural organic law states that the authority (*rectoría*) for policy-making lies in the hands of the state, and so this leads to a monocultural

> policy, a policy of massification in which is not considered the diversity of the curriculum from the communities and different ethnicities. It not even maintains the richness of our culture and its diverse nationalities in the Ministry's policy of school uniforms, where we see a loss of cultural identity. (Indigenous Union Leader, personal communication, March 5, 2013)

Over time, the broader concentration of power and the state-centric approach of the Correa government undermined the potential power of the *Buen Vivir* metaphor to inspire collective action, more profound democratic transformations, and the emergence of a clear educational alternative.

> Overall, as the government pursues *Buen Vivir* politics, they can be characterized as utterly centralized, hierarchic and technocratic. They aim at maximum control, stability through social and public management-type planning and accountability while regarding every opposing force as a threat. (Waldmüller, 2014)

7.2 *Not a Zero-Sum Game*

Given the shift in power between the state and social actors during Correa's presidency, it is not surprising that new areas of conflict opened up around education reform. These conflicts became more visible about two years into Correa's first term in 2009, when the Ministry began to focus on executing various strategies related to quality. The most contentious points were around the implementation of a national evaluation of teachers and students and the creation of national standards.

Within education, critics saw a turn towards a more neoliberal education reform package that included teacher evaluations, merit pay, and educational standards. These neoliberal reforms combined well—they said—with increased centralization of education policymaking in the state under the rationale of strengthening institutional authority.

A report from the meeting of a large forum of civil society organizations in education introduces one of the emerging cleavages around the state's concept of governance:

> After decades of deterioration, there has been a rapid race to renew the strength of the government since 2007. However, one of the costs of this new process is the diminishing role of society and its gradual eclipsing. Due to this Administration's style and their emphasis on political expediency, effectiveness and results, only one actor (the central government) have dangerously remained on the stage. (Luna Tamayo, 2009, p. 16)

An interview with a former high-level ministry official from the Alfredo Palacio (2005–2007) Administration expressed a similar critique:

> Correa has a very centralist and statist spirit. He defines education as a sector that is not decentralizable. Under this understanding, education is the responsibility of the national government and not the local government, and everything done in the territories is part of that sectoral governance. The current process is one of deconcentrating. That is solely administrative, not content related to or centered on educational quality. They have created local districts to pay salaries, administer resources, and to comply with what the center says. (Ex-official from Palacio Administration, personal communication, February 23, 2013)

Many critics on the left recognized the historical importance and significance of rebuilding the state's authority as a necessary means to recuperate public schooling. However, they also expressed consternation that that process of the state consolidating its power reduced the spaces for democratic dialogue and debate around education. Even more concerning was Correa's framing of opposition groups as corrupt, self-serving, and a threat to the public interest:

> We do not share the idea that strengthening the state is a zero-sum game, that the power that the state has to recuperate they have to take from someone else. So, the strengthening of the state implies the weakening of civil society organizations, universities, social movements that were traditionally present in public deliberations. (Civil Society Representative, personal communication, February 26, 2013)

7.3 *The "Technopopulist"*

Many critics accuse Correa and the Ministry of Education of being technocratic. They make these claims despite the progressive rhetoric of a new model of development based on *Buen Vivir* and a new Constitution that prioritizes citizen participation.

In 2009, when the Ministry initiated the reform strategies that dealt with quality, including teacher evaluations and standards, there was increasing opposition from various social actors such as the Teacher's Union, indigenous movements, and educational activists. Many leveled the critiques at the style of government that had taken shape during Correa's presidency. They had hoped for an alternative and a new vision of society and saw Correa's reform strategies as more of the same. Here an ex-Minister of Education and prominent leftist critic in education summarizes her view:

> The term "educational revolution" has been used in various countries and processes over recent years as a substitute for educational reform, which is fatigued and discredited. Let us reserve the term educational revolution for a more substantive and radical change, which implies a shift in the educational paradigm. In the Ecuadorian case, the paradigm did not change. It is an educational reform with classic characteristics. It is centered on the formal educational system, vertical, authoritarian, technocratic, homogenous, not participatory, and generated from the outside. (Torres, 2014)

7.4 *The Moral of the Story: A Conservative Political Project*

The moral of the story from the counter-narrative perspective is that Correa has constructed a political discourse based on populist elements that masks a more conservative notion of governance focused on the centralization of decision-making in the state and mostly in the Executive Power. This populist discourse employs a unique blend of socialist, social movement and indigenous symbols and rhetoric. However, from the counter-narrative perspective, reforms have become less participatory over time and in substance reflect a narrower technocratic concept of education reform.

How do we explain these contradictions? From a meta-governance theory perspective, this disjuncture can be seen as the state attempting to reconfigure its power and maintain control over social actors within the context of globalization. Carlos De la Torre refers to Correa as a "techno-populist." De la Torre extends Weber's concept of charisma as a form of domination, arguing that Correa's discourse and style of governance is a combination of populist charisma and technocratic rationalism. De la Torre argues that these are not necessarily opposing systems of dominance. De la Torre defines populism as a "polarizing and Manichean discourse used to arrive in power and govern while technocracy is a discourse used by experts that appeal to science as a way to transform society to benefit the common good (De la Torre, 2013, p. 10)." Correa effectively combines both tactics to consolidate and legitimate the concentration of power.

The irony in this story is that most civil society and social movement leaders were in favor of strengthening the state as Correa took power. However, the aggressive concentration of power in the state under Correa was not what they envisioned. Over time the rift between Correa's government and social sectors widened, undermining the possibility for more profound transformations in education.

8 Synthesis and Reflections

This final section examines competing policy stories, applying various lenses (theoretical and historical) to tease out the broader metanarratives and implications for educational change and governance theories that emerge. The implicit argument in the framing of this study is that governance, participation and education reforms interact with one another in complex and sometimes unexpected ways. These complex interactions are rooted in historical, political power dynamics. Complexity is ripe terrain for explanatory policy narrative analysis. The scrutiny highlights some of the paradoxes and policy tradeoffs that emerge as discourses and practices in these three areas intersect. By juxtaposing narratives, a more nuanced and intricate picture of the political economy of education reform appears, allowing for several vital insights into policymaking focused on quality.

8.1 *The Setting: A Story of Decline*

The overall policy story began for most of those interviewed with a description of the decade or so before Correa took office. Interestingly, both the dominant and the counter setting as described by those interviewed for this study seemed to overlap. The typical background story was what Stone (2002) would call a story of decline. In general, there was a shared notion that neoliberalism had contributed to destabilizing the political and economic situation in Ecuador. Fiscal crises and austerity had "hollowed out" the state, severely limiting its ability to follow through on any policy. This weakness contributed to political anarchy, excessive intromissions from international organizations in setting the policy agenda, and increased conflict between groups.

The ultimate effect of the application of neoliberal policies on education in Ecuador was increased inequality and a decline in quality. Reiterating Bermeo (2008), it was illusory to talk about an education system in Ecuador. There was no evidence of a system per se, but somewhat isolated schools and actors doing whatever they could or wanted. A few of those interviewed (but not the majority) did not draw a causal link between neoliberal policies and this decline. Instead, they pointed to longer-term historical developments such as regionalization, weak institutions, fragmented politics, political patronage and clientelist traditions that led to gridlock.

When Correa took office, there seemed to be an overall widespread consensus across groups that the sector needed severe reforms to address both equity and quality. There was also a common assumption across groups that to strengthen the state was a prerequisite to have a more proactive role. Also, there was palpable excitement across narratives around the possibility of a new vision of society and development. There was also a growing expectation after the drafting of the Constitution that traditionally marginalized groups would continue to play a central role in reimagining and to refashion a new social order and institutions.

8.2 *The Plot: What Kind of State? What Kind of Education?*

The stories began to diverge, and conflicts and disagreement became more acute at about the time when Correa and his government started to advance their policy agenda in different sectors. The question of the need to rebuild and strengthen the state shifted to the query of what kind of state Correa was building in practice. Was it an inclusive, democratic, intercultural and decentralized state or was it a centralized, insular, bureaucratic one?

8.3 *Governance, Participation, and Quality*

Within education, there seemed in the first few years to be a general acknowledgment of the need to be pragmatic. After all, the system was basically on life support and barely had a pulse. As described in more detail above, the priority focused on recuperating what the Ministry termed *Rectoría*, or authority and control over the school system. Stability, continuity, and rationality were some of the critical criteria in discourse that were applied to reshape the sector. However, the mode by which *rectoría* was constructed in discourse and pursued by the Ministry created new disagreements and conflicts. The Ministry definition of *rectoría* emphasized central state authority and control. Public education became synonymous with "state-run," and not necessarily with broader principles that ensured "publicness" in education such as free, laic, or compulsory (Scholar, personal communication, March 7, 2013).

Policy decisions were seen to fall precisely within the government's purview and domain. It may consult with social groups, but the decision-making locus was ultimately in the hands of the central policymaker. Participation was recast in most instances by the government as information sharing and validation of existing plans. Direct citizen participation was seen as desirable while conceiving as a threat collective group and union participation. Discursively, the Ministry questioned the representativeness and democratic legitimacy of leaders of influential civil society and union groups. In many ways, this critique was valid. The Union, with its sole focus on wages and frequent use of mass disruption, had fatigued the general public, including progressives. As several respondents highlighted, the discourse of the Union did not evolve with the changing context. Their cognitive frames and identity were entrenched in an extreme adversarial form of countervailing power (Fung, 2002; Kim, 2014).

Rectoría implied a central definition of the curriculum across the country. Discursively, the government painted the previous situation as anarchy (curricular, administrative), thus justifying a more central top-down approach. Central control was vital for ensuring equity and even quality. This argument made sense in many ways given the past mounting of the problem. Previous laissez-faire pluralism had led to different education systems for different classes. Those with resources ended up receiving higher quality while those with low income usually received inferior quality services. Equity entailed establishing a common core curriculum for everyone and, similarly, to frame standards and evaluation as a tool to foment participation and to help the state redirect resources to those that needed them most.

The counter-narrative disputed this concept of policy formulation and quality as narrow, technocratic, state-centric, and centralized. From the counter perspective strengthening the state did not necessarily imply concentrating the state; bolstering of the state was not a zero-sum game. Local diverse communities required different solutions. They demanded more agency in determining their educational ends and means. For decades, teachers and communities had been the object of development and education policies; not subjects with the outfit to shape and make policy.

Over time, there is evidence of policy learning and adaptation from high-level officials. Several of those interviewed acknowledged that mistakes were made along the way and blamed a more profound authoritarian cultural tradition embedded in the practices of the state and civil society actors. That is a policy story of helplessness in the face of an impersonal weight of history and traditions. Several officials recognized that deeper change could only happen by empowering local agents, schools, and teachers. At the same time, however, they were also convinced that given the experience of abandonment and chaos in the 1980s and 1990s, that autonomy without some form of quality control and accountability was a recipe for failure.

Correa and his government's application of *rectoría* was a double-edged sword. With the impulse to advance reform and break through potential gridlock that had characterized the sector for decades, Correa sometimes used force, symbolically and literally. The rhetorical threats employed by Correa may have been useful in the short-term for advancing elements of the reform, but in the longer-term, these threats only reinforced the general mistrust of government policies. Even if many of the strategies suggested made sense given the context or in the long term would benefit the public interest, opposition groups often rejected them because of their tone, origins, or just because that is what opposition groups do. They critique, they refuse, and they resist.

9 Moral of the Story: The Paradox of Power

One of the central insights of this study is that advancing quality reforms may first require the concentration of power, particularly in contexts where there are strong veto actors, gridlock and a contentious view of the reform package. However, compliance as a top-down governance strategy does not necessarily lead to better outcomes over time, particularly in contexts characterized by higher levels of diversity and complexity. Furthermore, top-down compliance does not significantly contribute to policy legitimacy or fuel sustainability. Thus, governors may introduce elements (often market-related in their logic) that shift the focus of institutions and actors to performance outcomes. Theses outcomes tend to be predefined by experts and governors a priori. Those couple with systems of sanctions and rewards, as well as methods of surveillance. The underlying assumption is that competition between individuals and groups for scarce resources will motivate behavior change. Unfortunately, this approach to governance through market competition can create perverse incentives and distortions, especially given that education is a public good (Klees, 2008).

Finally, emergent capabilities deal with the ability to respond to the more complex, unpredictable and locally rooted aspects that characterize the problem of enhancing quality. Here issues of values, identity, morale, and culture become salient. Differences and conflict are inevitable given the diversity of groups. Therefore, nascent capacities may focus more on the process and ways to constructively manage conflict and tensions, so they contribute to innovation and improvement, rather than undermining them. These emergent competences thus may be more linked to capabilities that are supportive, responsive, creative, and collaborative problem-solving. This approach has advantages, particularly when it comes to promoting collaborative problem-solving at the local level, where agents have more information on the specific issues at hand.

This gradually changing description of governance from compliance to performance, to emergence, implies a linear historical process similar to the democratization sequence argument made by Crozier et al. (1975) and later by Fukayama (2004). Without certain levels of compliance, it is difficult to shift towards performance on a system-wide level. If people don't get paid, if the books don't arrive, and if the teacher or student does not attend with consistency, then it is nearly impossible to focus on second-level processes of learning and improvement. Moreover, performance, often achieved through external pressure, is essential but often insufficient for broader change. Finally, emergence, which deals with the inner core of change (identity, morale, attitudes, affinities), is fostered more through spontaneous, organic networks.

The paradox of power lies in the fact that the application of specific forms of control to solve one dimension of the problem (i.e., policy decisiveness) exacerbates other aspects of the difficulty, like policy adaptability. It is also multidirectional, meaning that certain policy discourses create counter-reactions, new political identities and new political dynamics over time. For instance, many social actors in the case of Ecuador seem stuck in more adversarial forms of countervailing power. Decades of abuses of state power, institutional corruption, and mistrust shaped those political identities. These different identities and politics that once helped transform and democratize Ecuadorian society now may limit the ability of political and social actors to collaborate to construct a new society as envisioned in the Constitution and concept of *Buen Vivir*.

10 Lessons Moving Forward, Ecuador and Beyond

Thus, what are the lessons learned from this policy study for Ecuador and other countries in the process of rebuilding state capacity to manage educational reforms with a post-neoliberal agenda? Grugel and Riggirozzi (2012) define post-neoliberalism as:

> Reclaiming the authority of the state to oversee the construction of a new social consensus and approach to welfare and a set of economic policies that seeks to enhance or rebuild the capacity of the state to manage the market and export economy in ways that not only ensure growth but are also responsive to social need and citizenship demands. (pp. 2–3)

This study of Ecuador illustrates the problematic path of reclaiming state authority in a context where local and global pressures pull the state in different directions, and also where the grammar of schooling and politics limit reform processes and outcomes. Ensuring economic growth while being responsive to social needs and citizenship demands likely require necessary tradeoffs in the short and mid-term. Both policymakers and citizens need to learn to navigate these tradeoffs.

Situating Ecuador's education reform within this specific historical context helps to provide a more nuanced picture of the politics of education reforms and generates several vital lessons. These lessons are contextually bound, and additional cases are needed to deepen and confirm their applicability to other contexts.

10.1 *Lesson 1: Jumpstarting Progressive Reform Processes May Require a Concentration of Power*

The first set of lessons deal with the issue of governance in post-neoliberal settings. The policy story captured here makes clear that a weak state with no autonomy or capacity to formulate and implement public policies compromises the possibility of reform in social sectors severely. Furthermore, a proactive and capable state (not to be confused with size) is a pre-requisite for advancing certain types of policy reforms. In specific political contexts characterized by gridlock and political fragmentation, such as in Ecuador in 2006, the concentration of power may be needed initially to advance reforms dealing with educational quality politically. The strength of power allowed Correa and the Ministry to recuperate some of the autonomy that the state lost during previous decades to international donors and local interest groups. This autonomy cleared space for the government to set and advance a bolder reform agenda in the education sphere.

10.2 *Lesson 2: Building State Capacity to Manage Reform*

Centralization or concentration of power in and of themselves will not likely lead to better social policy outcomes. In the case of Ecuador, the government under Correa combined centralization with a focus on rebuilding state capacity. Within the education sector, this entailed a long and arduous process that consisted of a multi-pronged strategy focused on three courses. First, restructuring of the educational bureaucracy to better focus on policy reforms. Second, renewing the human talent pool within the educational bureaucracy with qualified technocrats and on the front lines with motivated, adequately remunerated, and qualified teachers. Third, focusing on performance and accountability through the use of standards and evaluations.

Interestingly, some of the specific policies implemented by the progressive state in Ecuador, such as performance standards and evaluation, have been associated with neoliberal reforms and in particular with the new public management approach. However, in Ecuador, there was a clear political prioritization of social policy reforms backed by significant increases in public investment in education (including a threefold rise in teacher salaries) which contradict the fundamental tenets of neoliberalism that called for rolling back the state through decentralization, austerity in public spending, and privatization of public services.

10.3 *Lesson 3: Leadership and Continuity in Reform*

Correa and his government have invested considerable political and financial resources into education reform despite the potential for conflict that this involved. One key lesson from Ecuador is that leadership, starting at the highest levels, is critical for successfully advancing reform efforts. Correa's rhetorical ability, his activist stance, and his strategic use of communication were crucial for securing support for the reforms. There were various strategic decisions along the way that demonstrate the political savvy of the government, particularly the decision to sequence the education reform, starting with equity and following up with more difficult qualitative improvements. The initial focus on increasing investment and tripling teacher salaries helped to create momentum and counter-arguments that would be very useful for the second more contentious phases of reform.

Continuity and persistence were critical. Initially, Correa's decision to continue with a 10-year plan provided much-needed stability and continuity. That agenda harmonized with a more specific set of educational strategies that were pursued with tenacity over the past five years. Correa maintained high-level officials (ministers and teams) in their positions for three or more years, on average. That is unusual in Latin America, where the average tenure of a Minister of Education is between 1.5 and two years. Continuity in leadership, clarity of vision and persistence in reform efforts are vital for complex social policy reforms.

10.4 *Lesson 4: Shifts in Governance Need to Occur over Time*

The fourth main lesson from Ecuador and for other progressive states in similar historical situations is that more profound transformations in the education system, such as improvement of educational quality, most likely require strategic mixes of governance modes (hierarchy and networks) over time.

In contexts such as Ecuador in 2006, it may require an initial concentration of power through the hierarchy where there was a total lack of governability and where state planning and decision-making did not operate by excessive international influence and powerful local groups that benefitted from a weakened state. In this context, recuperating the state's authority and control over the sector and ensuring necessary levels of compliance across actors in the system is required before advancing to higher order and more complex change. However, at some point, hierarchical forms of governance become limited in their ability to support local problem-solving in education at the school and community levels. Thus, they need to be complemented (not replaced) with more horizontal networks and bottom-up participation from critical actors. Getting the right governance mix, which is contingent on historical and political trajectories of institutions, is fundamental for improving education, not just expanding it.

Notes

1 Those interviewed included: Two Ministers of Education from the Correa period. Two Vice-ministers of Education from before and during the Correa period. Four Sub-secretaries of Education (three from the Correa period and one from the previous administration of Alfredo Palacio). Two high-level Ministerial teams (one focused on educational standards and the other side on the traveling cabinet). Two active teacher union leader members (President of the National Teacher Union (UNE) and UNE's national representative for indigenous communities). Four representatives from prominent international organizations (UNICEF, UNESCO, Care, and the German Cooperation). Four representatives from prominent and active civil society organizations in the educational space (Contrato Social, Grupo Faro, Educiudanania, and PREAL). One scholar with expertise in education. Three school principals (two from rural and one from urban schools. Two school teachers (one from an urban and the other from a rural school).

2 The Ecuadorian 10-year education plan included the following policy goals: Policy Goal 1: Universalization of early childhood education from 0 to 5 years. Policy Goal 2: Universalization of general basic education from primary to tenth grade. Policy Goal 3: Increase in enrollment for secondary students to achieve at least 75% enrollment of youth in the corresponding age group. Policy Goal 4: Eradication of illiteracy and strengthen continuing education for adults. Policy Goal 5: Improvement of physical infrastructure and equipment of the educational institutions. Policy Goal 6: Improvement of the quality and equity and implementation of a national system of evaluation and social audit process of the educational system. Policy Goal 7: Revalorization of the teaching profession and improvement of initial teacher training, ongoing professional development, work conditions and quality of life. Policy Goal 8: Increase of 0.5 GDP annually in education sector spending with the goal of reaching 6% GDP investment in education per year (as mentioned above, investment in 2006 was around 3% of GDP).

References

Ball, S. J., & Junemann, C. (2012). *Networks, new governance and education.* Bristol: Policy Press.

Bermeo, F. (2008). *Organización territorial del sistema educativo a nivel local; Proyecto Espacios Locales de Inclusión y Calidad Educativa (ELICE).* Quito, Ecuador.

Bevir, M., & Rhodes, R. A. (2010). *The state as cultural practice*. Oxford: Oxford University Press.

Board, P. A. (2006). *Quantity without quality: A report card on education in Latin America, 2006*. Washington, DC: PREAL.

Bourgon, J. (2011). *A new synthesis of public administration: Serving in the 21st century*. Montréal: School of Policy Studies, Queen's University.

Bowen, J. D. (2015). Rethinking democratic governance: State building, autonomy, and accountability in Correa's Ecuador. *Journal of Politics in Latin America, 7*(1), 83–110.

Bruns, B., & Schneider, B. R. (2016). *Managing the politics of quality reforms in education: Policy lessons from global experience*. Background Paper: The Learning Generation. International Commission on Financing Global Education Opportunity, New York, NY.

Carnoy, M., Gove, A. K., & Marshall, J. H. (2007). *Cuba's academic advantage: Why students in Cuba do better in school*. Stanford, CA: Stanford University Press.

Centeno, M. A. (2002). *Blood and debt: Nation-state in Latin America*. College Park, PA: The Pennsylvania State University Press.

Collier, P. (2008). *The Bottom Billion: Why the poorest countries are failing and what can be done about it*. New York, NY: Oxford University Press.

Cohen, J. L., & Rogers, A. (1995). A proposal for reconstructing democratic institutions. In E. O. Wright (Ed.), *Associations and democracy* (pp. 7–98). London: Verso.

Crozier, M., Huntington, S. P., & Watanuki, J. (1975). *The crisis of democracy: Report on the governability of democracies to the Trilateral Commision*. New York, NY: New York University Press.

De la Torre, C. (2013). El tecnopopulismo de Rafael Correa:¿ Es compatible el carisma con la tecnocracia? *Latin American Research Review, 48*(1), 24–43.

Fischer, F. (2003). *Reframing public policy: Discursive politics and deliberative practices*. New York, NY: Oxford University Press.

Fukuyama, F. (2004) *State building. Governance and world order in the 21st century*. New York, NY: Cornell University Press.

Fukuyama, F. (2011). *The origins of political order: From prehuman times to the French revolution*. New York, NY: Farrar, Straus and Giroux.

Fung, A. (2002). *Collaboration and countervailing power. Making participatory governance work*. Cambridge, MA. Draft paper. Retrieved from http://www.archonfung.net/papers/CollaborativePower2.2.pdf

Gallegos, F. R. (2010). Fragmentación, reflujo y desconcierto. Movimientos sociales y cambio político en el Ecuador (2000–2010). *Observatorio Social de América Latina, 11*(28), 17–48.

George Washington University. (2009). *Contribution of government communication capacity to achieving good governance outcomes*. The George Washington University's Elliott School for International Affairs Linder Commons Room. Rapporteurs' Report, Washington, DC.

Grindle, M. S. (2004). *Despite the odds: The contentious politics of education reform.* Princeton, NJ: Princeton University Press.

Grugel, J., & Riggirozzi, P. (2012). Postneoliberalism in Latin America: Rebuilding and reclaiming the state after crisis. *Development and Change, 43*(1), 1–21.

Hajer, M. A. (1995). *The politics of environmental discourse: Ecological modernization and the policy process.* Oxford: Clarendon Press.

Huntington, S. (1968). *Political order in changing societies.* New Haven, CT: Yale University Press.

Jones, M. D., & McBeth, M. K. (2010). A narrative policy framework: Clear enough to be wrong? *Policy Studies Journal, 38*(2), 329–353.

Jones, M. D., Shanahan, E., & McBeth, M. (2014). *The science of stories: Applications of the narrative policy framework in public policy analysis.* New York, NY: Palgrave Macmillan.

Kim, D. Y. (2014). Transformation of countervailing power in collaborative governance: A case study of the Shi-Hwa sustainable development committee. *Korean Journal of Policy Studies, 29*(3), 53–77.

Klees, S. J. (2008). A quarter century of neoliberal thinking in education: Misleading analyses and failed policies. *Globalisation, Societies and Education, 6*(4), 311–348.

Klees, S. J., Samoff, J., & Stromquist, N. P. (2012). *The World Bank and education: Critiques and alternatives.* Rotterdam, The Netherlands: Sense Publishers.

Levi-Faur, D., & Gilad, S. (2004). The rise of the British regulatory state: Transcending the privatization debate. *Comparative Politics, 37*, 105–124.

Lora, E. (2007). *The state of state reform in Latin America.* San Francisco, CA: Stanford University Press.

Luna Tamayo, M. (2009). Introducción. *Aportes ciudadanos a la revolución educativa, 16.* Quito: Contrato Social.

Luna Tamayo, M. (2014). *Las políticas educativas en El Ecuador, 1950–2010: Las acciones del Estado y las iniciativas de la sociedad* (Unpublished Ph.D. thesis). Universidad Nacional de España, Madrid, España.

Migdal, J. S. (1988). *Strong Societies and Weak States: State-Society relations and state capabilities in the Third World.* Princeton, NJ: Princeton University Press.

Minteguiaga, A. (2014). *Las oscilaciones de la calidad educativa en Ecuador, 1980–2010: Estudio sobre políticas, planes, programas y proyectos gubernamentales de "escuelas de calidad" (1980–2010).* Quito: IAEN, Instituto de Altos Estudios Nacionales.

Olson, K. M. (2007). Rhetorical leadership and transferable lessons for successful social advocacy in Al Gore's an inconvenient truth. *Argumentation and Advocacy, 44*(2), 90–110.

Peters, B. G., & Pierre, J. (1998). Governance without government? Rethinking public administration. *Journal of Public Administration Research and Theory, 8*(2), 223–243.

Rhodes, R. A. (1997). *Understanding governance: Policy networks, governance, reflexivity and accountability.* Buckingham: Open University Press.

Rhodes, R. A. (2012). Waves of governance. In D. Levi-Faur (Ed.), *Oxford handbook of governance* (pp. 33–48). Oxford: Oxford University Press.

Roe, E. (1994). *Narrative policy analysis: Theory and practice*. Durham, NC: Duke University Press.

Saravia, M. (2009, May 8). Alberto Acosta, economista: "El reto de Correa es construir poder mas horizontalmente. *Diario Rio Negro*. Retrieved from https://www.rionegro.com.ar/debates/alberto-acosta-economista-el-reto-de-correa-es-construir-poder-mas-horizontalmente-GBHRN1241751411240

Schattschneider, E. E. (1935). *Politics, pressures and the tariff*. New York: Prentice Hall.

Sørensen, E., & Torfing, J. (2007). Introduction governance network research: Towards a second generation. In E. Sørensen & J. Torfing (Eds.), *Theories of democratic network governance* (pp. 1–21). London: Palgrave Macmillan.

Spreen, C. (2001). *Globalization and educational policy borrowing: Mapping outcomes-based education in South Africa* (Doctoral dissertation). Columbia University, New York, NY.

Stone, D. A. (2002). *Policy paradox: The art of political decision making*. New York, NY: Norton.

Tolofari, S. (2005). New public management and education. *Policy Futures in Education, 3*(1), 75–89.

Torfing, J. (2012). Governance networks. In D. Levi-Faur (Ed.), *Oxford handbook of governance* (pp. 99–112). Oxford: Oxford University Press.

Torres, R. M. (2014, August). I Encuentro de Experiencias, Sueños y Pensamientos Educativos Humanos en Ecuador. *Red de Educación Alternativa, Saraguro, Ecuador*.

Torres, R. M. (2006, December 15). Por qué vote en blanco por el plan decenal de educación (2006–2015). *Otraəducacion*. Retrieved from http://otra-educacion.blogspot.com.co/2011/01/por-que-vote-en-blanco-por-el-plan.html

Waldmüller, J. M. (2014). Buen vivir, sumak kawsay, 'good living': An introduction and overview. *Alternautas, 1*, 17–28.

Wier, M. (2006) When Does Politics Create Policy? The Organizational politics of change. In I.Shapiro, S. Skowronek & D. Galvin (Eds.), *Rethinking political institutions the art of the state* (pp. 171–186). New York, NY: New York University Press.

Whitman, G. (2009). Esfero rojo, esfero azul. Impacto de las reformas educativas financiadas internacionalmente en las prácticas en el aula en el Ecuador. In C. Arcos Cabrera & B. Espinosa (Eds.), *Desafíos de la educación en el Ecuador: Calidad y equidad* (pp. 67–155). Quito: Flacso.

Yanow, D. (2014). Thinking interpretively: Philosophical presuppositions and the human sciences. In D. Yanow & P. Schwartz-Shea (Eds.), *Interpretation and method: Empirical research methods and the interpretive turn* (2nd ed., pp. 5–26). Armonk, NY: M.E. Sharpe.

CHAPTER 7

From the Indicative to the Imperative: Colombia, the Most Educated in 2025?

René Guevara Ramírez and Sandra Milena Téllez Rico

> The institution of an identity, which can be a title of nobility or an insult ('you're nothing but a ...'), is the imposition of a name, that is, of a social essence. To institute, to assign an essence, a competence, is to impose a right to be that is also an obligation to be (or an obligation to be so). It is to signify to someone what he is and to indicate to him that he should conduct himself according to that signification. In this case, the indicative is an imperative.
>
> PIERRE BOURDIEU, *Language and symbolic power*, 1991

∵

Abstract

This chapter situates the analysis of educational policies in Colombia, identifying the inclusion of problems constituting government agendas. For this purpose, the synchrony-diachrony relationship is observed to account for the Colombian educational system, in its mounting configuration of policies and its double meaning (service and right), during the years 1988–2010. Subsequently, we report on consistent achievements of the period of the national government (2014–2018), placing its diagnostic commitments on government action, and the symbolic efficacy of incrementalism. We reconstructed the path of education reform in a work that does not intend to evaluate nor prescribe guidelines for Colombian educational policies. The context is within the framework of Colombia's entry into the OECD.

1 Introduction

After a process that had lasted 7 years, on May 30, 2018 Colombian President Juan Manuel Santos Calderón signed in Paris the agreement that recognized

 | DOI: 10.1163/9789004413375_008

Colombia's entrance into the Organization for Economic Cooperation and Development (OECD). The search for this status had been given impetus in his first National Plan for Development in the following manner: "We have begun the process for entering the OECD, which is something unthinkable only a few years ago" (DNP, 2011, p. 21).

Indeed, the administrative report of the Ministry of Education (MEN, abbreviation in Spanish) from the first period of that government, 2010–2014, reaffirmed this goal (MEN, 2014). Nevertheless, joining the OECD would involve an assessment of Colombian public policies, as well as their improvement through acceptance of the recommendations provided by the OECD, principally those regarding the reduction of inequality.[1]

> One of the items of assessment for said entrance into the OECD specifically involved education: Colombia ... is the first country that will be evaluated in education; until now this criterion has not been considered by the (OECD) in the process of new member entry. Yet Colombia's education system is already familiar with OECD projects and initiatives. Since 2006, Colombia has been participating in international student evaluations (PISA) which measure student learning amongst 15-year-olds from different OECD countries and the world. (MEN, 2014, p. 54)

To be sure, the education sector plan of the following governing period, included in the "National Development Plan 2014–2018. All for a New Country with Peace, Equity, Education," expressed the Strategic Lineaments of Education Policy.[2] Indeed, its title established the tone of the government's strategy: "Colombia, the Best Educated in 2025." Yet this title resonated with strategies enunciated at much the same time: two development plans of regional authorities (Medellín, 2004–2007; Antioquia, 2012–2015) had already highlighted this strategy. In the first one, "Development Plan 2004–2007: Medellín, Commitment of the Full Citizenry," the execution of one of its plans, named "Medellín, The Most Educated," would end up becoming the overall planning strategy. The later Development Plan (2012–2015) showcased the title, "Antioquia, The Most Educated." While noting the shift from "more" to "best," one can certainly appreciate the notion that education would be central to government action and the deliberations of the Colombian public agenda: more education, better education.

We should note that the Presidential strategy discussed here did not imply any change in the direction of education policies, much less the existence of a new program of concrete government action as a guarantee of admission to the OECD. On the contrary, as we will observe in this chapter, it was continuity that marked the policy sphere. The education policies contemplated for the years 2014–2018 would be "more of the same," as a popular expression puts it. The operationalization of such policies would rely on the incremental application of accumulated policies, from the 1980s up to the present: a little more than 30 years of policies, now fortified.

Indeed, the final governing period of the 1980s (1986–1990) really responded to the critical administrative and financial situation of public schools (basic and intermediate); that's when the basis for subsequent action would be established. The decade from 1992 to 2002 saw significant efforts aimed at creating favorable conditions for the implementation of the legal and constitutional provisions for Colombian education, with a focus on the changing relationship between the central government and the regional governments in the design of education policy.

From 2002–2010, education policies whose design and implementation had yielded positive results at the local level were implemented at the national level as well. In this way, the full set of public actions in the education sector would, on the one hand, end up constituting the necessary antecedent for the presidential decision to join the OECD (announced in 2011); on the other hand, moving forward these same actions would now be included among the full set of issues characterizing the policy agenda for the Colombian education system: coverage, quality, efficiency, and financing.[3]

As Rivas (2015) reconstructs it in his regional study, those years in Colombia saw the exhaustion of the State-school relation in education that had prevailed before the 1990s resignified by a particular kind of decentralization: the municipalization, or better yet, the remunicipalization of education.[4] From its republican beginnings in the middle of the 19th century, Colombia has preserved this centralist-federalist tension in spite of the establishment and maintenance of a centralist political structure from the 1886 Constitution.

Here we present an analysis aimed at comprehending how government actions accumulated throughout the final decades of the 20th and the first decades of the 21st century constitute a configuring *continuum* of an education policy agenda that structures the current system. By situating the expression "the best educated" as a question in the title, we mean to open up critical analysis of the matter rather than ratifying a strategy whose logic is formulated via evaluative understandings of education policy strategies that accommodate dominant schemes of perception.

2 Methodological Inferences for a Theoretical Problem

Luis Aguilar (1992a, 1992b) has argued that an analysis of policies that postulates education policy as an object of study must examine governmental action—as process and as cycle. Accordingly, the definition of problems for inclusion in a policy agenda favors certain methodological implications that derive from this theoretical problematic.

Specialists in this type of policy analysis indicate two types of agendas, one public and one institutional. The first type, developed by Aguilar in his introductory text (1992b) and based on Cobb and Charles Elder (Cobb y Elder, 1984; en Aguilar, 1992b), is constituted by *issues* (*cuestiones*) deserving of attention by government authorities, and would represent an agenda "composed of all the issues that the members of a political community jointly perceive as deserving of public attention and as matters that fall into the legitimate jurisdiction of existing governmental authority" (Aguilar, 1992b, pp. 31–32). This agenda might have various synonyms: systemic, public, or constitutional. Thus, its primary function is to contribute to establishing the democratic "health" of a country by identifying the way that specific individuals or groups situate and position themselves on a given matter. Here the primary analytic concern is with how particular interests become universalized, and through what procedural mechanisms.

Typically during electoral processes (for the executive or legislative branch), communication media attempt to contribute to, without trying to influence, this type of public agenda by means of discussion or definition of its contents; they do so through the diffusion, discussion, and analysis of citizen surveys undertaken with the purpose of identifying the *primary social problems* of that moment. Previously the same media will have broadcast, in different formats, notes, stories, or news summaries related to "coinciding" matters, and in this way will have managed to establish in the surveys themselves such problems as constituting the "citizens' concerns for the candidates."

Our interest here corresponds to the other type of agenda: the governmental. Aguilar presents two of its synonyms, institutional or formal, and conceptualizes this type of agenda as that which contains

> ... matters explicitly accepted for active and serious consideration by authorized decision-makers. Therefore, any set of matters accepted by any governmental entity at local, state, or national levels would constitute an institutional agenda .... (1992a, p. 32)

This would be an agenda characterized by its specificity, concreteness, delimitation—indicating the definition of the problem whose theoretical backdrop corresponds to the problematic implied in the creation of the governmental agenda. It can be further stated as follows:

> ... completely intertwined with the definition of the problem is the government's need to examine its possible courses of action and to consider

> if it can in fact do something (and at what cost): if action itself make any sense. In sum, the attention to, definition, and feasibility of the problem are determining aspects of the process by which the problem (matter, issue, demand) obtains its character as *agendum*: something about which action must be taken. (Aguilar, 1992a, p. 30)

Following Aguilar's approach requires us to make clear that studies about governmental agenda indicate that authorities will determine which problems are those that become the object of action: "objects that public officials have decided that they must act upon or that they've considered acting upon" (Aguilar, 1992a, p. 29). Consequently, in our case the sources upon which we draw to reconstruct the contents of education policy agendas are primarily documentary—education sector plans as linked to national development plans—and we bring these into dialogue with other studies at moments that the analysis requires them.

However, before we can an analyze government action, we must locate the "*thing unto itself*" (*la cosa en si*) only after specifying a peculiarity of the Colombian education system: the magnitude of the private sector's involvement in educational institutions and its competition with the official government system for gaining enrollment at different levels of schooling.

3 The Colombian Educational System: Past in the Present

According to information from the MEN, based on existing education legislation (laws: General Education, Higher Education, and parliamentary decrees) the Colombian formal education system is comprised of four levels: preschool, basic (*primaria* and *secundaria*), middle, and higher education, with their corresponding grades, ages, and purposes. Table 7.1 conveys the basic information.[5]

The preceding information allows us to introduce our goal of identifying the conditions of possibility favorable to the governmental resolution of educational problems. Accordingly, we situate the action that the government undertook to meet educational demand, as well as the public's satisfaction with the supply to such demand, in a kind of market of symbolic goods (Bourdieu, 2002) within which educational capital marks a space of social competition.

In terms of research, this relation remains bound by a double delimitation: legal and statistical. The first involves a historical construction of its double meaning (as both right and service), from its republican origins up to the present. This conception is novel among national histories in the region

TABLE 7.1 Colombian educational system (formal)

	EPBM registration 2015: 10'239.145 / Urban: 76% – Rural: 24%	Levels (#)	Years: Denomination	Age
	1. Preschool education (EIAIPI). Purpose: "It forms the biological, cognitive, psychomotor and socio-affective aspects."	3	Initial	3 years
			Preschool	4 years
			Transition	5 or 6 years
			Years	From 7–11 years
2. Basic Education	a) **Basic Primary**: Develops communication skills, mathematical knowledge, artistic training and values, understanding the physical, social and cultural environment, among others. Participation: 9% of total enrollment (MT).	5	Compulsory Years: 1°, 2°, 3°, 4°, 5°	
2. Basic Education	b) **Basic secondary**. Purpose: "Encourages the development of logical reasoning, scientific knowledge of science, history and the universe, the development of critical thinking, among others." Participation: 44% of MT.	4	Compulsory Years: 6°, 7°, 8°, 9°	From 12–15 years
	3. High School. Purpose: "It promotes the understanding of universal ideas and values and the preparation for higher education and for work, through its two technical and academic modalities." *Participation: 34% of MT.*	2	10°, 11°	16–17 years
	complementary cycle **Normal School**. Purpose: "To train teachers (non-professionals)."	2	12°, 13°	
	4. Superior		Duration	
Undergraduate	i) *Professional technician*. Purpose: "To instruct in trades of an operative and instrumental nature."		2-3 years	
Undergraduate	ii) *Technological.* Purpose: "To prepare for trades, academic training programs and specialization."		3 years	
Undergraduate	iii) *Professional or undergraduate.* "To educate in scientific or technological research, in specific disciplinary areas and production of knowledge."		4-5 years	
Postgraduate	• *Specialization.* Purpose: "It seeks to perfect or deepen in a certain area of discipline, profession or occupation."		1 year	
Postgraduate	• *Master's degree.* Purpose: "It seeks to expand and develop knowledge for the solution of disciplinary, interdisciplinary or professional problems and to train in research in a specific area of science or technology."		2 years	
Postgraduate	• *Doctorate.* Purpose: "To train researchers at an advanced level."		3 years	
Postgraduate	• *Postdoctoral.* Purpose: "Most advanced level of postgraduate training research."		1 year	

SOURCE: BASED ON INFORMATION FROM THE MINISTRY OF NATIONAL EDUCATION AND EDUCATION LAWS

surrounding Colombia, which adhere more to the classic distinction between public and private.

> The foundational terms about the nature of the educational service is provided by our Political Constitution. For example, there it indicates that it's a matter of a person's right, as well as being a public service with a social function; the State assumes the obligation to regulate and exercise full supervision over this educational service in order to assure its quality and the completion of its purpose, which is the best possible moral, intellectual, and physical education of pupils. [The Constitution] also charges the State with guaranteeing adequate provision to assure that all children

and youth (*menores*) have the necessary conditions met for access to, and persistence in, the education system.[6]

Any analysis of the configuration of the education policy agenda in Colombia must recognize that "problems" themselves are interpellated in which the education system was first established. Its fundamental trait—the relationship between supply (school buildings/institutions) and satisfied demand (enrollment)—betrays the determining presence of the private sector, whose participation is not merely complementary, but identical, to that of the government.

The second half of the twentieth century indeed began with the government controlling supply and demand in primary education; it was not until the 1990s that the private sector competed effectively at this level. But it was not until 1984 that the government caught up with private enrollment in preschool and secundaria, and thenceforth began to progressively overtake it. Even though public enrollment passed private enrollment by 1975, it was not until the middle of the 1990s that this occurred in preschool education. This analysis serves to indicate the importance, sense, and significance of the notion of education as a "public service": it is an expression meant to encompass a specific conceptualization of the State in the Colombian educational field and the manner in which problems of education policy and their methods of solution are interlinked.

4 The Remaking of Policy Management: 1988–2002

The decade of the 1980s saw the accumulation of a set of problems related to three educational matters: (1) decentralization of governance and financing; (2) school building consolidation; and (3) teacher professionalization. These problems would command priority attention and mark the formation of policies: the matters related to educational access/coverage/expansion as well as persistence/quality/efficiency would determine the substance of the policy agenda. However, only when matters of access and coverage had been satisfied, at the same time that the prevailing model of state (departmental) educational management had been exhausted, were conditions favorable for focusing attention on the key matters of the agenda.

The first matter, political decentralization, was begun during the administration of Virgilio Barco (1986–1990); municipalization was tied to school funding. Municipalization was accomplished through reform of the Ministry via two laws: the Administrative Deconcentration law, which was then modified by a second law called Administrative Decentralization.[7] Later still, school funding was moved from the *Situado Fiscal* of 1993, which became insolvent five years later, to the General System of Participations (SGP), created by a 2001 law aimed at regulating resources and the authority to offer educational services.[8] This transitional period involved the redistribution of administrative responsibilities between the central government, departments, and municipalities, with the latter required to be certified according to criteria defined in the law if population exceeded one hundred thousand.

At the beginning, the central level designed the policies while their implementation fell to the municipal and departmental secretariats. The transfers were accompanied by the Regional Educational Funds (*Fondos Educativos Regionales*) created by the central State to harmonize efforts at local implementation—even though this didn't necessarily correspond to national intentions. The departments and municipalities administered the teaching posts paid in large part by the MEN. All of this was remedied by the ministerial reform, which made the local level responsible for efficiency and the attainment of specific objectives. But even though the central government guaranteed the financing, the actual assignment of resources obeyed a different logic: adjudication by local census.

The second set of policy issues had to do with consolidating school buildings as a step to resolving the problem of continuity between primary and secondary school, thereby guaranteeing a complete course of study up through 9th grade. This action cleared the field for the later institutionalization of an extended school day. The school day eventually became a transformational policy for schools during the second decade of the twenty-first century.

The final set of policy issues from this period involved the pre-service professionalization of teachers consistent with the 1979 reform of the Teaching Statute, reformed again in 2002. The latter established a public competition based on merit for entering the teaching profession. This measure sought to supersede experience and seniority as the primary means of professional advancement. It also allowed for the entrance of unlicensed professionals into the public teaching force.

The decade of the 1990s also signified a crucial moment for the definition of routes of action in accordance with the new legal and constitutional provisions for the education sector. For example, one of these involved the institutionalization of school governments in each educational establishment, as well as the strategic elaboration of Institutional Educational Project (PEI); in both cases, the participation of parents, alumni, and other representatives from the local community was required.

At the national level these were times for thinking about the connections among education, science and development, one sign of which was the creation of the so-called Assembly of Sages (*Misión de Sabios*), one of the first academic and intellectual gatherings charged with proposing a "road map" (*cartas de navegación*) for transforming the country through educational processes. The year 1995 marked the drafting of the first ever Ten-Year Plan for Education (1996–2005); the Plan included a section devoted to configuring means of educational action with the participation of communities and interests outside, but complementary to, the education sector itself.[9]

One final matter that also embodies the transformation in policy design has to do with the unintentional conversion of the national capital, Bogotá, into a kind of education policy laboratory from 1998 to 2001. Local reforms would end up having national significance during the next policy cycle. The 1998 city government—the fifth elected by popular vote since 1988—undertook a series of administrative reforms designed to configure information systems for education policy decision-making in the city. Most of these reforms involved the management of teachers and school infrastructure and favored linking information-decisions-resource distribution to student enrollment. The institutional modernization of that time was oriented to strengthening local schools, the evaluation of student competencies, equipping classrooms with computers and Internet connections, and the implementation of the program of "*colegios en concesión*."[10] The requisitioning of textbooks was decentralized by direct consultation with local schools. The Bogotá Network of Public Libraries was also created, and after a few decades this lessened problems of reading and writing and increased the number of books read on average by Colombians, according to a survey conducted in 2018 by DANE.[11] The periodic ministry report at that time characterized the change in the following manner:

> … from the middle of the 1970s this model began to show serious political, administrative, financial, and pedagogical problems, and these only worsened over the next twenty years. There was a basic contradiction between national government policies, which provided almost the totality of all financing, defined norms and objectives, and tried to influence local implementation through decentralized entities, and the action of Education Secretaries from the departments and municipalities, who managed and transferred teachers with complete autonomy and without assuming any responsibility with regards to the efficiency or financing of the system. (MEN, 2010, p. 25)

By the end of the 1990s these problems of school financing and administration were no longer the primary concern, though to be sure they had not been completely resolved (Ongoing strikes by the National Federation of Teachers show ample evidence of this). Still, the magnitude of these problems was minimized in order to focus on finding solutions for another set of problems whose importance has remained central—one might even say classic—up to the present moment—quality and coverage, according to different educational levels.

For example, up until the 1990s coverage remained the priority in primary basic education. Upon eclipsing 90 to 95 percent coverage rates for primary, and comparable rates for middle school, policy priorities progressively shifted toward the other ends of the education spectrum: preschool and higher education.

5 Policy Consecration: 2002–2010

A summative statement of the 2002–2010 period expressed the conviction of those who spearheaded a number of policies that were consolidated in Bogotá from 1998 to 2001, and which would become national policies when that city's Secretary of Education was named national Minister of Education.[12]

> The Education Revolution deeply addressed the concerns and objectives that the country had formulated over the course of recent decades and it put them into practice. It transformed the educational entities and the Ministry in such a way as to widen educational opportunities for all and assure that they were of high quality. More than the gains in coverage—which represents, in any case, an important quantitative change—the real transformation occurred by drastically improving the Ministry's capacity for management and technical assistance with the support of a reliable and user-friendly information system, as well as the consolidation of a quality assurance system based on assessment tools closely linked across all levels that generated very strong incentives for improving educational quality. (MEN, 2010, p. 38)

From this we can understand the initial phrasing of this chapter, since in the matter of education policies the Colombian experience can be characterized as an accumulation, punctuated yet sustained, to the point of progressively generating the conditions for strengthening an education system that ended up being included amongst the set of assessments for their entry into the OECD.

The National Ministry of Education was reorganized once again in 2003 to align it with the educational structure of the country. Previously, its internal structure was constituted by a minister, vice-ministers of management directorates (General Secretary, for example) and a whole set of other linked or subordinated entities. Based on the diagnosis initiated during the previous educational administration (2000–2002), the 2003 MEN ended up constituted into two Vice-Ministries in charge of each component of the education system, with other internal directorates: The Vice-Ministry for Preschool, Basic, and Middle Education and the Vice-Ministry for Higher Education. The goal: better coordination, integration, and efficiency in the management of these different policy sectors.[13]

The information systems were also crucial both in official policymaking and citizens' decision-making. For the former, the systems helped policymakers with calculating school enrollment, assigning resources, and creating or reconfiguring institutions; for the latter, the systems allowed families to be better informed for their school preferences. Support systems for ministerial management and help for local entities were also strengthened. Policy design occurred thematically, according to education level, and included evaluative indicators of schools' management. Educational assessment was strengthened as a strategy for improving quality (e.g., the PISA exams), and so too was the education sector's ability to increase access for all school-age children.

More than serving as a chronicle, apology, or critique, the forgoing description shows the shape and direction of policy change. In other words, it offers a view of how, following the adjustments of the 1990s, the Colombian educational agenda at the start of this century was characterized by a focus on other issues: quality, coverage, and information, all flowing from the re-design of technical and governmental instruments.

For this reason, we agree with Axel Rivas (2015) when he writes that:

> In the 90s the practice of teaching was the stumbling block of all education reforms. The majority of countries in the region sought to transform the curriculum, administration, and system assessment. Decentralization and school autonomy appeared as the promised land for most reform thinkers. Teaching was seen as something secondary or perhaps unchangeable because of the power of teachers' unions. (p. 120)

Resolving the issues of the 1990s was a region-wide concern, despite certain national differences. Rivas locates us in the present moment of governmental action for education:

Something ruptured with the shift to a new century. The hypothesis about needing to privatize school management or decentralize to the local level revealed its risks and limitations. A new era began with the arrival of international assessments of educational quality, especially starting with the launch of PISA in 2000. The results of the successful countries produced a wave of studies about causes and explanations (Rivas, 2015, pp. 120–121).

From 2010 on, with the information resulting from the accumulation of many evaluations of school quality in hand, it could be seen that results were similar across schools regardless of their socioeconomic condition. The policy gaze now fixed its attention on another matter. It was no longer what it had been up till the start of the 21st century: problems of law, management, finance, curricular structure, student's socio-economic conditions, or educational administration at different levels. Now attention was firmly centered on teachers. From this point forward there would be a whole new wave of actions designed to increase educational quality, all of which was clearly articulated in Colombia's National Development Plan. According to Rivas (2015):

> Education policy approaches could finally evaluate entire systems during periods of change with demonstrable improvements in learning outcomes .... The conclusions reached by such evaluations were widely distributed: the selection, training, and professional trajectory of teachers were together the linchpin for quality improvement .... No longer were proposals centered around privatizing school management being recommended unless they could be supported by empirical evidence from evaluations .... Everything began to revolve around teaching .... "The only limit (*techo*) to educational quality is the quality of teachers" ... A new-old hypothesis took flight on the new century's policy agendas .... Teaching once again occupied the center, but reform paths did not converge. In many cases, pressure for better learning outcomes was increased, even as the social and cultural complexity of classrooms soared as well. Teaching was experienced as an ever more demanding job. (p. 121)

In this way, for each policy issue each successive government designed its own program; policy design on these issues were thus not completely continued, but rather reconfigured with slight variations: quality, at the heart of monitoring teacher training as part of evaluating the effectiveness of the whole school; coverage, with the conceptual tension of equality-equity added to the couplet of right-service; efficiency, very close to process achievements and results; and financing, determined by subsidies to regular supply and demand.

6 Teachers: The Best Educated ...?

The document titled "Colombia, the Best Educated in 2025" contains the *Strategic Recommendations for Education Policy of the National Education Ministry* (CLE henceforward). While it is true that this document emerged out of the National Development Plan 2014–2018, titled *Everyone for a New Country: Peace, Equity, and Education*, its specific focus on education favored the identification of those issues where the government would be focusing its attention and defining its options for action.

According to Aguilar's (1992b) approach, one key moment in the study of policy agendas consists of identifying and weighing the issues the government has decided to act upon and, consequently, how it defines those issues for action in terms of investing public resources for their solution. Making this approach explicit also helps to identify—or to reaffirm, in our case—the structure of the policy agenda.

The issues: The initial CLE document includes strategic recommendations with the following terminology:

1. Full school day (*Jornada única*)
2. Teaching excellence—teacher scholarship program
3. Teaching excellence—"Everyone Learns" program (*Todos a aprender*)
4. Teaching excellence—teacher guidance and supervision (*acompañamiento*)
5. Policy of teaching excellence
6. Teacher evaluation
7. Incentives for educational quality
8. Colombia Learns and Teachers' Network, total connection amongst teachers
9. Bilingual Colombia
10. Illiteracy-free Colombia
11. Preschool education
12. The modernization of middle school education
13. National reading program "Reading is my Story" ("*Leer es mi cuento*")
14. ICETEX Funds, higher education, the focus on regional development
15. ICFES, better knowledge
16. Financial sustainability of the higher education system
17. The master plan for regionalization (PMR)
18. The national system for tertiary education (SNET)
19. Being smart pays (*Ser pilo paga*).[14] Improving higher education

Reordering these points by thematic affiliation yields eight specific issues: full school day, preschool education, modernization of middle school, better access to quality higher education, teacher excellence, illiteracy-free Colombia, the national plan "reading is my story," and bilingual Colombia. And even if this thematic grouping into 8 (action design) corresponds to the CLE content, in the first report (action implementation) only 5 remained explicit (MEN, 2015a, 2017, p. 1) Teacher excellence, (1) Full school day, (2) Bilingual Colombia,

(3) Illiteracy-free Colombia, and (4) Access to quality higher education. The other issues ended up subsumed by these five, even as it is possible to discern the others by properly *navigating* the design of the Ministry's annual reports, whose format is not necessarily the same (there was a change of Education Minister in 2016).

Taking the policy guidelines as a whole, the emphasis on the theme of quality indicated by "teaching excellence" comprises a percentage of 37% relative to the MEN's overall strategic plan; this is congruent with the "new wave" of education policy development in the region. The First Report of the MEN (2015b) aligned with the National Development Plan and its recommendations states the following:

> Today's scholarship recognizes that one of the primary determinants in the learning process and student performance is the level and quality of teacher training and the pedagogical practices employed in the classroom. Therefore, improving teacher quality is one of the fundamental challenges required to position Colombia as the most highly educated in Latin America. (MEN, 2015a, p. 10)[15]

The second set of issues covered in the guidelines correspond to higher education (32%); some of these items can be found in another report by the OECD about higher education in Colombia (SNET), while the remaining issues reflect issues particular to higher education policy: coverage, quality, financing.

Retaining their singularity are the matters related to literacy, reading, and bilingualism. The first seeks to declare Colombia as a territory free of illiteracy. The second implements actions leading to the integration of reading and writing in the everyday lives of all Colombians. The third positions a command of English as a crucial competency for participating in the contemporary labor market.

7 The Substance of the Issues

Teaching excellence. Even as they situate the teacher at the heart of the diagnosis, the seven strategic recommendations that make up this program retain strong links to schools and students. Likewise, at the heart of the set of recommendations the evaluation of student achievement (*Pruebas Saber*) occupies a central place. Thus, the improvement of teaching quality is anchored in the fact that teaching occurs in a school and is related to the assessment and performance of the students. Regarding the teachers' characteristics, governmental action has determined that graduate training, work recognition/incentives (symbolic, economic), and assessments centered on classroom practice will contribute to the improvement of educational quality.

Full School Day (Jornada Unica). This corresponds to the recommendation expressly linked to the guarantee of "students' effective enjoyment of their right to education ... as a normative mandate." Thus, "as a strategy for time management to deepen the development of basic competencies ... (this recommendation) seeks to augment the time that students remain at school and increase the amount of time on task to strengthen academic work." The intent of this recommendation is based on a point in the 1994 General Education Law, which clearly expresses asymmetries between the normative goal and its implementation. From a different point of view, however, this allows us to observe how much of the law's content gets implemented or not according to government priorities.

> This Law was initially effectuated through Decree 1860, in 1994 .... The articles referring to the school day were then partially abrogated through Decree 1850, in 2002, thereby postponing the effective implementation of the full school day for reasons principally related to problems of coverage and lack of resources .... It has been 20 years since the General Education Law, during which the implementation of the single-shift school day as public policy has been postponed. (MEN, 2015b, p. 11)

Bilingual Colombia. Strategy aimed at the teaching of English in both basic and middle education as a "real priority of the official education system" (MEN, 2015a). Accordingly, teachers should make an important effort to update their competencies in this language and use it both in curriculum design and learning materials for the students.

Illiteracy-Free Colombia. The perspective of this recommendation relates to the "development of basic competencies in language use, mathematics, social sciences, natural sciences, and citizenship competencies, integrated across all cycles." All of this is to be realized through the hiring or establishment of contracts with operators charged with implementing programs focused on youth and adults, with the aim to reduce the rate of illiteracy. This shall be a literacy that contributes to accessing information for decision-making; accessing services; and entering the labor market with better wages (MEN, 2015a, p. 11). The plan rests on the notion of forming human capital and is centered on the education-labor market relation.

Access to high-quality higher education. The designation of this policy goal is identical to that expressed by a government from many years prior, and which ended up being incorporated into institutional programs of the ICETEX with the acronym ACCES. This is a grant-making entity for financing enrollment in higher education programs of notable academic quality. This policy recommendation intends to incentivize an increase in high quality (accredited) higher education, and to act as a kind of provocation for other universities to make further progress toward accreditation, both at the program and institutional levels. The governmental orientation consists of a strategy of incentives aimed at improving quality and increasing coverage by making available a set of economic resources for high quality institutions of higher education. Up to this point, we have seen various issues related to the study of governmental action and its relation to norms. We have also established the compositional logic of the Sector Plan.

With regard to government action a reading of the CLE document left this first impression: "If you do this, you will receive ...", "... to receive more, you must do this." One would have to ask if this orientation corresponds to a renovated type of the old stimulus-response relation, as applied to the space of government action. It remains an open question if this deeper behaviorist presumption can account for an understanding of the action implied by this type of policies: requiring an individual or institution to emulate others in pursuit of the resources they might obtain as a result of making available additional funds for quality. This is how it was expressed in the contents of the recommendation for *Incentives*, which can be economic and be received in exchange for improved performance indicators.

Another observable issue corresponds to the relationship between government action and normative implementation, shown, previously, in the example of the entire school day. The General Education Law of 1994 prescribed its implementation, on the one hand, while, on the other hand, its realization was postponed without detracting from the operation of the Rule of Law (Decree 1860 of 1994).

Conversely, we also have cases in which the legal norms express a particular ordering of the education system and yet government action creates a different form of organization without contravening the law; in effect government action operates with a force that is analogous to the normative content of the law itself (as in the case of the SNET, created by government action without basis in the Higher Education Law). Starting with the latest National Development Plan, individuals who aspire to obtain resources (through government programs) to finance their access to higher education must only seek enrollment in accredited higher education programs. It's a matter of changing the functioning of the system without changing the law.

There are also those who might suppose that with the law a new order of things would be created, but what appears to happen is just the reverse: the law consecrates an order of existing things, the law's promulgation resolves preexisting antagonisms and relegates them to the past. This happens in such a way that those who abide by the new norms will thenceforth consider that a new reality exists because of them. This points to the importance of reconstructing the underlying histories of public decisions.

One issue that is not currently present on the education policy agenda as such, but which continues to orbit around the space of government action, concerns the matter of corruption—the investigations undertaken by fiscal, disciplinary, and judicial authorities of the country have failed to produce any sanctions in the public management of schools. The modernization (or privatization) of State entities during the 1990s were justified on the basis of inefficiencies in public administration, in addition to the increased benefits that resulted from the collective bargaining agreements signed with unions. Nevertheless, for the education sector the Comptroller's report makes plain how in recent years SGP resources designated for the School Nutrition Programs of some of the country's Departments have been re-routed or subject to irregularities of content and cost. It would appear that the corruption surrounding the use of public resources was not cleaned up with the increased presence of the private sector; on the contrary, it may have metastasized. This is yet another issue remaining on the agenda for 2018–2022.

Design/Logic of the Sector Plan. One identifiable characteristic of the Plan is its integrated design. While previous plans offered recommendations organized by educational level, here the policy issues traverse all such levels and are interconnected with other sectors of government action in the National Development Plan. In contrast to the recent past (perception), currently there are evaluation systems guiding decision-making. Another aspect is that government actions are to match the diagnosis in terms of efficacy or the achievement of goals by means of improving the diagnosed situation.

In sum, the methodological implications of our approach have led us to present specific understandings of the underlying logic of policy design in terms of the particular means of their documentation. In this case, we have focused on education sector plans, with particular focus on the most recent one as a cumulative expression of a kind of work that represents a government achievement (in the present) without this having been the motive of previous governments. In this manner, reconstructing government actions since the middle of the 20th century (diachronic analysis) contributes to identifying, in a practical way, the way in which "constructing upon that which has been constructed" would strengthen the thematic agenda of Colombian education policies around the issues already indicated. This analysis always enables us to understand why the government inaugurated on the 7th of August 2018 would announce among its first concerns a review of the education system's financing of school incentives and the indicators determining resource allocation within the more general existing "System of Participations" (see below).

In terms of policy cycles, then, it would appear that a practical incrementalism brings with it an ability to take advantage of windows of opportunity like the presidential succession to review what has been done on matters of quality, coverage, and efficiency, with an eye to fine-tuning, in this case, the financial component. While the primary government concern in education from 2001–2010–2018 centered on quality, equity, and efficacy, changing the means of financing the system appears to have become a priority for the period 2018–2022, just as it had been at the end of the 90s.[16]

8 Closing-Opening

The entry of Colombia to the OECD on May 30th, 2018, marked a difference, shifting from an indication (expression of a purpose) to an imperative (mandate, fulfillment) whose primary effects are yet to be seen in the domain of decision-makers and in their corresponding spaces of recognition and implementation. Colombia has now been added to the prior entry of Mexico (1994) and Chile (2010), two education powerhouses in the Latin American region. While Mexico has a quantitatively larger education system, Chile has become a policy pioneer for decision-makers on the issues already discussed here. Along with Peru, Colombia also shares a place with both of these countries in the Pacific Alliance, created in 2011. In addition, Peru and Brazil have ties to the OECD—the first with specific programs since 2014, the second as a *key partner* since 1994.

Together Mexico, Chile, and Colombia end up forming a kind of regional version of "first amongst equals" (*primus inter pares*) whose outcome will become apparent upon the execution of best practices in the policy realm, relying on the technical expertise of the OECD. In the case of Colombia, the education reports delivered by the OECD in 2012 and 2016 constitute a kind of navigational chart. The implementation agenda outlined in their Review of National Polices or 2016 Report lays out the education system into 4 components (preschool and integral attention to early childhood-EIAIPI; basic primary and secondary-EBPS; middle/high school; and higher education) with a total of 12 improvement goals and 33 recommendations. These cover issues ranging from access-coverage to quality, efficiency-relevance, financing, system structure, learning, the teaching force, school management, equality of opportunity, and equity.

On a different note, the goal of Colombia being the best educated after the current government (2018–2022) and then to be evaluated by the following government (2022–2026) must be established by the National Planning Department as a safeguard for the assurance of good-faith actions. To project itself as the "best educated" in a region with high levels of inequality, in which Colombia occupies a less than honorable place despite economic growth and the continual improvement of macroeconomic indicators, leads one to remember the call for modesty typical of the social etiquette of prior days. One need only refer to CEPAL studies or the UN's Millennium Development Goals to see that our region has made advances that, paradoxically, make our deficiencies even more visible. It's no surprise then that the OECD recommendations include the goal of equity and equality of opportunities.

Meanwhile, whether or not the country manages to become the best educated (as a primary concern of its governing elite), the education policy agenda will experience a flashback resulting from the assessment conducted by the General System of Participation (SGP) by the Comptroller General of the Republic at the end of 2017.[17] The Comptroller informs us that even though the model for transferring assigned resources to finance education and health to the country's departments was changed in 2001, its implementation was postponed till 2008 as the final year of a transition period. Even then, a new constitutional modification (Legislative Act of 2007) further postponed its implementation till 2016. In that year, the Comptroller began an assessment whose results show that, from 2001–2017, regional disparities in resource distribution and usage increased. Thus, in both the case of resource distribution and the Single School Day initiative we can see how policy implementation may be postponed in spite of apparent legal obligations.

It's worth noting that the state presence across all levels of schooling was quite disparate during the 20th century, since its involvement in preschool and secundaria was only comparable by the end of the century to its prevalence in basic primary education in the 1980s and 1990s. These were the years when the foundations were laid for the transformation of institutional mechanisms. By noting this we mean to indicate that even though our arrival at the present moment is the result of the accumulation of a set of prior actions, future outcomes remain indeterminate. It remains to be seen if future studies will be able to determine if a more highly qualified public teaching corps can effectively increase higher educational quality as measured by assessments administered in the education system and linked to participation in international exams. Raising the level of teachers' training will have positive consequences in their remuneration because of the increase in their overall career seniority score. This could allow for indirect assessments of the training received in master's and doctoral degree programs to which teachers will have had access by means of grants through the Teacher Excellence program.

In sum, the central paradox confronting the assemblage of Colombian education policies comes back to the fact that, despite certain signs of progress in education, the levels of social inequality have not only remained but increased, thereby boosting regional, social, and school disparities. In the final analysis, the school—its reforms and it policies—continue to contribute to the reproduction of social inequalities in the manner described for France in the 1970s by Bourdieu and Passeron. In a re-edition of *Reproduction* (1970), the first author reiterated one of his central theses from that research, affirming that the school "… *contributes* to reproducing the distribution of cultural capital, and with that, the structure of the social space" (Bourdieu, 1989, p. 125).

Studying the theory of symbolic violence as it applies to the schooling field enables us to better understand pedagogical action and pedagogical authority, as well as the pedagogical work of teachers in relation to their teaching systems. But studying this theory also contributes to a re-reading of government action (Guevara & Téllez, 2018) with the goal of understanding policies from a standpoint in which socially *configured* resources are doubly enacted (objectively and subjectively): in the end, a double reading for a double construction. Such a reading likewise reintroduces the diachronic dimension with an eye toward establishing the agencies implicated in the construction of social realities through government action; its contribution aims to denaturalize (historicize) the manner in which the purpose, content, and reach of the dominant policy perspective was established (naturalized). Colombia now forms part of the OECD, whose recommendations will thus cease to be indicative and be converted into imperative commands. What will persist is the doubt about whether Colombia can become the best educated in 2025.

Notes

1 This is how it ended up documented in the 2 assessments of education policy conducted by the OECD (2012, 2016).

2 The title of a MEN policy document which contains exactly the same broader government strategy recommendations articulated for 2014–2018. Later the document would be finally titled, "Colombia: The Best Educated."

3 This chapter forms part of Project DPG-456-17 of the National Pedagogical University (UPN). The studies of the Policy Group-UPN are based on a first attempt at translating a relational approach to social research in sociology (Corcuff, 2010), in which the re-reading of certain scholars (e.g., Bourdieu, 1987, 2001, 2002, 2003, 2013)

favors the development of a research methodology in which the construction of objects concurs with the configuration of the theoretical problematic. In a publication still in press (Guevara & Tellez, 2018), we delineate a first version of the accumulated work. This chapter is based on that relational imbrication in which the theoretical problematic enters into tension with a methodology oriented toward establishing links between two moments of governmental action: the diachronic and the synchronic. At the same time, to speak of policies requires us to explain the Colombian education system upon which we can identify the constitutive issues of the corresponding (policy) agenda.

4 (Translator's note) I conserve this awkwardly literal translation of the Spanish municipalizacion to indicate a form of federalist decentralization that attempts to place more decision-making power in the hands of local cities or counties rather than provinces or "departments," as they are called in Colombia. A traditional "federalist" arrangement places considerable power in the hands of the constituent states, or departments; new decentralization policies may try to reduce the power of departmental governors for even greater local control.

5 At this time, we refrain from making any kind of value judgment about the use of the term System to signify the entire set of institutions and resources that constitute Colombian education. It is employed because that is the term used in government policy action. At a later time, we might establish how the aforementioned structuring of education came to be denominated the Colombian Education System. The sources are governmental: https://www.mineducacion.gov.co/1759/w3-article-231235.html; http://www.colombiaaprende.edu.co/html/home/1592/article-235863.html; https://www.mineducacion.gov.co/1759/articles-205294_archivo_pdf

6 https://www.mineducacion.gov.co/1621/article-196477.html

7 The first law was passed on February 11th, 1988, the second on February 15th, 1989. The result of both laws is the restructuring of the National Ministry of Education and the redistribution of responsibilities between and amongst departmental (state) governments and mayoralties.

8 Article 356 of the 1991 Political Constitution had stipulated the distribution of national income and revenue to the departments (entidades territoriales) for the purpose of financing education and healthcare "... in proportion to the number of actual and possible users of these services, and also taking into account the financial capacity and administrative efficiency of each respective territorial entity." In addition, the new law clarified and jointly effected the transfers that had not been put into practice after the 1991 rule, which had stated that the resources should be distributed according to "the population served and to be served, the apportionment between rural and urban populations, fiscal and administrative efficiency, and equity" (MEN, 2010, pp. 29–30).

9 The following ten-year plans corresponded to the decades 2006–2016 and 2016–2026.
10 The scheme of the schools translates into local administration, which has demonstrated the experience and quality in educational and administrative management. https://www.mineducacion.gov.co/cvn/1665/printer-153912.html
11 National Department of Statistics. governmental entity responsible for producing, integrating and arranging statistical information for strategic purposes in the national public administration.
12 Cecilia María Vélez was Bogotá's Secretary of Education from 1998–2000; she continued on as municipal Secretary for the next mayor's administration but was then named National Minister of Education when a new President was elected, 2002–2006. Upon that President's re-election, she served 4 more years in the position, 2006–2010.
13 The Andrés Pastrana government (1998–2002) had 2 ministers, the second serving from 2000 to 2002.
14 A government program begun in 2015 which subsidizes demand by providing grants to low-income students with the best results on university admission exams. Enrollment is financed for students entering any institutionally accredited university regardless of actual cost.
15 Nevertheless, the document lacks a reference section, thus making it impossible to identify thesource that supports the assertion.
16 A recent study by the Comptroller General of the Republic titled "Redistributive effect of results and perspectives in the health and education sectors," published at the end of 2017, indicates the need to review the Education system because of regional disparities accumulated during implementation.
17 The SGP is a legal mechanism, based on Law 60 from 1993, which determines how the school budget is to be distributed. The sense of "Participation" is with regard to which level or instance of government must "participate" in the distribution of their own funds.

References

Aguilar, L. (1992a). *La hechura de las políticas*. México City: Editorial Porrúa.

Aguilar, L. (1992b). *Problemas públicos y agenda de gobierno*. México: Editorial Porrúa.

Bourdieu, P. (1970). *La reproducción*. Mexico City: Fontamara.

Bourdieu, P. (1987). *Cosas dichas*. Buenos Aires: Gedisa.

Bourdieu, P. (1991). *Language and symbolic power* (J. B. Thompson, Ed.; G. Raymond & M. Adamson, Trans.). Cambridge: Polity Press.

Bourdieu, P. (2001a). *Poder, derecho y clases sociales*. Bilbao: Editorial Desclée De Brouwer.

Bourdieu, P. (2001b). *Estructuras sociales de la economía*. Barcelona: Anagrama.

Bourdieu, P. (2001c). *¿Qué significa hablar? Economía de los intercambios lingüísticos*. Madrid: Akal.

Bourdieu, P. (2002). *Razones prácticas*. Barcelona: Anagrama.

Bourdieu, P. (2003). *Cuestiones de sociología*. Madrid: Istmo.

Bourdieu, P. (2013). *La nobleza de Estado*. Buenos Aires: Siglo XXI Editores Argentina.

Contraloría General de la República. (2017). *Sistema general de participaciones. efecto redistributivo de resultados y perspectivas en los sectores de salud y educación*. Retrieved from https://www.contraloria.gov.co/resultados/publicaciones

Corcuff, P. (2015). *Las nuevas sociologías. Principales corrientes y debates, 1980–2010*. Buenos Aires: Siglo XXI Editores Argentina.

Dirección Nacional de Estadística (DANE). (1958). *Anuario general de estadística*. Retrieved from http://www.dane.gov.co

Dirección Nacional de Estadística (DANE). (1968). *Censo general de población*. Retrieved from http://www.dane.gov.co

Dirección Nacional de Estadística (DANE). (1971). *Boletín estadístico número 243*. Retrieved from http://www.dane.gov.co

Dirección Nacional de Estadística (DANE). (1972). *Boletín estadístico número 249*. Retrieved from http://www.dane.gov.co

Dirección Nacional de Estadística (DANE). (1977). *Boletín estadístico número 306*. Retrieved from http://www.dane.gov.co

Departamento Nacional de Planeación (DNP). (1991). *Plan de apertura educativa*. Retrieved from http://www.dnp.gov.co

Departamento Nacional de Planeación (DNP). (2011). Plan Nacional de Desarrollo. 2010–2014. Prosperidad para todos. *Más empleo, menos pobreza y más seguridad*. Retrieved from http://www.dnp.gov.co

Departamento Nacional de Planeación (DNP). (2015). Plan Nacional de Desarrollo 2014–2018. Todos por un nuevo país. *Paz, equidad, educación*.

Departamento Nacional de Planeación (DNP). (n.d.). *Planes nacionales de desarrollo*. Retrieved from https://www.dnp.gov.co/Plan-Nacional-de-Desarrollo/Paginas/Planes-de-Desarrollo-anteriores.aspx

Guevara, R. (2017). *El campo político en universidades públicas latinoamericanas*. Bogotá: Editorial Aula de Humanidades.

Guevara, R. (2014). Institucionalización del predominio privado en la educación superior colombiana. Prefiguraciones del campo de políticas. *Revista Nodos y Nudos, 4*(36), 4–16.

Guevara, R. (2012). *Nominación rectoral y colegios electorales universitarios. Casos: UAM, México. UPN, Colombia* (Doctoral thesis). Universidad Autónoma Metropolitana, Unidad Xochimilco, México.

Guevara, R. (2009). Universidades públicas, autonomía política universitaria y elección de rectores: prefiguración del Campo Político Universitario. *Revista Pedagogía y Saberes, 31*, 69–76.

Guevara, R., & Téllez, S. M. (2018). *Una apuesta situada: la educación superior como objeto de investigación.* Bogotá: Universidad Pedagógica Nacional.

Lucio, R., & Serrano, M. (1992). *La educación superior: Tendencias y políticas estatales.* Bogotá: Universidad Nacional de Colombia.

Ministerio Nacional de Educación (MEN). (2010). Revolución educativa. 2002–2010. *Acciones y lecciones.* Retrieved from https://www.mineducacion.gov.co

Ministerio Nacional de Educación (MEN). (2014). Informe de gestión. 2010–2014. *Educación de calidad: el camino para la prosperidad.* Retrieved from https://www.mineducacion.gov.co

Ministerio Nacional de Educación (MEN). (2015a). Colombia. La mejor educada 2025. *Líneas estratégicas de políticas educativas del MEN.* Retrieved from https://www.mineducacion.gov.co

Ministerio Nacional de Educación (MEN). (2015b). *Colombia. Informe de gestión.* Retrieved from https://www.mineducacion.gov.co

Ministerio Nacional de Educación (MEN). (2017). *Informe al Congreso de la República. 2016–2017.* Retrieved from https://www.mineducacion.gov.co

Organización para la Cooperación y el Desarrollo Económicos (OCDE). (2012). Revisión de políticas nacionales de educación. *La educación superior en Colombia.* Retrieved from https://www.mineducacion.gov.co

Organización para la Cooperación y el Desarrollo Económicos (OCDE). (2016). *Revisión de políticas nacionales de educación.* Retrieved from https://www.mineducacion.gov.co

Rivas, A. (2015). *América Latina después de PISA: Lecciones aprendidas de la educación en siete países (2000–2015).* Retrieved from Retrieved from https://www.cippec.org

Téllez, S. (2013). *Académicos: carrera, trayectoria y libertad. Estudio binacional por contraste: UDFJC (Colombia) – UAM-A (México)* (Doctoral thesis). Universidad Autónoma Metropolitana, Unidad Azcapotzalco, México.

Téllez, S. (2014). La libertad académica vigilada a través del lente de la evaluación: Tensión entre la estructura organizacional y la acción del académico. In R. Ramos (Ed.), *La profesión académica: organización y representaciones sociales en educación superior*. Mexico City: UAM. UABC. UACH.

Téllez, S., & Guevara, R. (2016a). Una relectura de estadísticas sobre la educación superior en Colombia. *Revista de Investigaciones UCM, 16*(28), 42–53.

Téllez, S., & Guevara, R. (2016b). Informe del proyecto DPG-434-16. *Estudios sobre cambio institucional en Universidades Públicas colombianas.*

Téllez, S., & Guevara, R. (2017). *Informe del proyecto DPG-456-17.* Universidades Públicas: Políticas, casos, comparación.

UNESCO. (2001). *Situación educativa de América Latina y el Caribe. 1980–2000.* Retrieved from http://www.unesdoc.unesco.org

CHAPTER 8

Education in El Salvador: Recent Political Economy of Education Policy

D. Brent Edwards Jr.

Abstract

The purpose of this chapter is to summarize and extend previous research on the political economy dynamics of policy implementation in El Salvador, with the focus being on the years from the early 1990s to the mid-2010s. Two goals accompany this purpose. The first is to provide insights that complement and update the limited (analytic) literature on the history and political economy of education policy in El Salvador. The second goal is to derive lessons that may be relevant more broadly, beyond El Salvador, by being attentive to the conditions in which education policies are more or less likely to be implemented. The chapter goes beyond a focus on official reform processes at the national level to examine, as well, the often-invisible role of international organizations and international reform trends—integral as they are to contemporary reform dynamics. In sharing these insights and drawing tentative lessons, I hope that this chapter contributes, first, to the literature on the history of education policy in El Salvador and, second, to the documentation that addresses the ways that policy implementation in a given country is affected by dynamics that span the local, national, and international levels.

1 Introduction

The purpose of this chapter is to summarize and extend previous research on the political economy dynamics of policy implementation in El Salvador, with the focus being on the years from the early 1990s to the mid-2010s. Two goals accompany this purpose. The first is to provide insights that complement and update the limited (analytic) literature on the history and political economy of education policy in El Salvador (e.g., Gillies, 2010; Gomez, 2011; Lindo-Fuentes & Ching, 2012; McGinn & Warwick, 2006; Moncada-Davidson, 1995). The second goal is to derive lessons that may be relevant more broadly, beyond El Salvador, by being attentive to the conditions in which education

 | DOI: 10.1163/9789004413375_009

policies are more or less likely to be implemented. The chapter goes beyond a focus on official reform processes at the national level to examine, as well, the often-invisible role of international organizations and international reform trends—integral as they are to contemporary reform dynamics. In sharing these insights and drawing tentative lessons, I hope that this chapter contributes, first, to the literature on the history of education policy in El Salvador and, second, to the documentation that addresses the ways that policy implementation in a given country is affected by dynamics that span the local, national, and international levels (e.g., Brown, 2014; Steiner-Khamsi & Waldow, 2012; Vavrus & Bartlett, 2009; Verger, Novelli, & Kosar-Altinyelkin, 2018).

Three separate cases are at the center of the analysis presented here. These are, first, the "Education with Community Participation" (EDUCO) program; second, the policy of gender equality in education; and, third, the policy initiative around civic values education. The study focuses on the years 1990–2005. The reason for bounding the study in this way is fundamentally political. Following a decade of civil war, the early 1990s were a time of significant activity in El Salvador related to education policy and politics, and the year 1990 corresponds to the origins of the politics around the EDUCO program. As for the upper bound, 2005 was the year in which the guiding education policy document of the post-war time—i.e., the Ten-Year Plan (1995–2005) (or TYP)—expired; it was also the year that the next education policy (Plan, 2021) of the new presidential administration (which began in 2004) took effect. Thus, the period 1990–2005 saw not only a transition to peace (in 1992) but also represents a period in which El Salvador extensively engaged in education policy reform, with the first significant period of post-war education policy and politics coming to an end by 2005. Overall, the present chapter does not claim to reflect all political economy or reform dynamics during these years, but instead highlights dominant features of this period and provides insights into the experience of three different policies within those dynamics.

As for the dimension of international influence, during 1990–2005, the education sector alone received over $552 million in development assistance and loans from the Inter-American Development Bank (IDB), the United States Agency for International Development (USAID), and the World Bank (Gillies, 2010).[1] This time period thus provides an opportunity to examine various aspects of policy implementation empirically. It allows for consideration of how international organizations and policy trends, as well as developments in the political-economic context during and before the 1990s, initially and subsequently shaped reform possibilities, and with what implications for practice.[2]

The underlying research on which this chapter is based was conducted during 2010–2013 and published in a more extensive form in Edwards, Victoria, and Martin (2015)—an article which also contains more extensive references for the findings shared in this chapter. That research drew on more than 70 interviews as well as a thorough review of policy documents and archives within and beyond El Salvador. While a more detailed discussion of data and methods are in the publication mentioned above, it is worth noting here that I conducted additional interviews in January 2015 with representatives from the education research community, the government, and the World Bank. These interviews serve as the basis for the tentative reflections offered in the epilogue of the present chapter on the political economy dynamics of education reform in El Salvador since the early 2000s, as the Ten-Year Plan was winding down and critical actors were preparing for the next primary education policy document.

2 The Political Economy of Policy Implementation: Analytic Framework

The primary interest here is to understand policy implementation. Following Gillies and colleagues (2010), this research draws on systems thinking, which encourages us to focus on three fundamental and interactive dimensions—those being the technical, the institutional, and the political. The technical dimensions of education refer to those "core elements" which constitute the existence of education reform. They are the building blocks that give life to policy in practice. The institutional dimensions of an education system establish the parameters within which technical elements operate. For this, one must be attentive to the system's institutional framework (i.e., the "existing policies, procedures, norms, incentives, and mental models" that may support or discourage reform), institutional capacity (i.e., the "core ability of [the] organizations" that make up the education system), and resources (financial, material and human)—because together these three aspects of the institutional dimension of education systems "create the incentives (or disincentives) for the effective implementation of technical solutions" (Gillies, 2010, pp. 37–38). Lastly, the political dimension undergirds and permeates the implementation of education system reform. The fundamental issue here is who has a stake in the success (or failure) of reform, and how do they exercise their agency to foster or stifle its realization in practice.

Overall, the utility of this framework is that it is both sensitive as well as comprehensive. That is to say, it enables analysis of many specific factors (technical, institutional, political), while also promoting the identification of overall driving forces, which can "shake up or energize a society, and may facilitate or impede change" (Gillies, 2010, p. 39). However, in identifying the driving forces of change, more emphasis is placed in the present chapter on the international political-economic lens than in Gillies (2010). While Gillies' (2010) framework includes "culture and history," "civil war," "financial crisis," and "national elections" as issues to be considered as part of the context, the research shared here seeks to interpret policy implementation from a structural perspective more explicitly. That means recognizing how—both during and before the 1990s—specific actors as well as broader political economic dynamics within and outside the state (i.e., from the local and international levels) influenced and constrained the actions of the state and even altered the composition of government itself. This additional layer of analysis will allow us to more meaningfully explain the nuances of why certain policies have been more extensively implemented than others in the case of El Salvador during the 1990s and early 2000s. In line with the focus described here, the next section dedicates considerable space to unpacking El Salvador's internal and external contexts during the 1980s.

3 Country Context

While each of the cases discussed in this chapter has its particular characteristics, they all came on the heels of a distinct national and international context at the end of the 1980s and early 1990s. Nationally, the civil war consumed the decade of the 1980s. That struggle was between the Salvadoran government and the Farabundo Martí National Liberation Front (FMLN), an organization of five rebel groups fighting for social and economic opportunities for the poor majorities as well as political participation and access to the justice system. On the education front, during the years of the armed conflict, the government substantially reduced the budget for education, which led to the closing of schools. By 1989, the coverage of primary education reached only 69% of the national demand, and for those who were in school, the repetition rate was 19%, making access and retention two of the most significant challenges of the time.

On an international level, in the context of the Cold War, the U.S. presidential administrations of Carter and Reagan financed the Salvadoran armed forces against the FMLN. In all, by the end of the war, the U.S. government had contributed approximately $6 billion in the form of military aid and economic assistance. Despite such backing, it was not until late 1989, with the election of Alfredo Cristiani as President, that an administration would assume control of the Salvadoran government that was open to those free-market economic policies that the United States preferred. Importantly, in the years before Cristiani's election, due to a lack of support for the preferred economic policies of the United States, USAID established and funded think tanks and NGOs in El Salvador. That was done to create conditions favorable to the goals of the U.S. government, including neoliberal economic reform, strengthening democratic institutions, and stabilizing social problems. Such institutions, along with USAID and the World Bank, would subsequently play essential roles, in particular through their ability to produce reports designed to shape the debate around education policy.

Before proceeding, three issues from the above-described context should be highlighted. First, the conflict shifted from one that was internally-focused to one that was—for reasons of Cold War politics—heavily influenced by United States military and social aid. Second, the United States, through USAID, purposefully worked to strengthen specific Salvadoran business and political groups that it knew would, in turn, support its preferred neoliberal economic policies. Third, in an attempt to ensure acceptance of its organizational preferences, USAID facilitated the creation of new and powerful institutional policy spaces, spaces that would serve to promote credible alternatives to the Duarte administration (of 1984–1989) and public agencies for the development of policy proposals. These are the essential structural conditions that the education sector continued to confront in the 1990s, when the three initiatives investigated here were implemented.

4 Three Cases of Policy Implementation in El Salvador

With the signing of the Peace Accords in January 1992, an official process began which led to the development in 1995 of sector-wide education policy. This three-year process entailed extensive research, dialogue, and collaboration.[3] Moreover, the result—known as the Ten-Year Plan (TYP)—was a document that was intended to guide education reform until 2005. While each of the three policy initiatives investigated was part of that over-arching policy statement, the case descriptions below show that policy implementation in each case was influenced less by official policy and more by the intersection of international involvement with the Salvadoran political economic context and with the technical, institutional and political characteristics of each policy initiative.

5 *Educo* Program

The EDUCO program began in the early 1990s. It was famous for decentralizing the management of education from the central to the community level.

To that end, it formally gave, among other things, the authority for contracting teachers to parents in rural communities. It was among the first programs of its kind and would go on to inspire similar reforms in dozens of countries around the world.[4] Part of EDUCO's appeal, moreover, resulted from its thorough and convincing implementation.

From late 1991 onwards, the EDUCO program was expanded and implemented rapidly and extensively, and it came to serve as the driving force for reform within the Ministry of Education (MINED) during the 1990s. This rapid expansion came after a brief pilot program in early 1991 and was only possible because teachers' unions did not oppose it and because both the MINED and the World Bank came to see that this program aligned with their constraints and priorities. That is, it would help them increase access to education quickly and through a model that would be of interest to other organizations and countries (as further discussed below). Numerically, while the EDUCO program started as a pilot in only six schools in January 1991, at the end of 1994, it already covered 2,316 teachers and 74,112 students. Ten years later, in 2004, these figures had risen to 7,381 and 378,208, respectively.[5] Approximately 55% of rural public schools, which make up two-thirds of all schools in El Salvador, would operate under the EDUCO program. These figures are a consequence of the incredible success that the program experienced—an accomplishment that resulted from the alignment and reinforcement of the technical, institutional, and political dimensions of education reform.

Technical dimension—Technically speaking, the EDUCO program was constituted by a particular set of arrangements that had the community level at the center. To begin with, a group of five parents from each community was elected to form a Community Education Association (in Spanish, *Asociación Comunal para la Educación*, ACE). That was an entity with legal status and charged with contracting and paying (with funds transferred from the MINED to the ACE via bank account) the teacher(s) that would work in their schools. These ACEs were also thought to act as accountability levers that reduced teacher absenteeism and resulted in increased teacher effort in the classroom, especially since teachers hired on one-year contracts may be renewed at the discretion of the ACE. With the funds provided by the MINED, each ACE additionally had the responsibility of purchasing the necessary didactic materials. The MINED, on the other hand, was responsible for the following: facilitating the creation of the ACEs, training the members of the ACEs in administrative and accounting procedures, setting the minimum criteria for teacher selection by the ACEs, designing and providing curricula, and overall coordination, supervision, and monitoring of the program as it was scaled up.[6]

Institutional dimension—Institutionally, the EDUCO program received a significant amount of attention to guarantee that it had a solid foundation. Over time, both the MINED and the World Bank ensured that this program was grounded in an institutional framework, that the necessary leadership capacity was in place, and that adequate resources were dedicated to it. At first, the legal basis of the EDUCO program was provided by a presidential decree in June 1991 that was required by the World Bank as a loan conditionality. This decree established that communities could, in fact, be responsible for contracting teachers. The General Education Law (written with technical support from the World Bank) reinforced their legal basis in 1996, which stated that all schools should be managed through decentralized modalities, and again in 1998 when another presidential decree further specified the procedures and regulations that governed the EDUCO program. Loan documents from the mid-1990s also show that the $11.1 million in technical assistance provided by the World Bank was directed at such issues as "designing a new organizational structure" for the education sector (World Bank, 1995, p. 29). To that end, EDUCO was incorporated gradually into all the MINED's departments, and no longer existed as a separate entity, that is, as an add-on to the central bureaucracy.

Along with legal grounding, creating institutional capacity was also a priority. At first, the core ability of the MINED to pilot and scale up the program was provided by the UNESCO consultant, who became an employee of the MINED and the first coordinator of the EDUCO office, which at first operated independently of the rest of the MINED and directly under the Minister of Education. In 1994, EDUCO's first coordinator trained and handed control over to a Salvadoran counterpart. Doing so facilitated ownership and ensured sustainability as the program continued to be scaled up and finally incorporated into the MINED's formal organizational structure. Yet, before the World Bank would provide a second loan to expand the program, it ensured that that personnel of which it approved were selected and appointed, as indicated in loan documents; in addition, the World Bank dedicated key staff to the project who worked closely with the MINED for 15 years as the EDUCO program was augmented. One interviewee, an ex-Minister of Education who formerly worked in the EDUCO office, affirmed that each of the World Bank's consultants between 1991–2006 was integral to helping the MINED make "good decisions" concerning the design, expansion, and institutionalization of the program. Each of the measures described above was purposefully aimed at making sure that the implementation of the EDUCO program was guided both by international consultants and MINED staff with sufficient capacity.

Lastly, to operationalize EDUCO, immense financial, material and human resources were provided. In financial terms, while the EDUCO pilot began with

$300,000 in funding from UNICEF, loan documents reveal that it subsequently was backed with a series of loans that totaled $69.3 million, primarily from the World Bank and the IDB between 1991 and 2006.[7] Complementing international loans were funds from the government's budget. As the government expanded the education system and increased funding across the board—a requirement of the structural adjustment loans El Salvador had signed with the World Bank—it also augmented financing to the EDUCO program, which it came to see as its primary mechanism for addressing access. By 2001 the MINED provided $45 million in funding each year to sustain the program's recurrent costs.

Not surprisingly, with these funds, the MINED was able to develop both material and human resources. In the mid-to-late 1990s, the MINED not only developed a series of new curricular resources for EDUCO schools, but it also provided training to ACE members throughout the country as well as MINED supervisors, who offered periodic assistance at the school level. EDUCO was a well-resourced program—financially, but also in material and human resource terms.

Political dimension—While President Cristiani and his Minister of Eduaction, Cecilia Gallardo, were both interested in substantial reform of the education system from the outset, the dedication of the UNESCO consultant and the intensity of the technical advisors from the World Bank ensured, together with the structural constraints and the country context, that the reform pursued would align with international trends of the moment. Over time, additional factors served to bolster the political commitment to EDUCO. These factors included not only knowledge within the MINED that EDUCO represented an innovation in which World Bank officials were personally invested but also an awareness that EDUCO was a model that other countries were eager to learn from and emulate.[8] Moreover, a series of positive findings on this program from World Bank evaluations as well as the President's Award for Excellence from this institution in 1997 kept the program in the spotlight and helped to promote the model around the world.[9] Other international organizations such as IDB and UNESCO have since featured EDUCO as a best practice for increasing educational access in a participatory, efficient, and effective manner, despite questionable evidence, as further discussed later. In the words of one former MINED employee, encouraging feedback and persistent attention of this nature from the program's beginnings made it clear that—in political terms—"EDUCO was the goose that laid the golden egg." MINED personnel knew that EDUCO was not only going to make El Salvador an exemplar for other countries to follow, but it would also lead to the individual success of those associated with its development.

In the end, one sees how, in a particular historical context, a cycle in which focused and unwavering support from international donors for a specific strategy led to heightened political commitment at the national level. That produced well-resourced experimentation and extensive implementation, which resulted in positive evaluation and additional international interest, which reinforced national commitment, both politically and financially. That then further encouraged implementation, and so on.

Ultimately, concerning EDUCO, if one thing is clear, it is that this program, even before it entered the TYP as official national education policy, received both the political backing and economic and technical resources necessary to ensure its' implementation and institutional longevity. These features of the EDUCO case set it apart from both gender policy and values education in El Salvador.

6 Gender Equality Policy

In the early 90s, the need to address gender inequality in El Salvador was obvious. For example, while 25% of men over the age of 14 had never studied in school, 30% of women were in that situation. Moreover, at the primary level, reports showed that there was a difference of enrolment between girls and boys of up to 11%. Similar circumstances existed at the secondary and university levels. Against this backdrop, efforts were made throughout the 1990s at developing and implementing a gender policy which would address equality. The process of forming the first National Women's Policy was a long and slow one with origins in the early 1990s (and prior) in which international commitments (e.g., at the Fourth World Conference on Women in 1995) played a key role as local women's groups, national NGOs, and governmental institutions engaged with the issue of gender equality. While there were multiple milestones along the way to a formal policy, for this chapter, it is most relevant to note that the aforementioned efforts and commitments led, first, to the creation in 1996 of the Salvadoran Institute for the Development of Women (or ISDEMU, for its acronym in Spanish) and, second, to the National Women's Policy (NWP) in 1997.

Regarding implementation, this case shows how a lack of systematic efforts, combined with other factors, failed to operationalize that policy fully. Despite the collaborative manner in which the NWP was born, the official reports of neither the MINED nor ISDEMU show that there was a systematic, committed implementation of the gender equality policy. These institutions only carried out isolated and generic activities, which often did not correspond to the original objectives. Technical, institutional and political terms explain the lack of successful implementation.

Technical dimension—The NWP called for many things concerning education. These included: Research on guaranteeing equal opportunities for men and women; increasing women's and girls' access to formal and non-formal education; implementing training programs that modify discriminatory practices in educational settings; and revising national curricula to promote principles of equal opportunities for men and women at all educational levels.

The NWP was converted to practice in education through an assortment of disconnected activities. On the part of ISDEMU, according to their 1998 report, these activities included (a) five projects on gender inequality, trainings, and workshops on a range of gender-related issues for 1,258 participants plus 100% of MINED technical staff, as well as (b) a review of curricular materials in education—funded by USAID and IDB—in order to eliminate gender bias. More generally, though ISDEMU's reports found that there was broader access to literacy and primary education for girls during this period, the annual reports of the MINED from 1997 to 1999 not only failed to mention specific actions that it carried out related to gender equality, but also failed even to acknowledge the existence of the NWP.

From 2000–2004, gender-related activities improved somewhat, due to the many actions that were taken. Concretely, the MINED did the following: (1) Recognized the NWP in their annual reports, (2) provided awareness training on discriminatory practices to teachers and technical staff, (3) hosted talks on gender equality, (4) created 5,000 methodological guides on gender for educators, (5) funded non-sexist literature projects with a local women's NGO, (6) opened an office to receive reports and set norms on sexual abuse in schools and discrimination against pregnant students, and, lastly, through the support and requirements of the European Economic Community's technical and financial aid, (7) incorporated gender issues into both the literacy and secondary technical education curriculum. Clearly, and encouragingly, the number of gender-related activities increased over time; what did not change, however, was the sporadic and isolated nature of them, a feature that partially resulted from the institutional context of the gender equality policy.

Institutional dimension—Institutionally, while there was a defined framework within which the NWP was to operate, this structure was not without its initial problems. For instance, though ISDEMU was an entity that was intended to work with NGOs and across all public ministries, including the MINED, the institutional arrangement was a complex one that diluted and hindered ISDEMU's ability to stimulate actions within each ministry. This situation was addressed in 2000 when the Minister of Education finally formed a follow-up commission comprised of representatives from across the MINED's offices to ensure that the NWP was incorporated into the annual planning processes of the MINED. A second step taken by the MINED that gave the NWP institutional backing was the creation of a new "Education for Life" unit within the central ministry's offices, which was responsible for issues related to gender equality and sexuality, among other things. The director of this unit served as an additional link with the ISDEMU and provided updates on how the MINED was handling the NWP's educational aspects. The design of the institutional framework of the gender equality policy—though complex and diffuse—was thus strengthened over time.

The same cannot be said for institutional capacity. That is, while there existed technical expertise on gender issues within the MINED in the 1980s—thanks to a massive gender-sensitive, educational program during 1982 related to population growth and funded by the United Nations—by the 1990s, "those specialists who worked with this program had been transferred to other positions, due in large part to the indifference of mid-level MINED managers," as one interviewee from the MINED affirmed. Subsequently, by the time the NWP started, the MINED's technical capacity for gender issues had either been dispersed or assigned other responsibilities. Technical expertise was neither available nor developed within the MINED to mainstream gender in educational planning and priorities.[10] In part, this was because its implementation did not entail the participation of civil society, as did the writing of the NWP. The inter-institutional commission formed within the MINED was composed of only MINED representatives in the early years.

Insufficient, inconsistent, and unsustainable financing similarly confounded the realization of the NWP, beyond short-term projects, training and fringe aspects of the curriculum. Funding for gender in education flowed primarily from international sources, such as USAID, the Spanish Agency for International Cooperation and Development, and the European Economic Community. Moreover, it was directed to specific projects and not complemented by the government's funds. A prime example is the $32.6 million in funding provided by IDB and the World Bank, a small portion of which went to revising school curricula to remove, among other things, gender biased content. Not surprisingly, these projects operated as islands of privilege that enjoyed—due to the resources and clout of the sponsoring international organizations—not only funding but also technical know-how, institutional capacity, and political support from Salvadoran officials.

Political dimension—Difficulties in planning and resources reflect a lack of commitment from principal political and institutional actors to the topic, particularly given the numerous simultaneous reforms the MINED was tackling during the 1990s and early 2000s. As the World Bank (1996) noted, "motivation to take actions on the gender issue in the face of constraints and other competing demands ... is often lacking" (p. 51). On the other hand, the political backing was not forthcoming during the 2000s due to the religious affiliation of some mid- and upper-level MINED officials who were not interested in ideas of gender equality because they conflicted with the conservative gender roles supported by the Catholic Church, to which they belonged. In the end, the Millennium Development Goals of 2000 did succeed in raising the profile of gender equality as a priority and did generate some fresh actions on the part of the MINED. Still, the issue of gender never became a central concept or focus for education reform (either generally or for the national curriculum) behind which either the Minister of Education or other high-level officials in the MINED threw their weight. One thus sees how reform pressure and initiatives from the local and international levels can be complicated by the disposition of crucial MINED actors, for whom, in this case, the success of the gender policy would not impact their career because it was not seen as vital by the government, not the way that EDUCO was.

7 Values Education

In the post-civil war context, values education became a central focus for many actors because they saw it as a way to consolidate peace and strengthen democracy in El Salvador. Indeed, during 1991–1995, multiple programs and forums were developed by various international organizations that focused on education for democratic citizenship (USAID), tolerance and solidarity (the German Agency for Technical Cooperation), and education for a culture of peace (UNESCO). As will be discussed, these efforts largely preceded or diverged from official policy, as embodied in the Ten-Year Plan, which called for the "teaching of human, ethical, and civic values" (MINED, 1995, p. 11). The level and style of implementation that values education policy experienced reflected the variegated way in which education sector stakeholders had individually approached it. It was implemented intermittently, with the assistance of external organizations, and in a way which showed that it was an ad hoc policy that did not represent a high national priority.

Technical dimension—A series of isolated and minimal actions taken in the late 1990s constitute the extent to which the values policy of the government was enacted in practice. To be specific, in 1997, a series of instructional guides for basic education were developed, distributed to teachers, and intended to provide ideas for how teachers could incorporate values education—i.e., a focus on "good habits" and "acting with responsibility"—into the traditional subjects (MINED, 1999, p. 102). The year 1998 was then declared by the MINED to be the "Year of Values." A calendar was developed, with each week dedicated to highlighting a different humanistic (e.g., friendship), ethical (e.g., truth) or civic (e.g., democratic participation) value. The same was done again in 1999, except this time the year was dedicated to solidarity and each month honored a separate value (e.g., family, honesty, human rights).

Apart from the efforts of the MINED, both major newspapers in El Salvador—*El Diario de Hoy* and *La Prensa Gráfica*—contributed in 1998 to bringing attention to the issue of values. *El Diario de Hoy* did this by creating for children a weekly section titled "Learning Human and Civic Values" (MINED, 1999, p. 104). *La Prensa Gráfica*, on the other hand, called on students to write essays on peace, democracy, and liberty; to create values-related murals; and to develop a community project which would require teachers, students and parents to work together.

Thus, in practice, the substance of the policy was scant, and the most significant aspects were arguably not sponsored by the MINED, but rather by national newspapers. Seen in this light, it is understandable that, in the year 2000 and beyond, documents continued to call for and to propose the development of specific programs that would respond to the intentions initially established in the MINED's Ten-Year Plan of 1995. To that end, over the duration of the TYP, "political discourse appropriated the concepts related to a culture of peace, but the practice of these concepts was never realized" (Gómez, 2012, p. 113). This was due—at least in part—to a lack of institutional resources.

Institutional dimension—The implementation of education policies cannot, of course, occur without a clear framework, adequate capacity and sufficient resources—all of which were lacking regarding the development of the MINED's values education policy. That is not to say, however, that no structures existed. For example, the Salvadoran government created in 1995 an inter-institutional commission to coordinate all entities in the execution of the UNESCO-funded Culture of Peace program. Participants apart from the MINED with a stake in education reform generally and values education specifically included: the National Coordination Council, the Executive Committee, the Technical Committee for Projects, the NGO Consortium Committee, and the National Commission on Preschool Education. Thus, the problem was not a lack of structures, but rather an over-abundance of them, and the fact that unambiguous lines of responsibility for developing and implementing values education activities never were established.

With everyone and no one in charge of values education, the incentive to develop capacity within the MINED did not exist. As a result, the issue of values education was broached only once during teacher training—as part of professional development in 1998 (MINED, 1999). The only other instance of capacity building—made possible in 1998 with USAID funding and attended by teachers and MINED officials and specialists from multiple levels—was a one-day national conference on the relationship between preschool education and the teaching of humanistic, ethical and civic values.

A shortage of resources was another recurring issue. There is no evidence that the MINED dedicated funds to implementing values education, apart from those required to develop related instructional guides, create calendars, and include the theme as one element among many in professional development during 1998. Although UNESCO offered in 1994 to invest $32 million in programs and projects related to realizing a culture of peace, in the absence of specific proposals from NGOs and the government, these funds went untapped. Of course, the lack of specific proposals at that time stemmed from political dynamics during the late 1990s and early 2000s.

Political dimension—While the idea of values education was of interest to multiple actors of crucial importance to El Salvador's education reform, the political commitment required did not materialize to ensure that this policy affected practice in a meaningful way. Put differently, values education, in addition to lacking a coherent institutional framework, also suffered from the absence of political will.

UNESCO's representative to El Salvador tried to combat this situation. After helping to organize the National Forum on Education for a Culture of Peace, Francisco Lacayo gave a series of talks during 1994–1995 in which he encouraged the Salvadoran government to design specific—and sustainable—programs and indicators that UNESCO could support and that the government could monitor to promote a culture of peace. Politically, however, neither these suggestions nor other efforts at developing values education gained traction.

That was for four reasons. The first is that, concerning UNESCO's culture of peace program, the initiative did not have a single institutional home with a director that cared to shepherd it. The second is that the approaches to values education between UNESCO and the government did not align well. The third reason, as Gómez (2012) explains, is simply that the political will of the Minister of Education mainly was dedicated to other policies and programs, i.e., EDUCO and the overall "modernization" of the MINED. Finally, from 1999–2004, an additional political obstacle was the personal—and conservative—religious orientation of crucial MINED officials, who were more comfortable with teaching about values from the perspective of (Catholic) morality, rather than from the perspective of the active, engaged, and democratic citizen.

8 Cross-Case Discussion: Policy Implementation within Political Economy Constraints

Regarding Gillies' (2010) framework, the technical dimension of policy implementation links closely with the institutional and political dimensions. However, as has been shown in the case of El Salvador during the 1990s, policy implementation is also affected by how these latter dimensions interact and intersect with international trends and with the structural constraints of the state over time. The degree to which each of these aspects aligns—or doesn't—thus impacts the extent to which policies are broadly and/or thoroughly implemented according to their technical dimensions, as specified in the policy. The implication is that it is not only actors and ideas from the international realm that impact national-level political and institutional dynamics, but also that national-level political preferences and other local-level constraints can facilitate or impede the selection and implementation of a policy's technical elements. The cases presented here have provided multiple examples of how these elements combine, and with various consequences for implementation.

In many ways, the case of EDUCO represents the perfect storm. First, at the time when the government's attention began to shift to education reform (i.e., the late 1980s and early 1990s), international trends were focused on the ideas of participation and decentralization in development. Second, because of structural changes to the political-economic context during the 1980s, key functionaries of the government were predisposed to being open to the dominant—i.e., neoliberal—conception of these ideas. That is, thanks to the machinations of the US government (often through USAID), new organizations were incubated in El Salvador that—both—hosted actors who were sympathetic to the international political-economic reform agenda of the United States and also promoted their activities and channeled these actors into the government when the right-wing party secured the presidency in 1989. In this way, the Salvadoran government became one which, by the late 1980s, was oriented towards the neoliberal reform agenda emanating from Washington and strategic international organizations and actors, such as the World Bank, USAID, and the Chicago Boys (i.e., U.S.-trained economists from Chile).

With the above in mind, one sees how these international currents and structural developments also impacted the MINED and how it approached education system reform. Put differently; one sees that the structural events experienced by the Salvadoran state during the 1980s opened vital spaces in which the dominant international trends could circulate. The implication, in terms of Gillies' (2010) framework, is that the structural developments facilitated by the international actors impacted the political dimension within the education sector by reducing the range of acceptable options that key political figures (such as the Minister of Education) could choose, and by incentivizing the adoption of reforms that resonated with international trends. Stated simply: Major education reform in El Salvador in the early 1990s was being financed by USAID and by the World Bank, and, thus, if President Cristiani or Minister Gallardo wanted to have any success with their reform initiatives, they would have to select options that aligned with these institutions' preferences. That is how mutually-beneficial political buy-in from crucial governmental actors at the national level emerged in the case of EDUCO.

With this alignment of international trends, structural constraints, and political buy-in, the institutional dimension of the EDUCO reform was not in jeopardy. Over time, the Minister of Education, the World Bank, and others ensured that this program had a solid legal grounding, ample financial resources, and consistent technical support. Seen from this perspective, EDUCO's extensive implementation in practice is an outcome that should be expected.

The case of gender equality policy provides alternative lessons, which received support in certain areas but not others. For example, while gender equality policy benefitted from grassroots-level pressure in addition to high-profile international conferences and the inclusion of gender in such global agendas as Education For All, this policy lacked the necessary political backing from actors in the MINED. This absence of support from political players who are responsible for guiding reform at the national level was a central challenge in the creation of a focused and functioning institutional framework. In large part, the implication in practice was that international organizations interested in the gender theme directed their resources to specific projects or particular actions. The MINED, for its part, eventually acknowledged the NWP and minimally contributed to the operation of ISDEMU (the entity charged with working across government ministries on gender issues) and to the development of its internal institutional supports. However, in the end, though multiple education-related aspects of the gender equality policy (as embodied in the NWP) were carried out over the course of a few years, it was not the case that these provisions of the NWP consistently or thoroughly were implemented.

The above finding is to be expected when one considers that—beyond the absence of political and institutional footing—the structural context of the time did not advance the cause of gender equality. Recall that the dominant political-economic relations in which the Salvadoran government was involved in the 1990s focused on the improvement of democratic processes and the reform of economic and social policy along neoliberal lines. Gender equality policy thus found itself in an uphill battle for attention at a moment when the majority of the MINED's energy was funneled into EDUCO, which, unlike the gender policy, meshed with the over-arching reform principles that guided the government's actions. In such a situation, the findings suggest, internationally-popular reform ideas and resources from international actors can help to place issues on the agenda—and can even encourage the development of policy. But they cannot overcome either a lack of policy will on the part of governmental actors or a structural context that is slanted towards the realization of alternative policy goals.

Unlike the EDUCO and gender cases, there was not a particular international trend or a subset of over-arching concepts (e.g., participation, decentralization) that dominated the conversation around values education. And to an even greater extent than with the gender equality policy, values education was marginalized concerning the attention and priority they were given in that there was no consensus among international organizations regarding the focus of values education.

Each of the principal global actors involved (the German Agency for Technical Cooperation, UNESCO, USAID) in values education programs and policies had a different perspective. Yet one might expect that USAID, as a dominant actor operating from a Cold War mindset, would have attempted in the early 1990s to ensure that a focus on democratic values would prevail in education policy and curriculum. That was not the case. Robinson (1996) suggests one reason for this: Though USAID took steps during this time to fund isolated projects related to the teaching of democratic values, the focus of USAID, as an entity that advances US foreign policy, was centered on the development of democracy, but only insofar as this institution saw democracy—and the promotion of select national actors—as a means of assuring the implementation of the preferred economic policies of the United States in a stable political context. Relatedly, the evidence collected shows that education in democratic values was, for USAID, a programmatic add-on, something that received minimal attention in practice. Likewise, the German Agency for Technical Cooperation and UNESCO—neither of which had the resources or gravity of USAID—worked on their narrow values-related projects, each with a different focus.

Furthermore, and importantly, governmental actors had their own conception of values education. In the end, as was discussed, those political actors involved in the making of the Ten-Year Plan of 1995 (where the policy around values appeared) preferred to couch the teaching of values in human, ethical and civic terms. Add to this situation the fact that values education also lacked—both—the push at the grass-roots level that gender equality policy had and the system of community-level self-management that predated

EDUCO, and it becomes clearer why the values education policy floundered in practice the way that it did.

Finally, one can consider how the MINED's shortage of funds, capacity, and attention (given competing demands on time and energy) limited policy implementation. Though the MINED was the one to elaborate the values education policy, it could not, on its own, assign the resources or create the institutional arrangements necessary to move beyond a superficial operationalization of the policy. This is thus an example of how the technical aspects of policy will not be implemented without the necessary political will or institutional resources.

On the whole, then, the experience of values education policy is the reverse of the gender equality policy. In the past, national political preferences were reflected in the policy, but the policy did not, in turn, match the preferences of international actors or the dominant issues at the heart of the education reform efforts in El Salvador. As a consequence of the above, values education policy was the least prevalent and least extensively implemented policy of the three discussed.

9 Implications

In taking a further step back, the findings of the case studies lend themselves to the elaboration of three hypotheses regarding how the elements of interest here interact and, in so doing, impact policy implementation. The postulations offered here correspond, in order, to the cases presented in this chapter.

- Extensive implementation: Policy implementation will be extensive when there is alignment among international trends, structural constraints (both at the local level and concerning global political-economic relationships), and policymaker preferences. This is so because, in these conditions, it is highly likely that adequate and appropriate institutional frameworks, arrangements, capacity, and resources will be provided by involved and interested national and international actors.
- Moderate implementation: A policy's technical aspects will be moderately (and perhaps disjointedly) applied when global trends and international organizations are in favor of the strategy in question but where the reform context and governmental policy actor interests are directed towards the realization of other plans. In this case, international organizations finance isolated actions and local actors continue pushing their agenda (and perhaps put into practice programs that mesh with their prerogatives). Implementation of official policy will only occur insofar as interested international

actors secure approval from the necessary government officials (e.g., in the MINED) and then dedicate financial resources and technical specialists with know-how.

- Minimal implementation: This level of execution will result when there is no clear international trend, an unfavorable structural context (i.e., the gravity of the reform environment is moving towards other ends), and a policy focus on the part of politicians and essential governmental functionaries that does not align with the interests of those international actors that would otherwise provide a range of institutional supports. With each dimension of the context pulling in a separate direction, involved actors implement programs and take actions that align with their preferences. In this way, practice is marginally impacted, and not necessarily in line with the content of official policy.

Future studies should further investigate the propositions presented here, with the goal being to "develop generalizable frameworks that can account for relationships between context and outcomes" (Rhoten, 2000, p. 616).

10 Conclusion

While this study deals with the issue of international influence, it has shown that such encouragement is not alone in determining policy outcomes. That is an essential contribution since at times scholars are quick to ascribe significant powers to certain international organizations. As has been shown, although international actors and ideas can be very impactful, their influence is heightened or reduced depending on both the structural constraints of the reform context and the predilections of crucial governmental policy actors.

Of course, as has also been shown, developments in the underlying political-economic context can themselves affect the preferences of state officials and the nature of the spaces in and through which the technical aspects of reform are elaborated. In other words, political-economic developments can help to tilt in one direction or another the environment in which the formation and implementation of policy occur. That is an important observation because it implies that looking at policymaking and implementation at a given point in time cannot be fully understood without incorporating two points into the analysis: First, how constraints upon a particular country have changed over time and, second, the way that the state (or the institutions that make up the government) was altered or otherwise reconstituted over the course of many years (e.g., through the influence of particularly powerful international actors and/or other political-economic forces). To that end, the findings of the present chapter should be extended by comparing them with the conclusions of other literature on the historical contexts of education policymaking in El Salvador and Central America more broadly (Edwards, 2018c).

11 Epilogue: Education Policy Dynamics Since the Early 2000s

An additional way to extend the insights of the present chapter is to comment on more recent years. Since the early 2000s, the making, funding, and implementation of education policy has continued to be characterized by "policy negotiation," in that it reflects a mix of international and national priorities, constraints, and resources (Edwards, 2013). That has been true of both Plan 2021, the over-arching policy document developed for the presidential administration of Antonio Saca (2004–2009), as well as for the more recent Social Education Plan, designed for the administration of Mauricio Funes (2009–2014). In the former, the priorities of USAID and the World Bank—related, respectively, to financing for educational equity and the extension of compulsory schooling to 11 grades—were included alongside the many other priorities of the government, which related, for example, to introducing alternative delivery models and to enhancing the competitiveness of the education system by creating programs for the introduction of science and technology in schools and English language learning, among other strategies.

In the case of the Social Education Plan, interviewees comment that the incoming Minister of Education adapted ideas from Italy and Uruguay that informed the model of "Fulltime Inclusive Schools." The government has experimented more recently with this approach as one prong of its strategy to make schools more inclusive, to place schools at the center of culture, and to extend school hours for extracurricular activities. While Edwards, Martin, and Flores (2017) provide further discussion, it bears mentioning here that this model of Fulltime Inclusive Schools came in the wake of an essential structural development in El Salvador that had significant implications for education governance. That is, this model, which seeks to bring together students, families, and schools in a collaborative fashion (as opposed to a model based on accountability, as in the case of EDUCO) became the focus of education governance once the EDUCO program was phased out (starting in 2009; see Edwards, 2018c, for more). The elimination of the EDUCO program was a development which occurred thanks to a campaign promise made to teachers' unions during the lead-up to the election in 2009 of the first president from the left-wing FMLN party, following 20 years of presidents from El Salvador's most prominent right-wing party.

As with the 1990s, education policies since the early 2000s operate through programs, and they depend on funding. International organizations have continued their trend of subsidizing individual programs that align with their missions and priorities. A few of the many possible examples include USAID backing programs related to job skills, employment, and children at risk; UNESCO providing resources for orphaned children; UNICEF supporting the revision of early childhood curriculum; and the World Bank supporting the development of education standards, standardized testing, and the publication of educational indicators, among other things, for the Fulltime Inclusive Schools. For its part, the government has had some successes with implementing programs independently, as with the recent programs (a) to provide free school snacks to 1 million students to improve nutrition and to remove barriers to student retention (at a cost of $5.6 million) and (b) to provide uniforms, shoes, books and supplies to all students in order to encourage access and retention (via an investment of $80 million). In at least one circumstance, the government has used World Bank funds to further its interests, as in the case of in-service teacher training, which has consistently been raised as a critical issue since 2014 by the Minister of Education.

At times, though, the government faces challenges in the implementation of its plans. That has been true with what is perhaps its most significant recent initiative, associated with the Social Education Plan. To give form to the ideals of this Plan, the MINED commenced an "Integrated Systems" approach to accompany its emphasis on "Fulltime Inclusive Schools."[11] The integrated system aspect is embodied in practice through the creation of networks of up to 10 schools in close geographical proximity, to facilitate the sharing of materials and human resources. Though it is not always apparent at each level of the education system how the various ideals of this model are to be woven together in practice, the notion of fulltime inclusive schools should ideally be reflected in three crucial features. These are, first, expanded services beyond general curriculum topics (e.g., sports and recreation, music, arts, science, and technology—delivered through additional hours of schooling and in hopes of reducing violence) and, second, more participation of local sectors (e.g., community members, local business owners, churches, NGOs) in the life of the school as a way to enhance social cohesion, respond to local needs, strengthen governance, improve quality, and (unofficially) raise additional resources from the local level, a necessity given the expense of the model

Despite the lack of clarity, this model of Integrated Systems of Fulltime Inclusive Schools began in 2011 with 22 schools, then expanded to 38 schools in 2012, with technical assistance and funding from Italy, World Bank, and USAID. By mid-2015, 259 Integrated Systems were created and benefited 2,082 schools in 92 towns. Initial plans proposed placing all schools into integrated systems by 2019 with an investment of US $98.47 million from the World Bank together with Italian cooperation, USAID, and Salvadoran government funds, but the strategic education plan for the 2014–2019 period of government, while including the Fulltime Inclusive School strategy, does not even mention the Integrated System model. It seems that the government dropped the integrated systems approach before the effects or successes of the program were known. Although additional investigation is necessary, initial insights suggest that three factors caused the downfall of this ambitious model. First, the organizational and legal complexity of it in practice (mainly related to control at the school level over sharing resources). Second, the prohibitive cost for the government of additional services and support that it requires. And third, the impracticality of student mobility among schools in the clusters due to the dangers of crossing gang territory. Thus, although a number of international organizations were willing to contribute funds and assistance, the problem is that, while the interests momentarily aligned among the MINED and the donors, it does not seem that there has been sufficient political will to raise or to invest the public funds necessary to support the scaling up of this program. It also has not been possible to resolve the dominant issue of gang violence. Concerning the framework of this chapter, the limitation is not only financial and political in nature, but also relates to the broader social context.

In closing, I address essential relationships and structural constraints. More recently, since the transition to two consecutive FMLN presidential administrations in 2009, the government has asserted its leadership through the "donor roundtable," through which it seeks donor collaboration on its priorities, but this seems to be a matter of style rather than a substantive difference in the locus of control. The roundtable existed previously, but international organizations could work directly with the MINED, and it is reported that previous MINED leaders preferred it that way, whereas now the government prefers to coordinate international organizations through the Ministry of External Relations, which runs the donor roundtable. Nevertheless, cooperation is still a negotiation between national priorities and the main concerns of donors, as it was in the early 1990s, before the end of the civil war. And even though the MINED and the national government are not in the dire situation that they were in at that time, the fact is still that the MINED relies on external financing and donations for many reforms, since it cannot fund all that it would like to (Edwards, Martin, & Flores, 2017). As such, the MINED may have ideas for reform and may be able to garner international support for them, but challenges remain when it comes to mobilizing sufficient political and economic support for reforms that entail significant investments or radical departures from current practice.

Notes

1 In comparison, consider that the total budget for education in 1992 was approximately USD$109 million (MINED, 1994).
2 While the present research is primarily concerned with policy implementation, previous research has focused exclusively on international influence in the process of policy formation for the three initiatives examined here (e.g., Edwards, 2013, 2017; Edwards, Martin, & Victoria, 2015).
3 See Edwards (2018c) and Edwards, Martin, and Victoria (2015) for more on this three-year process.
4 For more on the origins and subsequent trajectory of this policy, see Edwards (2018c).
5 While the EDUCO program was initially only intended as a strategy to provide education at the preschool level and in grades 1–3, it was subsequently expanded in 1994 to cover through grade 6 and then again in 1997 to cover through grade 9. After 2005, even some high schools became EDUCO schools.
6 For additional details on the technical aspects of the EDUCO program, see Edwards (2018c).
7 This sum was particularly influential given that 96% of the MINED's budget went to teachers' salaries in the early 1990s.
8 As other research has shown (Edwards, 2013), it has been important to MINED officials in El Salvador to know that the reforms implemented resonate with international experts and international experience.
9 Edwards (2016) and Edwards and Loucel (2016) provide critical discussions of these evaluations. Edwards (2018a) reviews non-World Bank studies of the EDUCO experience at the sub-national and community level and reveals problematic and detrimental aspects of its operation in practice.
10 Gender mainstreaming means the creation of equal opportunities for men and women in public policy.
11 This and the following paragraph are adapted from Edwards, Martin, and Flores (2017).

References

Brown, C. (Ed.). (2014). *Globalisation, international education policy & local policy formation: Voices from the developing world.* New York, NY: Springer.

Edwards Jr., D. B. (2013). International processes of education policy formation: An analytic framework and the case of Plan 2021 in El Salvador. *Comparative Education Review, 57*(1), 22–53.

Edwards Jr., D. B. (2016). A perfect storm: The political economy of community-based management, teacher accountability, and impact evaluations in El Salvador and the global reform agenda. In W. Smith (Ed.), *Global testing culture: Shaping education policy, perceptions, and practice. Oxford Studies in Comparative Education* (pp. 25–42). Oxford: Symposium.

Edwards Jr., D. B. (2017). Policy formation in the context of global governance: Rational, organizational, and political perspectives on policymaking in El Salvador. *International Journal of Educational Development, 52*, 81–96.

Edwards Jr., D. B. (2018a). Accountability through community-based management? Implications from the local level implementation in El Salvador of a globally-popular model. In K. A. Heidemann & R. A. Clothey (Eds.), *Another way: Decentralization, democratization, and the global politics of community-based schooling* (pp. 44–60). Rotterdam, The Netherlands: Sense Publishers.

Edwards Jr., D. B. (2018b, March 25–29). *Education in Central America: Trends, tensions, and trade-offs*. Paper presented on a "presidential session" at the conference of the Comparative and International Education Society, Mexico City.

Edwards Jr., D. B. (2018c). *The trajectory of global education policy: Community-based management in El Salvador and the global reform agenda*. New York, NY: Palgrave MacMillan.

Edwards Jr., D. B., & Loucel, C. (2016). The EDUCO program: Impact evaluations, and the political economy of global education reform, Education. *Policy Analysis Archives, 24*(49), 150.

Edwards Jr., D. B., Martin, P., & Flores, I. (2017). El Salvador: Past, present and prospects of educations. In C. M. Posner, C. Martin, & Y. Martin (Eds.), *Education in México, Central America and the Latin Caribbean* (pp. 141–168). New York, NY: Continuum.

Edwards Jr., D. B., Martin, P., & Flores, I. (forthcoming). Teacher education in El Salvador: Politics, policy, pitfalls. In C. Wolhuter (Ed.), *International handbook of teacher education* (2nd ed.). Athens: Atrapos.

Edwards Jr., D. B., Martin, P., & Victoria, J. A. (2015). Different policies, distinct processes: Three case studies of international influence in education policy formation in El Salvador. In C. Brown (Ed.), *Globalisation, international education policy & local policy formation: Voices from the developing world* (pp. 39–58). New York, NY: Springer.

Edwards Jr., D. B., Victoria, J. A., & Martin, P. (2015). The geometry of policy implementation: Lessons from the political economy of three education reforms in El Salvador during 1990–2005. *International Journal of Educational Development, 44*, 28–41.

Gillies, J. (Ed.). (2010). *Education system reform and aid effectiveness: The power of persistence* (USAID and Equip 2). Retrieved from http://www.equip123.net/docs/E2-Power_of_Persistence.pdf

Gómez, A. (2011). Una genealogía de la educación en El Salvador. *Revista Latinoamericana de Estudios Educativos, XLI*(3–4), 73–117.

Gómez, A. (2012). Educación para la paz en el sistema educativo de El Salvador. *Ra-Ximhai, 8*(2), 93–126.

Lindo-Fuentes, H., & Ching, E. (2012). *Modernizing minds in El Salvador: Education reform and the Cold War, 1960–1980*. Albuquerque: University of New Mexico Press.

McGinn, N., & Warwick, D. (2006). La planeación educativa: ¿Ciencia o política?, *Revista Latinoamericana de Estudios Educativos, XXXVI*(1–2), 153–182.

MINED. (1994). *Memoria institucional: Periodo junio de 1989-junio de 1994*. San Salvador. MINED.

MINED. (1995). *Lineamientos generales del Plan Decenal*, 1995–2005. San Salvador: MINED.

MINED. (1999). *En el camino de la transformación educativo de El Salvador*. San Salvador: MINED.

Moncada-Davidson, L. (1995). Education and its limitations in the maintenance of peace in El Salvador. *Comparative Education Review, 39*(1), 54–75.

Rhoten, D. (2000). Education decentralization in Argentina: A 'global-local conditions of possibility' approach to state, market, and society change, *Journal of Education Policy, 15*(6), 593–619.

Robinson, W. (1996). *Promoting Polyarchy: Globalization, US intervention, and hegemony*. New York, NY: Cambridge.

Steiner-Khamsi, G., & Waldow, F. (2012). *World yearbook of education 2012: Policy borrowing and lending*. New York, NY: Routledge.

Vavrus, F., & Bartlett, L. (Eds.). (2009). *Critical approaches to comparative education: Vertical case studies from Africa, Europe, the Middle East, and the Americas*. New York, NY: Palgrave MacMillan.

Verger, A., Novelli, M., & Kosar-Altinyelkin, H. (Eds.). (2018). *Global education policy and international development: New agendas, issues and policies*. New York, NY: Bloomsbury.

World Bank. (1995). *El Salvador: Basic Education Modernization Project: Staff appraisal report*. Washington, DC: World Bank.

World Bank. (1996). *El Salvador: Moving to a gender approach: Issues and recommendations*. Washington, DC: World Bank.

CHAPTER 9

Education and Teacher Education in Cuba: Revolución and Perfeccionamiento

Mark Ginsburg and Gilberto Garcia Batista

Abstract

This chapter examines the reforms of education and teacher education in Cuba during different historical periods, seeking to document as well as explain the occurrence of such reforms giving attention to both national and global economic, cultural, and political dynamics. It briefly discusses developments prior to the 1959 "Triumph of the Revolution" (Spanish colonial period, 1510–1898, and United States neo-colonial period, 1898–1958), but goes into more detail on what have been labeled as the four revolutions or *perfeccionamiento* initiatives in education, which began in the following years: 1961, 1975, 2001, and 2008. It also analyzes the changes initiated in the 1990s during the "Special Period in the Time of Peace." It concludes by noting that the reforms of education and teacher education enabled Cuba to continue on its socialist path, in the face of significant challenges (not the least of which has been the blockade and other hostile actions by the U.S. government) as well as contributed to Cuba's laudable achievements with respect access, equity, and quality of education.

1 Introduction

In an article written almost 30 years ago, Ginsburg and colleagues (1990, p. 497) concluded that education reforms "would more likely occur during periods of economic crisis and restructuring in the world system and relate to other economic, cultural, and political crises in nation-states." In this chapter we focus on the reforms of education and teacher education in Cuba during different historical periods, seeking to document as well as explain the occurrence of such reforms giving attention to both national and global economic, cultural, and political dynamics. In the case of Cuba, however, the terms "revolución" and "perfeccionamiento" seem more appropriate than reform, with the former Spanish word meaning "revolution" and the latter translated as "perfecting" or "improvement" (García Isaac, 2018).[1]

 | DOI: 10.1163/9789004413375_010

We will briefly discuss developments in education and teacher education in Cuba prior to the 1959 "Triumph of the Revolution" (Spanish colonial period, 1510–1898, and United States neo-colonial period, 1898–1958), but devote more space to what have been labeled as the four revolutions or perfeccionamiento initiatives in education, which began in the following years: 1961, 1975, 2001, and 2008 (Lutjens, 2007; Massón Cruz et al., 2011; Quintero López, 2011). And, while not labeled as a revolution, we will also examine changes initiated in the 1990s during the "Special Period in the Time of Peace."[2]

The post-1959 developments in education and teacher education in Cuba are significant to analyze given what has been achieved in terms of access, equity, and quality (e.g., see Breidlid, 2007; Carnoy & Werthein, 1980; Gasperini, 2000; Gómez Castanedo & Giacchino-Baker, 2001; Griffiths, 2009; Lutjens, 2000, 2007; Sánchez Collazo & Sánchez-Toledo Rodríguez, 2002/2016; Saney, 2004; UNESCO, 2004; UNESCO IBE, 2010; Wolfensohn, 2001).[3] For example, concerning educational quality, at least as defined by performance on standardized tests, Cuban third, fourth, and sixth-grade students scored substantially higher than those in all other Latin American countries on tests of literacy and numeracy. Those studies were conducted by performance on standardized assessments, in 1997–1998 and 2006 by UNESCO's Laboratorio Latinoamericano de Evaluación de la Calidad de la Educación (Latin American Laboratory of the Evaluation of Educational Quality) (Carnoy & Marshall, 2005; Granimian, 2009; LLECE, 1998, 2007).

2 Spanish Colonial Period, 1510–1898

Kolivras and Scapaci (2009, p. 124) indicate that "Columbus landed in Cuba in 1492, but it was not until the second decade of the sixteenth century that Diego de Velázquez established seven original frontier settlements called villas." During the sixteenth, seventeenth, and eighteenth centuries, there was no systematized school organization (Buenavilla-Recio et al., 1995). The colonial pattern of education involved "a relatively small elite of plantation owners, bureaucrats, and professionals educat[ing] their children in private schools or abroad. A few public, religious, and charity schools existed for the urban middle strata, leaving children of the large rural lower class unschooled" (Paulston, 1971, p. 376; see also Alarcón de Quesada, 2011; Cruz Taura, 2008). The limited forms of education provided during the Spanish colonial period in Cuba featured a major role for the Church and clerics. "Spanish rulers and the Catholic Church designed and implemented limited educational programs to meet their own ends" (Paulston & Kaufman, 1992, p. 134; see also Buenavilla-Recio et al., 1995; Ginsburg et al., 2010).

In 1842 the Spanish government promulgated its "Plan of Public Education" (Plan de Instrucción Pública) toward developing public primary education in its colonies of Cuba and Puerto Rico (Buenavilla-Recio et al., 1995) and in 1880 it promulgated the Plan of Public Education of the Colony (Plan de Instruccion Publica de la Colonia) toward implementing public secondary education (Paulston, 1971). Moreover, the 1842 Plan called for the creation of a normal school to prepare primary school teachers, and this institution was subsequently established and operated in Guanabacoa from 1857 to 1868. In recommending the creation of this institution, Jose de la Luz y Caballero (1800–1862) insisted that teachers should "be able to help develop patriots" and they "be the most moral of all citizens" (quoted in Buenavilla-Recio et al., 1995, p. 101). Also, in 1842, the University of Havana was "transformed by Spanish authorities into a secular institution, having been founded in 1728 as the Real y Pontificia Universidad de San Jeronimo de La Habana (Buenavilla-Recio et al., 1995, p. 10).

During the 19th century, Cubans undertook three wars of independence: 1868–1878, 1879–1880, and 1895–1898 (Loyola Vega, 2001). According to Cruz-Taura (2008, p. 5), as "the metropolis-colony relation deteriorated during the nineteenth century, Cuban intellectuals voiced concern over the accompanying decline of education in the island" and viewed education as an essential element in establishing an independent nation (see also Johnson, 1995). For instance, "the apostle of Cuban independence, José Martí (1884) articulated the role of education in his maxim 'To be educated is the only way to be free'" (Quintero López, 2011, p. 55). And those involved in the independence movements emphasized that among the purposes of education were to make people literate and "prepare them to be able to participate as citizens ..., to develop their political consciousness, and to ... [build] a feeling of the unity of all Cubans" (Buenavilla-Recio et al., 1995, p. 62). Thus, during the 10-Year War, the Cuban independence leadership founded *escuelitas* (little schools) in military camps to promote literacy among the combatants.

3 United States Neo-Colonial Period

As Cubans were on the verge of winning their independence, the first U.S. military intervention took place in Cuba in 1898. And on 1 January 1899, U.S. President William McKinley signed an order, in accord with the Paris Treaty between Spain and the U.S., designating Cuba to be under U.S. rule (Cruz-Taura, 2008; Esposito Rodriguez, 1985). Despite protests from many Cubans, the U.S. military occupied Cuba during the periods of 1898–1902 and 1906–1909, and then dominated the island economically and (indirectly) politically from 1909 to at least 1933 (Ginsburg et al., 2010; Lutjens, 2007; Paulston, 1971; Paulston & Kaufman, 1992; Pedagogía '93, 1993; Schultz, 2018).

US intervention in Cuba was not only military, political, and economic, but also cultural and educational. Thus, in 1900, the U.S. administration issued Military Order No. 226, "the first educational law that [replaced] the legislation enacted by the colonial administration [and] that, in fact, created a secular, non-socially segregated, Cuban Public-School System" (Esposito Rodriguez, 1985, p 16). Also, in 1900, the U.S. administration issued Military Order No. 368, which placed the training and selection of teachers under the control of the occupation authorities. As Epstein (1999, pp. 243–244) reports:

> Leonard Wood, who governed from 1900 to 1902 … aimed almost single-handedly to transform Cuba into a mirror of society in the United States … Wood used schools to disabuse the islanders of their Spanish ways and prepare them for assuming the burdens of enlightened citizenship. Under the guidance of Lieutenant Matthew E. Hanna, Cuba developed a public-school system that conformed to laws patterned after those in Ohio. The curriculum included instruction in English from the earliest grade on, and the teaching subjects used textbooks translated from the American.

Not surprisingly, many Cubans criticized the culturally imperialist nature and the "poor performance of the public education system established during the U.S. occupation of Cuba "… [which] reflected the economic, political, and social relations of neo-colonial development" (Lutjens, 2000, p. 2). However, it is important to recount the positive moves, at least initially, of the U.S. administration:

> As part of an impressive reconstruction package, the authorities established a Board of Education in 1900 under the leadership of Enrique José Varona [1849–1953]. … The Board arranged new school districts and had created nearly 3600 classrooms for 172,000 students (10.9% of the island's population) by 20 May 1902, the day of the promulgation of the Republic of Cuba. Initiatives for teacher training led to the founding of the [Faculty] of Education at the University of Havana, summer programs for Cuban teachers at Harvard University, and to the opening of normal schools [for teacher preparation] in each province by 1915…[4] The Cuban Constitution of 1901 (Title IV, article 31) guaranteed the civil right to offer and receive instruction in any subject. (Cruz-Taura, 2008, p. 5)

In 1909 the U.S. officials enacted two relevant laws: La Primera Ley Escolar Cubana (the First Cuban School Law) and El Primer Código Escolar [the First School Code], which represented steps toward professionalizing and Cubanizing the training, placement, and supervision of teachers (Esposito Rodriguez, 1985; Paulston, 1971). Then in 1915, the Cuban government enacted a law that created seven normal schools (*escuelas normales*) for female teachers (two in Havana and one in each of the five provincial capitals), and in 1934 these were transformed into coeducational teacher education institutions (Badía, 1993, p. 11).

In 1940 Cuba approved, though did not fully implement, a new Constitution. It made mandatory primary schooling and specified that basic secondary education (grades 7–9) should be free (Schultz, 2018). At the same time in "Title V, Section II [the Constitution] guaranteed private schools the right to teach religion and to instruct any subject through methods and contents of their choice" (Cruz-Taura, 2008, p. 7).

Thus, although "in 1926 Cuba led all other Latin American countries in the percentage of children in school," by the early 1950s "all but three Latin American countries claimed higher primary school enrollment ratios than those of Cuba" (Paulston, 1971, p. 378). Further signs that the initial efforts during the U.S. neo-colonial period had not been fully successful or had not lasted include the striking inequality in educational opportunities across social classes, racial groups, and rural/urban residents; the apathy and absenteeism among teachers; and graft and corruption at all levels of the system (Breidlid, 2007; Carnoy, 1990; Epstein, 1999; Lutjens, 2000; Paulson, 1971). Moreover, as Berube (1984, pp. 83–84) documents:

> [P]rior to the [1959] Revolution, the socioeconomic background of parents largely influenced education ... [And] education was a happenstance affair. Although schooling was compulsory from 1900 on for students from the ages of six to fourteen, not all students attended. In 1907, slightly over 30 percent of children aged five to fourteen attended school; by 1919, 28.7 percent were in school. A high of 63 percent was reached in the prosperous years 1925–1926. There are no statistics for the 1930s, but after depression and a world war, the total was 58.1 percent in 1950. By 1955, that had dropped to 51 percent.

Furthermore, in 1955, there were 679 public, 478 private, and 326 religious primary and secondary schools, as well as three public universities and six private universities (Schultz, 2018). And on the eve of the Triumph of the Revolution, in 1958, there were six official, secondary-level normal schools (one in each of the provincial capitals) as well as three schools of education (*facultades de educación*) at the three public universities in existence: Havana, Las Villas (in Santa Clara), and Oriente (in Santiago de Cuba) (Pedagogía '93, 1993).

4 Triumph of the Revolution and First Educational Revolution, 1959–1974

On 1 January 1959, while the forces led by Ernesto *Che* Guevara controlled Santa Clara and those led by Camilo Cienfuegos were advancing on Havana, Fidel Castro Ruz entered Santa Clara and declared the Triumph of the Revolution, celebrating the exodus of Fulgencio Batista (1952–1958), the last "president" serving during U.S. neo-colonial rule (Alzugaray, 2008). The armed struggle undertaken by Fidel and the rebel army of the July 26 Movement had resumed in 1957, after an unsuccessful start with the attack on Moncada Barracks in 1953, followed by Fidel and others being imprisoned but released and then regrouped in exile in Mexico (Kolivras & Scapaci, 2009; Roucek, 1964). As Fidel recounted over a decade later:

> On January 1, with the military downfall of the Batista regime, nothing was left. There was no legislative power in the classic sense, no judicial power, nothing. Then we established a de facto revolutionary government, and in that context, instituted by decree new laws. (Fidel Castro, 1971, p. 14, quoted in Valdés, 1976, p. 2)

And education was a major focus of the revolutionary government. While Massón Cruz et al. (2011, p. 44; our translation) suggests that the first educational revolution began in the year 1961, she explains that "essential educational changes had already begun before 1961." The revolutionary government's educational initiatives were foreshadowed by remarks made by Fidel Castro Ruz in 1953. After being sentenced for his role in the assault on Moncada Barracks, Fidel in his *History will Absolve Me* speech stated that "a revolutionary government would initiate a comprehensive reform of our education ... to adequately prepare the generations who are called upon to live in a happier homeland" (Castro, 1983; quoted Massón Cruz, 2016, p. 195). Paulston (1971, p. 386) reports that "[i]n the first year, the government built more than 3,000 new public schools, and 7,000 additional teachers entered classrooms to teach more than 300,000 children attending school for the first time." Then in December 1959, the government issued Law 680, which emphasized the use of child-centered, active-learning pedagogies and re-established school councils, decentralizing responsibility for governing the expanding educational system (Schultz, 2018).

With respect to higher education, Alarcón de Quesada (2011) explains that "[o]ne of the government's first measures was the broad-based Scholarship Plan, directed to facilitate education for thousands of students from the hinterlands" as well as that "[a]t the same time, wide-ranging university reforms began. These included attempts to modernize teaching and teaching methods, to encourage the previously unknown study of some sciences and technologies... and to create university campuses throughout the country, launching what we call the 'Universalization of the University.'" These efforts included the creation of the university-level Preparatory School for Peasants and Workers (*Facultad Preparatoria Obrero-Campesina*), "which attempt[ed] to link farming, industry, and higher education more closely ... [by preparing] industrial workers and peasants aged eighteen through forty for university study" (Paulston, 1971, p. 389).

However, the first educational revolution in Cuba can be seen to commence in 1961, labeled by leaders as the "Year of Education" and highlighted by the National Literacy Campaign, which began in January 1961. According to MacDonald (1985, p. 55; see also Roucek, 1964), "after fifteen months, the illiteracy rate was down from 24% to 4% ... [The campaign] was mediated by large numbers of enthusiastic amateurs ... whose only contact with teacher training had been a quickie eight-day course on how to use the teaching materials."[5] Moreover, in 1962, the Cuban "government launched the 'Battle of the Sixth Grade" to improve the educational level of the more than 700,000 adults," who had benefited from the literacy campaign (Paulston, 1971, p. 387).[6]

Several prominent political/military developments occurred just before, during, and after the period of the Literacy Campaign. In February 1960, Cuba and the Soviet Union signed their first commercial agreement and, in May 1960, re-establish diplomatic ties. In July 1960, Cuba authorized further nationalization of U.S-owned businesses and properties, and the U.S. initiated sanctions against the importation of Cuban sugar, launching its trade embargo (or blockade) against Cuba. In January 1961, the U.S. broke off diplomatic relations with Cuba, and in April 1961, a U.S.-funded mercenary group attempted to invade Cuba at the Bay of Pigs (Alarcón de Quesada, 2011; Breidlid, 2007; Martínez Sánchez, 2015; Schultz, 2018).7 In the wake of these events, Fidel Castro Ruz declared the socialist character of the Revolution (April 1961) and the Cuban government nationalized all private schools (July 1961) (García Ramis, 2004; Griffith, 1998, 2009; Paulston, 1971; Pedagogía '93, 1993). And in October 1962, Cuba was the site of a major confrontation between the U.S. and the Soviet Union; known as the "Cuban Missile Crisis" or the "October Crisis," the dispute revolved around efforts to install nuclear missiles in Cuba (Franklin, 2015; Ramírez Cañado y Morales Domínguez, 2014).

In the context of such international political dynamics and given the goals of the "socialist" revolution, the Cuban government's commitment to expanding access to education was based on increasing literacy and numeracy as well as developing the population's economically relevant technical knowledge and skills. In addition, government leaders were motivated to engage in the political socialization of adults as well as children (Carnoy, 1990; Ginsburg et al., 2010; Griffith, 1988, 2009; López-Hurtado et al., 1996; Paulston & Kaufman, 1992). For example, Fidel Castro Ruz (1960, quoted in Aldama de Pino & Casañas Días, 2018, p. 89; our translation) stated that "the first problem of the revolution is how to... overcome the influence of old ideas... and how the ideas of the revolution are going to gain ground." And, as recounted by Ernesto *Che* Guevara (1970, p. 259, quoted in English in Turner Martí, 2014, p. 20), an important role of education is "the removal of the defects of the former society from the people's conscience..." In this regard, Lutjens (2000, p. 3) observes that:

> the expansion of formal schooling became part of a vision of the transformation of Cuban society that centered on *Che* Guevara's socialist 'new man.'[8] "To build communism, a new man must be created simultaneously with the material base," wrote Guevara [1973, p. 343], and to achieve this, "society as a whole must become a huge school." The Cuban model stressed values of cooperation, discipline, sacrifice, and moral motivation, calling for participation in defending and developing the revolution and international solidarity. (See also Guevara, 2002, 2017)[9]

Closely associated with *Che's* ideas for education's role in the cultural development and political socialization are the concept of work-study and the importance of moral rather than material incentives (Breidlid, 2007; Carnoy, 1990; Cruz-Taura, 2008; Griffith, 1998, 2009; Lutjens, 2000; Paulston, 1980).[10] In the words of Ernesto *Che* Guevara (1970, p. 165; quoted and translated into English in Turner Martí, 2014, pp. 45–46): "The combination of study and work ... is the best type of education for the youth who are preparing for communism: the type of education where work loses the kind of obsession it has in the capitalist world to become a rewarding social duty that is carried out with joy, singing revolutionary songs, in most fraternal comradeship and human contact that invigorates and enriches all the participants."

One of the boldest initiatives undertaken by the Cuban government concerning the work-study principle was the "Schools to the Countryside" program, which started in 1965–1966. In this program, urban students and teachers relocated for part of the school year to a rural area during the harvest season to do farm work as well as continue their academic studies. In 1972, in the context of "the radical 'Revolutionary Offensive" (*Ofensiva Revolucionaria*), which was launched in 1968, this program evolved into the national project of "Secondary Schools in the Countryside" (*Escuelas Secundarias Básicas en el Campo*) (Carnoy & Werthein, 1983; Gasperini, 2000; Griffith, 1998; Lutjens, 2000). According to Carnoy (1990, p. 184), as a result of "the 'schools in the countryside' ... [a]cademic performance did apparently increase, and dropouts decreased. ... Collective consciousness was probably raised as well ... But the schools did not come close to financing themselves."

To achieve its educational goals, Cuba's revolutionary government needed teachers and, thus, it had to devote attention and resources to teacher education, both preservice and in-service (Carnoy, 1990; Ginsburg et al., 2010). As Fidel Castro Ruz expressed it in a speech on 10 April 1963 (Ministerio de Educación, 1977, p. 20): "Teachers have in their hands an extremely important assignment, because they are the ones who begin to develop children's mentality, to teach them the first letters and, at the same time, to inculcate habits of social life, and to forge in each child a future citizen of the republic." The revolutionary government's goal of creating the "new socialist person" required the "emergency training of thousands of teachers" (López-Hurtado et al., 1996, p. 14). This was the case not only because of the planned dramatic expansion of schooling but also because of "the exodus of thousands of Cuba's professionals and trained personnel in the first few years [after 1959], including half of Cuba's teachers" (Lutjens, 2000, p. 4; see also Berube, 1984; Ginsburg et al., 2010). There was also a need to reorient teachers who stayed, to ensure their commitments to reaching all students and to promoting the nationalist, socialist line of the new society.

Thus, in June 1961 the government established tertiary-level Pedagogical Institutes (ISPs—*Institutos Superiores Pedagógicos*). García Ramis (2004) reports that initially, the ISPs had three types of programs: (1) short-term, emergency training for the in-service primary school teachers who intended to meet the qualification to become a licensed teacher; (2) regular preservice primary school teacher training programs for individuals who had at least completed the six years of primary schooling and would graduate with a high school diploma; and (3) in-service training for primary school teachers with or without a license to elevate their cultural/political, scientific, and psycho-pedagogical level.

Also, in 1961, the government created 5-year teacher education programs in conjunction with the *Plan Minas del Frío-Topes de Collantes*. These targeted individuals who had at least a sixth-grade education to prepare them to be directors and assistants in public early childhood centers (*círculos infantiles*), which the government was establishing. Then in 1965, the government instituted provincial schools of preparation and development of personnel for early childhood centers (*escuelas provinciales de formación y superación de personal para círculos infantiles*), which recruited students who had completed at least the sixth grade.

And in 1963, the government created the Industrial Pedagogical Institute (*Instituto Pedagógico Industrial*), This institution prepared teachers who had responsibilities for supervising practical workshops and teaching technical subjects of mechanics and electricity located in the Technical School of the Liberty Education City (*Escuela Técnica de Ciudad Escolar Libertad*) which housed the Institute. Subsequently, in 1973, the government created the Pedagogical Institute for Technical and Professional Education (*Instituto Pedagógico para la Educación Técnica y Profesional*), and, in 1974, established the Pedagogical Centers (*Centros Pedagógicos*) in the seven secondary-level Polytechnic Institutes (*Institutos Politécnicos*), which aimed to prepare teachers for technical subjects and workshops in these institutes.

In 1964 the revolutionary government created schools of education at the then existing universities: Havana, Las Villas (in Santa Clara), and Oriente (in Santiago de Cuba). These schools offered higher education programs to prepare lower and upper secondary school teachers (*enseñanza media básica y superior*). Before developing these programs, the Ministry of Education had recruited secondary teachers from university graduates in Letters and Philosophy, Physics-Mathematics, Physics-Chemistry-Mathematics, or Engineering (García Ramis, 2004). Furthermore, in 1968, the Ministry started in each province a "school of primary teacher preparation" (*escuela formadora de maestros primarios*), which served students who had completed at least six grades of primary education.

On 16 February 1970, *The Granma* announced the development of the "Plan to Title/Qualify Teachers" (*Plan de Titulación de Maestros*). According to Paulston (1971, p. 388), this "plan presents the rationale and tactics for certification of some 26,031 primary and secondary school teachers or some 40 percent of the existing teaching corps. ... The Plan was designed to prepare 'teachers who understand the essence of the educational process [, who have] ... a mastery of the subjects they teach [, and who are] ... capable of teaching children not encyclopedic facts, but how to learn." Then, in 1970, the government created the first schools of preschool educator preparation (*escuelas de formación de educadoras de círculos infantiles*), offering a four-year program for students who had completed at least the eighth grade.

In 1972 Cuba initiated its "Pedagogical Detachment" (*Destacamento Pedagógico*) "Manuel Ascunce Domenech." This 5-year *emergente* program recruited individuals who at least had completed the 10th grade to prepare them to teach in lower secondary schools (*escuelas de nivel medio or secundarias básicas*), to serve the rapidly growing number of students at that level. As part of the program, the future secondary teachers continued their own upper secondary school studies while also receiving pedagogical preparation as well as taking on classroom teaching responsibilities starting in their first year in the program (Garcia Ramis, 2004; Ginsburg et al., 2010; Griffiths, 1998).

Second Educational Revolution, 1975–1990

Massón Cruz et al. (2011, p. 47) identifies 1975–1990 as the period of the second educational revolution in Cuba, dividing this period into two moments: 1975–1986 and 1987–1990. However, to understand the impetus for this educational revolution, we need to consider developments at the beginning of the 1970s.

The year 1970 was significant as the deadline for Cuba's "second development strategy (1964–1970), ... [which featured] a 'big push' to produce a record of ten million tons of sugar in 1970" (Fitzgerald, 1987, p. 35). However, although the 1970 sugar harvest set a record of 8.5 million tons, the failure to reach 10 million tons provoked concern and debate about Cuba's economic system, the impact of moral versus material incentives for work, the functioning of the government bureaucracy, and the content and processes of education (Valdéz, 1976). For instance, Horowitz (1976, p. 72) explains that "when this moral economy proved incapable of producing a gigantic sugar crop ... [and] when the moral economy degenerated into unpaid labor time, then a considerable amount of the 'romance' of the revolution vanished ..."

Criticisms of the education system surfaced during the First National Congress of Education and Culture, held in Havana in April 1971 (Griffiths, 1988). And one of the Congress' "main recommendation to remedy the series of failures in the system was to devote more resources to the proper training of Marxist teachers" (Cruz-Taura, 2008, p. 8). Moreover, the Congress directed the Ministry of Education to undertake "a diagnostic study of Cuban education at all levels ... [which] resulted in the Plan for the Improvement and Development of the Educational System of Cuba (*El Plan de Perfeccionamiento y Desarrollo de Sistema Nacional de Educación de Cuba*)" (Fitzgerald, 1987, p. 69). Also, in 1972, Fidel Castro Ruz discussed the shortcomings of the school system during a speech to the Second National Congress of the Young Communist League, stating in part that "the Revolutionary educational system had not yet created the 'new socialist man' ... [H]e lamented that 'we still don't have the new man, and we no longer have the old one ... The discipline of the old man is gone, and we don't have the new man with corresponding discipline ... self-discipline and awareness of his obligations and tasks'" (quoted in Berube, 1984, p. 106).

In December 1975 the First Congress of the Communist Party of Cuba (PCC) was convened (Gonzales, 1976; Stubbs, 1989), and among various actions, it approved the above-referenced Plan de Perfeccionamiento. The Plan "provided the guidelines for improving the quality of education in closer association with the Communist Party in order to better satisfy economic and ideological goals" (Cruz-Taura, 2008, p. 9). Additionally, based on the Plan, the "13 grades of schooling became 12; the primary level of education included two cycles, with students remaining with the same teacher in grades one through four. Teacher training was stressed, and reorganization of the curriculum required a change in 1,350 school programs and more than 600 textbooks. A separate Ministry of Higher Education emerged in 1976, while the arrangements of [People's Power] *Poder Popular* redistributed some of the responsibilities of the Ministry of Education to the municipal and provincial levels" (Lutjens, 2000, p. 4).

The Party Congress also approved the Party Platform, which "[a]ccording to Raúl Castro [Ruz], in his remarks opening the Congress, the Party Platform had been discussed in over 110,000 meetings in which over four million citizens had participated" (Gonzales, 1976, p. 4). Among other elements the Platform stated that: (a) "the improvement of education [*perfeccionamiento de la educación*] is a continuous process;" (b) "socialist pedagogy is incompatible with memory-oriented, schematic, and verbalizing teaching;" (c) "as part of economic and labor education of youth, the combination of study with work will continue to be developed;" and (d) "one will work to elevate the professional ethics of educators ... for developing the socialist personality of the new generations... with a firm internationalist conviction" (PCC, 1975, our translation; see also García Isaac, 2018).

Furthermore, the Party Congress approved "Cuba's first socialist Constitution, which was later endorsed by 97.7 percent of the voters in a national referendum on February 15, and enacted on February 24, 1976" (Gonzales, 1976, p. 6; see also de la Cuesta, 1976). And, as Quintero López (2011, p. 56) explains, "the Constitution of the Republic of Cuba in force since 1976 establishes in several articles the fundamental principles and objectives of education, according to which the Socialist State, as the power of the people [...] shall ensure [...] that no child be left without schooling, food and clothing; that no young person be left without the opportunity to study; that no one be left without access to the studies, culture, and sports" (see also García Isaac, 2018; Massón Cruz et al., 2011; Schultz, 2018).

In the wake of the First Congress of the PCC, in 1975–1976, Cuba launched a campaign to restructure the educational system, based on the "Plan de

Perfeccionamiento" mentioned above (Gonzales Joy García Mena, 2018). The campaign "involved revamping the elementary school into two stages: a first-through the fourth-grade cycle and a fifth-through the sixth-grade cycle. ... In addition, the plan revised all textbooks and teachers' manuals. The focus now was on how well the schools performed in national examinations and promotion rates. ... Under the perfecting plan, teachers remain with their students from the first to the fourth grade" (Berube, 1984, pp. 108–109).

The "Perfeccionamiento" campaign also focused particular attention on—and allocated additional resources to—teacher education (Lutjens, 2000). For instance, in October 1976, the Cuban Ministry of Education promulgated Resolutions No. 658/76 and 659/76, which focused on improving the "political, scientific, ideological, and technical–pedagogical formation" of teachers. According to Garcia Ramis (2004, pp. 9–10; our translation), these resolutions and subsequent actions:

> ... integrated into a single subsystem—the System of Preparation and Improvement of Pedagogical Personnel (*Sistema de Formación y Perfeccionamiento del Personal Pedagógico*)—the institutions dedicated to initial preparation and ongoing development of educators. The pedagogical faculties, which up to this moment existed in the country's universities, were converted into Higher Pedagogical Institutes (*Institutos Superiores Pedagógicos* or ISPs), as independent pedagogical universities under the Ministry of Education ... [ISPs] were progressively increased until there was one in each province and two in the capital. ... [And the government] renamed the primary teacher preparation schools as pedagogical schools (*escuelas pedagógicas*) and constructed new buildings for them in each province.

Beginning in 1976–1977, moreover, these teacher education institutions implemented new study plans (Plan of Study A) to prepare graduates of lower secondary schools to obtain an "educational license" (*licenciado de educación*) for teaching in primary schools. There was also a program for graduates of upper secondary schools to prepare them to obtain a bachelor's degree (*licenciatura*) in education for teaching in secondary schools. Plan of Study A was structured around four content areas: "sociopolitical (4.7%); general education (61.5%); psycho-pedagogical (24%); specials (4.6%); and facultative subjects (4.8%). The sociopolitical cycle familiarized teachers with the Marxist–Leninist theory" (Kolesnikov, 1983, p. 346; see also Ginsburg et al., 2010; Massón Cruz et al., 2011).[11]

Toward the end of the 1970s and into the 1980s significant economic and political developments occurred that informed Cuba's policies in education and other sectors. As Griffiths (1998, pp. 204–205) states, the "economic recovery that began in the first half of the 1970s moved into recession by the end of the decade, as the national economy continued to feel the impact of [falling] world commodity prices and a growing hard currency foreign debt. The early 1980s [however]… brought generalized, though uneven industrialization, expanded consumption, and economic growth."

In 1982 the ISPs began to implement Plan of Studies B, which included an expansion of the *licenciatura* program to five years. That provided more "space for practical preparation, with the increase in time available for the students to be in schools, accompanied by ISP faculty members" (Massón Cruz et al., 2011, p. 56; our translation).

However, the economic situation once again created challenges for Cuba during the mid-1980s, as Griffiths (1998, p. 205) chronicles: "By 1985 the government again confronted domestic economic problems, linked to Cuba's terms of foreign trade and a large, hard currency foreign debt. Potential political problems also returned in the face of a domestic austerity strategy in response to these problems, and increased levels of inequality as a result of the decade's economic reform …."

In this context, the Third Congress of the PCC was begun in December 1985, and at a delayed session held in July 1986, Fidel Castro Ruz announced the beginning of an initiative termed "Rectification—the Campaign to Rectify Errors and Negative Tendencies" (Stubbs, 1989). This campaign initially targeted "deficiencies in economic performance, including the neglect of the social and political dimensions of production" (Lutjens, 2000, p. 6). However, given the centrality of education for achieving the goals of Cuba's Revolution, it is not surprising that when he launched the Rectification campaign:

> Fidel [Castro Ruz] publicly criticized teachers, and school education more generally … In his July 26 speech in 1986, Fidel … also specifically addressed the problem of these tendencies and practices for the teaching of political subjects … [And in] a speech to close the Fifth Congress of the UJC [*Unión de Jóvenes Comunistas*] in April 1987, he stressed the need for cadres and school teachers to model desired socialist and revolutionary behaviour, morals, attitudes, and the application of Marxism-Leninism, adding: 'We might have a teacher teaching Marxism, 400 hours in a semester if you like, and if they are a bad example to their students, all the books and the 400 hours of Marxism-Leninism are worthless.' (Griffiths 1998, pp. 292–294; see also Griffiths, 2009, p. 54)

5 The "Special Period" of the 1990s

In 1992, ISPs initiated Plan of Study C, which focused the preservice teacher education programs even more strongly on teachers' work, the curriculum, and other dimensions of the reality of schools (Massón Cruz et al., 2011, p. 56; see also Gómez Castanedo & Giacchino-Baker, 2001; Gasperini, 2000; García Ramis, 2004). According to Diáz Fuentes (1996, pp. 141–142), the new plan of study combined the following principles: (a) achieving a solid patriotic and citizen preparation; (b) reinforcing professional motivation; (c) solving the problem of insufficient cultural development of students in school; (d) preparing in work and for work; (e) reinforcing the pedagogical, psychological, and sociological preparation [of teachers]; and (f) preparing pedagogues differently from those trained in other university programs. And in 1993, ISPs began to offer a five-year *licenciatura* program to prepare preschool teachers (Aquino 1994; Ministerio de Educación, 1994; Pedagogía '93, 1993).

This curricular reform in ISPs was initiated three years after the demise of the CMEA [Council for Mutual Economic Assistance] and approximately one year after the collapse of the Soviet Union (Griffiths, 1998). As a result of these transformations of Cuba's main trading partners, Cuba's GDP "declined 40% between 1990 and 1994 and foreign exchange receipts dropped 75% ... The economic crisis ... rippled throughout the economy: imports declined; food production and consumption contracted precipitously; energy resources shrank; and savings disappeared (Ritter, 2004). U.S. policy contributed to the crisis with legislation (Torricelli [Law] and Helms-Burton [Law] in 1992 and 1996, respectively) that strengthened an embargo that is estimated to have cost the island more than US$70 billion over the years" (Lutjens, 2007, p. 173; see also Kolivras & Scarpaci, 2009; Ludlam, 2012).

Breidlid (2007, p. 622) observes that the "economic problems had immediate effects on all spheres of life. The regime's introduction of tourism and dollars to compensate for the economic losses meant an exodus of teachers from the teaching profession to tourism, where salaries were much higher. The education system thus regressed into a state of emergency, if not crisis, where teachers were suddenly in short supply and where the budget for education in 1998 had decreased by 45% compared with 1989 ...." However, despite the challenges that Cuba faced during the "Special Period," Fidel Castro Ruz in 1993 articulated with pride that Cuba retained its commitment to providing education as a human and constitutional right (Alarcón de Quesada, 2011). He expressed it in the following manner: "'How can it be explained that a country that has lost 75% of its imports, a country that has to work with 40% of the fuel that it had [at its disposal]—and all as a consequence of the disappearance of the socialist camp and the disintegration of the USSR, countries with which we had 85% of our trade and just prices for our products—… that not a single school has been closed, not a single child has been left without a teacher" (Castro Ruz, 1993, p. 5, quoted in Lutjens, 2000, p. 1).

Additionally, after adopting reforms to its Constitution in 1992 (Schultz, 2018), Cuba reinforced the role that education would play in developing citizens and workers. As Griffiths (1998, p. 302) reports, in the "context of the collapsing Soviet Union and Eastern Europe," civic education was incorporated in the school curriculum in order "to strengthen the schools' treatment of moral, juridical and civic aspects … [and] contribute to the development of knowledge, capacities, habits, abilities, sentiments, values and norms of behaviour required for the ethical formation of the new person …"

The challenges of the "Special Period"—and the introduction of tourism and other private-sector economic activities –continued throughout the 1990s to undermine the cultural/ideological commitments of many Cubans, especially youth. Fidel Castro Ruz (1997), in a speech delivered at the opening of the 1997–1998 school year, said: "So for us, education is decisive: the creation and development of values in the consciousness of children and young people from an early age, and today it is more necessary than ever […] to save our independence, to save our Nation, to save our Revolution" (quoted in Quintero López, 2011, p. 70).

And in 1999 Cuban "authorities launched a campaign called 'The Battle of Ideas' to mobilize the new generation for the defense of the revolution" (Breidlid, 2007, p. 622; see also Font, 2008; Lee, 2015). As Domínguez García et al. (2014, p. 16; our translation) report, "The Battle of Ideas was directed toward the educational, cultural, and political-ideological reinforcement of the population and in particular the youth, with the objective of … guaranteeing their social insertion in studies and work." By 2000, "programs mobilized voluntary labor to upgrade public facilities of all kinds," class sizes were "radically reduced" to 20 in primary schools and 15 in lower secondary education, and university programs were located in all municipalities as part of a drive toward the "universalization of access to tertiary education" (Ludlam, 2012, p. 46). Besides, the Ministry equipped with one or more television sets and computers each school throughout the country (Breidlid, 2007). Furthermore, the government opened upper secondary-level professional/technical schools focused on preparing social workers (Griffiths, 2009).

In line with the shifting foci and emphases in primary and secondary education, efforts also were made to reform and enhance the quality of teacher preparation programs. The "development and improvement of teachers [were] directed ... to perfect the professional preparation and to elevate the scientific level in order to respond to the qualitative changes that have taken place on the different subsystems of education and the [nation's] educational policy" (Pedagogía '93, 1993, p. 29). And as Aquino (1994, p. 20) indicates, "work continue[d] to be devoted to improving the level of practicing [primary] schools' teachers, who graduated from intermediate level pedagogical training, through workers' courses" in a primary school license (*licenciatura*) program. One aspect of these and other teacher education programs involved efforts to strengthen teachers' motivation to remain in the profession and foster their cultural/ideological commitment to the collective goals of the Revolution. Also, in 1999, the government increased teachers' salaries by 30%, though it seems that "this salary hike was insufficient to compete with the tourist industry" (Breidlid, 2007, p. 623).

In this context of teachers exiting the profession for private-sector jobs and the reduction of class sizes, the government re-established *emergentes* programs to recruit and train teachers. Additionally, in 2000, "the Cuban Ministry of Education began training 4,000 specially recruited *emergentes*... graduates [of] upper-secondary schools... *Emergentes* were offered a "fast-track" into primary and lower-secondary school teaching through an intensive two-year program, of which the first year was comprised of all academic coursework and the second of supervised teaching" (Snell Goldstein, 2012, pp. 34–35; see also Carnoy et al., 2007; Griffith, 2009).

6 Third Educational Revolution, 2001–2009

Massón Cruz et al. (2011, p. 50) states that "in the act initiating the 2001–2002 school year, Fidel Castro [Ruz] announced that Cuba would begin a new educational revolution, which he called the 'Third Educational Revolution'" (see also Breidlid, 2007; Lutjens, 2007). An essential element of this educational revolution was the establishment in 2001 of a bachelor's degree (*licenciatura*) in General Comprehensive Education, designed to prepare lower-secondary school teachers to teach a range of subjects and work with a group of students for three years, grades 7–9. According to Breidlid (2007, p. 624):

> [A] new concept, the comprehensive junior secondary teacher, *profesor integral general*, was introduced. In contrast to the earlier system, where teachers taught their specialized subject, teachers are now expected to teach all subjects with the exception of foreign languages, computing, and the arts. ... The focus is on interdisciplinary teaching, in an attempt

> to avoid the earlier fragmentation of school subjects. Much attention is also paid to the social aspect of learning ... It is hoped that the *profesor integral general* will be able to cater to the whole student group and their individual needs to a greater extent than earlier when teaching was fragmented between different specialist teachers. (See also Addine Fernández & García Batista, 2005; Massón Cruz et al., 2011)

Gómez Castanedo and Giacchino-Baker (2010, p. 102) elaborate on the features of this new teacher education program:

> During the first year, all participants take core classes to ensure that they have adequate foundations in psychology, pedagogy, and sociology... Starting in the second year and continuing through the rest of the programs, students are placed in a school in the city where they live. This school is meant to serve as a 'micro-university' where experienced teachers become mentors to [teacher education program] students in the areas of professional preparation while also helping them with their university studies... [which the participants pursue] at Higher Pedagogical Institutes [ISPs] at satellite campuses created in all participating cities.

Thus, in this period, the training of educators was deepened, promoting creative professional performance in their pedagogical activity to develop systematically their students' personality. That involved modifying the curricula to incorporate a multidisciplinary approach in the general pedagogy course, highlighting relationships among the various components of the school curriculum, and promoting a dynamic teaching-learning process.

Furthermore, in 2003, the ISPs began implementing revised plans of studies (*planes de estudio C*). The revised plans of studies prepared lower secondary school teachers in multiple subject areas but also focused their learning on a general field of study: Exact Sciences (Mathematics and Physics), Natural Sciences (Chemistry, Biology, and Geography), and Humanities (Spanish Literature, History, Marxism-Leninism, and Civics). Similar to the *emergentes* program, students participated in an intensive year at one of the main campuses of an ISP, now labeled universities of pedagogical sciences (*universidades de ciencias pedagógicas*), followed by four years working in micro-universities and attending classes at municipal campuses (Ministerio de Educación, 2003).

The elaboration of teacher education programs in plans of study "C" was a complex task, posing a series of scientific requirements, both for particular subject areas and for pedagogy. For instance, efforts were made to integrate the knowledge, skills, and attitudes focused on the three components of the programs: academic courses, labor/teaching practice, and research. Furthermore, the following principles served as the basis for the design of the plans of studies C:

- Training and reinforcement of the professional motivation through the direct and systematic engagement of the future teacher with the reality of schools.
- Making the training process at work and for work as a condition of the students' revolutionary preparation and their professional performance.
- Increasing pedagogical and psychological development so that the future professional knows the learners in depth and, thus, can direct the pedagogical process effectively.
- Preparing the graduate as an educator, who is considered first and foremost, to be a teacher.
- Achieving flexibility, allowing its updating and modification when necessary in solving problems, and pursuing technical-scientific development.

7 Fourth Educational Revolution, 2008–2018

The year 2008 served up two additional challenges to the Cuban economy: (a) the global economic crisis, sparked by the meltdown of financial institutions in the U.S. and (b) the destruction wrought by Hurricane Gustav in August (Ludlam, 2012, p. 42). As described by Hickling-Hudson et al. (2012, p. 3), the results were the displacement of "many thousands of workers from wage-earning jobs in state enterprises and government offices, pushing them into self-employment, family businesses, cooperative enterprise, or unemployment." In this context, Cuba experienced "a very important moment of new transformations ... [to] enable continually improving the outcomes of education in relation to previous moments that became important landmarks [the 1960s, 1970s, 1990s, earlier 2000s] in the history of Cuban education" (Quintero López, 2011, p. 58). We refer to this period starting in 2008 as the fourth educational "revolution" or fourth "improvement" of the Cuban education system. The initiatives covered all the levels of the system and introduced greater flexibility in curriculum and degree program design, allowing institutions to take into consideration aspects of the provincial or local context.

The fourth revolution initiated just after Raúl Castro Ruz assumed the presidency of Cuba, as a result of Fidel's resignation due to his health issues (see Gonzáles Santamaría, 2017). Raúl declared the end of the "Battle of Ideas", closed rural boarding schools, scaled back the University for All (*Universidad para Todos*) initiative, and called for an expansion of technical vocational programs (e.g., agronomy, computer science, education/pedagogy, medicine, and sports) (Hickling-Hudson, 2012, p. 3). Besides, the government made efforts to strengthen entry exams and academic rigor in schools and universities, while also legalizing private tutoring (in 2010). Furthermore, there was a renewed emphasis on moral education and the family's role in cultural/political socialization.

Concerning teacher education, in 2010, the government re-opened the upper secondary-level pedagogical schools (*escuelas pedagógicasor preuniversitarios vocacionales de ciencias pedagógicas*), the ones closed in 1976 when teacher preparation became a tertiary education activity exclusively. The programs in these re-opened institutions focused initially on preparing preschool, primary school, and special education teachers, and, subsequently, organized teacher preparation for primary-level English teachers (in 2013) as well as lower secondary teachers of history and mathematics (in 2017) (Quintero López, 2011). Students attending these programs studied the same subjects as students in academic pre-university institutions, but also took classes in theory and practice of education and undertook field-based teaching practice (Escobar-Lorenzo et al., 2013; García Batista & Addine Fernández, 2013).

Meanwhile, at the higher education level, ISPs initiated programs in line with new plans of study (*planes de estudio D*). Interestingly, the new plans of studies for programs to prepare lower secondary teachers once again focused on specific disciplines (Massón Cruz et al., 2011, p. 58). More generally, the new programs are designed to prepare educators who would be prepared to:

- Scientifically conduct the educational process at the school, ensure the full personal development of the student expressed in the knowledge of contents, the supporting methods and the ethical standards shown in their professional performance.
- Vocationally orient the student to the specialties the country needs the most.
- Interact with the family so as to play a significant role in the full development of their students.
- Use scientific methods to provide solutions to problems encountered in their work.
- Be politically, legally and culturally prepared and capable of communicating effectively, to serve as a linguistic model to students.
- Identify their own enhancement needs and act to meet them.
- Be committed to [their own and their students] political-ideological work and full general cultural development (Quintero López, 2011, pp. 65–66).

Yet another change in higher education was instituted in 2016. Except for the Havana-based institution, named for Enrique José Varona, universities of pedagogical sciences (*universidades de ciencias pedagógicas*) were incorporated as schools of education in provincial universities as part of an initiative to encourage more collaboration across fields. In the same year all university bachelor's degrees (*licenciaturas*), except for medicine, were shortened from five to four years in length, which required new plans of study to be implemented. In the case of pedagogical schools and the lone remaining University of Pedagogical Sciences "Enrique José Varona," the revised plans of study applied to programs for preparing preschool, primary schools, and special education teachers as well as lower and upper secondary teachers of various academic subjects/disciplines and technical/vocational areas.

It is also essential to observe the variety of in-service professional development activities that are not only available but also actively pursued by educators in Cuba. These activities include diploma programs, individual university courses, and training workshops but also specialized conferences, informal scientific debates, and exchange of experiences among colleagues, and individual or group field investigations or action research (Castillo Estrella, 2002). Ongoing administrative—peer—and self-evaluations of a teacher's performance of their various roles shape all these activities. All of those planned and carried out primarily from the workplace, which implies less time and resource expenditure, as well as immediate feedback from improving professional practice.

8 Conclusion

In this chapter, we discussed the developments in education and teacher education in Cuba briefly before the 1959 "Triumph of the Revolution," providing a basis for comparing what transpired after 1959. We examined the Spanish colonial period (1510–1898) as well as the United States neo-colonial period (1898–1958). We then examined in more detail what have been labeled as the four revolutions or perfecting/improving (*perfeccionamiento*) initiatives in education, which began in 1961, 1975, 2001, and 2008, while also devoting attention to an important period of change in the 1990s, which has not been labeled as a revolution but is referred to as the "Special Period in the Time of Peace."

In our discussion, we sought to identify national and international economic, cultural, and political dynamics that have shaped the timing and focus of Cuba's "reforms" in education and teacher education. At the same time, we analyzed how the planned and implemented changes were directed to address concerns generated by these dynamics. Constructing workers and citizens in and for revolutionary Cuba—what characterized as the "New Person"—remained the focus. And this focus required attention to organizing and reorganizing schooling and higher education to facilitate the development of academic and technical knowledge and skills as well as cultural values and political/ideological commitments. And, given the critical role that teachers play in accomplishing such goals, the educational revolutions always included efforts to alter and improve the preservice and in-service education of teachers. These changes in teacher education were designed to attract sufficient numbers of people to pursue the profession of teaching and to equip them with the necessary knowledge and skill as well as desired cultural values and political/ideological commitments.

Finally, one may debate how "revolutionary" the educational changes undertaken by Cuba since 1959 have been. However, there is little question that the initiatives pursued enabled Cuba to continue on its socialist path, in the face of significant challenges, not the least of which has been the blockade and other hostile actions by the U.S. government. Moreover, these *perfeccionamiento* efforts have contributed to Cuba's laudable achievements with respect to access, equity, and quality of education.

Notes

1 Indeed, as Ludlam (2012, p. 49) suggests in relation to economic changes pursued in Cuba after the demise of the Soviet Union in 1991, it is more appropriate to speak of "the 'updating' of the Cuban model ... [since] the word 'reform' is avoided due to its association with the collapse of socialism elsewhere ..."

2 We would like to thank C. Francisco Lau Apó (2017) for his work in developing a detailed chart of historical developments in teacher education in Cuba as part of a project of the Asociación de Pedagógos de Cuba.

3 One should also note Cuba's important contribution to educational development internationally (Hickling-Hudson et al., 2012). Examples of this international solidarity approach include the facts that: (a) Cuba "sent more than 22 000 teachers abroad between 1973 and 1985" (Lutjens, 2000, p. 18); (b) "roughly 185,000 Cubans [, including teachers,] participated in international missions during the ten-year period from 1998 to 2008, and they were active in 160 countries around the world" (Corona González et al., 2012, p. 46); and (c) in 2004 "there were 27,585 foreign students in higher and secondary education in Cuba, and of them 15,308 were scholarship students" (Lutjens, 2007, p. 184).

4 Thus, during the summer of 1900, 1,273 Cuban teachers (out of a total of 3,400 in Cuba) participated in a six-week summer teacher professional development program at Harvard (Schultz, 2018). The government decided to send Cuban teachers to Harvard and other U.S universities response to a protest by the Asociación Pedagógica, the Asociación Nacional de Maestros, and other educators to an

initiative to staff Cuban schools with U.S. teachers (Esposito Rodriguez 1985, p. 18; see also Epstein, 1999). These Cuban educator organizations initially accepted these summer school teacher education programs but argued that such programs should be organized in normal schools in Cuba and staffed by Cuban teacher educators (Buenavilla-Recio et al., 1995; Esposito, 1985; Paulston, 1971).

5 However, while the literacy campaign was undoubtedly a resounding achievement, one should note that before the literacy campaign "Cuba's illiteracy rate was not high by Latin American standards" (MacDonald, 1985, p. 55; see also Breidlid, 2007, p. 620).

6 Fitzgerald (1987, p. 70) reports that "[i]n 1980, the Cubans declared victory in the 'Battle for the Sixth Grade' and in the [subsequently declared] struggle for the ninth grade in 1985" (see also Lutjens, 2000, p. 5).

7 The invasion attempt is part of a long list of bombings, attempted assassinations, and other terrorist activities sponsored or undertaken by the U.S. government against Cuba, beginning almost immediately after the Triumph of the Revolution in 1959 (Franklin, 2015; Ramírez Cañado y Morales Domínguez, 2014).

8 It seems more appropriate to translate the term, "el hombre nuevo," as the new person, since "over half of those who volunteered to teach in the literacy campaign was female and over half of the beneficiaries of the campaign were also female, meaning that women were instrumental to the project of creating a nation of 'New Men' and ... thereby asserted a 'New Woman" (Herman, 2012, p. 95).

9 Fitzgerald (1987, p. 45) elaborates on Che's distinction between moral and material sources of motivation: "[T]o permit the high rates of capital formation and the labor-intensive development projects considered necessary to develop the material base of the future society, they needed a New Person who would work long and hard, not for personal advantage, but for the good of the community."

10 Fitzgerald (1987, p. 76) notes that work-study "was promulgated as a principle of Cuban education ... [in] Resolution 362 [of 1964, which] ... called for educational programs that would combine 'physical labor with intellectual work, and both of these with life."

11 Moreover, in 1977 "volunteers from the ...[previously discussed] 'Manuel Ascunce Domenech Pedagogical Brigade' [were] called upon to undertake internationalist service in the Popular Republic of Angola. Ministerial Resolution 663/77 grouped these volunteers to form the 'Che Guevara Internationalist Pedagogical Brigade'" (Griffiths, 1998, p. 120).

References

Addine Fernández, F., & García Batista, G. (2005). *La interacción: núcleo de las relaciones interdisciplinarias en la formación de profesores de perfil amplio* (Una propuesta, Curso 44). La Habana: Congreso Internacional Pedagogía.

Alarcón de Quesada, Ricardo. (2011). Cuba: Education and Revolution. *Monthly Review, 63*(3). Retrieved from https://monthlyreview.org/2011/07/01/cuba-education-and-revolution/

Aldama de Pino, M. A., & Casañas Díaz, M. (2018). *Filosofía de la educación de Fidel Castro (1945–1981)*. La Habana: Editorial Universitaria Félix Varela.

Alzugaray, C. (2008). *Crónica de un Fracaso Imperial: La Política de Eisenhower contra Cuba y el Derrocamiento de la Dictadura de Batista*. La Habana: Editorial de Ciencias Sociales.

Aquino, R. (1994). *Cuba: Organization of Education, 1992–1994*. Report of the Republic of Cuba to the 44th international conference on public education. Havana: Ministry of Education.

Badía, A. (Ed.). (1993). *La educación en Cuba: Pasado, presente y futuro*. Washington, DC: Cuban American National Foundation.

Berube, M. (1984). *Education and poverty: Effective schooling in the United States and Cuba*. Westport, CN: Greenwod Press.

Breidlid, A. (2007). Education in Cuba—An alternative educational discourse: Lessons to be learned? *Compare, 37*(5), 617–634.

Buenavilla-Recio, R., Cartaya-Cotta, P., Joanes-Pando, J. A., Silverio-Gómez, M., Santos-Echeverría, N., Martínez-Hernández, M., Benítez-Rojas, J., Orille-Azcuy, L., & Echeverría Martínez, I. R. (1995). *Historia de la pedagogía en Cuba*. La Habana: Editorial Pueblo y Educación.

Carnoy, M. (1990). Education and the transition state. In M. Carnoy & J. Samoff (Eds.), *Education and Social Transition in the Third World*. Princeton, NJ: Princeton University Press.

Carnoy, M., Gove, A. K., & Marshall, J. H. (2007). *Cuba's academic advantage: Why students in Cuba Do Better in school*. Stanford, CA: Stanford University Press.

Carnoy, M., & Marshall, J. (2005). Cuba's academic performance in comparative perspective. *Comparative Education Review, 49*(2), 230–261.

Carnoy, M., & Werthein, J. (1980). *Cuba: Cambio económica y reforma educativa, 1955–1978*. Mexico City: Editorial Nueva Imagen.

Carnoy, M., & Werthein, J. (1983). Cuba: Training and Mobilization. In J. Simmons (Ed.), *Better schools: International lessons for reform*. New York, NY: Praeger.

Castillo Estrella, T. (2002). *La superación de los docentes de la escuela: una necesidad para la calidad de la educación. Trabajo presentado en el Congreso Pedagogía 2003*. Pinar del Río: Instituto Superior Pedagógico "Rafael María de Mendive."

Castro Ruz, F. (1953). *Carta al Sr. Ramón Castro* (East Prison, September 5).

Castro Ruz, F. (1960). Discurso en el Acto con los Empleados del Comercio (La Habana, 5 de junio). Quoted in Miguel Ángel Aldama de Pino and Mirta Casañas Díaz, Mirta (2018). *Filosofía de la educación de Fidel Castro (1945–1981)*. La Habana: Editorial Universitaria Félix Varela.

Castro Ruz, F. (1971). *Granma Resumen Semanal* (28 November). La Habana: Granma.

Castro Ruz, F. (1983). *La historia me absolverá*. La Habana: Editorial de Ciencias Sociales.

Castro Ruz, F. (1993). Discurso en la Clausura de Pedagogía '93. *Granma,* (9 February), 3–6.

Castro Ruz, F. (1997, September 1). *Speech delivered at the official opening of the school period, 1997–98*. Havana: Ministry of Education.

Corona González, J., Hickling-Hudson, A., & Lehr, S. (2012). Challenging Educational underdevelopment: The Cuban solidarity approach as a mode of South-South cooperation. In R. Preston, A. Hickling-Hudson, & J. Corona González (Eds.), *Capacity to Share: A study of Cuba's international cooperation in educational development* (pp. 35–52). Gordonsville, VA: Palgrave Macmillan.

Cruz Taura, G. (2008). *Revolution and continuity in the history of education in Cuba.* Retrieved from https://www.ascecuba.org/asce_proceedings/revolution-and-continuity-in-the-history-of-education-in-cuba/

De la Cuesta, L. A. (1976). The Cuban socialist constitution, its originality and role in institutionalization. *Cuban Studies/Estudios Cubanos, 6*(2), 15–30.

Díaz Fuentes, A. D. (1997). El sistema de formación inicial y continua del personal docente de Cuba. *Revista Educación y Pedagogía, 9*(17), 137–151.

Domínguez García, M. I., Rego Espinosa, I., & Castilla García, C. (2014). *Socialización de adolescentes y jóvenes: Retos y oportunidades para la sociedad cubana actual.* La Habana: Editorial de Ciencias Sociales.

Epstein, E. (1999). The peril of paternalism: The imposition of education on Cuba by the United States. In N. McGinn & E. Epstein (Eds.), *Comparative perspectives on the role of education in democratization.* New York, NY: Peter Lang.

Escobar-Lorenzo, R., Leyva-Figueredo, A., & Mendoza-Tauler, L. (2013). La formación de los estudiantes en aulas pedagógicas. *Ciencias Holguín, XIX*(1), 1–11.

Esposito Rodriguez, B. (1985). *Apuntes del movimiento de los trabajadores de la educación* (1899–1961). La Habana: Editorial Ciencias Sociales.

Fitzgerald, F. (1987). *Managing socialism: From old cadres to new professionals in revolutionary Cuba.* New York, NY: Praeger.

Font, M. (2008). Cuba and Castro: Beyond the 'battle of ideas.' In M. Font (Ed.), *Changing Cuba in a changing world.* New York, NY: CUNY Graduate Center.

Franklin, J. (2015). *Cuba-Estados Unidos: Cronología de una historia.* La Habana: Editorial de Ciencias Sociales.

García Batista, G., & Addine Fernández, F. (2013). *Transformación de la institución educativa.* La Habana: Editorial Pueblo y Educación.

García Isaac, Y. (2018). *Las políticas y sistemas educativos.* Presentación de powerpoint para el curso de educación comparada, Universidad de Ciencias Pedagógicas "Enrique José Varona."

García Ramis, C. L. (2004). *Situación de la formación docente inicial y en servicio en la República de Cuba.* La Habana: Instituto Central de Ciencias Pedagógicas.

Gasperini, L. (2000). *The Cuban education system: Lessons and dilemmas.* Country Studies, Education Reform and Management Publication Series, Vol. I, No. 5. Washington, DC: The World Bank.

Ginsburg, M., Belalcazar, C., Popa, S., & Pacheco, O. (2010). Constructing worker-citizens in/through teacher education in Cuba: Curricular goals in the changing political economic context. In J. Zajda & M. A. Geo-JaJa (Eds.), *The politics of education reforms* (pp. 137–163). Dordrecht: Springer.

Ginsburg, M., Cooper, S., Raghu, R., & Zegarra, H. (1990). National and world-system explanations of educational reform. *Comparative Education Review, 34*(4), 474–499. Retrieved from http://www.jstor.org/stable/1188294

Gómez Castanedo, S., & Giacchino-Baker, R. (2001). Current programs and issues in Cuban teacher education today. *International Journal of Curriculum and Instruction, 3*(1), 15–23.

Gómez Castanedo, S., & Giacchino-Baker, R. (2010). Teacher education in Cuba: Keeping promises to the past and to the future. *International Perspectives, 4*(Spring), 94–108. [Reprinted from K. Karras & C. Wolhuter (Eds.). (2010), *International handbook on teacher education worldwide: Training issues, and challenges for the teaching profession.* Athens: Atrapos Editions.]

Gonzales, E. (1976). The party congress and poder popular: Orthodoxy, democratization, and the leader dominance. *Cuban Studies/Estudios Cubanos, 6*(2), 1–14.

Gonzales Jo, B., & García Mena, Y. (2018). *Estudio comparado sobre el proceso de Formación Profesional de Cuba y Alemania. Trabajo Final de Educación Comparada.* La Habana: Universidad de Ciencias Pedagógicas "Enrique José Varona."

Gonzáles Santamaría, A. E. (compilador). (2017). *Raúl Castro y Nuestra América: 86 discursos, intervenciones y declaraciones.* La Habana: Editorial Capitán San Luis.

Granimian, A. (2009). *How much are Latin American students learning? Highlights from the Second Regional Student Achievement Test* (SERCE). Santiago, Chile: Partnership for Educational Revitalization in the Americas.

Griffiths, T. (1998). *The development of secondary school education in revolutionary Cuba, 1959–1991: A world-system approach* (Doctoral dissertation). University of Newcastle, Australia.

Griffith, T. (2009). Fifty years of socialist education in revolutionary Cuba: A world-systems perspective. *Journal of Iberian and Latin American Research, 15*(2), 45–64.

Guevara, E. "Che" (1970). *Obras, 1957–1967.* La Habana: Casa de las Américas.

Guevara, E. "Che" (1973). Man and Socialism in Cuba. In B. Silverman (Ed.), *Man and socialism in Cuba: The great debate.* New York, NY: Atheneum.

Guevara, E. "Che" (2002). *Man and socialism in Cuba.* La Habana: Editorial de Ciencias Sociales.

Guevara, E. "Che" (2017). *El Socialismo y el hombre en Cuba* (pp. 253–272). La Habana: Editora Política. [Tomando de Ernesto Che Guevara (1977). Ernesto Che Guevara: *Escritos y discursos,* tomo 8. La Habana: Editorial de Ciencias Sociales.].

Herman, R. (2012). An army of educators: Gender, revolution and the Cuban literacy campaign of 1961. *Gender and History, 24*(1), 93–111.

Hickling-Hudson, A., Corona González, J., & Preston, R. (2012). Introduction: Cuba's capacity to share. In R. Preston, A. Hickling-Hudson, & J. C. González (Eds.), *Capacity to share: A study of Cuba's international cooperation in educational development* (pp. 1–10). Gordonsville, VA: Palgrave Macmillan.

Horowitz, I. (1976). Authenticity and Autonomy in the Cuban Experience: Toward an operational definition of revolution. *Cuban Studies/Estudios Cubanos, 6*(1), 67–74.

Johnson, L. (1995). Education and Cuba Libre, 1898–1958. *History Today, 45*(8).

Kolesnikov, N. (1983). *Cuba: Educación popular y preparación de los cuadros nacionales, 1959–1982*. Moscow: Editorial Progreso.

Kolivras, K., & Scarpaci, J. (2009). Between corporatism and socialism: Navigating the waters of international education in the Dominican Republic and Cuba. *Journal of Geography, 108*(3), 121–131.

Laboratorio Latinoamericano de Evaluación de la Calidad de la Educación (LLECE). (1998). *Primer estudio internacional comparativo sobre lenguaje, matemática y factores asociados en tercero y cuarto grado*. Santiago: UNESCO.

Laboratorio Latinoamericano de Evaluación de la Calidad de la Educación (LLECE). (2008). *Segundo estudio internacional comparativo sobre lenguaje, matemática y factores asociados en tercero y cuarto grado*. Santiago: UNESCO.

Lau Apó, C. F. (2017). *Cronología de la formación de educadores en Cuba*. La Habana: Asociación de Pedagógos de Cuba.

Lee, C. (2015). *Achieving quality education through centralized teacher training in Cuba*. Comparative Education Term Paper, College of Education, University of Maryland.

López-Hurtado, J., Chávez, J., Garcés, M., Esteva, M., Ruiz, A., & Pita, B. (1996). *El carácter científico de la pedagogía en Cuba*. La Habana: Editorial Pueblo y Educación.

Loyola Vega, O. (2001). Liberación Nacional y Cambio Social (1868–1998). In E. Torres-Cuevas & O. L. Vega (Eds.), *Historia de Cuba, 1492–1898: Formación y liberación de la nación* (pp. 230–400). La Habana: Editorial Pueblo y Educación.

Ludlam, S. (2012). Aspects of Cuba's strategy to revive socialist development. *Science & Society, 76*(1), 41–65.

Lutjens, S. (2000). Política Educativa en Cuba Socialista: Lecciones de 40 años de reformas. In M. Monereo Riera y J. Valdéz Paz (Eds.), *Cuba: construyendo futuro* (pp. 1–23). Barcelona: Fundación de Investigaciones Marxistas/Viejo Topo.

Lutjens, S. (2007). (Re)reading Cuban educational policy: Schooling and the third revolution. In I. Epstein (Ed.), *Recapturing the personal: Essays on education and embodied knowledge in comparative perspective* (pp. 163–194). New York, NY: Information Age Publishing.

MacDonald, T. (1985). *Making a new people: Education in revolutionary Cuba*. Vancouver: New Star Books.

Martí, J. (1884, May). Maestros ambulantes. *La América*.

Martínez Sánchez, R. (2015). *Girón: Razón de la victoria*. La Habana: Casa Editorial Verde Olivo.

Massón Cruz, R. M., Llivina Lavigne, M. J., & Arencibia Sosa, V. (2011). *Estudio comparativo en la formación de profesores de secundaria básica*. La Habana: Ministerio de Educación.

Ministerio de Educación (MINED). (1977). *Documentos directivos para el perfeccionamiento del subsistema de formación y perfeccionamiento del personal pedagógico*. La Habana: MINED.

Minsterio de Educación (MINED). (1994). *Cuba: Organization of education 1992–1994*. Report of the Republic of Cuba to the 44th International Conference on Public Education. La Habana: MINED.

Ministerio de Educación (MINED). (2003). *La escuela como microuniversidad en la formación integral de los estudiantes de carreras pedagógicas*. La Habana: MINED.

Partido Comunista de Cuba (PCC). (1975). *Plataforma de Partido Comunista de Cuba*. La Habana: PCC.

Paulston, R. (1971). Education. In C. Mesa-Lago (Ed.), *Revolutionary change in Cuba* (pp. 375–398). Pittsburgh, PA: University of Pittsburgh Press.

Paulston, R. (1980). Impacto de la reforma educativa en Cuba. *Revista Latinoamericana de Estudios Educativos, 10*(1), 99–124.

Paulston, R., & Kaufman, C. (1992). Cuba. In P. Cookson, A. Sadovnik, & S. Semel (Eds.), *International handbook of educational reform* (pp. 85–99). New York, NY: Greenwood Press.

Pedagogía '93. (1993). *La educación en Cuba: Aspectos fundamentales*. La Habana: Ministerio de Educación.

Quintero López, M. (2011). Education in Cuba: Foundations and challenges. *Estudos Avançados, 25*(72), 55–71.

Rámirez Cañado, E., & Morales Domínguez, E. (2014). *De la confrontación a los intentos de 'normalización': La política de los Estados Unidos hacia Cuba* (segunda edición ampliada). La Habana: Editorial de Ciencias Sociales.

Ritter, A. (2004). The Cuban economy in the twenty-first century: Recuperation or relapse? In A. Ritter (Ed.), *The Cuban economy* (pp. 3–24). Pittsburgh: University of Pittsburgh Press.

Roucek, J. (1994). Pro-communist revolution in Cuban education. *Journal of Interamerican Studies and World Affairs, 6*(3), 323–335.

Sánchez Collazo, A., & Sánchez-Toledo Rodríguez, M. E. (2002/2016). La pedagogía cubana: sus raíces y logros. In G. García Batista (Ed.), *Compendio de pedagogía* (pp. 36–44). La Habana: Editorial Pueblo y Educación.

Saney, I. (2004). *Cuba: A revolution in motion*. London: Fernwood Publishing/Zed Books.

Schultz, R. (2018, February). *Turning points in the history of education in Cuba, 1898–2018* (Powerpoint presentation). Havana: CASA-Cuba.

Snell Goldstein, A. (2012). Teaching in the shadow of an Empire: Teacher formation in Cuba and the United States. In M. Ginsburg (Ed.), *Preparation, practice, and politics of teachers: Problems and prospects in comparative perspective* (pp. 31–47). Rotterdam, The Netherlands: Sense Publishers.

Stubbs, J. (1989). *Cuba: The test of time*. London: Latin America Bureau (Research and Action) Limited.

Turner Martí, L. (2014). *Notes on Ernesto Che Guevara's ideas on pedagogy*. Halifax & Winnipeg: Fernwood Publishing.

UNESCO. (2004). *The EFA global monitoring report 2005: The quality imperative*. Paris: UNESCO.

UNESCO International Bureau of Education (IBE). (2010). República de Cuba: Datos. In *Datos Mundiales de Educación* (7th ed.). Geneva: UNESCO International Bureau of Education. Retrieved from http://www/ibe.unesco.org/

Valdés, N. (1976). Revolution and institutionalization in Cuba. *Cuban Studies/Estudios Cubanos, 6*(1), 1–37.

Wolfensohn, J. (2001). *Learn from Cuba*. Washington, DC: World Bank. Retrieved from www.twnside.org.sg/title/learn.ht

CHAPTER 10

Hills and Valleys of the Mexican Reform: Politics and Contentions

Carlos Ornelas

> Some critics may choose to portray the contemporary school reform movement as a nefarious conspiracy on the part of evil plutocrats hoping to destroy America's [or Mexico's] schools, but in fact, the vast majority of reformers (ourselves included) are well-meaning people who are acting in good faith and trying to do right by kids.
>
> JAY P. GREENE AND MICHAEL Q. MCSHANE, *Learning from school reform failures*, 2018

∵

Abstract

In this chapter, I analyze the main political components of the Mexican education reform of the Peña Nieto administration. I synthesize how both the reform proposal and the reactions of diverse actors contribute to re-map the Mexican basic education system. I combine divergent theoretical perspectives to discuss the Mexican reform in comparison with the GERM or Global Education Reform Movement, led by intergovernmental organizations, mostly the OECD. I elaborate based on three frameworks. The first body of concepts derives from the neoinstitutionalist sociology referred to as the world culture. This approach sees national educational reforms in a path towards the construction of a world culture that creates institutional isomorphism worldwide. The second standpoint, which I call cultural neo-imperialism, provides concepts of domination. Authors adherent to this perspective see the intervention of the intergovernmental organizations as part of a global tendency to make education an instrument of neoliberal world order. The third outlook is known as the lending and borrowing approach. It claims that national governments and educators alike take concepts and tools from *traveling policies* posted in the

 | DOI: 10.1163/9789004413375_011

international arena. Finally, I mix the approaches with the Mexican education reform unveiling the dialectics between the national and the global.

1 Introduction

At the outset of his six-year term, President Enrique Peña Nieto launched an ambitious project of education reform. It showed a political purpose: to recover the control of the basic Mexican school system (from pre-school through lower secondary), which top loyalists of the corporatist National Education Workers' Union (SNTE) had seized through decades of political action. The President also made clear that his principal aim was to eradicate harmful traditions of retiring teachers: at that time, they could still bequest their teaching posts, called *plazas*, to relatives or, if they did not have kinsfolks with appropriate credentials, they could sell their plaza outright to the highest bidder. Over their careers, unethical teachers could even rent their plazas while working elsewhere. By the end of 2012, the incoming Revolutionary Institutional Party (PRI) administration coped with the existing political context by forging an unusual alliance with the right-wing Party of National Action (PAN)—which had just lost the Presidency after twelve years in power—and the left-wing Party of the Democratic Revolution (PRD). Together they signed the Pact for Mexico, a program of structural reforms aimed at an overhaul of the economy, governance, and programs for social development. According to the President, education reform would lead the way (Presidencia de la República, 2012). The supporters of the Pact agreed to use two kinds of tools to stroll the reformist path: political and legislative.

Four key words—*purpose, tradition, context*, and *tools*—form the axes for building a political narrative about the struggles around the changes, and of the roles of the principal political and institutional actors in the Mexican education reform.

By the end of his six-year tenure, President Peña Nieto could exhibit vast achievements of the education reform he launched. Through legislative action, the government and its allied parties had attained constitutional amendments, changes to the General Law of Education (LGE), and two new laws. One law provides autonomy to the National Institute for the Evaluation of Education (INEE), while the other designs a whole new institution to manage labor relations and to regulate the professional careers of teachers and administrators. The General Law of the Professional Teaching Service provides tools to dismantle the corrupt corporatist behaviors of existing teachers, but also to warrant a new professional ethics, based on merit, competition, and performance. However, this aspect of the reform is still under siege by dissident teachers' organizations grouped around the National Coordinator of Education Workers (CNTE) and MORENA, the Party which won the federal elections, both the presidency and the majority in Congress, on July 1, 2018.

In his classic work *Still the Century of Corporatism?* Philippe Schmitter alludes to the difficulties in settling the concept in operational and useful terms. It has united so firmly with a unique political culture, as the type of regime or macrosocial configuration that becomes, in the best of cases, something descriptive rather than analytical. However, after going through a significant set of literature and intellectual currents, he arrived at what he called an operational definition. For Schmitter, corporatism is the opposite of democratic pluralism: "[...] an interest intermediation system, where a limited number of non-competitive groups obtain a license from [or are created by] the state, which grants them a monopoly in their respective categories in exchange for controlling their leadership and their demands" (Schmitter, 1974). This type of political organization of the masses and institutions was the critical feature of the regime of the Mexican Revolution and still holds a hegemonic muscle in the larger unions, especially on those of the public sector, like the SNTE.

Throughout the first 18 months of his administration, Peña Nieto appeared as an armed prophet, as Machiavelli would say. He was in command. The National Congress and state legislatures responded to his initiatives (Machiavelli, 2003). At that time, he appeared as a young, energetic leader catalyzing a sequence of changes: eleven structural reforms, involving 58 amendments to the Constitution, 81 changes in secondary laws, 21 new legal systems and 15 old regulations repealed (Beltrán del Río, 2014). The international press called these important changes *the Mexican moment*. Yet, political failure to deal successfully with dissident teachers' organizations, systemic corruption, the inability to stop criminal violence, and other uncontrollable effects of the political context, disarmed Peña Nieto. International affairs, such as the election of Donald Trump as President of the United States, even further reduced his political capital. In his last year in office, the President has looked like prey for many adversaries. The political context was ultimately unfavorable to him and the reform: corporatist traditions are striking back, and although current government officials defend the changes brought by reform, no other political forces are doing so. Thus, the struggle for education reform will continue.

In this chapter, I argue that the Pact for Mexico proposed an education reform that incorporated traits from global discussions but mostly was in response to local issues and conflicts. After hitting highs and low, successes and defeats, the outcome of that reform is still in question.

2 Global and Local Perspectives

In the field of comparative and international education, many theoretical standpoints vie with one another to explain education reforms. Although those theories frequently overlap in concepts, their adherents' debate about the meaning and content of educational phenomena worldwide. Three of those perspectives are most relevant to help elucidate the *similarity* in education reform around the globe: the world culture theory; the cultural neo-imperialism perspective; and the borrowing and lending approach.

Authors favoring the world culture theory understand the development of education as a way towards a single global ethos. According to a leading world culture theorist:

> At the nation-state level, comparative studies have shown that educational systems around the world are much more similar than would be predicted by the extreme variations among them in levels of development and cultural traditions. And they tend to change in parallel ways, affected by world fashions. [...] these structures tend, isomorphically, to reflect legitimate models, and to change along with changes in these models. (Meyer, 2007, pp. xi–xii)

World culture scholars have produced a considerable bulk of literature on education reforms to demonstrate their claims about isomorphism. However, since not everything in the world of education is entirely similar, Wiseman and Matherly (2009, pp. 334–335) concur with others: "This process occurs as these associations and programs follow established and accepted scripts for legitimate activity and content. Within the established structures and norms there will be some 'loose coupling' of day-to-day activity."

Radical authors challenge such a claim for legitimacy. In the opinion of these dissenters, the World Bank and other intergovernmental organizations, like the OECD, impose models of education reform that follow the hegemonic inclinations of global capitalist development (Klees, Samoff, & Stromquist, 2012; Lingard, Martino, Rezai-Rashti, & Sellar, 2016; Stromquist & Monkman, 2014; Tröhler & Lenz, 2015; Turner & Yolcu, 2014). This is the cultural neo-imperialism view. In his classical work, *Education as Cultural Imperialism*, Martin Carnoy observed the role of education in empire-building of European military powers as tools of colonization of Third World countries. The colonial states imposed their culture on the peoples of Africa, Asia, and Latin America, as well as on the poor whites and blacks of the United States through internal colonialism. The central powers aimed to impose—sometimes by use of military strength—in the colonized territories a school system to instruct a local elite at the service of the colonizers. For Carnoy, imperialism was a stage in the expansion of capitalism, and its cultural content (mainly, schools) was a structural policy willfully adopted by the central powers to dominate the mind of the colonized peoples. Thus, education became an architectural feature in the process of economic exploitation (Carnoy, 1974).

With the rise of the term globalization and the vast amount of intellectual work about global phenomena, the expression of imperialism has lost ascendancy. Some still argue that globalization exalts its features as the natural, historical development of humankind towards a global society, or globalism, while in fact it has strong ideological and intellectual bases. According to them, the ideology underlying globalism is neoliberalism, which is the belief that the free market delivers benefits and that its workings should be as unrestricted as possible. The neoliberal orientation supposedly established its ideological hegemony not only in economic and financial matters but also in education and society (Takayama, 2015; Turner & Yolcu, 2014).

Although these radical authors do not identify the workings of the intergovernmental organizations on education as a form of cultural imperialism, they do associate them with a process of imposition of educational policies on national education systems. In fact, they argue, the importance of the global market for formal schooling does not evolve by some spontaneous development of capitalism. Global institutions such as the World Bank, the OECD, and to a lesser extent, UNESCO, have sown the fundamental criteria for a Global Education Reform Movement, or GERM (Sahlberg, 2015). The idea of GERM—Sahlberg argues—evolves from the increased international exchange of policies and practices. It is not a formal global policy program, but rather an unofficial educational agenda that relies on a particular set of (neoliberal) assumptions to improve education systems "[...] GERM has emerged since the 1980s and is one concrete offspring of globalization in education. It has become accepted as 'a new educational orthodoxy.'"

Stromquist and Monkman (2014) pinpoint four indicators of globalized education reform, or GERM. First, the criteria employed by firms for efficiency and productivity are being extended to schooling, sometimes in an inappropriate fashion. Second, the focus has shifted from a child-centered curriculum to economy-centered vocational training. Third, education is losing ground as a public good to become another marketable commodity instead. Fourth, there is a reduction in teachers' autonomy, independence, and control over their work, while workplace knowledge and direction find their way increasingly into the hands of administrators.

Starting from the idea of Sahlberg and taking the early conceptualization of Carnoy, I would say that GERM is not a formal policy program, but it does provide the grounds for a theory that can reasonably be named cultural neo-imperialism. In contrast with the old fashion of colonization by conquest and the use of military forces, now, the intergovernmental organizations lead the way for education reforms worldwide by employing propaganda, scholarly works, and mainly assessment tools, such as PISA, TALIS, TIMSS, PIRLS, and others. The products of many authors (like Carnoy, 2015; Klees, Samoff, & Stromquist, 2012; Stromquist & Monkman, 2014; Sellar & Lingard, 2013; Turner & Yolcu, 2014) illustrate how the globalism ideology comports with substantial public relations activities of OECD. They also show how the tasks of scholars employed by the World Bank and the spread of evaluation devices and rankings of educational institutions, shape the intrusion of those organizations into the politics of many nations (Klees, 2012).

The authors of world culture theory and those that favor a cultural neo-imperialism view disagree on political orientation, but they agree that globalization has become the driving force for education reforms since the 1980s. Still, although many scholars show examples of how those globalization organizations fight for instilling their outlooks in nations and regions of the world, they fail to recognize the contradictions and particular political relations between governments, political parties, and domestic actors. It seems that for some of those researchers, the national ruling classes or the alliances in control of the government have no distinct aspirations or ways of doing politics. They tend to see local governing groups as loyal followers of international tendencies, at best; or just like puppets, at worst.

Still, other scholars emphasize the importance of local political struggles in motivating national authorities to promote education reforms, even as the governments that carry out those reforms may borrow ideas from abroad (Ginsburg & Cooper, 2007; Rappleye, 2012; Rust, 2007; Steiner-Khamsi, 2012). The borrowing and lending approach, Steiner-Khamsi argues, represents a shift in comparative and international educational scholarship because of the inconsistencies of those authors who do not consider the idiosyncrasies of national politics—and national turmoil, I may add—where local governments appropriate and retool "itinerant ideas," such as those of GERM. Further, Steiner-Khamsi asserts that national politics should be the core for the study of education reforms: "These inconsistencies end up making sense once we apply an interpretive framework that pays attention to the 'socio-logic' [...] of cross-national policy attraction or acknowledges the political and economic rationale for policy borrowing. The terrain under scrutiny should be the local policy context" (p. 5).

Carney, Rappleye, and Silova (2012) illustrate the connections between those two modes of interpreting the increasing homogeneity of educational systems worldwide, which they name convergence, and Tröhler (2015) calls harmonization. Although they focus their criticism on world culture theory, someone can also apply it to all approaches that appeal to globalization as the driving force of culture, like the cultural neo-imperialism outlook. Carney and colleagues stress that "[…] both sides of the debate offer complementary perspectives in explaining the interaction between the global and the local: world culture theorists are charged with documenting global phenomena while their opponents' content themselves with analyzing their local variations."

The scrutiny of the Mexican education reform demands more than seeing it as an imposition of global forces or merely as a national movement. Instead, Robert Arnove's conceptualization of the relationships between global trends and national engagements offers a good starting point:

> Common prescriptions and transnational forces, however, are not uniformly implemented or unquestionably received […] a dialectic is at work by which these global processes interact with national and local actors and contexts to be modified and, in some cases, transformed. There is a process of give-and-take, an exchange by which international trends are reshaped to local ends. (Arnove, 2013, p. 2; see also Tröhler, 2015)

In other words, to explain education reform drives in a given country demands a theory of the state and political power, although such theory may be implicit. The assumption is that the state is also an arena for conflict and power struggles, and thus education is a part of those struggles. The Mexican case can perhaps serve to illustrate these themes.

3 Hills and Valleys of the Mexican Reform

In the Pact for Mexico, the allies displayed the purpose of the education reform. "For this [to achieve quality and equity in education], [the parties] promote a legal and administrative reform in educational matters with three initial and complementary objectives. First, increase the quality of basic education that should reflect better results in international evaluations, such as PISA. Second, increase enrollment and improve quality in secondary and higher education systems. Third, that the Mexican government regains control (*rectoría*) over the national education system, maintaining the principle of secularism (Presidencia de la República, 2012). The first aim reveals the influence of the "traveling policies." The reference to PISA was an indicator that the architects of the Pact reduced the concept of educational quality to students' performance on standardized tests. It elicits globalization and globalism. The second goal implies more expansion than change, but this still is part of GERM in its earlier iteration, "Education for All." The third one discloses the political purpose of the state rulers: to recover control over the school system that past governments first gave to the SNTE's leaders on operational matters only and then they ceded to them increasingly important decision-making matters. The SNTE's loyal cadres thereby colonized the Mexican system of basic education (Ornelas, 2008, 2010).

The dialectics of the global and the local were noticeable not only by the reference to PISA but also because of other tools announced in the text of the Pact for Mexico, echoing almost literally recommendations the OECD made to the Mexican government in 2010. Those were: (1) to establish an Educational Information and Management System, based on a census of schools, teachers, and students; (2) to consolidate the National System of Educational Evaluation, granting full autonomy to the National Institute for the Evaluation of Education; (3) to provide schools greater autonomy on management issues; (4) to make the transition to full-time schools (students in primary education in Mexico have only 20 hours per week of direct instruction, 200 days per year); (5) to provide students with laptops with Internet connectivity; (6) to create a professional teaching corps (this was the greatest source of political controversy); (7) and to strengthen pre-service education of teachers and their in-service training (OECD, 2010). There were other aims for high school (upper secondary), which were less controversial because in that sector the SNTE has no control.

Once the political parties signed the Pact, the government pursued a twofold strategy: legislation and political maneuvers, which implied both bargaining and repression.

President Peña Nieto organized a symbolic political show in the National Anthropological Museum on December 10, 2012, escorted by the chiefs of the PAN and the PRD. He enacted the ritual to announce that the following day his administration would send to the Legislative Power an initiative to amend articles 3 and 73 of the National Constitution.[1] In that ceremony, the Secretary of Public Education, Emilio Chuayffet, used an imperative tone. He narrated how the past—governments of both the PRI and the PAN—had lost control of basic education and given it to the operatives of the SNTE. "[The SEP] is an archipelago," he said.[2] He also alleged that the state apparatus did not know how many teachers were working in the school system, nor did they know exactly what job educators were doing, nor how much they were earning. Chuayffet described as anarchy the handling of basic education. That was why the government had to recover the exercise of authority over the school system (Chuayffet Chemor, 2012). It was a political war cry.

Given the agreement of the leaders of the three major parties, the Federal Congress approved the proposal by December 20, only with minor changes; and 20 state legislatures ratified it by January 21, 2013 (Ramírez Raymundo, 2013). The constitutional amendment contained the aims expressed in the

Pact; and although the word did not appear in the text, "merit" became a value almost equal to justice, freedom, and democracy. The most substantive part of the reform modified existing teachers' career incentives and evaluations since their entrance into the teaching profession.

Commitment 12 of the Pact for Mexico set the basis for the establishment of the Professional Teaching Service as a system of competition based on merit to fill the positions of new teachers or those that were left vacant due to retirement or illness. The idea of merit, however, was reduced to the organization of opposition contests, through standardized tests. The addition of a paragraph to Article 3 of the Constitution proclaimed the new meritocratic basis of entering into the profession as opposed to the corporatist tradition of bequeathing or marketing teaching plazas. This amendment sowed the seeds of a profound change in the lives of both in-service teachers and prospective educators:

> Also, admission to the teaching service and the promotion to positions of management or supervisory functions in the basic and upper secondary education provided by the state will be carried out through competitions that guarantee the suitability of their [teachers'] corresponding knowledge and skills. The regulatory law shall establish the criteria, terms, and conditions of the mandatory assessment for admission, promotion, recognition, and permanence in the professional service. (Article 3, fraction III Mexican Constitution, as of February 26, 2013)

Nevertheless, through debates in the Senate and Federal Chamber of Deputies, legislators diminished the amendment's original purpose. They eliminated the "teeth" of the amendment; even if teachers did not manage to pass the three stages of mandatory assessment in four years, they would not lose their jobs but rather be transferred to lower administrative duties. Still, such a change did not reduce the opposition of the leaders of all factions of the SNTE. The labor boss of the largest faction, the one that controlled most of the operations of the corporatist union, organized a "National Crusade in Defense of Public Education and its Teachers." The heads of the dissident organization, the CNTE, were even more radical in their opposition to the changes (Ornelas, 2014). It is likely that leaders in both organizations wished to maintain existing privileges and keep control of teachers' professional career path.

Using the tools of the law, President Peña Nieto ordered the arrest of Elba Esther Gordillo, who'd been "lifetime leader" of the SNTE since 1989. The government accused her of money laundering, tax evasion, and theft of union funds. The capture of Ms. Gordillo took place on February 26, 2013. Such a move disciplined the larger faction of SNTE; the new leader, Juan Diaz de la

Torre—who was second in command—immediately agreed with the Secretary of the Interior not to oppose the reform. Up to this point, though, the traditional CNTE practice of popular struggle and mobilization—sometimes with violence—made the government follow a different strategy. Instead of repressing teachers who committed acts of obstruction and violence—like stopping the traffic on major highways, closing airports, setting fire to public buildings, assaulting trucks, vandalizing department stores, creating circulation chaos in many cities, and effecting wild-cat strikes in schools—the president decided to bargain with them. He charged such a responsibility to the Secretary of the Interior (Segob) rather than the Secretary of Public Education (Fernández, 2013; Ornelas, 2014).

For almost 40 years, the CNTE has nurtured a tradition of struggle against both their opponents within the union (SNTE) and the government. Although the CNTE has democratic roots in the late 1970s, fighting against corruption and defending teachers' rights, their leaders soon did what they criticized in the other faction. Through mobilization they conquered many higher administrative positions, put state governments under siege, and achieved substantial concessions to their demands. They colonized the management of the school system in some of the poorest and most educationally backward states: Chiapas, Guerrero, Michoacán, and Oaxaca. According to Rubio and Jaime, both SNTE and CNTE leaders developed new tools beyond the corporatis tradition: blackmail and threat (Rubio & Jaime, 2007).

From April to November of 2013, the CNTE utilized its tactics and thereby obtained many concessions from the Secretary of the Interior. Among those concessions were the granting of automatic teaching posts to graduates of Teachers' Colleges (*Escuelas Normales*), the suspension of pre-service assessments as a pre-condition of employment in those four states, and the commitment to incorporate into states' laws portions of the dissidents' proposals, even if they contravened the General Law of the Professional Teaching Service. Although the Interior Ministry denied the under the table bartering, *Reforma*—a national newspaper—made public how the Ministry in fact violated the law (Del Valle, 2013).

According to many polls published in March and April 2013, arresting Ms. Gordillo gave Peña Nieto credibility in his reformist proposals (Beltrán & Cruz, 2013; Cámara de Diputados Centro de Estudios Sociales y de Opinión Pública, 2013). Also, although it was a centralist move, the re-centralization of the teachers' payroll—achieved by reforming the Fiscal Coordination Law in September 2013—was applauded by most observers because it represented a savings of millions of dollars and the retreating of the power of the SNTE sections in the states. In this way, the central government weakened the state governors who, in any case, had never acquired enough strength to cope with local leaders of the SNTE. The image of President Peña Nieto was of a man with a high vocation for power. It even seemed as though he wished to revive "the imperial presidency," like in the times of the regime following the Mexican revolution.[3]

Conversely, bargaining with the CNTE diminished his trustworthiness and thus lessened the legitimacy of the reform. Many civil organizations grouped into "The Citizen Eye, or *Ojo Ciudadano*," led by *Mexicanos Primero* (Mexicans First), demanded transparency and integrity from the government when dealing with the various teachers' factions. Still, the alliance signed in the Pact for Mexico started to break apart in 2014. From the right, the PAN rejected the fiscal reform while the leftist PRD disliked the changes in energy policies favoring privatization. Furthermore, scandals of corruption of the President himself, the Secretary of Finance, and many other public officials, including state governors of all parties, bit by bit dismantled government credibility. Also, the killing of four students of the Rural Teacher College of Ayotzinapa by the municipal police of Iguala and the disappearance of another 43, revealed the inadequacy of the Executive Chief to deal with emerging issues outside of the political script designed at the outset of his presidency.[4] Thus, from being the "man in charge," the President became a vulnerable head of state. Therefore, his credibility came down, and his opponents gained political terrain, especially Andres Manuel López Obrador (AMLO), who won the presidential election on July1, 2018. Peña Nieto received yet another political blow at the end of his term. On August 7, 2018, a District Court absolved Elba Esther Gordillo of the charges brought against her by the government in 2013. Although she is now over 70 years old, and her health is weak, she may seek to return to her privileged position. Thus, the education reform—and others, like the one on energy—are likely to be turned back.

Still, the new constitutional amendment and the creation of the new bylaws have spread important institutional changes. Even though the government took suggestions from the OECD, some of these were used as tools by the dominant union group to take back control—though not entirely—of the school apparatus. Later, the new Secretary of Public Education, Aurelio Nuño, commenced the design of an aspiring curricular reform.

4 Political Brawls and Institution Building

For decades the leaders of the SNTE—and their allies in the press and academia—said that their primordial function was to defend public education and its teachers. They argued that any criticism of the low quality of education, the failures of the bureaucracy, or the deficiencies and poor training of teachers ultimately was aimed at privatizing the public-school system. They blamed the World Bank and the OECD for attacking teachers and claimed that those intergovernmental organizations were supported by business and conservative civil society groups as well as by the neoliberal forces of the PRI and the PAN (Hernández Navarro, 2013). The union leaders argued that society should protect the SNTE and its factions from the assaults of the nefarious forces of neoliberalism.

In the administration of Peña Nieto, the OECD has provided the main recommendations for education reform. Still, the OECD did not impose such recommendations on the government of Mexico; rather, the SEP, with Josefina Vazquez Mota at the head, sought the expert advice of the organization (OECD, 2009). The Pact for Mexico then considered the recommendations and adapted them to its ends to address the political context, apparently with good design and efficient mechanisms.

The power struggle between the governing group and the leaders of the SNTE and CNTE also involved institutional tools; in those, the top bureaucracy had the initiative. The purposes set out in the Pact for Mexico became pieces of the law; even the amended Constitution was ordered to suit the new Educational Information and Management System (SIGED). To establish this apparatus, the National Institute for Geography and Statistics (INEGI) conducted a national Census of Schools, Teachers, and Students of Basic and Special Education. Even though the OECD had recommended the creation of such a system, the signatories of the Pact for Mexico nationalized the issue and elevated it as a matter of paramount importance.

The census only covered 90 percent of the expected universe because the CNTE boycotted the collection of data in their territories. However, it exhibited dramatic figures that affected the political debate: The census identified more than 39 thousand aviators (as they are popularly known; these are people on the payroll who "fly around" without doing any educational work at all). Also, it showed more than 31 thousand legally "commissioned" employees, who enjoyed a license by agreement between the union and the SEP, as well as more than 110 thousand other "commissioned" employees doing administrative work. The jewel of the findings: almost 115 thousand workers who had resigned, were retired or even deceased continued cashing their checks (The Economist, 2014). Between the dead, retired, commissioned, and aviators, the government was spending about 1.4 US billion dollars a year.

A set of new mechanisms and institutions furnished the reform that in turn empowered the official government bureaucracy:

- SIGED became a new apparatus to foster transparency. SIGED not only struck at the heart of corporatist traditions defended by SNTE leaders but also has become an information repository for the Mexican education system's statistics. On its website, the SEP provides access to open data.

- The reform included the consolidation of the National System of Educational Assessment (SNEE) led by the INEE, but now with the participation of the both the federal and states' governments. The SNEE goes beyond what the OECD proposed in 2010. It provides a set of tools for what Guy Neave (1990) termed the evaluator state. Its overall strategy includes: (1) objects, methods, parameters, indicators, and assessment procedures; (2) based on the results of the assessments but also on political judgments, the INEE stipulates guidelines that the authorities should follow; (3) qualitative and quantitative indicators of quality and equity; (4) design and distribution of data to all parties; (5) the encouragement of a culture to foster assessment (INEE Act, article 17).
- Using the tools of the evaluator state, the government ended the inheritance and selling of teaching plazas. Furthermore, as of 2017, the SEP implemented and pushed the states' authorities to do the same, so that the winners of the open competition choose where they like to work, according to the vacant plazas and their position in the rankings.
- The first edition of teacher performance assessment created much turmoil in September-November 2015. The opposition propaganda was effective in saying that the government designed the evaluation to dismiss teachers. Teachers' uncertainty about their plazas generated anxiety and all type of protests. Thenceforward, INEE took a step back and accepted some criticism, such as the perception that the evaluation instruments might be discriminatory in certain ways. In the end, though, it seems that the institutionalization of assessment is a *fait accompli*.
- Information and assessment serve well the purposes of centralizing power, yet the control of economic resources is the mightiest instrument of all. The reform of the Fiscal Coordination Act in September 2013 created the Fund of Contributions for the Educational Payroll and Operational Expenditure (FONE). As of January 1, 2015, the Departments of Finance and Education together manage teachers' and other workers' payroll; the states have no more money to do so, although the governors still appear to act as patrons of their teaching personnel. Using FONE, with data from 1.4 million teachers and education support employees, has allowed SEP and the states to regularize more than 44 thousand plazas of teachers who'd been doing administrative work for the local authorities. That represented a savings of more than 220 million US dollars per year (as of June 2017).
- The government gave another blow to the SNTE with the substitution of the Teachers' Career (*Carrera Magisterial*, a program of monetary incentives

that the government created in 1993) for the Program of Promotion in the Function for Incentives in Basic Education. Parity commissions of the SEP and the SNTE officially had managed *Carrera Magisterial*, but given the power of SNTE's leaders, union cadres had in fact controlled it. The SEP alone now operates the new system. It has been a significant power shift.

– Another part of institution making was a massive program of school rebuilding and maintenance not in the Pact for Mexico but dictated by political pragmatism. This program had tangible consequences. In 2015 the government securitized the school infrastructure budgets and launched the Certificates of National Educational Infrastructure (CIEN, or 100); this is a stock exchange instrument designed to provide resources to carry out a program of school building and maintenance. So far it has been successful: the government used it for its primary purpose, but also for restructuring school buildings damaged by the September 2017 earthquakes that affected many parts of the country (Ornelas, 2018).

Max Weber pointed out that when bureaucratic rationality is at work, and the officialdom performs with efficacy, the government constructs credibility. Thus, the head of a state with legitimacy has more political tools to achieve his/her ends (Weber, 2014). The Peña Nieto administration kept pace and gained momentum in 2013 and 2014. It seemed that his watchword, "For an effective government," was becoming a reality. He had all the instruments of a centralist state to carry out his political aims: to recover state control over education, weaken corporatist traditions, and to discipline SNTE factions. However, corruption and the changing political context deteriorated his presidency; still, those developments have not stopped the march of the education reform. SEP has kept stride and managed to advance in its purposes, albeit with changes in the top of the bureaucracy.

5 Armoring the Reform

Regardless of the fact that the Constitution (article 40) establishes that Mexico is a democratic, representative and federal Republic, the political system is centralist. Although the president no longer has all the powers of the imperial presidency, the structure of government remains presidential. Much of what happens in the government depends on how the president manages the tools of power. Due to its size, and the colonization of its administration by the SNTE leaders, the running of the public education system is vertical, bureaucratic and riddled with corruption (Ornelas, 2010, 2012).

The Peña Nieto government's education reform aimed to change those traditions. Then again, the issue is complex because of the history of colonization, bureaucratic routines, and the dimensions of the system. The Mexican institutional arrangement is gigantic; more than 25 million students in basic education, more than five million in high school; more than one million 900 thousand in training for work; and almost four million in higher education. More than two million educators attend this universe in nearly 260 thousand schools (Peña Nieto, 2017).

The arrival of Aurelio Nuño to the leadership of the SEP in August 2015 was more than a change of Secretary. It was a shift of direction. The previous Secretary, Emilio Chuayffet, had fulfilled the tasks of consultation for the new educational model, but political untidiness created the militant opposition of the CNTE and the fraught negotiations with the Interior Ministry; his health also deteriorated. Chauyffet's last act of power consisted in negotiating, jointly with the governor, Gabino Cué, the "recapturing" of the State's Institute of Public Education of Oaxaca (IEEPO) for the authorities. Although there are reasons to suspect that Mr. Chuayffet had wanted to muscle forth such a move at least one year before, the Interior Minister had been opposed and maintained its politics of giving concessions to CNTE leaders of that state.

Since April 2013 the dissident teachers of Oaxaca and the other "rebel" sections of Chiapas, Guerrero, and Michoacán, continued with their protests, including sit-ins and walkouts in Mexico City and Oaxaca. They made mistakes though. The biggest one was to reject the offer of the Undersecretary of the Interior, Luis Miranda, on June 4, 2015, in which Oaxaca teachers were guaranteed their "right to remain," recognizing "their labor rights and political, administrative, economic, social, legal and union achievements." That would have meant to keep the control that CNTE's leadership had over the IEEPO. Yet the CNTE leaders insisted that the government repeal the constitutional reforms and revoke its secondary laws. They threatened to boycott the June 7, 2015, elections, but they did not succeed.[5]

For the government, the situation in Oaxaca was already unsustainable. The SEP had to suspend the scheduled evaluations, but the President resented the social pressure and made his displeasure known in the press, in ceremonies with businesspeople, and in the criticism of political parties. A sum of factors forced him to act both as a fox and as a lion, as recommended by Machiavelli. The decree of July 20, 2015 indicates that the government had carefully studied how to erase all union influence on management. Such a verdict refunded IEEPO and gave the local authorities control over school system management, teachers' affairs, and appointment of schools' principals and supervisors. It was a maneuver designed to decolonize the governance of education in Oaxaca. It was announced and enforced on the first day of schools' vacations, and so it was difficult for the leaders to convince their followers to march; to call for a strike was impossible. Accordingly, President Peña Nieto acknowledged the formal rules; it was Governor Cué who led the way, while his envoys showed the support of the federal government. It was a mighty blow that set the stage for a new Secretary of Public Education.

As reported in the press, the new Secretary, Aurelio Nuño, from his first day fine-tuned his use of power. His first step was to snatch away from the Interior Minister any negotiation that had to do with the education sector. Secondly, he developed an aggressive discourse against the "bad teachers," threatening layoffs if they did not comply with the teachers' performance test or if they missed more than three days of class; he also bullied the governors who did not support the reform (Hernández, 2016).

Since his arrival at the SEP, Aurelio Nuño showed a willingness to move the reform towards curricular and pedagogical issues. The purpose was to bring the ideals of the *reform* closer to teachers, to modify the unfavorable political context, and to continue dismantling the corporate traditions. He showed signs of a political vocation. Every Monday he visited a school and sent messages, his picture appeared on the press' front pages, and he appeared on those TV shows most viewed by students and rank and file teachers. He also wrote editorials for the daily press where he announced in plain language the plans of the government. He moved like a fish in water.

The Secretary's strategy was working out. The CNTE was losing pace and it appeared that the reformist way was on the straight track. Dissident teachers accepted the evaluations and graduates of the Rural Teachers' Colleges entered the teaching profession according to the new rules. However, in June 2016 local and federal police forces tried to open a highway the nonconforming CNTE teachers had blocked for more than one month. It was the Nochixtlán incident, which resulted in 8 civilian deaths.[6] Even though he had no command over the forces of public order, the rebel teachers charged Secretary Nuño with the unfortunate outcome. It was a blow to his policy.

The reader will recall that the SNTE had monopolized not only the labor representation of teachers, but it had also replaced the authorities in their relationship with them. Therefore, the Secretary made another important shift: SEP staff prepared a document for a public enquiry to discuss a new model for education delivery. The educational model of 2016 presented the pedagogical approach of the educational reform. It was a kind of white paper where the SEP was fully involved in the core of education: it expanded the notions of "School at the center," inaugurated the new curricular approach, and set before the voice training (*formación* is a word in Mexican Spanish that connotates education in a more wide-ranging way than instruction) to professional teacher development (Nuño, 2016; Secretaría de Educación Pública, 2017a, 2017b). It was an ideological and political turn; teachers always demanded first quality training, then professional development.

SEP thus put under discussion that white paper and other three documents: (1) "A letter on the aims of education in the 21st century"; (2) The core document: *Educational Model 2016;* and (3) *The Curricular Proposal for Compulsory Education.* While the teachers remained the focus of the invitation, Secretary Nuño called a broader audience and considered a variety of political and institutional actors. The SEP organized 15 national forums that included a conclave with the Board of Governors (this was perhaps a formality that more than asking for their opinion was seeking to align them with the educational reform); dialogues with the Government Board of INEE; colloquia with legislators, both federal and state; and even corporate actors, such as the SNTE, the National Association of Universities (because of its bearing on upper secondary education, which had become compulsory in 2015), and the Councils of Social Participation in Education. He also invited many civil society organizations. The gathering of school principals, teachers—with special mention of teachers who speak indigenous languages—and students created an atmosphere of plurality. Scholars, businesspeople, and journalists also participated.

The consultation was huge: More than 200 state forums, with about 50 thousand participants; a roundtable on line for particular discussion for the school technical councils and groups of teachers, with almost 30 thousand participants, and more than 1.8 million visits to a webpage. There were 28 documents from organizations and academics. In short, the consultation provided a sea of information that, in a milieu like the Mexican one, loaded with distrust, was difficult to administer, let alone to organize. However, as James March and Johan Olsen (1996) have asserted, hiring experts gives prestige to politicians. From the beginning, the SEP involved the Interdisciplinary Program on Educational Policies and Practices (PIPE) from the prestigious Center for Economic Research and Teaching (CIDE).

The PIPE is a think-tank that was responsible for collecting and ordering the papers and other contributions to the Model proposed by the SEP. The value of the PIPE's final report lies in that it allowed the top bureaucracy of the SEP to arrive in March 2017 with a proposal which, if not wholly reworked, did reflect changes that arose from the consultation. In a section of the *Modelo educativo para la educación obligatoria* (Educational model for compulsory education), SEP criticizes the administrative tradition of the school system: "[…] by prioritizing compliance with norms and regulations, teachers are discouraged from collaborative work and waste opportunities for horizontal exchange" (p. 23). It also disapproved the style of supervision and advocated for the creation of a new school culture. It privileged the making of collective decisions (although still under the leadership of the principal) not only for the use of financial resources but also for curricular contextualization. The proposal called for a "school that must be a community that learns and improves" (p. 25), and that the school technical council (CTE) should be the collegial decision-making body. It was there that "… strategies must be established to evaluate the students' learning and to fight opportunely the factors that cause abandonment" (p. 27).

Given the context, it is possible to suppose that most of the "innovations" that the SEP incorporated between the 2016 proposal and the final version of the Model came from teachers and school principals. One can detect the changes in the matters that most interest them: curriculum, training and teacher professional development, and school administration. Nonetheless, the new educational Model arrived almost at the end of the six-year term of President Peña Nieto. His approval rating was at historically low levels, the new presidential campaigns were at their peak, and the education reform was in the crosshairs. Such a situation was not novel; Antonio Gramsci wrote that education is politics and politics is education (Gramsci, 1976). What maybe would be fatal for the President Peña Nieto is that the new group in power would overhaul the education reform. Both institutionally and politically, his government struggled to shield the reform so that it might resist the attacks of opposing groups. It seemed, before the July 1 election, that the need to amend the Constitution assured the continuation of the reform. However, after September 1, 2018 the left-leaning MORENA has a majority of Congress, and very close to the qualified majority (two-thirds of the votes) and more than the seventeen states' legislatures needed to amend the Constitution. Thus, the education reform is still at risk of being rescinded.

6 The Global and the Local

The Mexican education reform is not an isolated venture; it also is part of an all-embracing global education reform movement. Given the path of the Mexican education reform, it is feasible to assert that it imports elements from the international environment, but not mechanically. It is contradictory; it incorporates tools from neoliberal trends, but also from participatory models and upon implementation it acquires a particular profile.

Cuevas Cajiga and Moreno Olivos (2016) made a detailed tracking of the recommendations made by the OECD to Mexico in the 2010 report regarding teachers. The OECD put into perspective eight strategic orientations, "[...] based on the thesis that, to achieve better results for students, Mexico requires a rigorous system of selection, training, development, and evaluation of basic education teachers." Cuevas and Moreno documented that the education reform embodied such orientations. The "creation of the Professional Teaching Service and the autonomy of the National Institute for the Evaluation of Education concretized the OECD advice." The "nationalization" of the policy of the OECD, would mean, in the eyes of these radical authors, the confirmation of their theses about the dependence of the Mexican government in the execution of the educational reform. The OECD—as before the World Bank and UNESCO—inspired, if not designed, the leading neoliberal edges of changes in education (Navarro Weckmann, 2017). Therefore, according to such scholars it lacks cultural legitimacy because it does not consider the characteristics of the national school system, much less the traditions of Teachers' Colleges and Mexican educators.

Nevertheless, the reform is much more than teacher evaluation, although that is the central piece and the one that generated the most turmoil among educators. In the Model for Compulsory Education and the provisions for its implementation, references to the Global Educational Reform Model abound, both in the substantive parts (learning) and in the portion regarding authority and accountability (which the Model compiles under the heading of "governance"). The defenders of tradition perhaps would say that the ideas embodied in such proposals are alien to Mexican pedagogy, that the Mexican government imported them from abroad without considering what teachers know how to do and a positive school culture that took decades to consolidate. Perhaps some might grant some credence to the reform but highlight the absence of national roots. Others, such as Miguel Ángel Pérez (2017), predict the failure of the education reform, in particular the Professional Teaching Service, for dismissing Mexican teaching traditions in favor of globalizing influences.

Although the OECD is the primary focus of the authors who censure the educational reform, they would perhaps coincide with researchers from other latitudes who criticize the "new" approach of the World Bank. To be sure, the Educational Model for Compulsory Education puts the accent on learning and relegates teaching—and aspects such as school expansion—into the background. Antoni Verger and Xavier Bonal, in their criticism of the World Bank 2020 Strategy, state that one of its main characteristics is its desire to overcome input-driven reforms and place learning outcomes as the central objective. "Learning for all, and not simply access for all, is configured as the main priority ... While the strategies of the past recognized this goal, the new one gives more emphasis, establishing it in a context of evaluation and system reforms" (Verger & Bonal, 2014). Some would suggest that the emphasis on learning is not an accident, but a response to neoliberal proposals that demand more competent "human capital" for Mexico to embed itself in the world market.

Still, from another perspective, putting learning at the center of reform is an asset in the struggle against the authoritarian tradition of teaching and its rote pedagogy. Although at first glance one might note the neoliberal ideological reasons that the OECD reform suggestions were adopted, a deeper look shows how the strength of local politics caused mutations, sometimes abrupt, in the implementation of the reform.

Let's take the proposal of the program, "School at the Center." First, it takes up the idea of strong school leadership from the OECD recommendations. However, it revises the suggestion, and instead of assigning an almost dictatorial role to the school principal, it distributes the management tasks among the members of the school technical council, which includes the principal. That is an important nod to a more participatory approach. The principles of accountability and evaluation are present, but not 100% in the sense of the recommendations of the OECD. Rather, the program diminishes their scope: "evaluation for improvement," as suggested by some of the OECD's harshest critics. The most valuable asset: putting learning in the driver's seat and teaching in the passenger seat. In the founding documents of the Mexican reform and the program proposals for the School at the Center, there is no mention of rankings or competition for resources. The Model postulates that when autonomy is granted to meet the needs of schools the teachers—together with the principal—will construct their useful technical advice, supported by social participation commanded by parents and other social actors.

By replacing the competitive mentality with a rationale focused on student learning, the Model accommodated global expectations but adapted them to local conditions. The School management autonomy program, for instance, is a part of the purpose of the state recovering the control of education. Fair enough, little of that program can be shown to have local intellectual grounding. Many of its elements come from notions that permeate the international environment. Then again, while they did not come as a product of a global trend towards cultural isomorphism, as if by nature, neither were they imposed by intergovernmental organizations; it is not a case of coercion by cultural neo-imperialism. It was a tool devised by the Mexican central government to avoid the intrusion of SNTE and CNTE cadres and to erode the states' authorities in the allocation of funds and the monitoring of their application. The end expresses the ideology: money so that each school improves its infrastructure and it is their local community that decides. The political vision is tacit: to build bridges from the apex of power in the sector—SEP and the Secretary himself—to the smallest scale of the system; it was a struggle for supremacy in the control of education. The move bypasses the states' authorities and the cadres of different union factions.

To sum up: The ideological provision for the reform was available in the global environment, and the dominant group in the Mexican government (first with its political allies in the Pact for Mexico, and then on its own initiative) used them to prepare a unique program for the national context. They borrowed notions and procedures from lenders—some amorphous, others well-defined—on the global plane. The short time frame will dictate the final sentence. If the institutional changes are strong enough to endure a dialectics of control, as Anthony Giddens (1995) would say, they might guarantee an inevitable evolution, and secure achievements well beyond the Peña Nieto's term. The promises of improvement are apparent, but it will no longer be up to this government to fulfill most of them.

7 Closing Dicta

The Mexican government's purpose and the context in which the education reform unfolded serve to explain why the dominant group chose institutional and political tools to dismantle corporatist teacher traditions. Still, although the Peña Nieto presidency relied on proposals from the OECD and borrowed other traveling policies from GERM, I sustain that the primary driver of the education reform was the government's aim to decolonize the management of the school system. To do so, it had to diminish the power of the SNTE's factions and to deliver results. The Peña Nieto administration used elements of globalism but also appealed to power levelheadedness to dismantle the heritage of corporatism and thus achieve a significant degree of legitimacy.

True, the Mexican education system is similar in many of its constituent modes to others in the world. Since the institutionalization of the SEP, in 1921, one could think that it was designed isomorphically, as John Meyer might say, affected by world trends. Indeed, Mexican education development throughout the twentieth century followed dominant models and changed along with the modifications in other parts of the world, especially in the advanced countries. Even during the "socialist education" interregnum (1934–1940), Mexico imported notions from the USSR (Quintanilla & Vaughan, 1997). However, the introduction of corporatist traits into the Mexican political system and the institutionalization of the "imperial presidency" shaped a particular mode of domination. The "loose coupling" idea is insufficient to explain the power of

SNTE and its leaders, the rampant corruption, and the mode of corporatist control of teachers.

The education reform that began in 2012 indeed developed in parallel ways to what was going on in the world. Globalization is a reality, but it does not govern everything happening inside of a given country. The approaches of world culture and cultural neo-imperialism are linked to the obsession to see the world from a global perspective. Much of the research they do and the tests they conduct are valuable. Thanks to these studies, we understand the similarities of the educational reforms that proliferate in the world and understand part of the logic of convergence (or homogeneity or isomorphism). Nonetheless, they fail to explore adequately the dialectics between those tendencies and the national efforts. Although they recognize local particularities and aspirations of their rulers, in the final analysis they do not grant them degrees of autonomy of thought or political action. Some authors, such as Samir Amin (1998), conceive them as mere transmissions of the prevailing global order. In these visions—maybe—national interests are the object of study only to obtain evidence and arguments in favor of their theoretical perspectives.

Meanwhile, the promoters of the neoliberal approach pick up the suggestions of the GERM model to attack the unions of teachers. They argue that there are rights of individuals, but not of collective entitlements. Therefore, the OECD always proposes that school principals have the authority to hire, suspend, punish, assign tasks, set rewards and dismiss teachers, as happens in private companies and schools where principals are sometimes the owners (commendation 12 of the 2010 report). That would be the primary attribute of school principal leadership. In the name of administrative efficiency, they profile an exercise of power at the micro level that is vertical, where each actor (or agent) complies with his/her tasks by the regulations and conforms to the rules of the game. In essence, it transfers state authoritarianism to each school by diminishing the role that traditional bureaucracy represents. Such reference fits well with criticism like that made by Stromquist and Monkman about how intergovernmental organizations extend the same criteria to schooling as those used in capitalist firms for efficiency and productivity. Still, it does not match entirely with that the focus on basic education has shifted from a child-centered curriculum to economy-centered vocational training. The Mexican Model proposes a more humanist approach to preschool and primary schooling and mixed strategies for secondary and higher education. The School at the Center program shows this more humanistic, participatory side of the Mexican reform.

Stromquist and Monkman also argued that education is losing ground as a public good to become another marketable commodity. That's correct. In several parts of the globe, the defenders of the neoliberal approach combine the projects of school reforms with the privatizing trends (Turner, 2014; Zajda, 2006). They insist that education is a service (the concept of the right to education rarely appears in their vocabulary) and therefore the laws of supply and demand must govern the management of schools. However, neoliberals consider that the market by itself is incapable of regulating such an extensive and diverse service. For this reason, they demand the participation of the state so that, from a beginning model of autonomy, the schools can leap to the private sector. That is the ideological origin of the voucher programs in various parts of the world (McEwan & Carnoy, 2000) and the charter schools in the United States (Ravitch, 2014). The political longings are more varied and depend a lot on the contexts where those ideas have flourished. It is not the same to impose programs by dictatorial means, such as the vouchers in Chile at the time of Pinochet than to seek that the local legislatures of the United States allocate budgets for charter schools, even as private corporations operate them.

Not in complete opposition to neoliberal approaches, but with considerable differences in view, those who advocate the participatory model of school reform manifest a democratic and pluralist ideology. They criticize the vision of effectiveness following the molds of management in the business sector, but they support accountability. They link their conceptions of quality to equity and emphasize the risks of reforms dictated from the top down. In the Mexican reform, there is not an appeal to privatizing the school system. Quite the contrary, the state allocates more monies to the education sector, including for compensatory programs (though, inequality still is rampant throughout the system).

What is a neoliberal feature of the reform, and yes adapted from global trends, is the way that the new Professional Development Service reduces teachers' autonomy, independence, and control over their work, while workplace knowledge and direction find their way increasingly into the hands of administrators. However, I do not think that is a reactionary trait; before this reform, the work trajectory of teachers was in the hands of labor bosses, and corruption marked their entrance and promotion in the professional career. The Professional Teaching Service, like all coins, holds two faces. On one side is the eagle who in its claws charges the evaluator state with rules that some consider ominous against teachers. The other side presents the attributes of professionalism that the corporate system snatched from teachers over decades of clientelist practices. The General Law of Teacher Professional Development includes values such as merit, independence of criteria and a new work ethic based on responsibility, engagement, and performance. It tries to find the middle of the coin.

Robert Arnove, in his analysis of the dialectics between the local and global, outlined a research project. For him, the most important principles to be derived from the history of borrowing and lending is that there is no one best system, that all have strengths and weaknesses. He also posited that education systems reflect the tensions and contradictions of the societies of which they are a part. The history of Mexican education scripts attempts to reform every six years, though only a few have had lasting and profound effects on the school system and its principal actors: the teachers. In those efforts to reform, the reformist forces borrowed ideas and policies, but in the end, the local politics and contradictions determined their fate.

When it became law, The Professional Teaching Service contained the potential for an in-depth reform, and implied deep changes in politics, administration and practices and customs of the teaching profession. It is a long-term project that, however, given the Mexican political pendulum—consecrated in six-year terms—is ever at the edge of falling. It was the most controversial aspect of the reform; it was attacked by leaders of union factions that saw that their tools to control teachers' career trajectories—and thus privileges—were at risk. The new institution of teachers' labor relations was also the result of broad condemnation of harmful practices like selling and bequeathing teaching plazas.

The new president of Mexico, Andres Manuel López Obrador, when he was the candidate of MORENA, signed pacts with SNTE's factions to dismantle the education reform. Being president-elect, his nominated secretary of Public Education, Esteban Moctezuma, has repeatedly said that the government would send initiatives to Congress (where MORENA is now the leading force) to change the Professional Teaching Service Law. It is entirely possible that this Congress will enact changes that diminish the weight of performance assessment for teachers and weaken transparency mechanisms. Still, I do not think that the new group in power will dismantle the other institutional changes, like the information systems or the re-centralization of the payroll. Nor will they give back the control of the administrative apparatus to SNTE loyalists. The new president has a noteworthy power vocation. I estimate that he will not share governance tools. Although he may give some concessions to teachers who voted for him, I foresee that López Obrador will act as an armed prophet. National politics will take precedence over global influences.

Notes

1 Article 3 institutes the philosophy, aims and institutions of national education; it one of the most revised pieces of the Constitution. It started the principle of secular

education since 1917. Article 73 refers to the responsibilities and duties of State organs and the distribution of authority between the national and regional powers.

2 In 1921 the federal government established the Secretariat of Public Education (SEP) to found and organize schools, prepare teachers and conduct national education (Ornelas, 2018).

3 For more than 70 years of the PRI's regime, the President enjoyed meta-constitutional or informal powers. For example, he was the head of the PRI, appointing his successor, governors, Supreme Court ministers, senators and the majority of the Deputies of his party, as well as the Presidents of the most important municipalities. The President was the supreme judge of all social and political conflicts. Daniel Cossío Villegas said that the President of Mexico was a monarch for six years, while Enrique Krauze spoke of an imperial presidency. The presidential institution established the informal rules of the political game. The mediation of interests of groups of different nature and depth could only be done through official representation and in the ways that the presidential regime dictated: asking the president to solve all problems. He was the only ruler (Carpizo, 1978; Cosío Villegas, 1972; Krauze, 1997).

4 When narrating facts from the periods of the struggle between the government and other forces, I rely largely on newspaper accounts. It not worth citing many of them.

5 I base this and the following paragraphs on my recent book (Ornelas, 2018).

6 Eight people—none of them teachers—were killed when the police responded to the aggression (Excelsior, June 20, 2016).

References

Amin, S. (1998). *El capitalismo en la era de la globalización*. Barcelona: Paidós.

Arnove, R. F. (2013). Introduction: Reframing comparative education: The dialectic of the global and the local. In R. F. Arnove, C. A. Torres, & S. Franz (Eds.), *Comparative education: The dialectic of the global and the local* (4th ed., pp. 1–24). Lanham, MA: Roman & Littlefield Publishers.

Beltrán del Río, P. (2014, August 18). Las reformas: pasado y futuro. *Excélsior*.

Beltrán, U., & Cruz, A. (2013, March 4). Maestros aplauden captura de Elba. *Excélsior*.

Carney, S., Rappleye, J., & Silova, I. (2012). Between faith and science: World culture theory and comparative education. *Comparative Education Review, 56*(3), 366–393.

Carnoy, M. (1974). *Education as cultural imperialism*. New York, NY: David McKay.

Carnoy, M. (2015). *International test score comparisons and educational policy: A review of the critiques*. Retrieved from http://nepc.colorado.edu/publication/international-test-scores

Carpizo, J. (1978). *El presidencialismo mexicano*. Mexico City: Siglo XXI Editores.

Chuayffet Chemor, E. (2012). *Intervención durante la presentación de la iniciativa de reforma educativa* [Press release].

Cosío Villegas, D. (1972). *El sistema político mexicano: las posibilidades del cambio.* México: Cuadernos de Joaquín Mortiz.

Cuevas Cajiga, Y., & Moreno Olivos, T. (2016). Políticas de evaluación docente de la OCDE: Un acercamiento a la experiencia en la educación básica mexicana. *Archivos Analíticos de Políticas Educativas, 24*(120). http://dx.doi.org/10.14507/epaa.24.2283

Cámara de Diputados Centro de Estudios Sociales y de Opinión Pública. (2013). *Cápsula semanal de opinión pública LXII Legislatura: Repercusiones del caso Gordillo* [Press release].

Del Valle, S. (2013, November 7). Ablanda CNTE a Gobernación. *Reforma.*

Fernández, M. A. (2013). Saldo de la reforma educativa: avances, deudas y desafíos pendientes. *Animal Político*. Retrieved from http://www.animalpolitico.com/blogueros-el-blog-de-mexico-evalua/2013/09/12/saldo-de-la-reforma-educativa-avances-deudas-y-desafios-pendientes/

Giddens, A. (1995). *La constitución de la sociedad: Bases para la teoría de la estructuración* (J. L. Etcheverry, Trans.). Buenos Aires: Amorrortu.

Ginsburg, M. G., & Cooper, S. F. (2007). Conceptual issues in 'educational reform': Ideology, the state and the world economic system. In V. Rust (Ed.), *Educational reform in international perspective* (pp. 55–80). Bingley: Emerald.

Gramsci, A. (1976). *La alternativa pedagógica* (C. Cristos, Trans.). Barcelona: Novaterra.

Greene, J. P., & McShane, M. Q. (2018). Learning from school reform failures. *Phi Delta Kappan, 99*, 46–50.

Hernández Navarro, L. (2013, 22 de enero). La reforma educativa y la OCDE. *La Jornada.*

Klees, S. J. (2012). World bank and education: Ideological premises and idelogical conclutsons. In S. J. Klees, J. Samoff, & N. P. Stromquist (Eds.), *The world bank and education* (pp. 49–65). Boston, MA: Sense Publishers.

Klees, S. J., Samoff, J., & Stromquist, N. P. (Eds.). (2012). *The world bank and education.* Boston, MA: Sense Publishers.

Krauze, E. (1997). *La presidencia imperial: Ascenso y caída del sistema político mexicano (1940–1996)*. México: Tusquets Editores.

Lingard, B., Martino, W., Rezai-Rashti, G., & Sellar, S. (2016). *Globalizing Educational Accountabilities*. New York, NY: Routledge.

Machiavelli, N. (2003). *The Prince and other writings* (W. A. Rebhorn, Trans. original en 1503 ed.). New York, NY: Barnes and Noble Classics.

McEwan, P. J., & Carnoy, M. (2000). The effectiveness and efficiency of private schools in Chile's voucher system. *Educational Evaluation and Policy Analysis, 22*(3), 213–239.

Meyer, J. (2007). Foreword. In D. P. Baker & A. W. Wiseman (Eds.), *The impact of comparative education research on institutional theory* (pp. xi–xvi). Wagon Lane: Emerald.

Navarro Weckmann, M. (2017, 7 de junio). Una profesión que exige respeto. *Educación Futura.*

Neave, G. (1990). La educación superior bajo la evaluación estatal: Tendencias en Europa Occidental. *Universidad Futura, 2*(5), 4–16.

Nuño, A. (2016, January 25). La escuela al centro. *Milenio*.

OECD. (2009). *OECD-Mexico agreement to improve the quality of education in Mexican Schools*. París- Mexico City: Organisation for Economic Cooperation and Development Publishing.

OECD. (2010). *Establishing a framework for evaluation and teacher incentives: Considerations for Mexico*. París: Organisation for Economic Cooperation and Development Publishing.

Ornelas, C. (2008). The SNTE, Elba Esther Gordillo and the Administration of Calderón. *Revista Mexicana de Investigación Educativa, 13*(37), 445–469.

Ornelas, C. (2010). *Política, poder y pupitres: crítica al nuevo federalismo educativo* (2nd ed.). Mexico City: Siglo XXI Editores.

Ornelas, C. (2012). *Educación colonización y rebeldía: la herencia del pacto Calderón-Gordillo*. Mexico City: Siglo XXI Editores.

Ornelas, C. (2014). La oposición a las reformas. In G. Guevara Niebla & E. Backhoff Escudero (Eds.), *Las transformaciones del sistema educativo en México, 2013–2018* (pp. 360–375). México: Fondo de Cultura Económica.

Ornelas, C. (2018). *La contienda por la educación: globalización, neocorporativismo y democracia*. Mexico City: Fondo de Cultura Económica.

Peña Nieto, E. (2017). *Quinto informe de gobierno: Anexo estadístico*. Mexico City: Presidencia de la República.

Presidencia de la República. (2012). *Pacto por México*. Mexico City: Presidencia de la República.

Pérez, M. Á. (2017, July 26). El gran fracaso del servicio profesional docente. *Educación Futura*.

Quintanilla, S., & Vaughan, M. K. (1997). *Escuela y sociedad en el periodo cardenista*. Mexico City: Fondo de Cultura Económica.

Ramírez Raymundo, R. (Ed.). (2013). *La reforma constitucional en materia educativa: alcances y desafíos*. Mexico City: Senado de la República Instituto Belisario Domínguez.

Rappleye, J. (2012). *Educational Policy Transfer in an Era of Globalization: Theory – History – Comparison*. Frankfurt am Main: Peter Lang.

Ravitch, D. (2014). *Reign of error: The hoax of the privatization movement and the danger of America's public schools*. New York, NY: Vintage Books.

Rubio, L., & Jaime, E. (2007). *El acertijo de la legitimidad: por una democracia eficaz en un entorno de legalidad y desarrollo*. Mexico City: Fondo de Cultura Económica-CIDAC.

Rust, V. (2007). Introduction: The change, process and educational reform. In V. Rust (Ed.), *Educational reform in international perspective* (pp. vii–xiv). Bingley: Emerald.

Sahlberg, P. (2015). *Finish lessons 2.0: What can the world learn from education in Finland*. New York, NY: Teachers College Press.

Schimitter, P. C. (1974). Still the century of corporatism? *The Review of Politics, 36*(1), 85–131.

Secretaría de Educación Pública. (2017a). *Modelo educativo para la educación obligatoria: educar para la libertad y la creatividad.* Mexico City: SEP.

Secretaría de Educación Pública. (2017b). *Ruta para la implementación del modelo educativo.* Mexico City: SEP.

Sellar, S., & Lingard, B. (2013). PISA and the expanding role of the OECD in global educational governance. In H.-D. Meyer & A. Bonavot (Eds.), *PISA, power, and policy: The emergence of global educational governance* (pp. 185–206). Southhampton: Symposium Books.

Steiner-Khamsi, G. (2012). Introduction. Understanding policy borrowing and lending: Building comparative policy studies. In G. Steiner-Khamsi & F. Waldow (Eds.), *World yearbook of education 2012: Policy borrowing and lending in education.* New York, NY: Routledge.

Stromquist, N. P., & Monkman, K. (2014). *Globalization and education: Integration and contestation across cultures* (2nd ed.). Lanham, MD: Rowman & Littlefield.

Takayama, K. (2015). Provincialising the world culture theory debate: Critical insights from a margin. *Globalization, Societies and Education, 13*(1), 34–57.

The Economist, H. T. (2014, April 7). Education in Mexico: Phantom Teachers. *The Economist.*

Tröhler, D., & Lenz, T. (2015). Between the National and the global. In D. Tröhler (Ed.), *Trajectories in the development of modern school systems* (pp. 2–9). New York, NY: Routledge.

Turner, D. A., & Yolcu, H. (Eds.). (2014). *Neo-liberal Educational Reforms: A critical analysis.* New York, NY: Routledge.

Verger, A., & Bonal, X. (2014). All things being equal?': Policy options, shortfalls, and absences in the world bank education strategy 2020. In S. J. Klees, J. Samoff, & N. Stromquist (Eds.), *The world bank and education.* Boston, MA: Sense Publishers.

Weber, M. (2014). *Economía y sociedad* (New edition, revised, commented and annotated by Francisco Gil Villegas; J. M. Echavarría, J. RouraParaella, E. Ímaz, J. F. Mora, & F. G. Villegas, Trans.). Mexico City: Fondo de Cultura Económica.

Wiseman, A. W., & Matherly, C. (2009). The professionalization of comparative and international education: Promises and problems. *Research in Comparative and International Education, 4*(4), 334–335.

Zajda, J. (2006). Introduction. In J. Zajda (Ed.), *Decentralisation and privatisation in education: The role of the state* (pp. 3–27). Dordrecht, The Netherlands: Springer.

CHAPTER 11

Teacher Unions and Educational Reforms: The 90's in Argentina, Brazil and Mexico

Aurora Loyo

Abstract

In the 1990's, several Latin American countries launched a series of changes in the field of education. This has been a complex and uneven process. Teacher organizations, particularly teacher unions and others working in education have been relevant actors, responding to the establishment of those educational policies that would modify one or more of the parameters in which their members' activities were developed. This chapter examines such a problem. The path chosen consisted of contrasting three cases: Argentina, Brazil, and Mexico. The Mexican example is taken as the point of reference of this exercise because it is a country in which education reform, as international organizations have defined it, has been developed without experiencing significant irregularities up to now. The contrast will be examined in the following dimensions: (1) the teacher organizations (TOs) with emphasis on their structure and their links with the State; (2) the logic of the educational policies put into effect; and (3) the actions and reactions that these have triggered, such as teacher walkouts and mobilizations.

1 Points of Departure

Addressing the issue of teacher organizations in Latin America, and the role they have played with respect to the education reforms of the 90's, means entering into a subject dominated by a notorious polarization of viewpoints. Broadly speaking, we can say that we face two worlds that are clearly differentiated. On the one hand, is that of those who consider reforms to be primarily positive and consider a teacher organization as a main actor, but one which always or almost always hinders those processes. On the other hand, is that of the critics of the reforms, who are mainly interested in TOs in terms of the circumstances in which they resisted or mobilized to protest against the reforms. There is an additional bias in that the pro-reform authors, when referring to

 | DOI: 10.1163/9789004413375_012

TOs, tend to give privilege to the examination of positions adopted by the trade union leaders, whether in negotiation or confrontation. In contrast, the critics focus their attention on 'teacher movements' and on the groups and leaders who distinguished themselves during the protest days.

In this reflection we are interested in establishing communication lines between those two worlds; therefore, it is essential to identify first off certain blind spots that make it difficult to pose the problem in its proper dimension.

1.1 *What Are We Talking about When We Refer to "The Teachers"?*

No type of education reform can succeed if it does not have the support of the teachers. Tyrians and Trojans agree with this statement. However, what kinds of 'teachers' are being referred to? More often than not, it is an abstraction. That imaginary teacher in the literature on educational reform is an educator facing a group; once their centrality is recognized, analysts incorporate analyses and recommendations related to their vocation, initial formation, professional trajectory, and the possible ways to update their competencies. At the other extreme, for scholars who study TO movements, the imaginary teacher is the one who appears on the scene to resist neoliberal educational policies through strikes and mobilizations.

Notwithstanding, if we recognize the complex nature of a teacher, who is usually more liable to be female, we will see that she is a worker who operates in a given institutional framework. The rules that govern the classroom and the school are her immediate context, but the order of the school system, the union to which she belongs, and the educational system are not alien to her being. She is also a person whose aspirations are in no small extent conditioned and constrained by the institutional, social and political contexts in which she has developed. Thus, that teacher may be poor or feel very poor; she may be a member of the middle class or believe she is part of that middle class; she can feel that she is fortunate, even privileged, or consider that society is in debt to her; and she can have a feeling of security or vulnerability.

1.2 *What Do We Mean by Teachers' Organizations?*

The TOs in Latin America present considerable heterogeneity. In our countries, they are among the most energetic and combative union organizations. We cannot reduce the positions they adopted in the face of the reform to simply two; they make up a range of beliefs and actions that are not necessarily coherent or clear. Even though we know that the real signatories of contracts or pacts are the leaders, and that using initials such as SNTE, CTERA, CNTE (National Union of Education Workers in Mexico, Confederation of Education Workers of the Republic of Argentina and National Confederation of

Education Workers in Brazil) is simply a conventional way of naming them, we may fall into the error of reifying them. In our narratives, we use such acronyms unthinkingly to brand the TOs either as allies or opponents to the reforms. It is, therefore, necessary to remember that the leaders of such powerful organizations make up a social segment that must be characterized from the beginning by their specific interests, which are neither the same as those of the members of the TOs nor alien to them. Moreover, even in the most obvious cases of hierarchical control of these organizations, the members, the unionized teachers are there. Finally, it is worth remembering that the consensus that we can see in the positions of the TOs is never total and that dissent that does not go unnoticed is as important as the consensus.

1.3 *What Do We Mean When We Write about Education Reforms in Latin America?*

The extensive bibliography on this subject rests its interest and its value regarding knowledge on three critical issues. The reforms were different from country to country, but it is indisputable that they have general guidelines that are common to them. International organizations played a fundamental role in this. As a prescribing and data generation agency or as a direct source of financing, intergovernmental organizations were the chief architects of those general guidelines. In the case of the World Bank, the adjustment policies they imposed were concomitant to the reform cycle. In some countries, Mexico notably, incidence was greater through loans for educational programs. The Economic Commission for Latin America and the Caribbean (ECLAC) was also a center for radiating ideas in education discourse in all governments throughout the decade.

Though intergovernmental organizations designed the main guidelines of the reforms for Latin America, they were always limited by the local context. Such guidelines had to be adjusted and adapted to the specific realities of each country. Nevertheless, the topic was soon installed in academic debates and in that intermediate zone between scholars and decision-makers, in which the "experts" make their appearance.

Thinking about the reforms in areas not restricted to one nation allowed the introduction of productive discussions on the global front, as well as in national vs local relationships, on the transfer of knowledge, and related topics. The national and international promotion of the reforms favored a reasonably fluid exchange between scholars, government officials and foreign officials, but also union leaders, members of civil society organizations and churches, as well as entrepreneurs. The studies produced within the institutional frameworks under the theme of education reform in Latin America generally analyze a few selected national cases, whether for their relevance to a topic, or to use a specific approach, or because of the greater familiarity of the researcher with particular processes. Note that under this general format there have been essential works in which, although the comparison is present, the comparative method is absent.

As for what we generically group under the theme of teacher organizations and/or social movements of teachers in Latin America, academic production is much less abundant. Frequently those who describe and analyze the collective actions of teachers are part of TOs or related political parties and disseminate their work in different academic circuits.

Special mention deserves to go to the Latin American networks. Among their contributions is the publication of the Latin American Faculty of Social Sciences (FLACSO), Argentine headquarters in 1995, entitled: *Is it possible to coordinate educational policies?* (*¿Es posible concertar las políticas eductaivas?*). Three years later, the Program for the Promotion of Education Reform in Latin America and the Caribbean (*Programa de Promoción de la Reforma Educativa en América Latina y el Caribe*, PREAL)—known in the USA as Partnership for Educational Revitalization in the Americas—and the Argentine Headquarters of FLACSO, launched another project with the name of Teacher Unionism and Educational Reform in Latin America. After several seminars, Guillermina Tiramonti and Daniel Filmus compiled a set of reports on national cases; Mariano Palamidessi produced the final work. From another point of view, in 2003 the Latin American Policy Observatory/Public Policy Laboratory coordinated by Pablo Gentilli took the task of developing a chronology about social movements that have been a useful source of information, and that led to two books.

Another critical initiative came from the Konrad Adenauer Foundation that published a collection of studies on TOs in ten countries. In Brazil, scholars launched two more initiatives that remain active. One was the Latin American Network of Studies on Teaching Work, created in 1999. The other was the effort of the Working Group Education, Work and Social Exclusion (*Educação, Trabalho e Exclusão Social*) of the Latin American Council of Social Sciences (CLACSO) or *Red Estrado*, and the Network of Researchers on Communalism and Trade Unionism of Workers in Education (*Rede de Pesquisadores on Associativismo e Sindicalismo do Trabalhadores em Educação*). This last one began in 2009 and has held international seminars and published three books to date.[1]

Without being state of the art, the preceding considerations provide an idea of the collective efforts in which this chapter is inscribed. We reiterate that the problem analyzed here tends to generate discrepant interpretations, biased by political, ideological positions. However, in the corpus of individual research and work produced in the networks as mentioned above, it is possible to find clues to unravel both the prevailing logic of the reforms and the teachers' movements that have opposed the "reformist" policies. We want to leave aside the analysis scheme that sees the OD as allies or enemies.

The objective that we pursue is to put them in relationship with each other and from that, propose lines of interpretation. Our focus is on the teacher organizations. The dimensions we choose for doing such are the following: (1) The logic of the reform; (2) the teacher organizations, especially their structure and their founding brands; and, finally, (3) the responses of the TOs to the reforms.

2 The Logic of Educational Reform

In the 90's speeches on education reform became dominant. That does not mean that it was a different credo, therefore making it possible to differentiate, for example, between the positions of the World Bank and those of ECLAC, which is important and necessary. We can also observe dissimilarities in the language and the emphasis of the speeches issued by national governments. However, there is a hard core that we could separate analytically into elements of context and elements related to the field of education.

Education restructuring was raised within the framework of the reform of the State, which abandoned the principles of the welfare State, which to a certain extent had shaped the governmental policies of the previous phase. A second element consisted of the primacy of economic criteria in school management. Control of the variables in the managing processes was considered indispensable. Finally, intergovernmental organizations, notably the World Bank, intensified their influence through financing and direct advice to governments.

The first step consisted of catastrophic diagnoses of national education systems. Some of the dominant notes were: criticism of its bureaucracy, being excessive, expensive and inefficient. Likewise, its rigidity was highlighted, in terms of the structure and functioning of the education ministries, as well as in the slowness to adapt to change. Centralization and hierarchical control were other targets of criticism. About the first, the ubiquitous recipe was decentralization. The second issue recommended new participation schemes, as well as the inclusion of new actors in the field of education. The third core idea pointed to structural aspects of the education system: its high costs and low yields, as well as the lack of data that would allow quantifying precisely the different elements; also, the structure and duration of school cycles and the convenience of making changes to give privilege to the basic levels. Finally, within that framework, scholars and officials magnified the deficiencies of schools and teachers. The slogan was the need to have better-qualified teachers. Thus, the watchword of "professionalization" took force. It emphasized the urgency of establishing a set of coherent rules for the entry, promotion, and permanence of teachers, and to install evaluation and incentive systems. Regarding the schools, there was interest in extending the days of class and promoting more excellent use of time in the classroom. It was also recommended to improve the information systems at all levels of the education system, starting from the one generated by schools and suggesting an expansion of school autonomy.

As can be observed, the underlying logic gave privilege to almost the entire repertoire of recommendations, higher and better controls in the processes, which would result in higher levels of efficiency and effectiveness.

3 National Specificity

The general orientation of educational reform acted upon different national contexts and educational systems. In all three countries, the idea that education was of poor quality became prominent; it was on the wrong track and therefore educational systems required particular attention. However, it was in the decade of the 90's when the conditions matured enough to launch the reforms.

Argentina was a paradigmatic case because that was where the reform had a stronger legal component through the establishment of the Federal Law of Education of April 1993. Scholars who had analyzed the issue pointed out that it had as a background the National Pedagogical Congress, which developed in the government of Raúl Alfonsín, in the course of which several forces reached a consensus on the need to renew the normative framework of national education.

The discourse for redesigning the educational system of the 90's put the accent on the challenges derived from global economic and technological transformations. However, there was no doubt that the new objectives assigned to education would have to take place under unfavorable economic conditions that were hitting middle and subordinate classes hard. Thus, the proposed reforms would have to devise ways to address as far as possible the severe educational inequality. Another condition was to try to make the new policies acceptable for the most critical groups in the educational field, especially for the unions. The government therefore decided to take a risky approach, which involved significant changes in legislation, which at the same time touched on different aspects of the structure and organization of the education system, its financing, and priorities, while still introducing educational and pedagogical changes. Consequently, the Argentinian transformation process was the most ambitious and also the most controversial of the three cases under analysis (Tedesco & Tenti, 2001).

In Argentina, but also in Brazil, the budget deficit conditions were a central feature of reformism and therefore driven by the primary interest of redistributing financing for education. The Federal Education Pact established greater responsibilities for the Argentine provinces with political and social costs for the most impoverished regions.

In the case of Brazil, the Fundef (Maintenance and Development Fund for Fundamental Teaching and Appreciation of Teachers) was the principal means used to carry out the municipalization of funds. The total amount of the participation fund of the municipalities was very similar to that established for the states. The calculation for both took into consideration the number of students served according to the school census reports issued by the Ministry of Education, corresponding to the previous year. The aim was to distribute the financial resources in such a way as to make the universalization of fundamental education possible. In both cases, the results were mixed.

In Mexico, the reformist impetus was lower. There were no teams of experts comparable to those involved in Argentine education, nor was space created for innovations that did exist in some Brazilian states and municipalities. Therefore, the changes were more limited and gradual. Seen in perspective, however, in the Mexico of the 90's two trends emerged that would have a profound impact on the educational policies of the coming decades. The first was the targeting of social policies. The major programs, *Solidaridad and Progresa,* included an educational component that benefited families located in the most disadvantaged population deciles. Although Argentina also established compensatory programs through the Educational Social Plan (PSE), in force between 1993 and 1999, Mexico was at the forefront in this regard. The second tendency, concerning system administration, was decentralization, agreed in 1992 in the National Agreement for the Modernization of Basic Education, and whose central points were included shortly after in the General Education Law. Although secondary school was made compulsory, there was no restructuring design of the school cycles in the Mexican case analogous to the one put into practice in Argentina.

The central aspect of decentralization in the Mexican educational system was the transfer of control of basic education and teacher training schools from Federal administration to State governments. However, the central government's funding to the states did not suffer the abrupt shocks sustained in the Argentine provinces.

Despite the differences in the decentralization processes, both in amplitude and depth, and in their application rhythms, in the three countries, a paradox emerged. These processes did not arrive at a redistribution of power that would make broader and more balanced participation feasible in the most relevant decisions for the system as a whole. Those aspects of a normative nature inevitably remained in the hands of central government.

The core actions that we have described had their correlation in changes in the structure of the negotiations of the social actors of the educational field, notably of the TOs.

4 Teachers and Teacher Organizations: Areas of Conflict

The core ideas of the reforms touched vital points of the educational systems and affected both the teaching staff and their organizations. However, each national case had unique characteristics concerning priority objectives, strategies, rhythms and implementation modalities.

Although the reform made the quality of education its main motto from the beginning, the fact is that expansion of coverage and redefinition of the cycles of compulsory and basic education, combined with demographic dynamics introduced greater pressure to enlarge the demand for educational services. The scarcity of public resources to meet this demand was decisive in guiding the recommendations of the reforms towards policies and measures that frequently entailed adverse effects on working conditions, salaries and benefits for teachers. Within an economist's logic of the reform, the diagnoses emphasized an excessive proportion destined for wages and benefits, noting that it left very few resources for improving the infrastructure, or for innovation.

The trends observed in the average teacher salary in the 90's show differences in the three countries. At the beginning of the 90's, teachers' salaries were in a critical situation. The data indicate that throughout the 80's in Argentina, Brazil, and Mexico, the decrease in the real wages of teachers was accentuated. For example, the average salary of Argentine teachers lost half of its real value. In Brazil, with enormous regional disparities, several studies document on average a significant reduction between 1981 and 1985. The case of Mexico is again atypical because in the 90's, teacher remuneration experienced a vital recovery, although it barely managed to restore the losses of the previous decade.

It is not surprising then that educational organizations received from their bases the request for improvements in salary and benefits. In addition to facing up to these growing and continuous demands, the union leaders resented the drastic reduction of their influence in the discussion of the core ideas of the reform. They were even ousted from the decisions on administrative adjustments, and government officials considered the union presence uncomfortable when not superfluous. At the same time that governments were narrowing the scope of action of the unions strictly to wages or benefits issues, the door was opening to the participation of other social actors, not always well-received by the unions: parent associations, civil society organizations, and the business community.

Closely linked to the demand to improve educational quality, the reformist discourse pondered the importance of teacher professionalization. There was no governmental interest in introducing improvements in initial teacher training, but rather in investing in updating. Governments chose different modalities but always in the interest of reducing their costs.

The antagonism generated or accentuated in the course of the reform processes was exemplified in the language. Rosa María Torres provides an inventory of keywords that allude to what was called the *teacher's distress*. It is interesting to contrast those words with elements of the discourse used by reformers to characterize teachers (see Table 11.1). The same author concludes:

> Teacher opposition to decentralization in the 90's cannot be understood by itself or only from self-interest or nostalgia for a lost welfare State, but in the set of policies that in fact mark important ruptures with the educational model, school culture and the conquests and flags that have been part of traditional teaching ideology. The defense of the public school, free and universal, a central element of educational ideology in the Latin American tradition, has been embodied fundamentally by the

TABLE 11.1 Teacher distress (keywords)

Reform speech to refer to teachers	Perceptions of teachers regarding changes
Spending	Disorder
Problem	Uncertainty
Input	Requirement
Doers	Exclusion
Trained	Nostalgia
Beneficiaries	Impotence and stress
Responsible	Dignity, pride, belligerence

SOURCE: TORRES (2000, PP. 33–34)

> teachers and their organizations. Here, in the unrestricted defense of public school, lies, as stated, the vitality and tragedy of teaching. (Torres, 2000, p. 31)

Once these starting points are established, we will refer to the teacher organizations. And, according to our understanding their birthmarks is a core aspect.

5 The Main Teacher Organizations: Their Birthmarks

It is said, not without reason, that the founding moments leave a virtually indelible mark on the life of any organization. In this line, Julian Gindin provides an interesting study on teacher unionism. In the comparison of the cases of Argentina, Brazil and Mexico, it identifies as a fundamental variable the differential relationship that the State established with TOs in the consolidation period of labor relations (Gindin, 2008).

Based on that line of interpretation, we bring to our discussion critical points in the history of the TOs, starting with their background. The Mexican SNTE, Arentinian CTERA and the Brazilian CNTE all resulted from a process of integrating pre-existing organizations and incorporating their ideologies, forms of association and different traditions. Incorporation into a national union or a confederation does not dissolve them; they appear in the way of internal tensions of the new union structure. The conjuncture of the foundational moment is a second aspect to compare because it determines the form adopted by the relationship of the newly created organization with the State. We will begin with the Mexican National Union of Education Workers.

The government and groups of teachers founded the SNTE in 1943, more than three decades before the Brazilian CNTE and four decades before the founding of CTERA. During the 1930's, teachers and, in general, education, were subjected to intense politicization. On the one hand, since the late 1920's, the anti-clerical radicalism of the government and its political arm, the National Revolutionary Party, had led to a virulent response of militant Catholicism in what was known as the *Guerra Cristera*. When the government of Lázaro Cárdenas began, that conflict had subsided. However, the reform to Article 3 of the Constitution of 1934 that established that "education would be socialist" continued to provoke confrontations that reached the point where, in many rural communities, angry groups of peasants cut off the ears of rural teachers, considering them communists.[2]

President Lázaro Cárdenas (1934–1940) tried to unify the different teacher organizations. In the six years of his mandate, he did not succeed. The next government, headed by Manuel Ávila Camacho, operated a moderate political and ideological turn to the rightwing. The new political climate was conducive to the unification of existing TOs into a single union. Thus, the SNTE germinated. As soon as it was born it became one of the worker unions at the service of the State. During the Cardenista government a particular statute had been issued for these employees, a regulation that, while establishing and protecting full labor rights, framed them within a corporate structure.

The Statute of Workers at the Service of the State established that there would be only one union per agency of the Federal government; that the affiliation to these unions would have a mandatory character and that the quotas for the respective organization would be deducted automatically from the worker's salary. These three elements, together with the fact that these unions were part of the Federation of Workers' Unions in the Service of the State (FSTSE), which in turn, was integrated into the government party, branded the type of corporate unionism of Federal public employees. It was this normative framework that teachers and administrative workers from the Secretariat of Public Education (SEP) and teachers from states and municipalities, as well as a few from the private sector, became part of in 1943.

Between 1943 and the beginning of the 90's, the SNTE grew and became stronger. As for its internal political currents, since its early years, the union had already lost its initially open character in which groups of different political-ideological tendencies coexisted. At the beginning of the 90's, the robust nucleus of the union retained its political alliance with the government and its party, except for some sections, grouped in the National Coordination of Education Workers, where political orientation was leftwing and extreme leftwing. The foundational traits of the SNTE were still in force: union monopoly, compulsory membership, automatic deduction of union dues.

Such a condition as a corporate union contrasts sharply with the cases of the CNTE in Brazil. To appreciate the difference, we must consider some of the background of Brazil during the 30's, in which, even though an organized teacher unionism similar to the Mexican one might have been possible, a different direction was taken. The trade union movement, promoted in the government of Getulio Vargas (1930–1945), sought to unite each branch of activity in a single union. The legislation established that the entire base of representation must participate in the maintenance of their union, which gave rise to the so-called union tax, deducted from the salary of all workers. However, among teachers, there was stiff resistance to acceptance of this model.

The Brazilian education system was already decentralized, which meant that the states were directly responsible for the hiring and remuneration of their teachers. Teachers associations, open to negotiation and separated from the workers' movement and the left, had been formed in the states of the Federative Republic (for example, the Paulist Faculty Center or *Centro do Professorado Paulista*). The demands of these associations were mainly salary improvements, timely payment and the establishment of a unique retirement plan. Another of the claims of the Brazilian associative trend was the enactment of Career Plans (*Planos de Carreira*), meaning regulatory statutes for public officials.

It was not until 1960 that the Confederation of Primary School Teachers (*Confederação de Professores Primários do Brasil*, or CPPB) was born, which maintained a cooperative relationship with the government. The military dictatorship established in 1964 would lead to a marked change in the orientation of Brazilian organizations that culminated in the formation of the Workers Party (PT) and the Workers Central Union (CUT). The study of Amarilio Ferreira Jr. narrates the vicissitudes of the teacher's associations in that period. The leftist parties that had managed to survive the military-political repression had a powerful influence on the decisions of teacher movements. From the second half of the 70's, a significant number of teachers joined the organizations that opposed the military dictatorship, especially in large urban centers (Ferreira, 2014).

At the end of that decade, the struggles of the teachers were revived and radicalized, which gave birth to several organizations that struggled to expand their bases and increase their political participation. Between 1973 and 1978, the CPPB expanded its membership by including not only primary school teachers but also those from other educational levels; they organized great strikes and became the Confederation of Teachers of Brazil (CPB). The most important demand, due to its political-union repercussions, was the right to retire after 25 years of service. This conquest represented a point of inflection in the CPB that moved from the ideological influence of the military dictatorship to the sphere of social action on the part of the civilians, who were defending the democratic state of law.

In 1987 another breaking point occurred when the CPB joined the CUT, and in 1989, it was integrated with three other national entities, becoming the National Confederation of Education Workers (*National Confederação dos Trabalhadores em Educação*, the CNTE), which included not only teacher organizations but also associations that grouped counselors, supervisors, technicians, and administrators. In the process of unification, the leftwing parties, which were counting on mobilization of the masses, were important. With this backdrop, it was clear that the Brazilian CNTE would be different from the Mexican union.

In Argentina, the process leading up to the founding of CTERA has run along forked paths. Teacher unionism is an *ave raris*; a rare bird, and a late bloomer as well, which seems to go in the opposite direction from that of most unions (Nardachione, 2014). Between 1910 and 1940, Argentine teachers grouped into professional, non-union associations that were fragmentary and weak. There are several reasons why, i.e.: the majority of its associates were women, from the lower middle class; from 1920 on there was also a surplus of teacher training school graduates called *normalistas* (after the type of training they received), which reduced the possibility of the pressure from those associations; their membership was very heterogeneous, since there were certified and non-certified teachers, national and provincial, primary and secondary; for decades, the image of the teacher as an apostle persisted, which made it even harder for an educator to break the stereotypes to decide to intervene in the union and in the political world.

A drastic change came with Peronism, which was characterized by a more significant influence and intervention of the government in the life of the TOs. However, the teacher organizations, in general, reacted adversely. The first subject of questioning was the centralization, in the Ministry of Education, of crucial aspects of the teaching career. In addition, given the reluctance of the associations towards the Peronist government, Perón chose to support the creation of a national union linked to the government: the ADA (Assembly of Argentine Teachers) in 1950 and the Union of Argentine Teachers (UDA) in 1953. The first joined the National Confederation of Labor, the famous CGT, and the second entered into the CGP (General Confederation of Professionals). Antagonism against the government emerged with particular harshness on the occasion of the sanction of the Statute of Teachers. Even though this enactment gave stability and other rights to teachers, it also demanded their adherence to the government to make those rights operational. The leaders of the associations leaned towards the defense of their traditional autonomy from political power. An additional fact: religious education in the schools revived the debate and the liberal demands in favor of secular education.

After the military coup that overthrew Juan Domingo Perón, and after the return to democracy, Arturo Frondizi and his government applied the Teaching Statute contained in a previous decree. The Statute referred to two areas: the functioning of the educational system and the rights of teachers.

The next phase corresponds to the transformation of associations into unions. There is also an obvious tension between professional orientations and trade unionism. This antagonism grew in the sixties, and the unionist tendency won out. The need for teacher organizations to act together against the government of Juan Carlos Onganía and its educational reform was a great incentive for their unification. In that process, in 1972 several organizations founded the Unifying Central Unification of Education Workers (CUTE). In 1973, leaders of the organizations convened for a Unity Congress. More than 100 organizations attended and agreed on a declaration of principles expressing the approach achieved between the two orientations. During the second Unification Congress, the "professional sector" imposed its position because establishing the confederation as an organization instead of a federation delayed its entry to the CGT. As a result of this, the new type of trade unionism of CTERA was at the same time more leftist and more liberal than traditional Argentine trade unionism. At the organizational level, for example, mechanisms were instituted to ensure the participation of minorities. It established that the leaders would always have to act under the mandate of their fundamental bases and that national leadership would respond to the provincial organizations (Nardachione, 2014).

The paths traveled by Argentine and Brazilian teachers to organize themselves and achieve forms of unification that gave them greater strength left foundation marks that have survived in the form of underlying tensions. However, in our interpretation, the associative past, together with the experience of dictatorial regimes has resulted in one dominant orientation: the protection of a margin of autonomy for grassroots organizations; autonomy not only in terms of the second level organization to which they belong, but also of political parties and governments, regardless of their ideology. However, that margin of self-rule is broadened or reduced by following the ups and downs of national politics and is a matter of ongoing tension in teacher unionism.

Mexican teacher unionism does not have much in common with the TOs of the Southern Cone, and there are some substantial differences. The associative tradition that is still blooming in Brazil and Argentina did not exist in Mexico. Teachers' associations in Mexico were far behind in history and they have not been reborn. The opposition of the Brazilian and Argentine TOs to imposed fees and mandatory membership, which have been part of the defense of the autonomy of their organizations, do not correlate to Mexico, as shown in Table 11.2.

6 Teacher Organizations and Reforms

We have said that in the educational reforms of the 90's it is possible to identify a common nucleus. However, the priorities and forms of implementation of the policies, as well as the characteristics of the TOs of each country made the difference. The SNTE of Mexico established a broad agreement with the Federal government. In 1992, the union signed with the Federal government the National Agreement for the Modernization of Basic Education (ANMEB),

TABLE 11.2 Three educational organizations in contrast

	CTERA	CNTE	SNTE
Moment of origin	Unification Congress with more than 100 organizations. Tension between professionalism and trade unionism. More leftist and more liberal than traditional Argentine trade unionism.	Its foundation ran parallel to that of the Workers Party (PT). It was the result of a process that included the fight against the dictatorship. The state organizations have wide margins of autonomy.	It emerged at the initiative of the government within a policy of national unity and joins a federation of state workers with the government party.
Corporatism	Flatten	Flatten	Dominant (corporatism, in this case, explains both the success of the agreement and the violence of confrontation).
Associationism	Medium (expressed as a tradition linked to teaching as a profession and the importance of the autonomy of the TOs).	Medium	Very low
Position of the leadership	Confrontation	Confrontation	Agreement
Unrest	Intermittent	Intermittent	Intense and continuous
Internal dynamics	The teacher movements of the subnational organizations have their dynamics: unions, professionals and references to specific policies.	The movements of teachers of subnational organizations with high degrees of autonomy frequently included protests against the management of subnational governments.	The mobilizations of the *Coordinadora*, although they included union demands, also contained a radical political component and continuous confrontation with the national leadership of SNTE.

which gave way to a limited decentralization of the educational system which was carried out without significant upsets. That was considered an example of success in government-teacher union negotiations in Latin America. The agreement, in addition to the transfer of the administration of schools from Federal to State jurisdiction, established a second core policy, termed as the reevaluation of the teaching profession. Its main component was the so-called Teaching Career, a merit-pay system and a horizontal ladder that improved the income of teachers who adhered to its rules.

This successful government negotiation with the union leadership did not eliminate the conflict. Still, it concentrated on certain union sections which, while belonging to the union, had joined together in a political grouping opposed to the national leadership of the union: The National Coordinator of Education Workers. Section 22 of Oaxaca, the most influential group within this faction, carried out mobilizations in radical opposition to the governmental, educational policy. It denounced the change as a neoliberal policy imposed by international organizations. The government could not neutralize those teachers' nuclei, nor did it manage to accept as valid the issues proposed by the discourse on education reform. However, the protests generally stayed within the borders of the states without coming to represent a threat to the governance of the education system.

Another objective pursued by the Mexican government during the 1990's was to try to limit the influence of the union on matters vital to the progress of education, such as the meritocratic and non-clientelist assignment for teaching positions, and the appointment of school principals and supervisors. The government aimed at implementing an operation of the Teaching Career program outside union control. In those points, progress was limited.

The ANMEB reaffirmed the role of the union as the principal interlocutor of the government in educational policy. In the states, there were no significant changes either. Union power, valorized during the electoral periods to operate in favor of the candidates of the governing party, allowed the organization to recover in a short time the little political territory that the authority had reconquered for itself. In short, from the reformist perspective, the balance was mixed. It was possible to agree on limited decentralization of the educational system, and the SNTE leaders accepted and helped to disseminate the themes of the reform. These were the main achievements.

For the national leadership of the SNTE, the events of that decade showed that a strong national union, even with an opposition segment within it (the *Coordinadora*), is capable of defending itself on issues that are crucial for its integrity as a national group. I refer here to an alternative government project, which was reported shortly before the signing of the ANMEB, which sought to establish, along with decentralization of the education system, the segregation of ownership of labor relations. That would have implied a fragmentation of the national union into state unions. The project was successfully vetoed by the SNTE national leadership, with the support of a faction of the same government headed by Manuel Camacho, regent of the Federal District and political adviser to President Carlos Salinas de Gortari (Ornelas, 2008).

In the cases of Brazil and Argentina, the balance also shows a *chiaroscuro*. Most of the teacher mobilizations involved organizations linked to the two national confederations. The demands were more often economic ones, but many of them included a frontal criticism towards the orientation of educational policies, denouncing them as neoliberals imposed by international organizations. The constant unrest of the guilds determined a strong antagonism with the group of reformers.

A central aspect that emerges from the comparison between the three national cases is that although decentralization was a common theme of the reforms, it adopted modalities that affected very different forms and degrees of the teachers' working conditions.

In Mexico, the agreed decentralization gave more significant opportunities for negotiation to the union, given that, although the salary agreements between SEP and the National Executive Committee of the SNTE operated as the base, decentralization opened the door for local sections to undertake additional negotiations with state governments with positive results for its members. This is known as double negotiation. In Argentina, on the other hand, the call to bilateral national talks was a continuous demand, since the new scheme brought with it a greater shortage in teacher salary in the poor provinces. CTERA also fought in those years for the recognition of the teacher as an education worker with double union membership (provincial and national). Although there were mobilizations that did not obtain any concession from the governments, CTERA register as a triumph the Teacher Incentive Fund and its veto capacity on the Teacher Professionalization Project. That was the result of new trade union action strategies such as the installation of the White Tent in front of the Congress of the Nation in April 1997, lifted after a thousand and three days of protest and fasting.

The case of Brazil allows us to appreciate the importance of the political context to open or close the possibilities of an agreement. In 1989, the electoral defeat of Ignacio Lula da Silva began an interregnum that allowed the CNTE to negotiate the Pact for the valorization of teaching and quality of education (Pact pela valorização do magistério e qualidade da educação) of 1994. That settlement established the value of the national wage floor. The Chamber of Deputies discussed the draft Law on Guidelines and Bases of Education (LDB), promoted by the National Forum in Defense of Public School, which also included the salary floor. Still, the political context changed with the arrival to the presidency of Fernando Henrique Cardoso. The Pact was not respected, and the new government adopted the international guidelines for educational reform. The reformers in Brazil opted for municipalization and decentralized negotiation of labor relations. The teaching career was at the center of the confrontation between the TOs and the Federal and State governments. The CNTE maintained a fierce opposition to flexibilization of hiring, salary policies, and the teaching career. The CNTE's speech emphasized that these policies were part of the designs of international organizations and continuously aggravated the mercantilism and individualism that they entailed (Gindin, 2008).

7 Conclusion

The traditional struggles of the TOs in the three countries have distinctive marks. In Mexico, these traditions had their origin in the social revolution that began in 1910 but, as far as education is concerned, they experienced unprecedented impulses in the 1930's. In Argentina and Brazil, associationism was still predominant as a form of organizing the teachers; in Mexico the rural school and socialist education, with a nationalistic component, were the source of an idiosyncratic teaching tradition. The teacher who emerged from the revolutionary process identified her/himself more with the image of a social leader than with that of an apostle. Moreover, in the urban environment, she/he was conceived more as an education worker than as a professional.

Corporatism emerged as another exciting key in our comparison. The three countries, at different times, had charismatic leaders that promoted corporatist structures: Vargas, Cárdenas, and Perón. However, in Brazil and Argentina, these experiences were truncated by the overthrow of governments, so that corporatism at no time completely dominated the political and ideological spectrum of teaching. In the Mexican case, on the other hand, Cardenism established bases of stability and institutionalization that allowed corporatist forms to take hold and survive for decades.

The struggles against dictatorships in Argentina and Brazil modified the guidelines on which their educational organizations had previously worked. Both cases fortified the links between teachers, social organizations and political parties; hence the tensions between unionism and associative forms, between autonomy and integration or alliance with workers' leagues and political parties. The founding of the Argentinian CTERA and the Brazilian CNTE shaped arrangements to alleviate those underlying tensions. In the case of

Mexico, there was political stability with an authoritarian regime, but not a dictatorial one. The SNTE during the 60's and 70's continued to enjoy exceptional conditions of monopoly and state protection thanks to its organic link with the hegemonic party. This alliance diminished their combativeness, as well as their autonomy.

When we analyze the response of the TOs to the educational reform processes of the 1990's, we find that the founding brands of each organization are significant in understanding their subsequent development. As for the reforms themselves, there are two elements of greater weight: the type of decentralization of the reformist project and the type of link existing between the educational organizations, the governments and political parties.

The binomial centralization-decentralization is complex and concerns not only the education system but also the TOs themselves. The union structure points the finger at the features of the type of centralization now in effect. On the one hand, we must consider the fact that confederations join unions that act with margins of autonomy. In the Mexican case, however, there is a centralized national union that grants enormous decision-making power to its National Executive Committee.

The reformist projects postulated the benefits of educational decentralization in the manner of an irrefutable principle. National education systems range from the most centralized, the Mexican, to the most decentralized, the Brazilian. However, for the subject that concerns us, the most interesting things are (a) the implications that the decentralization project had for the educational organizations, and (b) the union capacity to limit or counteract this project. Even though in Mexico there was a temptation to use decentralization to fragment the national union by creating state unions, the political power of the SNTE in alliance with a governmental faction prevented this from being done. The decentralization that took place was limited, and the SNTE legally remained the owner of labor relations in the teaching profession. In the case of Brazil and Argentina, decentralization focused on financing problems. The resistance of the CTERA and the CNTE was combative in those years, putting a stop to some excesses and achieving essential social recognition of their unions in specific conjunctures.

The agreement on establishing decentralization in the Mexican case bore a more ancient and structural political alliance between the State and the union. The success of ANMEB, observed from a distance, is relative. On the issue concerning an effective decentralization of the most critical decisions for the educational system, as well as on the limitation of union power, its fruits were poor. As for Argentina and Brazil, the idea that trade unions were the biggest obstacle to reformist success obscures the fact that the very formulation of the policies included in education reform—upon being implemented in very problematic economic and political contexts—suffered from formulation errors and lack of modesty. To sum up, teachers' unions cannot and should not carry the blame for the limited results obtained by the educational reforms of the 90's in their most important objective, often forgotten, which is that the system must provide more and better education to their populations.

One last consideration: The teacher organizations were and will continue to be foremost actors in any process of educational reform. Several of the major topics such as professionalization and teacher evaluation remain valid in the current reformist agendas. Therefore, the experiences of the 90's are an invaluable source of learning. They invite us to identify the implications that each proposed measure may have on the working conditions of teachers, fully recognizing them as education workers. Finally, their opposition to reformist movements can prevent us from forgetting that the values and traditions of teachers, as well as the binary logic—guild and professional—of their organizations, will decisively guide their response to changes.

Acknowledgment

I thank Yoalli Navarro for her support in the compilation of bibliographic material, as well as the careful reading of and observations made to the initial version of this text.

Notes

1 To learn more, visit the league: http://www.anped.org.br/content/vi-seminario-internacional-da-rede-de-pesquisadores-sobre-associativismo-e-sindicalismo-dos. The new page is under construction.

2 On October 8, 1934, the Chamber of Deputies amended Articles 3 and 73 of Constitution to state that: "Education provided by the State will be socialist, and, in addition to excluding all religious doctrine, will fight fanaticism and prejudice, for which the school will organize its teachings and activities in a way that allows creating in the youth a rational and accurate concept of the Universe and social life" (Cámara de Diputados, 2019).

References

Braslavsky, C., & Cosse, G. (2004). Las actuales reformas educativas en América Latina: cuatro actores, tres lógicas y ocho tensiones. *Revista Electrónica Iberoamericana sobre Calidad, Eficacia y Cambio en Educación, 4*(2e), 1–26.

Cámara de Diputados (2019, June 19). *Constitución Política de los Estados Unidos Mexicanos. Reformas por periodo presidencial.* México City: Cámara de Diputados. Retrieved from http://www.diputados.gob.mx/LeyesBiblio/ref/cpeum_per.htm

Ferreira Jr. A. (2013). A Confederação dos Professores do Brasil e a aposentadoria aos 25 años en Associativismo e sindicalismo em Educação (teoría, hisórica e movimientos). In J. Gindin, Vieira Ferreira, & S. Dal Rosso (Eds.), *Associativismo e sindicalismo em tempos de mal-estar* Brasilia: Paralelo 15 (Rede Aste).

Fontoura, J., Gindin, J., & Gentili, P. (2008). *Los sindicados docentes y las reformas educativas en América Latina: El caso brasileño.* Brasil: Fundación Konrad Adenauer.

Gajardo, M. (2012). *La educación tras dos décadas de cambio. ¿Qué hemos aprendido? ¿Qué debemos transformar?* Santiago, Chile: PREAL 65 (December).

Gentili, P. Suárez, D. Stubrin, F., & Gindin, J. (2004). Reforma educativa y luchas docentes en América Latina. In *Educación y Sociedad, 25*(89), 1251–1274.

Gindin, J. (2008). Sindicalismo docente en México, Brasil y Argentina. Una hipótesis explicativa de su estructuración diferenciada. *Revista Mexicana de Investigación Educativa, 13*(37), 351–375.

Loyo, A. (2008). *Sindicados docentes y las reformas educativas en América Latina: México.* Rio de Janeiro: Fundación Konrad Adenauer.

Nardacchione, G. (2015). *Una rara avis en el sindicalismo argentino: los sindicatos docentes (1880–2001).* Buenos Aires: Universidad Nacional del Centro de la Provincia de Buenos Aires. Facultad de Ciencias Humanas. Núcleo de Estudios Educacionales y Sociales.

Ornelas, C. (2008). El SNTE, Elba Esther Gordillo y el gobierno de Calderón. *Revista Mexicana de Investigación Educativa, 13*(37), 445–469.

Palamidessi, M. (2003, December). *Sindicatos docentes y gobiernos: conflictos y diálogo en torno a la reforma educativa en América Latina.* Santiago, Chile: PREAL, No. 28.

Palamidessi, M., & Legarralde, M. (2006). *Sindicalismo docente, gobierno y reformas educativas en América Latina y el Caribe: Condiciones para el diálogo.* Washington, DC: BID/Red de Educación, No. 62.

Peraza, R., & Legarralde, M. (2008). *Sindicados docentes y las reformas educativas en América Latina: Argentina.* Río de Janeiro: Fundación Konrad Adenauer.

Tedesco, J. C., & Tenti, E. (2001). *Alcances y resultados de las reformas educativas en Argentina, Chile y Uruguay.* Buenos Aires: IIPE/UNESCO.

Torres, R. M. (2000). Reformas educativas, docentes y organizaciones docentes en América Latina y el Caribe. In A. L. Cardenas Colmenter, A. Rodríguez Céspedes, & R. M. Torres (Eds.), *Los docentes protagonistas del cambio educativo.* Bogotá: CAB/ Editorial Magisterio Nacional.

Postscript

Carlos Ornelas

At the end of an anthology such as this, the editor can hardly resist the temptation to add a final reflection, or to wrap up what the authors said, or to deduce logical conclusions. I did not escape such enticement. Still, I firmly believe that each pair of eyes sees different things in the same text, that each head construes different meanings from the same written words. That is a reader's right.

What I can say is that in the end, I think we have fulfilled what we proposed at the outset of the CIES Conference in Mexico City: to put together a collection of essays that would provide an overview of what is going on in education politics, policies, and practices throughout the Latin American region. What we found is a plurality of initiatives for education reform that, while sharing some common global features, show rather more strongly how the particularities of each country determine what unfolds, what changes, and what persists. The persistence of rooted practices is mainly due to the resistance created by long-standing traditions as well as diverse interest groups, especially leaders of teachers' unions.

The dialectics of the local and global are at play in each instance. Still, the analyses of the cases honor both national contexts and local traditions. Each author or pair of authors chose the theoretical perspective for the examination of their country's circumstances or the method of comparison in the case of teachers' unions. We agreed to work collectively, but not to think alike.

We offer the readers a compendium of studies on education reforms: the different methods reformers use to convince other actors to participate affirmatively, the distinct types of opposition by different social groups, and the endurance of practices that constitute the education systems of Latin America.

I only desire that each reader extract her/his conclusions and notice that, although it is not usual, we can benefit by seeing the world from the South to the North.

 | DOI: 10.1163/9789004413375_013